FIRESIDE

BY THE SAME AUTHOR

South Florida Cookery

The Shrimp Cookbook

Tropical Cookery

Encyclopaedia of Cultivated Orchids

Orchids—Their Botany and Culture

Cultural Directions for Orchids

The Major Kinds of Palms

Guide to Common Plants of the Everglades National Park

The Four Arts Garden of Palm Beach: A Catalogue

Editor, *Cookery Notes* (monthly publication)

COOKING WITH VEGETABLES

an encyclopedic treasury of recipes, botany and lore of the vegetable kingdom

ALEX D. HAWKES

illustrations by Bill Goldsmith

FIRESIDE

A FIRESIDE BOOK
PUBLISHED BY SIMON AND SCHUSTER

ISBN 0-671-20121-2
ISBN 0-671-22179-5 Pbk.
Library of Congress Catalog Card Number 68-25748
Designed by Betty Crumley
Manufactured in the United States of America

2 3 4 5 6 7 8 9 10 11

This book is affectionately dedicated to
three of the exceptional vegetable cooks in my life . . .

Mrs. Morris (Barbara) Cargill, "Charlottenburgh," Highgate, Jamaica
Mr. Edward A. Flickinger, "Bonsai House," Coconut Grove, Florida
and
Mrs. W. W. G. (May) Moir, "Lipolani," Honolulu, Hawaii

contents

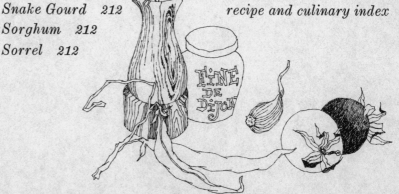

ACKNOWLEDGMENTS

A gratifying number of friends have assisted in various ways in the
writing of this book. I would like to express my sincere thanks to these, in particular.

Elizabeth Alston, Food Editor, *Look* Magazine, New York
Helen Barrow, Simon and Schuster, New York
Blanche Blackwell, "Bolt House," Port Maria, Jamaica
Bootsie Bowen, Miami, Florida
The late Katherine Hawkes Chatham, Coconut Grove, Florida
Craig Claiborne, Food News Editor, *The New York Times*
Consolidated Olive Growers, Lindsay, California
Joyce and Basil Densham, Mandeville, Jamaica
Polly and Phil Dross, St. Petersburg, Florida
Maude Drum, Coconut Grove, Florida
Dee and Tony Gason, "Turtle Cove," Port Antonio, Jamaica
Ruth Gray, Food Editor, *St. Petersburg Times*, Florida
Bertha Cochran Hahn, former Food Editor, *Miami News*
Miss B. S. Hawkes, Coconut Grove, Florida
The late G. A. Jagerson, Neenah, Wisconsin
Doreen Kirkcaldy and Jamaica Festival 5 Committee, Kingston, Jamaica
Charlie and Kirk Kirkpatrick, "Brandon Hill House," Montego Bay, Jamaica
Anton G. Maratos, Athens, Greece
Marguerite and Arthur Myers, "Rocaille," Stony Hill, Jamaica
Pat Read, Simon and Schuster, New York
Benita Robaina, Havana, Cuba, and temporarily Miami, Florida
Bill Straight, Miami, Florida
T. Sakata & Co., Yokohama, Japan
Jim Yeager, San Francisco, California

Thanks, too, to *Gourmet* Magazine and
Consolidated Book Publishers, Inc.,
for permission to reprint a few of my recipes
previously published by them.

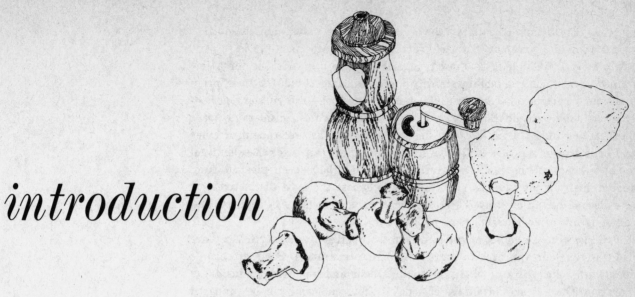

introduction

This is a book about vegetables, their origin, their botany, and particularly their cookery. It is, emphatically, not a vegetarian book, but one which takes up nearly 200 of the amazingly diverse plants throughout the world that are eaten by man, often in combination with meat and fish and other ingredients. In its pages I treat of the well-known, ''old-fashioned'' kinds of vegetables such as the potato and the squash and the tomato. And I also introduce—for the first time to many readers, I suspect—a great array of ''new'' vegetables which have only in recent years become generally available in our domestic stores and markets. These include such wonderful, and sometimes weird, species as the plantain, the breadfruit, the chayote, the bok-choi, and on and on.

Collecting the material for this book, and writing it, has been an exciting experience for me. I am primarily a botanist-horticulturist, the author of a dozen published volumes in these fields. But at an early age I became interested in food and cookery. My maternal grandmother, who was from Scotland, declared when I was quite young that every young gentleman should learn how to cook—and cook well! So this started things off, and since I have remained a happy bachelor, the knowledge has often been of use to me and has, in fact, become a strong secondary interest in my life. I have written three cookbooks on regional or special topics, and I have for several years now put out a monthly publication, *Cookery Notes* (whose subscribers have broadened my culinary horizons, as I hope I have theirs).

A World of Vegetable Cookery is a result of combining my interests in botany and cooking over a number of years. My researches on my particular botanical specialties—orchids, palms, bromeliads, and certain other groups of plants—have taken me to many parts of the globe. Everywhere I have traveled I have had the opportunity to note the good things that appear from the kitchen or cook-pot or campfire.

Though I have been collecting recipes for the use of all types of vegetables for a considerable number of years, it is only within comparatively recent date that many of the less familiar ones have become available in the United States. This is, to me, very exciting, since this condition opens up a wondrous new field of inventive cuisine.

By and large, these exotic ''new'' vegetables are easily prepared, exceptionally flavorful and nutritious, and often easily located. For example, in my neighborhood supermarket in Coconut Grove, Florida, I now find daily supplies of everything from plantain and boniato and chayote and malanga to bok-choi, in addition to an overwhelming array of all the old favorites of our American tables.

Oddly enough, though these "new" vegetables have been with us for a few years now, and their availability steadily increases, suggestions for their preparation and service are lacking in contemporary cookbooks and culinary periodicals (except my own monthly *Cookery Notes,* which devotes considerable space to these exotic edibles). In *A World of Vegetable Cookery* I have brought together what I believe to be a rather comprehensive sampling of recipes for these unusual vegetables—and for the familiar favorites, too. They have been gleaned from friends in many lands overseas (I have tried to choose the most distinctive versions collected during my travels), from kitchen cronies in my own country, and from happy inventive hours spent in my own kitchen.

The recipes run the gamut of the menu, from appetizers to desserts. They are varied, too, in their approach to ingredients and preparation. Some are classic recipes, with long years of tradition behind them and requiring painstaking preparation. Others take advantage of today's short cuts and can be prepared and served easily and quickly. While I do not generally approve of canned this or precooked that in good cookery, nevertheless the era of convenience foods is upon us and, judiciously used, they can contribute to a meal.

The acquiring of these recipes has been a fascinating series of experiences. In the text that follows I make note of some of these. For instance, a trek into the high cool mountains of British Honduras in search of rare plants, brought not only the desired botanical specimens, but also a group of distinctive recipes from the charming Indians with whom I stayed. Since I did not speak their language, and they did not know either Spanish or English, the actual setting down of these instructions on paper was a lengthy, sometimes hilariously confused, session!

Oftentimes, once I have obtained one of these recipes, I am confronted with certain considerable problems in trying it out in my own kitchen—which I always believe in doing. For though a person, whether a montane Indian from British Honduras or a sophisticated New Yorker, may be an excellent, enterprising cook, she (or he, in many cases) often does not convey the full instructions for the dish under consideration. An essential, perhaps infinitesimal, ingredient has been omitted, or some crucial mixing or blending has been skipped. Or perhaps a special ingredient is just too hard to come by in the average American store (though this is, happily, an increasingly rare occurrence in these days of specialty food shops and gigantic supermarkets), and I am forced to substitute something else. It all takes time and patience—and it is all most enjoyable, and sometimes a bit fattening.

Sometimes the question is raised: What *is* as vegetable? A number of our common vegetables—tomato, eggplant, cucumber, the innumerable kinds of squash— are technically fruits, but we consider them vegetables because they are served during the main part of a meal. Others, new to us, from the tropics—the breadfruit, jakfruit and akee—are in this same fruit-vegetable category. Botanically we consider vegetables as falling into the following basic groups: leaf, stem, root and tuber, flower and bud, seed and seed pod, fruit-vegetable, and fungi.

In this book the vegetables have been arranged for ease of reference, in alphabetical sequence of their most widely known common names. The botanical index is especially comprehensive, to accommodate the multitudinous common names that are applied in differing parts of the globe (and in our own markets) to these edible plants.

In addition, the text gives the generally accepted botanical name for each vegetable, and the particular family of plants into which it is placed. The botanical name for a plant is a universally accepted one, while the common, vernacular names fluctuate so widely everywhere as to be of no serious identifying use. For instance, beans are beans in some places, but peas in others. One kind of bean (or pea, if you wish) is called *this* here, but *that* somewhere just next door. Chicory is chicory in one country, endive in another—and vice versa. In our country, too, many of the exciting "new" vegetables appear under more than one of their foreign common names, especially when one finds them in the ethnic markets, and because of this I have taken special pains to indicate as many of these as possible in the text.

There is no essential reason for designating that a particular plant belongs to the Daisy Family or the Soapberry Family or the Goosefoot Family. But I think it adds a bit of interest when one can avow to one's family and guests that the vegetable array at the table contains members of these, and other, alliances!

Vegetables have been used by man since the earliest recorded times. The primeval landscape contained species of plants which were found to be edible by our ancestral species. Historians assure us that the ancient Babylonians and Egyptians and Chinese (our Oriental friends have always been specialists in superb vegetable cookery) all made abundant use of the edible plants around them.

Today we appear to appreciate vegetables even more than in the past. Vastly improved transportation and storage systems make countless types of fresh vegetables available in our domestic markets throughout the year. When a particular seasonal vegetable is not to be found in perfect fresh condition, it can often be encountered on the grocery shelves or in its cold bins, either in a can or frozen package, or even dried. In addition, many gardeners have discovered the pleasure and ease of raising vegetables, especially the less familiar ones, which can be found in many seed catalogs.

When selecting fresh vegetables, the good cook should take time to choose only those which are in perfect condition, unblemished and obviously of recent harvest. In many cases, the life span of a vegetable is exceedingly brief—fresh corn, to name just a single example, notably deteriorates in flavor within hours after being picked.

Prepare your vegetables, especially the fragile green leaf or stem types, as promptly as possible. If storage is necessary, wrap them securely in protective wax paper or a kitchen towel and keep them in the refrigerator's special compartment. I find, in most instances, that it is better to cook fresh vegetables and reheat them than to delay in their preparation—even though the average vegetable should be eaten immediately after cooking.

Vegetables should be cooked only until just done. Never, please never, overcook them! Many a potential vegetable enthusiast has been turned into a vegetable hater by youthful exposure to gray pastelike potatoes or sodden wedges of flavorless cabbage. But today's good cooks are learning the art of vegetable cookery: brief cooking in a minimum amount of water (or in seasoned stock as a flavorful alternative), and the imaginative use of recipes from other parts of the world where vegetables are highly regarded. In the inventive cookery of the East—from Indonesia and India to Japan and Korea and China—some of the most famous and delectable creations consist primarily of beautifully cooked vegetables, with just a touch of meat, used as seasoning. You will find examples of such dishes throughout the book.

Similarly, as many other recipes in the book demonstrate, the cuisines of Spain and Mexico, of Italy and France and of many Caribbean and South American countries offer distinctive and unusual ways of preparing vegetables—alone and in combination with meat, with seafood, and with other vegetables.

As a vegetable aficionado, I like to think that many of my fellow countrymen share my enthusiasm. From my childhood in northern Maine, where I used to participate in the creative preparation of the fresh spring and summer vegetables (the glories of fiddleheads picked from the river's bank!) and those hardy roots and tubers stored in our cellars during lengthy frigid winters, I have favored these edibles over almost everything else. Wherever I have traveled or resided—from Coconut Grove to Calcutta, Kissimmee or Kennebunkport to Kingston—I have happily tried vegetables which were themselves new to me, or in fashions previously unencountered, and have brought back instructions for their preparation. Today, in fact, I often plan my menus around one or more pristine-fresh special vegetables of the season, rather than around the meat course!

Treat all vegetables as if they were precious luxuries, even though their cost may be minimal when compared with that of other items of the daily menu. Afford each vegetable the attention its character so richly deserves, and you, your family, and your guests will be more than amply pleased and rewarded.

I hope that through perusal of these pages, and of Mr. Bill Goldsmith's enchanting drawings, new light will be cast on the exciting culinary possibilities of the vegetables of the world.

A. D. H.

Coconut Grove, Florida

AKEE

Akee—sometimes spelled Ackee or Achee, and also known as Vegetable Brains or, in Spanish, *seso vegetal* —is one of the most extraordinary of all of the vegetables of the world. The edible part is the mature fat yellowish-white inch-long aril, creased like a tiny brain, each one set next to handsome ebony seeds in a large vivid scarlet fruit. These fruits hang all over the beautiful glossy-leaved big trees, like Christmas ornaments, and in their season open into three parts, to expose seeds and arils.

The Akee has gained considerable notoriety because of the fatalities suffered by incautious persons eating arils which are either immature or overripe. Despite this sinister reputation, the Akee is an extremely popular vegetable in several parts of the world.

The tree, an indigene of Guinea and adjacent parts of West Africa, is known by botanists as *Blighia sapida* (of the Soapberry Family). The generic epithet was bestowed to honor Captain William Bligh, infamous for his part in the mutiny on HMS *Bounty*. *Blighia* has become extensively naturalized in Jamaica and is cultivated as a handsome ornamental in many warm countries, including extreme southern Florida.

The arils of the Akee fruit, firm and rather oily, and variously compared with cooked brains or scrambled eggs, are occasionally eaten raw, but more often are prepared in the varied appetizing styles popular in Jamaica.

Canned Akees imported from Jamaica are now available in gourmet shops. The fresh fruit-vegetable should not be utilized unless the cook can identify precisely the stage of maturity at which it can be eaten, but the tinned product may be used safely and enjoyably.

IN JAMAICA, the classic way with this strange fruit-vegetable is with saltfish, which we know as salt codfish. Here is a recipe I encountered during a happy stay at Turtle Cove, near Port Antonio, Jamaica.

Akee and Saltfish Turtle Cove
Serves 6.

1 16-ounce can akees
1 pound dried salt codfish
3 thick strips lean bacon, diced
2 large onions, cut into thin rings
⅛ teaspoon dried thyme
1 small clove garlic, mashed
1 large tomato, cut into wedges
1 tablespoon butter
Pinch fresh-ground black pepper

Soak the salt codfish overnight in water to cover. Drain off and discard water next day, and cover again with fresh water. Boil fish until just tender, and drain. Bone and shred the fish. Drain canned akees. In a skillet, fry the diced bacon until crisp. Drain off part of bacon fat, then add onion rings, thyme, garlic, and tomato, and fry over low heat until onions are soft. Reserve some of cooked onion rings for garnish. Add shredded saltfish and akees to the skillet, with the butter and black pepper, and cook, stirring carefully, for 5 minutes. Serve garnished with reserved onion rings.

HERE is an unusual appetizer version of the illustrious akee which I first encountered at a cocktail party at the home of Mr. and Mrs. Arthur Myers, at Stony Hill, overlooking the sprawling city of Kingston.

Akee-Cheese Hors d'Oeuvre
Serves 8 to 10.

1 16-ounce can akees
4 slices lean bacon
2 tablespoons finely chopped onion
1 egg
small squares fresh crisp toast
⅓ cup freshly grated sharp cheese
1½ tablespoons freshly snipped chives

Using a skillet, fry the bacon until crisp, remove and drain, then chop or crumble. Fry the onion in part of the bacon fat, stirring often, until soft. Break egg into bacon fat and onion, and soft-scramble. Drain liquid from akees, and fold them into egg mixture, heating through over low heat. Place liberal servings of akee mixture on small toast squares, top with grated cheese, snipped chives, and the crumbled bacon, and run under preheated broiler until cheese is melted. Serve very hot.

THE akee is the national fruit of Jamaica, even though there it is customarily prepared as a vegetable. Here is an elegant casserole from the kitchen of Mrs. Fay Gearing, of Mandeville, the pretty island town which is famed for its English atmosphere.

Akees au Gratin
Serves 4 to 6.

1 16-ounce can akees
2 cups rich white sauce
1 cup grated sharp Cheddar cheese
4 tablespoons fresh-grated Parmesan cheese
1 cup cooked fresh or canned green peas
¼ cup fine-chopped onion
½ cup sliced fresh or canned mushrooms
¼ cup crisp bread crumbs

Butter a medium-sized casserole. Drain the akees thoroughly. To the rich white sauce, add half of the grated cheeses, plus the peas, onion, mushrooms and akees. Turn into casserole, sprinkle with remaining Cheddar cheese, then bread crumbs and remaining Parmesan. Bake in preheated 350° F. oven for 30 minutes, and serve while very hot.

ANNATTO

The Annatto, or Annotto, a singularly attractive flowering small tree of the West Indies and South America (*Bixa Orellana*, of the Bixa Family), is extensively cultivated in the tropics. A product derived from it is highly important in good cookery in many lands. This is the orange-red pulp which surrounds the seeds of the heart-shaped, prickly scarlet fruits—which open on maturity to display these colorful seeds.

This pulp is soaked off in water, the seeds removed, then the liquid is reduced by boiling until a reddish-orange powder remains. This is offered commercially in this and other countries as Annatto, or as *achiote, bija,* or *bijol.*

Extensively used as a coloring material—in such diverse things as butter, cheese, chocolate, and even silk—Annatto powder is often called for as a special seasoning in the cuisines of Latin America and the Philippines. Vaguely like saffron, it is infinitely less costly than that spice, hence frequently figures in the preparation of such things as arroz con pollo, West Indian Okra Stew (page 159), and the like.

The seeds of the Annatto, fresh or dried, are also often stirred with lard or oil until this is well colored, and the strained seasoned substance used for cooking in such lands as Puerto Rico.

AROIDS

The large Arum Family, the Aroids, includes such varied plants as jack-in-the-pulpit, calla lily and the well-known Philodendron. In addition, a number of the several thousand different kinds of Aroids are used by man as vegetables, and several of these are even cultivated to a measurable extent. Taro and Malanga are both important Aroid crops in our markets, and are discussed in some detail on pages 141 and 228 of this book.

In a great many parts of the Pacific, species of the genus *Cyrtosperma* are grown for their large tuberous rootstocks. These, after cooking, are edible and form an important source of starch in the indigenous diet of many millions of Pacific island dwellers. Oddly enough, though these are spectacular big "elephant-ear" plants of considerable ornamental potential, they are virtually unknown in this country.

Alocasia is a sizable group of Aroids, like so many of its relatives with no generally accepted vernacular name, many species and hybrids of which are extensively cultivated for the extravagant form and coloration of the large leaves. The Giant Alocasia or *senteh* (*Alocasia macrorrhiza*) is raised in various countries of tropical Asia and adjacent island areas for its often immense thickened rootstocks. These are consumed as a starchy, bland-flavored vegetable after protracted boiling or baking to remove the toxic crystals of calcium oxalate which occur in all parts of these plants. The leaves and leaf stalks of other members of this genus are also eaten, in India and Malaysia, in curries, always after careful preliminary cooking.

Amorphophallus is one of the most remarkable aggregations of the Aroid Family. One species, laboring under the charming name of Stanley's Bath-Tub (*Amorphophallus campanulatus*), is cultivated in Malaysia and parts of Indonesia (with the name of *loki*), for its ponderous flattened tubers, sometimes weighing ten pounds apiece. These are used in the manner of the true Yams (page 246), after prolonged cooking. In this country, we grow it as a spectacular exotic, with its solitary dissected leaf taller than a man, and fantastic "flower" up to two feet across, which gives off a perfectly shocking fetor in its prime!

Another kind of *Amorphophallus,* the Devil's Tongue, Snake Palm, or *konnyaku* (*A. Rivieri*), is frequently seen as a startling ornamental in choice gardens in this country, where its foul-smelling inflorescences sometimes reach a length of three feet. In Japan the plant is extensively cultivated, the big tubers being made into a starch, which is prepared into a transparent cake used in certain dishes much in the manner of soybean *tōfu*. It is also formed into long crystalline threads, one of several kinds of cellophane noodles, or shirataki. These are available in our specialty markets either dried or packed in water in cans, and are commonly used by those of us who delight in such dishes as Sukiyaki.

ARROWHEAD

The Arrowhead (*Sagittaria sagittifolia,* of the Arrowhead Family, Alismaceae) is a native of the temperate and subtropical parts of the Old World, particularly the Orient. It has long been cultivated in China (as *chee-koo* or *t'sz-ku*), Japan (as *kuwai*), and Korea for its edible underground corms.

The plant, and several others of its group, is grown in this country as an ornamental in water gardens, for the handsome arrowhead-shaped leaves and showy erect spikes of white flowers. In suitable conditions, the Arrowhead is a rampant grower. In rich wet soil, each corm will rapidly send out eight or more runners, each of which soon forms a new corm at its end. These corms, as found in markets, principally in Hawaii and California, are roundish or somewhat cylindrical, and measure up to about one and a half inches long, and often almost as much in breadth. With a gray, bluish-gray, or yellowish skin, the flesh is pale yellow or buff-colored, with much the consistency and flavor, when cooked, of a sweet potato.

Arrowhead corms are very tasty when boiled in a small amount of salted water until firmly tender, then thin-sliced, chilled and served with a vinaigrette dressing, as a salad. Or cut the hot boiled corms into quarters and serve at once with butter and salt and pepper to taste.

A native North American Arrowhead, *Sagittaria latifolia*, extending through Mexico into Central America, also called Arrowleaf, Wapato, or Duck Potato, has long been used by the Indians as a potato substitute, the corms being either boiled or roasted. It has an especially fine nutty flavor, and good texture. Since it thrives in boggy spots, it could well become a popular market vegetable in many parts of this country.

ARROWROOT

The principal source of commercial Arrowroot is the fleshy underground rhizome of the plant known by the botanists as *Maranta arundinacea* (Maranta Family), a native of many parts of tropical America. It has long been cultivated commercially in such places as Bermuda and the West Indian islands of Jamaica and St. Vincent. Indeed, Bermuda or St. Vincent Arrowroot are accepted vernaculars for the species. Other common names, in the Spanish-speaking lands, are *ararú*, *sagú* or *sagú cimarrón*, or *yuquilla*.

Arrowroot is also grown for its attractive rich-green, long-stalked foliage in warm areas in this country around the Gulf of Mexico, and the species is seen as a pot plant in greenhouses throughout the world.

The edible rhizomes, four to eight inches long, and about an inch thick, have an ivory skin and crisp white flesh. They are occasionally found in our markets, notably in Hawaii (sometimes under the Chinese name *chok-woo*) and large mainland U.S. cities. They are customarily boiled in salted water until tender, scraped, and served with butter and salt or a touch of soy sauce. Their flavor is very bland, vaguely reminiscent of a subtle sweet potato.

Commercial Arrowroot in its customary powdered kitchen form is used as a thickening starchy agent. It is extensively utilized in the manufacture of biscuits and pastries, and special foods for infants and invalids.

ARTICHOKE* (GLOBE)

The Globe Artichoke (*Cynara Scolymus*, of the Daisy Family), a regal relative of the lowly thistle, is a native of southern Europe and northern sectors of Mediterranean Africa. It is extensively cultivated in this country—notably in California—for the budding flower heads, of which the edible parts are the fleshy bases of the leafy bracts, and for the thickened "bottom" of the complex bloom-cluster. Alternate vernacular names for this unique vegetable include French Artichoke, *artichaut* (French), *alcachofa* (Spanish), and *carciofo* (Italian).

The sizable prickly plant itself is attractive and, especially in its juvenile state, is occasionally seen as a garden ornamental in areas in which it thrives. The fresh vegetable is at its peak in our markets during the spring months. One should purchase heads with firm leafy bracts, these tightly pressed together, of uni-

* For Japanese Artichoke, see page 126; for Jerusalem Artichoke, see page 126–27.

form bright-green color, with no wrinkling, brown streaking, or spotting. Size is theoretically immaterial, but I personally prefer the medium-sized or smallish ones, obviously the younger ones, to the gigantic specimens.

Canned Artichoke Hearts—the innermost portions of the "globe" packed in a light brine solution or in seasoned olive oil—are extensively imported from France, Italy, and Spain. They are comparable in size and culinary usefulness to our frozen Artichoke Hearts.

The superb *fonds d'artichaut* are the circular wafers trimmed from the "bottoms" of the vegetable. In them, the subtle nutlike flavor of the vegetable is captured most intensely. They are the remarkable essence of the Artichoke.

To serve fresh Artichokes, allow one or two per person, depending upon individual fondness for this extraordinary vegetable and upon the remainder of the menu to be presented.

Boiled Artichokes
Serves 4.

4 *to 8 medium to medium-large fresh artichokes*
1 *to 2 tablespoons salt*
1 *to 2 tablespoons olive oil*

Carefully wash the artichokes, and break off (do not cut) the stem ends flush with the bases of the leafy bracts. Trim off any ragged ends with a knife. (One can trim off the sharp-pointed leaf tips with kitchen shears prior to cooking, but I object to this, on the basis that it ruins the pristine beauty of the globular heads.) Place in a kettle, preferably one which just accommodates the artichokes, upright side by side, add water to cover, plus the salt and oil. Bring to a quick boil, covered, then reduce heat and simmer for 30 to 40 minutes, or until one of the outside leaves is easily pulled off. Remove artichokes with tongs and drain them upside-down in a colander. Serve individually on plates large enough to accommodate the discarded leaves, or on smaller plates with a big communal bowl for the discards. Serve hot with melted butter or Hollandaise sauce, or cold with Homemade Mayonnaise or Vinaigrette Sauce.

SINCE the eating of an artichoke is a reasonably complicated business, one which requires time and attention for its full enjoyment, it is very much recommended that the vegetable be served as a separate course—usually after the appetizer (if any), or, following the European pattern, immediately after the meat course.

To eat an artichoke, pull off the leaves, one at a

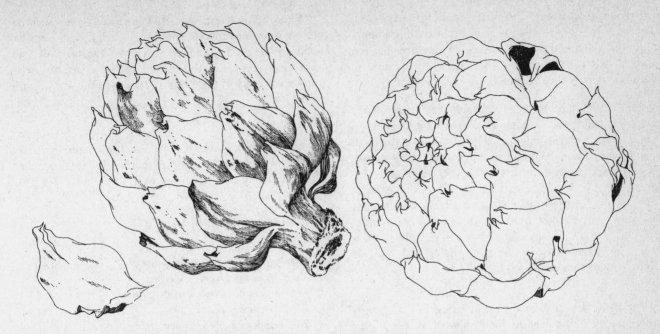

time. Hold the tip of the leaf in your fingers, and dip the fleshy base into the butter or sauce, then nibble off the tender fleshy part. The remainder of the leaf is discarded. The thin undeveloped leaves towards the center of the head are pulled away, the little bit of soft flesh consumed, and remnants discarded. The prickly-feathery ''choke'' beneath is removed in its entirety with a knife or sharp-edged spoon.

Then we come upon the *pièce de résistance* of the artichoke. This is the base, *fond*, or bottom, when trimmed a vaguely concave circle of supreme succulence. Cut this into pieces, dip into the butter or sauce, and relish its delicacy to the fullest degree.

Artichoke bottoms are fortunately also available in cans, imported from France or Spain. These may be eaten as they come from the can, but are more often sautéed slowly in a little butter until nicely browned on both sides. Serve hot as an elegant garnish with steaks and the like.

For a first-course appetizer, lightly spread pâté de foie gras on the hot, sautéed bottoms prior to offering. Or spread a very small quantity of Smithfield ham on the hot, sautéed bottoms, sprinkle lightly with freshly grated Swiss cheese, and run under a preheated broiler until the cheese melts. The latter is also delicious without the ham.

Boiled artichokes can be stuffed in various ways. These are basically prepared as indicated on page 18, but the globes are boiled for only fifteen minutes or so. Allow the vegetable to drain and cool somewhat, then carefully press the leafy bracts, a few at a time, downward to open up the heart of the matter. Remove the fuzzy choke. Place a good quantity of the stuffing mix-

ture of your choice in the middle of the artichoke and neatly tuck bits of it between the leaves as you re-assemble the structure to approximate its original appearance. Then set the stuffed globes on a rack in a sizable kettle over a small amount of boiling water, cover and steam over medium or low heat for about 30 to 40 minutes, or until done. Most versions of stuffed artichokes are best served hot, though in the Italian and Greek cuisines they are often served cold or at room temperature.

Favorite stuffing mixtures include seasoned coarse bread crumbs—anointed with olive oil and touched with oregano and mashed garlic—ground baked ham combined with bread crumbs, or minced scallions sautéed in light oil with coarse bread crumbs and a pinch of basil.

HERE is a rather showy version, utilizing canned salmon, which makes a memorable main dish for a light supper when accompanied by a glass of good wine, preferably a white or rosé.

Stuffed Artichokes Seattle
Serves 4.

4 *medium artichokes*
1 *7-ounce can red salmon, drained, flaked*
¼ *cup minced fresh parsley*
1 *small clove garlic, mashed*
¼ *teaspoon black pepper*
⅓ *cup coarse bread crumbs*
2 *teaspoons lemon juice*

Prepare boiled artichokes for stuffing (page 18). Thoroughly combine the salmon and other ingredients and stuff the artichokes. Arrange on rack over boiling water, cover container, and steam for 30 to 40 minutes, or until very tender. Serve while hot, preferably.

THE little Mediterranean artichoke hearts which are available canned in a seasoned oil, rather *à la grecque*, are, I think, perfectly delicious. When served, drained, just as they come from the container, they can scarcely be improved upon as an instant appetizer or as an ingredient in a flamboyant antipasto. The same companies that offer these also make available an unusual artichoke purée, to be used as a dip with crisp sesame-seed crackers. I like to add a bit of lemon juice and a touch of garlic powder to this purée, and chill it lightly prior to use.

SMALL artichoke hearts packed in salt water, available in tins from Spain, lend themselves especially well to stuffing, and make a unique hors d'oeuvre. My favorite version of these is as follows:

Stuffed Artichoke Hearts Diana
Serves 6 as appetizers.

1 15-ounce can tiny artichoke hearts in brine
1 6-ounce can tiny shrimp
1 tablespoon minced scallion tops
2 tablespoons minced celery heart, with a few leaves
1 tablespoon minced cooked beets
salt and pepper to taste
mayonnaise

Thoroughly drain the artichoke hearts and very carefully open up the center of the leaves to receive the stuffing. Drain the shrimp and chop very fine. Thoroughly combine with the scallion tops, celery, and beets. Season to taste and add enough mayonnaise (homemade, preferably) just to bind the mixture. Very carefully place small amounts of the shrimp-vegetable mixture in center of each artichoke heart, press them closed, and chill until ready to serve—for at least 1 hour.

USING canned artichoke hearts, another unusual hors d'oeuvre can be created.

Artichoke Hearts Roman-Jewish Style
Serves 6 as appetizers.

1 15-ounce can tiny artichoke hearts in brine
1 cup olive oil
½ small clove garlic, mashed
coarse salt

Thoroughly drain the artichoke hearts and pat them dry with paper towels. Heat the oil in a heavy skillet, adding the garlic, and in it fry the hearts until they are nicely browned and indeed almost crisp. Drain on absorbent paper towels, salt lightly, and serve while very hot.

CREAMED artichoke hearts are best made with the frozen vegetable, widely available in this country. This delicate, rich dish goes well with chicken or veal.

Creamed Artichoke Hearts
Serves 4 to 6.

1 package frozen artichoke hearts
1½ cups heavy cream
salt and freshly ground white pepper
1 to 2 teaspoons lemon juice
2 tablespoons finely chopped parsley

Fully cook the artichoke hearts according to package directions, draining them thoroughly. Bring the cream to the boil, and boil it until it is somewhat reduced in quantity—for about 10 minutes. Season to taste with salt, white pepper, and lemon juice. Arrange the drained hot artichoke hearts on a heated serving dish, pour the hot cream over, and sprinkle with parsley. Serve at once.

ASPARAGUS

Asparagus (a member of the Lily Family, known botanically as *Asparagus officinalis*) is a native of Europe. It still grows wild in fields in France, and has been in more or less extensive cultivation for more than two thousand years, having been known and prized by the Greeks and the Romans.

Today fresh Asparagus is a seasonal vegetable in our markets, reaching its peak during the month of April in most areas. California is our greatest Asparagus-producing state, where its somewhat specialized cultivation is practiced on a very large scale. The edible portion of the plant is actually the young sprouts, or spears, which arise from the underground woody crown. The plant grows on to bear graceful fernlike sprays with vivid red berries, these justly popular as decorations.

Several other kinds of Asparagus are frequent ornamentals in our gardens in warm climes, and in greenhouses elsewhere. Asparagus fern (*A. plumosus*) and *Asparagus Sprengeri* are the best known of these.

In our stores, I have been puzzled to see so many

people purposely buying the large, thick, older stalks of Asparagus. Don't do that! Unless the stalks are of one of the special "colossal" varieties imported at considerable expense from Europe, you will find the sleek slender spears better for all table purposes.

Pay attention to the cooking of the vegetable. Asparagus, overcooked, loses its delicate flavor. Each stalk should be slightly firm to the bite, *al dente.*

Asparagus can be used in many ways. It adapts itself very well to a variety of sauces—Hollandaise, Mornay, mayonnaise, vinaigrette, a light mustard, and even the exotic Maltaise (page 255). Superb creamed soups are prepared from it. Asparagus purée (of both the green and the bleached stalks) is a famous example of *haute cuisine,* and the chilled tips are extensively utilized as showy garnishes.

Probably the best version of Asparagus is the simplest one: steamed in a small amount of lightly salted water until just firm-tender, then served with melted butter, or homemade mayonnaise, a little salt and fresh-ground black pepper, and a touch of fresh lemon or lime juice. Or, if desired, tie stalks into bunches with kitchen twine. Then place them in lightly salted water to cook, covered, until just firm-tender. Special asparagus cookers are available from France, in which the bunches of stalks are steamed standing upright. One can also accomplish this, of course, in a sizable kettle with tight-fitting lid, or a double boiler with the upper portion inverted over the lower.

Preliminary preparation includes snapping off or cutting off the tough bottoms of the stalks, removing the scales and washing the stalks well.

THE average recipe for asparagus with lemon butter is a shade too "lemony" for my taste buds, so I cut down the amounts, with the following more subtle results:

Asparagus with Lemon Butter
Serves 4.

>2 *pounds fresh asparagus*
>¾ *cup butter*
>2 *teaspoons fresh lemon juice*
>*salt and freshly ground pepper*

Cook and drain the asparagus. In a small heavy saucepan melt the butter, mix in the lemon juice, and pour this over individual hot servings of the vegetable at table. Season to taste with salt and pepper.

HERE is another simple version of asparagus—a Dutch recipe from the Victoria Hotel in Amsterdam.

Holland Asparagus
Serves 4 to 6.

2 pounds fresh asparagus
⅛ teaspoon freshly ground nutmeg
¼ pound (1 stick) butter
2 hard-cooked eggs, finely chopped
1 bunch watercress, chopped

Cook asparagus until tender but still slightly crisp. Drain spears and arrange on a warmed platter. Sprinkle with nutmeg. Meanwhile, in a heavy saucepan, melt the butter, stirring constantly, and allow it to brown slightly. Serve the brown butter in a small heated pitcher, the chopped eggs in a bowl, and the chopped watercress in another bowl.

A QUICHE made with asparagus is at once a culinary showpiece and a delectable thing to consume.

Asparagus Quiche
Serves 4 to 6.

1 unbaked 9-inch pastry shell
2 pounds fresh asparagus
2 cups light cream
⅓ cup grated Parmesan cheese
⅓ cup grated Swiss cheese
4 eggs
salt and freshly ground pepper

Partially bake the pastry shell in preheated 400° F. oven for about 8 minutes. Cook and drain the asparagus. Cut the top 2 inches off each spear, reserving the rest for soups and other uses. Combine the cream, both kinds of cheese, eggs, and salt and dash of pepper together very thoroughly, and pour into pastry shell. Bake in preheated 350° F. oven for 30 minutes, or until the custard is almost set. Stick the asparagus tips upright into the quiche, so that the whole thing resembles some sort of outré forest. Return quiche to the oven until it is firm, not more than 5 minutes. Serve immediately.

ASPARAGI *alla parmigiana* is a delicate Italian version of our favored vegetable. Use freshly grated cheese, of course.

Asparagus Parmesan
Serves 6.

2 pounds fresh asparagus
½ cup melted butter
½ cup freshly grated Parmesan cheese

Cook asparagus until tender, yet still firm, and drain well. Arrange spears in a single layer in a buttered shallow baking dish. Pour the melted butter over them and sprinkle liberally with the cheese. Bake in a preheated 400° F. oven for 10 minutes, or until very lightly browned. Serve at once.

UNTIL recent years, the superb rapid Japanese method of stir-frying asparagus (and comparable vegetables) was little known outside of Oriental restaurants of note. But nowadays, happily, this system of cookery—which preserves all of the abundant nutritional value of the spears, plus their unique taste and texture—has grown popular in many homes. Be sure to serve the asparagus cooked this way immediately it comes from the stove, so that the sections do not become soggy! They form a fascinating addition to any menu, whether simple or ornate.

Asparagus Nipponese
Serves 4 to 6.

2 pounds fresh asparagus
3 tablespoons peanut or soy oil
1 tablespoon coarse salt

Cut the raw asparagus on an extreme diagonal into pieces about 2 inches long, discarding the tough bases or using them in soup stock. Cook in rapidly boiling salted water until partially tender, and drain very thoroughly. Immediately before serving time, heat the oil in a wok or large heavy skillet, and in it, over high heat, stir-fry quickly the asparagus pieces until they are lightly browned—they should be almost crisp, and the process should require about 2 minutes at most. Remove with slotted spoon and place them on paper towels to drain, dusting rather liberally with coarse salt. Serve without any delay.

HERE is a rich creation that must be offered as a solo course.

Asparagus with Chantilly Mayonnaise
Serves 4 to 6.

2 pounds fresh asparagus
2 cups Homemade Mayonnaise (page 255)
½ to ¾ cup whipped heavy cream

Cook asparagus until tender but still firm, drain thoroughly, and chill. To make Chantilly Mayonnaise, prepare Homemade Mayonnaise, chill it, and at last moment, fold in the whipped cream. Serve the asparagus spears liberally topped with the Chantilly Mayonnaise.

Asparagus lends itself to many kinds of salads. The secret of this one is in the cooking of the spears in the savory seasoned stock. I suspect that this will become one of your favorite ways with this marvelous vegetable.

Asparagus Salad Annette
Serves 6.

2 pounds fresh asparagus
1 cup chicken stock
½ teaspoon salt
¼ cup finely chopped onion
½ cup commercial "French" dressing
4 cups shredded lettuce
freshly ground black pepper
paprika
1 tablespoon chopped fresh parsley
anchovy fillets
tomato wedges
ripe olives

In a large heavy saucepan heat the stock, with salt and onion, to the boiling point. Cook the asparagus in this until just tender. Carefully remove the spears from liquid and arrange in a shallow dish. Pour your favorite commercial "French" dressing, the thick kind, over the spears, and turn several times as they cool. Refrigerate until well chilled. Serve marinated asparagus spears on individual salad plates on a bed of shredded lettuce. Sprinkle to taste with pepper, and dust with paprika and fresh parsley. Garnish each serving with an anchovy fillet or two, a couple of tomato wedges, and ripe olives.

Here is another unusual asparagus dish, a combination of hot and cold ingredients.

Brussels Asparagus-Lobster Salad
Serves 4.

20 cooked asparagus spears
4 to 6 hard-cooked eggs, peeled, halved
2 tablespoons butter
1 tablespoon granulated flour
1 teaspoon salt
¼ teaspoon white pepper
½ teaspoon sugar
1 cup light cream

1 cup chopped cooked lobster
1 teaspoon lemon juice
1 egg yolk
2 tablespoons cooking sherry
3 tablespoons freshly grated Swiss cheese

In a saucepan, melt the butter and stir in the flour, salt, white pepper, and sugar, mixing thoroughly. Gradually add the cream, and cook over a low flame, stirring constantly, until the sauce is thickened and smooth. Add the chopped cooked lobster and heat thoroughly. In a bowl, beat together the lemon juice, egg yolk, and sherry. Remove the sauce from the heat, and stir in the lemon-sherry mixture. Return sauce to low flame and heat through. Do not allow it to approach the boiling point. Arrange the hard-cooked egg halves and asparagus tips on serving plates, and liberally pour over the hot lobster sauce. Sprinkle each serving with cheese, and serve at once.

AVOCADO

The Avocado (*Persea americana*, of the Laurel Family), also known oddly as Alligator Pear, is one of those fruits which is most often treated as a vegetable at our tables. Originally from Mexico and Guatemala, the Avocado was introduced into South America in pre-Columbian days, being cultivated there by the Incas. In this country, commercial production, which is extensive, centers in two areas—South Florida and Southern California.

Though the wild Avocados, produced mostly during May and June on a stately tree as much as one hundred feet tall, are scarcely three inches across, development of many improved varieties here permits us to enjoy fruits ten or eleven inches in length, weighing as much as four pounds, for some nine months of the year.

An Avocado is ready for use when it yields slightly to gentle pressure at the bottom. In certain varieties found in our markets, the large seed rattles when the fruit is ripe, but this does not always hold true. Unripened Avocados should be set in a warm spot to mature. When cut, they darken, but if the seed is left undisturbed in the unused portion, and this is wrapped in aluminum foil or wax paper and refrigerated, this discoloration is minimal for a day or two.

There are a great many different ways to serve this luscious tropical vegetable—from soups or appetizers to hearty main dishes.

Certainly the best known Avocado hors d'oeuvre is that marvelous Mexican medley, Guacamole (pronounced wah-kah-*mow*-lay). There are infinite variations, but here is a good one. Crisp triangles of tortillas or corn chips are perfect for dipping, it seems to me.

Guacamole
Serves 6.

2 cups fork-mashed ripe avocado
¼ cup fresh lime juice
½ cup grated or finely chopped onion
¼ teaspoon salt
¼ teaspoon freshly ground pepper
4 to 6 drops Tabasco sauce
¼ cup finely chopped pimiento

Be sure the avocado (or plural, if necessary) used is a very good, smooth-ripe one. Add all other ingredients to the peeled, mashed avocado, except the pimiento, and blend thoroughly. For a less juicy version, reduce lime juice. Stir in pimiento lightly, and chill for at least 2 hours. Serve as an excellent and exciting dip at cocktail time.

EL SALVADOR, though one of the smallest countries in the Americas, is one of the most impressively picturesque, with a marvelous, almost always active volcano, Izalco, which can be viewed at close range from a posh resort hotel. The national cuisine is varied and excellent, and includes the following avocado and rice medley, which is ideally served with such things as chicken or pork.

Arroz con Aguacate (Saffron Rice with Avocados)
Serves 4.

2 medium-size ripe avocados
3 tablespoons butter
¾ cup chopped onion
1 small clove garlic, minced
1 cup raw long grain rice
½ teaspoon saffron (or Annatto, page 16)
2½ cups rich chicken stock
salt to taste

Sauté onion and garlic in butter in a heavy skillet with cover for 5 minutes. Add the rice and continue to cook, stirring constantly, until rice becomes slightly opaque. Combine saffron (or annatto) with chicken stock. Add to rice and bring to the boil. Cover, reduce heat and simmer until rice is tender, usually about

20 minutes. Peel avocados and slice or dice. When rice is tender, fold in avocado, reserving a few pieces for garnish. Season to taste with salt, garnish, and serve at once.

HERE is a hearty salad with Latin overtones, ideally suited for a summertime light supper.

Avocado Suzette
Serves 4 to 6.

2 medium-size ripe avocados, peeled, cubed
6 slices lean bacon
3 cups diced cooked potatoes
¼ cup finely chopped onion
1 tablespoon chopped scallion tops
2 hard-cooked eggs, coarsely chopped
1 tablespoon chopped pimiento
1 teaspoon salt
½ teaspoon freshly ground pepper
½ cup mayonnaise
2 tablespoons fresh lime juice

In a skillet, fry the bacon until crisp, then drain and crumble it. In a sizable salad bowl lightly toss together the potatoes, onion, scallion tops, eggs, pimiento, salt, pepper, and bacon. Chill for one hour. Combine the mayonnaise (homemade, preferably) with the lime juice, and fold this into the potato mixture at last minute. Then toss gently with avocado cubes and serve at once.

AVOCADO soups are justifiably popular in tropical America. Here are two pertinent delectable versions, one to be offered hot, the other chilled.

Avocado Soup Luisa
Serves 4.

½ cup mashed ripe avocado
1 can condensed cream of mushroom soup
1 soup can water
2 tablespoons dry sherry
1 tablespoon fresh lime juice
½ teaspoon salt
¼ teaspoon freshly ground black pepper
2 tablespoons minced scallion tops
2 tablespoons grated sharp Cheddar cheese

In a kettle, combine the soup with water and bring almost to the boiling point. Reduce heat and add all other ingredients except scallion tops and cheese. Heat through and serve quickly, each portion sprinkled with scallions and cheese.

Avocado Soup Acapulco
Serves 4.

1 large, very ripe avocado
2 cans consommé madrilène
½ cup commercial sour cream
1 teaspoon grated onion
⅛ teaspoon Cayenne pepper
⅛ to ¼ teaspoon chili powder
1 teaspoon minced fresh dill weed

Mash peeled avocado thoroughly with a fork—do not use an electric blender for this task, please. Combine with all other ingredients except the dill weed. Chill until firm and serve in chilled bowls, garnished with the dill weed.

WHEN I lived in Cuba, one of the edible delights which appeared with frequency in both restaurants and private homes was the following avocado salad.

Cuban Avocado Salad
Serves 3 to 4.

1 large avocado, chilled, peeled, and diced
1 medium-size fresh pineapple, chilled, peeled, and diced
2 tablespoons fresh lime juice
¾ cup mayonnaise
crisp lettuce for base

Blend together the lime juice and mayonnaise, and chill for an hour or so. Arrange cubes of pineapple (the canned variety can be used, and is, indeed, often substituted in Cuba) and avocado on lettuce leaves, and pour dressing over them. Garnish, if desired, with halves of maraschino cherries. Serve at once.

AMONG the many ways in which our splendid Florida avocados are served at my home is the following one. It is so unique that I customarily offer it as a special course, all by itself, prior to the meat.

Avocado à la Hawkes
Serves 4.

2 medium-size ripe avocados
1 tablespoon butter
1½ teaspoons tomato ketchup
1 tablespoon warm water
1 tablespoon wine vinegar
1 tablespoon Worcestershire sauce
¼ teaspoon salt

½ teaspoon dry mustard
5 whole cloves
1 tablespoon sugar
3 drops Tabasco sauce

In a saucepan, combine all ingredients except the avocados. Heat until the mixture comes to the boil, stirring often. Lower heat at once, and simmer, uncovered, for 10 minutes. Cut avocados in half and, of course, discard seeds. With sharp knife, make several cross cuts about ½ inch deep in the avocado flesh. Pour hot sauce into avocado halves, and serve at once.

IN BRAZIL, the avocado is known as *abacate,* and is a favorite ingredient in menus, whether simple or ornate. Here is a wonderful dessert from *a cidade maravilhosa,* Rio de Janeiro.

Brazilian Avocado Cream
Serves 4 to 6.

2 large, very ripe avocados
2 to 3 tablespoons fresh lime juice
1 cup sugar
¼ cup heavy cream
¼ teaspoon salt

Press avocado pulp through a sieve to make a purée. Thoroughly blend in other ingredients. Chill for at least two hours. Serve in chilled parfait glasses.

BAMBOO SHOOTS

The very young and usually ivory-colored sprouts of several kinds of Bamboo are extensively utilized in good Oriental cookery. These sprouts, severed just as they push above the soil, are exceedingly rapid in their growth, in some instances attaining a height of a foot or more during a twenty-four-hour span. Imported, canned, generally in a lightly salted liquid, from Japan and Honk Kong, they are readily available in our domestic markets today.

Bamboos are fascinating plants, actually gigantic grasses, of overpowering variety and botanical complexity, which reach their greatest development in the Asiatic tropics and subtropics. There they are extremely important, their stout stems being utilized to construct the walls and roofs of houses, curtains,

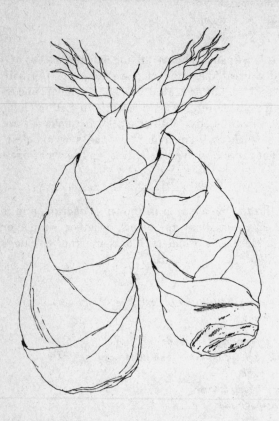

room partitions, baskets, and even ornate umbrellas. Though exceedingly rapid of growth, these prodigious plants—on occasion attaining heights of more than one hundred feet—by and large flower only one time, often some forty or fifty years from seed, and then perish. In some Asiatic lands, all of the common clumps of a given kind of Bamboo will flower simultaneously, then die down, and no specimens will be found until the seedlings germinate later on.

Canned Bamboo Shoots are not inexpensive, but a small amount of them in a given recipe goes a long way. Once the can has been opened, the unused portion of the shoots can successfully be saved by placing them in cold water, covered, and changing the water daily; the shoots should be used as soon as possible, however, since they rather quickly lose their unique nutty flavor and pleasant, crisp texture.

As is typical of almost all Oriental cookery, the Bamboo Shoots, either sliced or cubed, are added to the recipe so they just barely cook—full appreciation of their texture is most important.

HERE is a dish which is a great favorite in my home, where it is offered as one of several such creations for an elegant Chinese-Japanese-Korean dinner.

Bamboo Shoots and Shrimp
Serves 4 to 6.

> 2 cups cubed bamboo shoots
> 1½ pounds raw medium shrimp, shelled and deveined
> 2 tablespoons cornstarch
> 2 tablespoons Japanese soy sauce
> 2 tablespoons sake or cooking sherry
> ½ teaspoon ground ginger
> 3 tablespoons peanut or soy oil
> 1½ cups scallions, with tops, cut into ½-inch sections
> ½ cup drained canned tiny peas

Cut the raw shrimp into bite-size pieces. Combine the cornstarch, soy sauce, sake or sherry, and ginger, and marinate the shrimp in this mixture for 30 minutes. Using a wok or other large skillet, heat the oil to high degree, and add the shrimp pieces, stir-frying them for a minute or so, stirring constantly. Add the bamboo shoots and scallions and stir-fry them for not more than 2 minutes. Add the drained peas, stir through, and remove wok or skillet from the heat. Serve at once, with steamed white rice.

DICED or sliced bamboo shoots can also be added with attractive results to shrimp, lobster, or fowl salads. They form a distinctive ingredient in heated chicken or beef bouillon, or other clear soups, and in sizable chunks can well be incorporated into the fabulous Japanese tempura.

BANANA

In the United States, Bananas (*Musa paradisiaca* subsp. *sapientum*, principally) imported in huge numbers from Central and South America, have long been known as highly prized fruits. There are, however, interesting ways of preparing them as a vegetable. For this purpose, they should be utilized when only partially ripe, with conspicuous green tips and firm texture.

The spectacular big leaves of the commercial Banana plant are important as well to the connoisseur cook. In the tropics, these fronds—frequently six to ten feet in length and a couple of feet across—are used much as we do aluminum foil or parchment paper. While our modern products impart no flavor to the foods enclosed in their wrappings for baking or steaming, the *Musa* foliage adds an indefinably delicate touch (as well as a unique appearance) to all dishes in which it participates.

In Hawaii and other islands of the Pacific, all sorts

of wondrous things wrapped with pieces of Banana frond will be presented at festive tables, from portions of roast whole pig, baked in a special rock-lined oven in the ground, to soy-sauce-seasoned hamburgers and meatballs, to special concoctions of seafood or pork or beef as hot hors d'oeuvres.

ON THE Hawaiian island of Kauai I was served the following exciting version of Laulau, which is a sort of generic term for a wide array of steamed or baked appetizer (or, in larger quantities, main dish). The laulaus arrive at the cocktail table steaming hot in their handsome individual packets of banana fronds.

Kauai Laulau
Serves 8 to 10.

> *3 to 5 young banana leaves*
> *1 pound fresh salmon, cubed*
> *Hawaiian or kosher salt*
> *2 pounds slightly fatty pork, cubed*
> *2 pounds fresh spinach or taro leaves*
> *1 can bean sprouts, drained*
> *Japanese soy sauce*

Cut the fresh salmon (frozen fish can, of course, be used) into 8 to 10 equal cubes. Place in a container with a goodly amount of the coarse salt and cold water to cover, and soak refrigerated overnight. If salted fresh salmon (not smoked, please note) is available, omit this soaking process. Drain salmon cubes thoroughly. Prepare the banana leaves by trimming out and discarding the fleshy midrib and cutting the remaining frond into rectangles about 15″ × 8″. Wash these pieces thoroughly and drain only partially, so that a bit of moisture sticks to them. Arrange 2 or more pieces of the banana frond on a flat working surface and top with a liberal amount of the fresh spinach (or taro) leaves, these washed, drained, and torn into chunks. Add some of the drained canned bean sprouts to each laulau, together with one or more cubes of salted salmon. Cut the pork into 16 to 20 cubes, and add equal amounts to each laulau. Sprinkle to taste with Japanese soy sauce (be rather liberal), then distribute remaining bean sprouts over each portion, and top with remaining spinach or taro leaves. Fold the banana-frond pieces into envelopes enclosing everything and tie firmly with kitchen string. Using a large heavy kettle with cover, place the laulaus in a single layer on a rack above hot water, then cover, and steam for 3 to 4 hours, carefully adding additional water as needed. Remove laulaus and serve for your guests to untie on individual plates. If the recipe is used as a main dish, serve with hot white rice and a pineapple or citrus salad.

IN TROPICAL America, banana fronds are also used to enclose varied versions of tamales. In Mexico and Guatemala, corn husks usually serve as tamale wrappings, but in their warm lowland regions, and in most other parts of Central America, South America, and the West Indies, banana leaves comprise the envelopes.

Nicaraguan cuisine is little known outside of that spectacular land, but the national version of tamales, often indicated as the Nicaraguan national dish, is truly a culinary experience. They require a bit of time and effort, but are eminently worthwhile, served very hot with rice and red *frijoles* (kidney beans in a pinch), the latter cooked and refried in lard (Frijoles Refritos, page 46). There are about fifty authentic recipes for Nacatamales; here is my personal favorite.

Nicaraguan Nacatamales
Serves 8 to 10.

> *banana leaves (or parchment paper or aluminum foil)*
>   *for wrapping*
> *3 cups white cornmeal*
> *4 cups boiling water*
> *6 tablespoons butter*
> *2 teaspoons salt*
> *2 eggs, beaten well*
> *4 cups diced raw lean beef*
> *3 cups diced raw lean pork*
> *3 cups diced raw chicken*
> *4 cups cold water*
> *3 small cloves garlic, minced*
> *2 cups canned garbanzos, coarsely chopped*
> *⅓ cup light olive oil*
> *3 cups coarsely chopped fresh tomatoes*
> *1 cup coarsely chopped green pepper*
> *3 cups coarsely chopped onion*
> *½ teaspoon dried ground chili peppers*
> *½ cup finely chopped parsley*
> *3 teaspoons salt*
> *4 tablespoons cider vinegar*
> *2 teaspoons sugar*
> *3 teaspoons capers*
> *¾ cup seedless raisins, halved*
> *¾ cup thinly sliced stuffed olives*
> *⅓ cup fried crumbled lean bacon*
> *2 cups canned corn kernels, drained*
> *1 cup canned tiny green peas, drained*
> *⅓ cup diced pimientos*

Combine the cornmeal with a bit of cold water, then add this to a saucepan containing the rapidly boiling water, stirring constantly. Add the butter and the 2 teaspoons of salt. Over low heat, stirring occasionally, cook for 15 minutes. Remove from the stove and add the beaten eggs, stirring until a smooth dough results. Meanwhile, in a large saucepan combine the beef, pork, chicken, cold water, garlic, and garbanzos. Bring to a quick boil, then reduce heat and cook, stirring occasionally, for 30 minutes, or until meats are tender but not overly cooked. Drain thoroughly and chop coarsely. Using a large skillet with cover, heat the oil, and add the tomatoes, green pepper, onion, chili peppers, parsley, salt, vinegar, sugar, and cooked meat. Cover and cook over low heat for 15 minutes, stirring once. Remove from the heat and lightly mix in the capers, raisins, olives, bacon, corn, peas, and pimientos. Prepare banana-leaf wrappers by trimming out and discarding the fleshy midrib, cutting remainder into rectangles about 15″ × 8″. Wash these pieces thoroughly and drain only partially, so that a bit of moisture adheres to them. Parboil them until they are limp—usually about 10 minutes in rapidly boiling water, covered. Spread about 4 tablespoons of the cornmeal mixture onto the center of the pieces of banana frond (or parchment paper or aluminum foil), and pat it out into a very thin layer. Place about 2 or 3 tablespoons of the meat-and-vegetable mixture on one side of the cornmeal dough and roll it up carefully and tightly, sealing the edges as thoroughly as possible. Seal with a bit of warm water and more dough, if needed. Fold the blanched banana leaves around the nacatamales, and tie them firmly with string. Place them in one or two large shallow pots of salted water to cover, and cook over very low heat, covered, for about one hour. The nacatamales should be placed in layers only 2 deep at the most. Serve in their banana-frond coverings, hot or at room temperature. You may wish to offer a heated Creole sauce of some sort to spoon over these ornate delicacies, but this is strictly optional.

PLANTAIN

Recent years have seen the arrival in our markets of Plantains, or *plátanos*, imported from the Antilles or Central America. Though the fruit of a close relative of the "sweet" bananas, Plantains are treated as a vegetable, since they must be cooked to be edible. Ordinary bananas can, of course, also be cooked, and indeed many of the recipes suggested below apply equally well to them.

Plantains, of a number of varieties, are to be found at almost every meal on tables in the tropics, where they are served as a starch (often with potatoes, rice, and/or beans), in soups, as special accessory dishes, or even as showy desserts. Happily these utilitarian vegetables are being offered by good cooks in this country with increasing frequency.

These *plátanos*—like the other kinds of bananas, members of the Bird-of-Paradise (*Strelitzia*) Family —are sold, not in hands but individually, priced by the pound. It is not uncommon to find single specimens weighing two or more pounds, and they are often a foot or more in length and upwards of two or three inches in diameter. They are usually sold when very green-skinned. Ripening proceeds rapidly in a warm spot in the kitchen, whereupon they turn yellow, with irregular blackish-brown markings, and finally become a rather unfortunate dirty-black, often with patches of mold spotting the skin.

Basically, we can consider that Plantains come in three delicious flavors—green (*verde*), semiripe (*natural*), and very ripe (*maduro*). In pantries in many parts of the tropical world, one finds entire stalks of *plátanos*, which are used up in an amazing diversity of fashions as they change from green to very ripe.

When *verde,* or hard and green, Plantains are cooked as appetizers, incorporated into hearty soups, and served as distinctive vegetables in several variations.

BOILED green plantains are somewhat of an acquired taste for most of us in this country, though in lands to the south and elsewhere throughout the world they appear from breakfast to late dinner as a specialized vegetable. The recipe given below is from the Guianas, and is excellent when served with roast meats, if possible with side dishes of hot red or pinto beans and hot steamed rice.

Boiled Green Plantains Paramaribo
Serves 4 to 6.

2 firm green unspotted plantains
salted water
3 slices lean bacon
½ cup finely chopped onion
⅓ cup chopped green pepper
butter
salt and freshly ground pepper
fresh lime wedges

Peel the plantains under running cold water and cut transversely into chunks about 2 inches in length.

Without delay place in a big kettle of rapidly boiling salted water, cover, and cook until soft. Drain thoroughly. Meanwhile, in a skillet, fry the bacon until crisp, then remove to drain on absorbent paper towels. In a small amount of the bacon drippings, sauté the onion and green pepper until soft, and remove these with slotted spoon to drain. Chop the boiled plantains coarsely, combine with the cooked onion and green pepper, plus the crumbled bacon, then add butter and salt and pepper to taste. Serve hot, garnished with wedges of fresh limes.

THE GREEN plantains can also be lightly parboiled in salted water and added to such hearty soups as Juanita's Mondongo (page 77) or Ajiaco (page 143), or the following Nicaraguan specialty, which is a great personal favorite of mine. Its name signifies "Soup of the Poor," but it is a robust affair of considerable elegance.

Sopa de Pobre
Serves 4 to 6.

> 2 *firm green unspotted plantains*
> *large meaty beef soup bone*
> 2 *quarts cold water*
> 1 *teaspoon salt*
> 2 *to 3 tablespoons butter*
> 1½ *cups coarsely chopped onion*
> 2 *to 3 cloves garlic, finely chopped*
> 1 *pound lean stew beef*
> 2 *large green-ripe tomatoes, coarsely chopped*
> 1 *large green pepper, coarsely chopped*
> 5 *or 6 small carrots, sliced*
> 2 *cups diced potatoes*
> 4 *small yellow crookneck squash, sliced*
> 1 *cup fresh green corn kernels, or canned corn kernels, drained*
> *salt and freshly ground pepper*
> *fresh lime or sour orange wedges*

Place the soup bone in a big soup kettle with cover, add cold water and salt. Bring to a boil over high heat, skim off any scum that forms, then reduce heat and simmer, covered, for an hour or so. Meanwhile, in a skillet melt the butter and in it sauté the onion and garlic until they are just soft. Remove them with slotted spoon and add to the soup stock, first removing the soup bones and discarding them. In the same skillet cook the pieces of stew beef until they are well browned on all sides, removing them to the soup kettle as this is done. Add the tomatoes and green pepper to the skillet, and cook, stirring often, for about 15

minutes, then turn all of this into the soup. Cover again and cook soup over low heat for about 30 minutes. Then add the carrots and potatoes, and continue to cook until they are almost tender. Add the squash and either kind of corn, plus the green plantains, these peeled and cut into 1-inch chunks. Cover again and cook for about 10 minutes, correct seasoning, and serve the thick soup while very hot, with fresh lime or sour orange wedges to be squeezed in to personal taste.

ONE of the finest cooks from Cuba whom I have ever met is Sra. Benita Robaina, a charming lady who has been very cooperative in disclosing to me her special recipes for use in this book. Benita's way with twice-cooked green plantains is a particular treasure. She often serves it with such things as Cuban roast pork, or other versions of this meat, or ham, or beef. It is appropriate to offer one's guests thick wedges of limes or sour oranges to squeeze over the flattened *plátano* chunks. Though technically a side-dish kind of vegetable, a good platter of Benita's specialty, offered hot, is an intriguing accouterment with cocktails or beer!

Technically, the name for this delicacy is *plátanos chatines*, but Sra. Robaina has bestowed on them the nickname of *plátanos a puñetazos* (hit with the fist).

Benita's Green Plantains
Serves 4 to 6.

> 2 *firm green unspotted plantains*
> ½ *cup lard*
> *salt*
> *fresh lime or sour orange wedges*

Peel the plantains under running cold water and cut into transverse slices about ¾ inch thick. Place the unmelted lard in a skillet, with some of the plantain slices, and bring the heat to moderate degree. Cook the slices, turning once, until they soften slightly. Remove partially cooked slices with slotted spoon or spatula and place on a sheet of waxed paper on a level surface. Top with another piece of waxed paper, and with a sharp blow of the fist mash each plantain slice. Raise the heat under the lard, and return the mashed plantains to the skillet, to cook until lightly browned on both sides, turning once. Remove to paper towels to drain, salt to taste, and serve hot, with wedges of lime or sour orange on the side.

AN EXCELLENT cocktail accompaniment is crisp, salted chips of green Plantains, known as mariquitas. These are available, packaged much like potato chips, in some of our cities these days, but are better prepared fresh, as follows. When working with these *plátanos verdes,* peel them under running cold water, to avoid staining your hands—and do not peel them until ready to cook.

Mariquitas

> 3 *very firm, unspotted green plantains*
> 1 *cup peanut or soy oil*
> *salt, coarse kosher kind preferred*

Peel the plantains and cut them into wafer-thin slices under running cold water. Heat the oil in a deep skillet until very hot, and fry the plantain slices a few at a time until they are lightly browned on both sides. For best results, do not cook too many at once. Drain on absorbent paper towels, and while still hot salt them to taste—rather liberally. Serve while hot, or keep warm in the oven, or store in a tightly sealed jar in a dry cupboard. Mariquitas can be served at room temperature, but they are more widely appreciated when offered fresh and warm.

SEMIRIPE or *natural* plantains can be used in much the same way as both green and ripe ones, but they differ subtly both in texture and flavor. Here is a recipe which is designed, it seems, for use with fried, broiled, or baked fish. I first encountered this delicacy some years ago while searching for orchids and other rare plants in the lovely, cool highlands of Panama's Chiriquí province, but it is a recipe enjoyed in many other Latin lands as well.

Fish and Plantains
Serves 4 to 6.

> 2 *semiripe yellow plantains*
> *salted boiling water*
> 4 *small onions, peeled, thinly sliced*
> 2 *whole cloves garlic, peeled*
> *butter*
> *fish for frying, broiling, or baking*
> *fresh lime wedges*

Peel the semiripe plantains and cut into transverse chunks about 2 inches long, then cut each lengthwise into halves. Drop at once into a kettle of salted boiling water with the onion slices and garlic cloves, and cook, covered, for about 4 minutes. Drain thoroughly, discarding the garlic, but reserving the plantain chunks and onion slices. Arrange plantains and onions attractively in a shallow ovenproof pan and dot liberally with butter. Place in preheated 325–350° F. oven, and baste 2 or 3 times with the juices from the fish of your choice, as this cooks (either fries, broils, or—best—bakes). The plantains, when finished, should be very tender, but not mushy. If necessary, keep them warm for serving with the fish, with wedges of fresh lime.

THE RIPE and very ripe plantains, called *maduros,* in texture and flavor are very distinct from the green vegetable, and somewhat so from the semiripe variety. These *maduros* can be boiled slightly (as indicated for the *verde* plantains), and served seasoned to taste with salt and freshly ground pepper, possibly a dash of lime or sour orange juice, and even a drop of hot pepper sauce, to accompany almost any meat. When treated thus, they compare with a vaguely pulpy "sweet" banana, though their starch content is a bit more obvious.

A favorite way, especially with the ugly black-ripe *maduros,* is the following tropical side dish. A platter of nicely browned *maduros* goes well with pork or ham in any form, or even with hamburgers or beef hash.

Sautéed Ripe Plantains
Serves 4 to 6.

> 2 *black-ripe* maduro *plantains*
> 4 *to 6 tablespoons butter*
> *fresh lime wedges*

Peel the very ripe plantains and cut into tranverse slices ½ to ¾ inch thick. Sauté in butter over low or moderate heat until nicely browned on both sides, turning with spatula as needed. Drain on absorbent paper towels as cooked, and keep warm. Offer wedges of fresh lime (or sour orange) at the table with the hot vegetable.

ONE of the most unusual and memorable uses for these very ripe plantains is to be encountered on fine tables in the republic of Nicaragua. The *maduros* are cut into rather thick lengthwise slices and sautéed in butter, as in the preceding recipe, until nicely browned. These are then served, traditionally, with cooked small red beans which have been lightly refried in lard, and thick slices of deliciously piquant Chinandega *queso de crema*—a sort of farmer cheese. This forms a separate, palate-clearing course after the meat entrée, prior to an optional green salad, before the dessert. The flavor combination is initially a bit peculiar, but a second taste quickly convinces the participant that this is a unique culinary accomplishment!

Our friends in Central America also make use of

maduro plantains in the following recipe, a species of ground beef-*plátano* omelet which is indeed savory. The dish needs few accouterments save perhaps some crusty bread or rolls and a good bottle of beer or red wine.

Plantain-Beef Omelets
Serves 4 to 6.

2 *black-ripe* maduro *plantains*
4 *to 6 tablespoons butter*
1 *egg, well beaten*
¾ *pound lean ground beef*
½ *cup minced onion*
1 *large clove garlic, minced*
salt to taste
2 *or 3 dashes Tabasco sauce*

Peel the very ripe plantains and cut into transverse slices ½ to ¾ inch thick. Sauté these in the butter over low or moderate heat until they are soft and lightly browned on both sides. Remove slices as they are done and mash them thoroughly. Mix in the beaten egg, then all other ingredients. In the same skillet, reheat the butter (add a bit more if deemed necessary), and drop in the *plátano*-beef mixture by heaping tablespoons. Sauté these little omelets until well browned on both sides (the beef will remain rather rare), turning them carefully with a slotted spatula as needed. Serve while hot.

Now we arrive at the delights of the plantain when served as a delicious dessert. The lovely West Indian isle of St. Lucia offers this recipe.

Plantains St. Lucia
Serves 4 to 6.

2 *black-ripe* maduro *plantains*
4 *to 6 tablespoons butter*
1 *cup sugar*
2 *cups water*
½ *cup grated coconut*
unsalted crackers
cream-cheese cubes

Peel the very ripe plantains and cut into ¾-inch transverse slices. Sauté these in the butter over low or moderate heat until lightly browned on both sides, removing the pieces with a slotted spatula as they are done, and draining them on absorbent paper towels. Meanwhile, combine the sugar and water in a saucepan, bring it just to the boil, stirring often, until the sugar has melted. Add the coconut, mix well, and simmer for 10 minutes, uncovered. Arrange the plantain slices in an ovenproof shallow serving dish, and pour the sauce plus the butter from the skillet over them. Run under preheated broiler until thoroughly heated through, and serve at once with unsalted crackers and cubes of cream cheese—or slices of crumbly goat-milk cheese, if available.

ONE OF the most famous of Central American desserts is the following deliciousness, in which these banana relatives reach a sublime caloric height. As in the other dessert recipes, semiripe commercial "sweet" bananas can be substituted. The dish is known in Spanish as *maduros en gloria*, indeed an apt title.

Plantains in Their Glory
Serves 4 to 6.

2 *black-ripe* maduro *plantains*
¼ *pound (1 stick) butter*
1 *large package cream cheese, softened*
2 *tablespoons brown sugar*
2 *tablespoons white sugar*
1 *teaspoon cinnamon*
2 *tablespoons light rum*
1 *cup heavy cream*
whipped cream for garnish

Peel the very ripe plantains and cut into lengths of 4 inches or so; cut these pieces lengthwise into 2 or 3 slices. Melt the butter in a large skillet and sauté the slices, a few at a time, until they are nicely browned on both sides. Arrange half of the slices in the bottom of a buttered shallow baking dish or pie plate. Meanwhile, cream the cream cheese until it is very soft, then add the 2 kinds of sugar, cinnamon, and rum, and beat until the mixture is smooth and rather fluffy. Spread half of this mixture over the first layer of plantain slices. Top with remaining slices and the remaining cream-cheese mixture. Pour the cup of heavy cream over the top, and bake in preheated 375° F. oven until almost all of the cream is absorbed and the topping is lightly browned—usually about 15 to 20 minutes. Serve hot, with dollops of whipped cream.

A NICELY spiced *plátano* dessert is the following one which has evolved through the years in my Coconut Grove kitchen. If desired, it can be accompanied by lightly toasted thin slices of a good firm pound cake.

Baked Plantains Hawkes
Serves 4 to 6.

2 *black-ripe* maduro *plantains*
¼ *pound (1 stick) butter*
⅓ *cup dark-brown sugar*
½ *teaspoon cinnamon*
¼ *teaspoon nutmeg*
¼ *cup dry red wine*
2 *tablespoons water*

Peel the very ripe plantains and, unless they are very thick, arrange them whole in a large shallow baking dish; if more than 1½-inches thick, cut them lengthwise into halves. In a heavy saucepan, combine the other ingredients, and bring to the boil, stirring constantly. Simmer, uncovered, for about 15 minutes, stirring constantly. Pour this syrup over the plantains, and bake in preheated 325° F. oven until they are very tender and dark orange-colored. Serve while very hot.

BARLEY

Barley is today rather a neglected grain. Yet as a child, I was often offered it as a breakfast cereal, and my grandparents from Scotland delighted in its use in a wide variety of husky dishes, from unleavened cakes to stuffings for chicken to spiced puddings.

A member of the Grass Family (*Hordeum vulgare*), Barley and its antecedents probably came from the immense region extending from Syria to Baluchistan. It is one of those grains which has been grown by man for such an incredible length of time that its precise original habitat is unknown.

Today, "pearl" Barley is the form most often to be encountered in our stores. There is even, as one would anticipate in our modern times, a "brand new quick all purpose" variety to be had!

Barley is also cultivated as a source for the malt used in brewing beer, and the seeds (which is what we consume) are ground to make a flour of extensive international utility. The most famous use of Barley, of course, is in the distillation of Scotch whisky.

A number of soups of diverse ancestry—from Scotland to Poland to France—are particularly noteworthy because of their content of this grain. A favorite is this one, often encountered in fine kosher restaurants and in private Jewish homes. Ideally, it should be prepared a day ahead of time. Reheating improves its flavor (as it does most soups), and any

excess grease that forms can be skimmed and discarded when the soup has chilled.

Barley-Mushroom Soup
Serves 4 to 6.

¾ *to 1 cup pearl barley*
1 *meaty beef soup bone*
3 *quarts water*
3 *to 4 tablespoons liquid beef extract*
salt and pepper
2 *cups thinly sliced fresh mushrooms*
2 *tablespoons corn or peanut oil*

In a large soup kettle with cover, bring the soup bone and water to the boil. Skim off and discard any scum, and cook over medium heat, covered, for at least 1 hour. Remove the bone, and shred or dice the meat, returning all to the soup. Mix the beef extract with some of the soup, and stir into the pot, with salt and pepper to taste. The stock must be a very rich one. Sauté the sliced mushrooms in oil until they are nicely browned but still retain some firmness of texture. Turn into the soup, with the barley, cover, and simmer until the barley is tender, usually about 10 minutes. Do not overcook—and serve while very hot!

THE FOLLOWING version of baked barley—a kind of pilaf, as it were—is delicious with beef or fowl, veal or ham. In other words, virtually an all-purpose casserole!

Baked Barley Thomas
Serves 6 liberally.

1 *cup pearl barley*
4 *tablespoons butter*
1½ *cups thinly sliced fresh mushrooms*
2 *cups finely chopped onion*
½ *cup chopped scallion tops*
¼ *cup finely chopped green pepper*
5 *cups rich chicken bouillon or broth*

In a skillet, melt 2 tablespoons of the butter and over rather high heat quickly sauté the mushrooms, stirring constantly and with care, until they are well browned but still somewhat firm in texture. Remove mushrooms with slotted spoon, melt remaining butter in same skillet, and add onions. Over medium heat, sauté until just limp, and remove with slotted spoon. Preheat oven to 350° F., and grease a 2-quart casserole with cover. In skillet with butter, over high heat, quickly sauté the scallions and green pepper, stirring often, until they are just limp; remove these vegetables with slotted spoon. Reduce heat and add the barley to the skillet. Stirring often, cook over low heat, until it turns golden-brown in color, usually about 8 minutes. Remove skillet from heat and stir in sautéed mushrooms, onions, scallion tops, and green pepper, plus 2 cups of the rich chicken bouillon or broth. Turn into casserole, cover, and bake for 30 minutes. Carefully stir in 2 more cups of the bouillon or broth, cover again, and bake for 30 minutes more. The barley should be almost tender by this time. Add the 5th cup of bouillon or broth, mixing well but with care, to avoid mashing the vegetables, and bake uncovered for 15 minutes.

BASELLA

Basella, or Malabar Nightshade as it is often called (*Basella rubra,* placed in a family by itself, the Basellaceae) is occasionally encountered in the mainland United States as a slender annual vine grown in gardens for its succulent glossy green or purplish-red-flushed foliage, spikes of white, red, or purple flowers. As its second name indicates, it is an indigene of India —*basella,* in fact, being a native epithet along the Malabar Coast. It is also of some importance as a spinachlike vegetable in Hawaii and other warm regions of the world. Interestingly, in two contemporary catalogues from important purveyors of vegetable seeds, Basella is touted as a fine "new" vegetable.

Very easily cultivated, it is raised in rich, moist soil either from seed or from cuttings. Alternate vernacular names are Country Spinach, *niviti* or *pasali* (Ceylon), *pu-tin-choi* (China), and *tsuru-murasaki* (Japan).

A FAVORITE way with Basella in Hawaii is the following soup, which can be served with side portions of hot steamed rice as a pleasant light supper. Otherwise, the vegetable is best prepared as one would spinach, cutting the viny growths into suitable lengths prior to cooking very briefly.

Basella Soup
Serves 4.

1 *bunch basella*
¼ *cup dried tiny shrimp*
1½ *quarts water*
4 2-inch cubes soybean curd (tōfu)
1 to 2 *teaspoons soy sauce, Japanese preferred*

Wash the basella and cut into 3-inch lengths. Wash and drain the tiny shrimp (available from Oriental markets), and place in the water in a soup kettle with cover. Bring to a quick boil, then cover, and reduce heat so the liquid barely simmers. Add the cubes of soybean curd, cover again, and cook for 15 minutes. Then add the basella, cover once again, raise heat, and cook until vegetable is just tender. Season to taste with soy sauce, and serve while hot, without delay.

Beans

The multitudinous kinds of Beans used by man, in every part of the world, comprise as a class one of his most important basic, staple foods. The cuisines of many lands, from Mexico to Mozambique, would be measurably altered and restricted if these seeds were not available.

Though, in English, we generally group all of these "wonderful fruits" together simply as Beans, in actuality this category includes such diversities as peas, garbanzos, limas, green (snap or string) beans, and an incredible host of other edibles. All of these plants, whatever their names (and these vary to a frightfully confusing degree from region to region, even in the same country), are legumes, of the same great botanical family as the acacias, garden sweet peas, and the famed splendid flowering trees of the tropics, the royal poinciana and orchid trees.

ADZUKI BEAN

The Adzuki Bean (*Phaseolus angularis,* of the Legume Family) is an Asiatic species which has been very extensively cultivated for thousands of years in China, Manchuria, Korea, and Japan. The beans, small and varying from dark red to cream or black or mottled, are important in the *haute cuisine* of the Orient, hence are imported into this country, dried or in cans, in the latter either whole or in a coarse paste.

There are innumerable varieties of this tasty legume, including several which are ground into a meal, this made into compact festive cakes and candies. The dried beans are boiled in soups and stewlike combinations, or are very often added to rice, as in the following recipe. Kidney beans or other red beans may be substituted.

Adzuki Beans and Rice
Serves 6.

> 1 *cup dried adzuki beans*
> 3 *cups raw rice*
> 3 *teaspoons salt*
> 2 *tablespoons sake or dry sherry*
> 2 *tablespoons toasted sesame seeds*

Pick over and wash the beans. Place in a large pot with cover, and add cold water to cover. Bring to the boil, covered. Remove scum when this forms, then drain beans and place in fresh cold water. Return to the boil, repeating the process 3 times. Cook the beans over low heat, covered, until they are tender, adding a little water as necessary. Remove from the heat, allow beans to cool, and drain, reserving the liquid. Meanwhile, soak the rice in 2 changes of water, draining thoroughly. Add salt and sake (or dry sherry) to bean liquid, bring to the boil, and add the soaked drained rice plus the mashed or sieved beans. Lower heat, cover, and cook until the rice is tender, usually about 15 minutes. Serve either hot or cold, sprinkled with toasted sesame seeds.

BLACK BEAN

The Black Bean, or Turtle Bean as it is often called, is one of the literally numberless forms of *Phaseolus vulgaris,* that odd hodge-podge species which also includes kidney beans, navy beans, pea beans, and so on. Black Beans are widely used in the tropics of this hemisphere, where they are usually called *frijol negro* in Spanish, *feijão* in Portuguese.

Black Beans have an especially hearty, distinctive flavor, which many people like. They are commonly available in our markets dried, canned, or in various thick soups.

I do not ordinarily approve of the all too prevalent practice of combining the contents of several cans and calling it "cooking." But the canned soup prepared

from the Black Bean is so savory that it seems almost a waste of time to prepare a homemade batch. The following hearty potage, incorporating canned black bean soup as well as canned turtle soup, is superior fare, and I doubt that one could equal its flavor if one caught a green turtle and shelled the legumes. Note the subtle play on words, too, "Turtle Bean" being a synonym for our inky bean.

Turtle Bean Soup
Serves 4 to 6.

> 1 *can condensed black bean soup*
> 1 *can green turtle chowder*
> 1 *bean soup can water*
> 2 *tablespoons dry red wine*
> *salt and freshly ground pepper*
> *thin slices fresh lime*

In a kettle with cover, combine the undiluted green turtle chowder and the black bean soup with the can of water. Blend thoroughly, adding the wine, cover, and heat through. Do not allow to come to the boil, and simmer, covered, for a few minutes before serving. Season to taste with salt and pepper and top each portion with a thin slice of lime, this to be mashed with one's spoon prior to consuming the rich soup.

I VERY much enjoy the commercial canned black bean soups with a dollop of dry sherry or dry red wine added, just heated through, and served with wafer-thin slices of lemon or lime atop. Or sprinkle each serving with a bit of mashed hard-cooked egg yolk.

Then, consider the following delicious thick spread or dunk for cocktail time. Keep the mixture warm in a chafing dish and offer guests a selection of unsalted Cuban crackers, plantain Mariquitas (page 30), corn chips, and tortilla wedges.

Black Bean Spread
Makes about 2½ cups.

> 1 *can condensed black bean soup*
> 1 *8-ounce can tomato sauce*
> 1½ *cups shredded sharp Cheddar or Jack cheese*
> ¼ *teaspoon chili powder, or more*

In a heavy saucepan, combine the undiluted soup, tomato sauce, half of the cheese, and the chili powder to taste, mixing thoroughly. Cook over medium heat, stirring frequently, until the cheese has melted. Add remainder of the cheese, mixing thoroughly, and again cooking until cheese has melted. Keep warm in chafing dish to serve as a spread at cocktail time.

BRAZIL is the biggest bean-producing nation on earth. Average production of dried beans is more than twice that of this country. The bean there is the black bean, or *feijão,* and the national dish of Brazil is a wondrous array called Feijoada Completa. It would be impossible to list all the ingredients that might go into a *feijoada,* but here is the way I fix it on particularly festive occasions. It is a time-consuming business to prepare, and to consume, but with good company, good conversation, and lots of good beer, a *feijoada* is definitely a memorable method of utilizing black beans. It is pronounced, by the way, fay-zho-*ah*-da kom-*play*-ta.

Feijoada Completa
Serves 6 to 10 liberally.

4 *cups dried black beans*
1 *pound* carne seca (*sun-dried salted beef*)
1 *small smoked beef tongue*
1 *pound Portuguese sausages* (linquiça)
½ *pound lean bacon, in 1 piece*
2 *pigs' feet*
1 *pound lean stew beef, in 2 pieces*
2 *tablespoons lard*
2 *cups chopped onion*
2 *or 3 medium cloves garlic, mashed*
⅓ *cup chopped fresh parsley*
2 *teaspoons salt*
½ *teaspoon freshly ground black pepper*
Farinha de Mandioca (page 78)
Collards Brazilian (page 96)
4 *large seedless oranges, unpeeled, thinly sliced*
hot steamed or boiled rice

Soak the *carne seca* in water to cover overnight; this ingredient is essential to the authenticity and success of the recipe and is now available in specialty food shops in our large cities. Next day, pick over and rinse the beans. Place them in a very large heavy kettle, cover with cold water, cover container, and bring to the boil. Remove from the heat and allow to stand, covered, for one hour. Over medium heat, still covered, start cooking beans again. Drain the *carne seca* and cut it into 1-inch cubes. Soak tongue in water for 30 minutes, drain, and parboil in fresh water until the skin can be removed. Rinse sausages and drain. Place these meats, plus the bacon, pigs' feet and stewing beef, in a second large heavy kettle with cover, add water just to cover them, and simmer, with the lid on, over very low heat until all meats are tender. In a skillet, melt the lard and sauté the onion and garlic, with the parsley, until onion is soft. Season beans, which should now be tender, with salt and black pepper. Add about 1 cup cooked beans to the skillet,

and mash them rather thoroughly with a fork. Turn contents of skillet into the bean kettle, and add meats, plus most of their liquid—the mixture should not be overly soupy. Cover the kettle, and simmer for 20 minutes or so to blend flavors.

To serve, remove various meats from the beans, slice them, and arrange on a large heated platter—traditionally with the tongue in the middle, the smoked meats at one end, the fresh at the other. Pour the beans, undrained, into a large bowl, and offer a ladle. Offer a side bowl of Farinha de Mandioca. Place collards (or kale) in another bowl, and arrange orange slices on top of the vegetable. Each guest takes a large scoop of hot rice, tops it with beans plus some of their liquor, obtains a sampling of every sort of meat, collards, an orange slice, and sprinkles the entire array to taste with Farinha de Mandioca. In many Brazilian homes, white rum (*cachaça*) is offered as the liquid accompaniment for this stupendous repast, but I have found, through hilarious experiment, that good beer is safer.

IN BRAZIL *feijões* with rice are served in many homes at virtually every meal. Normally, the legumes are just boiled until tender in lightly salted water, and both they and the dark thickish liquid are poured over hot steamed or boiled rice. Here is a Haitian, more highly seasoned version of the Brazilian recipe, which is a staple at my house.

Haitian Black Beans
Serves 6 liberally.

1 *pound dried black beans*
2 *cups chopped onion*
1 *cup chopped green pepper*
2 *large cloves garlic, mashed*
2 *medium bay leaves*
1 *tablespoon salt*
½ *teaspoon freshly ground black pepper*
¼ *teaspoon oregano*
¼ *teaspoon mixed herbs*
3 *tablespoons cider vinegar*
½ *cup peanut or soy oil*
1 4-*ounce jar pimientos, chopped*

Pick over and rinse beans. Place the beans, with fresh water to cover, in a large kettle with cover, put on the lid, and bring to a quick boil. Remove from heat and allow to sit for one hour. Return to the heat and cook, adding a bit of water as needed, for 30 minutes. Add the onion, green pepper, garlic, bay leaves, salt, black pepper, oregano and mixed herbs, and continue to cook, covered, over medium heat until the beans are very tender—usually several hours. Add the vinegar, mixing thoroughly, and return to heat. About 15 minutes before serving, mix in the oil and chopped pimientos. Stir often during this final period to avoid scorching. Serve alongside or over hot steamed or boiled rice; especially good with pork or beef in various forms.

RUM and black beans have a considerable affinity, as is amply revealed in the following savory recipe. Serve with ham or pork, hot rice, and perhaps a salad such as a Caesar (page 137). Delightful!

Black Beans in Rum
Serves 6.

1 *pound dried black beans*
1½ *cups coarsely chopped onion*
2 *large cloves garlic, mashed*
3 *large stalks celery, coarsely chopped*
1 *medium carrot, scraped, chopped*
2 *tablespoons salt*
½ *teaspoon freshly ground black pepper*
2 *small bay leaves*
¼ *teaspoon oregano*
1 *tablespoon minced fresh parsley*
4 *tablespoons butter*
2 *jiggers dark Jamaica rum*
1 *pint commercial sour cream, at room temperature*

Pick over and rinse the beans, place them in a large kettle with cover, add water to cover, put on the lid, and bring quickly to the boil. Remove from the heat, and allow to stand, covered, for 1 hour. Then add the onion, garlic, celery, carrot, salt, pepper, bay leaves, oregano, and parsley, and, over medium heat—adding water as needed—cook, covered, until the beans are almost tender. Correct seasoning and remove the bay leaves. Turn the beans out into a casserole, add the butter and one jigger of the rum, mixing thoroughly. Cover and bake in preheated 350° F. oven until the beans are completely tender. Remove from oven, mix in the second jigger of rum, and top each hot serving with a goodly dollop of sour cream.

BONAVIST BEAN

The Bonavist Bean (*Dolichos Lablab,* of the Legume Family) is a very large twining vine with showy white, rose, or purple flowers, for which it is rather frequently cultivated as an ornamental in this country. In more tropical climes, this legume—also known as Hyacinth Bean, Monavist Bean, Lablab, or Motchai Bean—is very extensively grown as a food crop, both small pods and seeds being eaten.

The pods are often five inches in length, broad and flat, usually with lumpy or undulate margins, and contain small beans which vary from white or reddish to black, mahogany, or gray in color.

When the pods are first developed, and measure only a couple of inches in length, they are tasty when boiled until just tender, and served with butter and suitable seasonings, or when added to a Vegetable Curry (page 255). The beans are also typically boiled in salted water until tender, then mixed with hot rice, which is seasoned to taste—often with soy sauce and some grated onion mixed in.

BROAD BEAN

The Broad Bean (*Vicia Faba*) is extensively cultivated in the Old World, but in this country is grown mostly as a fodder crop for cattle. This is paradoxical, since we must import the considerable quantities of these beans which are utilized by a sizable percentage of our populace—notably those of Mediterranean ancestry.

The Broad Bean, presumably a native of North Africa and Asia Minor, has been cultivated by man since prehistoric times. It possesses many more or less distinct variants, and labors under such diverse additional epithets as Shell Bean, Windsor Bean, Horse Bean, English Dwarf Bean, *fève* (France), *faba* or *fava* (Spain, Portugal, and Italy), and *fool* (Arabic lands).

Unless the pods are very fresh and tender, they are not eaten, the beans being shelled out. These pods are large—as much as eighteen inches long—and rather heavy. The big, flat beans are generally peeled prior to cooking in liberally salted water (add a pinch of savory for an assist in taste).

Broad Beans are ideally served well drained and still hot, liberally dressed with butter, and seasoned to taste. The excellent canned Italian imports, called Fava Beans, are perfect for general culinary uses. The French enjoy them puréed, or dressed with a small amount of heavy cream. In these fashions, the legumes are particularly appropriate with ham, pork, and chicken.

THE FOLLOWING delicious Near Eastern dish uses the dried Broad Beans.

Broad Beans with Lamb
Serves 4.

1 *pound dried broad beans*
2 *cups cubed raw lamb*
3 *tablespoons butter*
1 *tablespoon olive oil*
½ *cup chopped onion*
1 *small clove garlic, mashed*
½ *cup water*
salt and pepper

Pick over dried beans and wash them. Place in boiling salted water to cover, and cook until beans are almost tender. Drain thoroughly. In a large skillet with cover, thoroughly brown the cubes of lamb in butter and oil, stirring often. Add the onion and garlic, and over low heat simmer for 10 minutes or so. Add the beans, water, and seasonings, cover skillet, and simmer until beans are very tender, usually about 20 minutes.

GOA BEAN

Two kinds of *Psophocarpus* (of the Legume Family) are cultivated in the tropics as food plants. One of these, *Psophocarpus palustris*, is grown to some degree, notably in parts of Africa, for its edible fleshy underground rhizomes and for the young pods.

The other, the Goa Bean (*Psophocarpus tetragonolobus*), presumably originally from India, is a rather important crop in warm countries of Asia, and in recent years has been grown in this hemisphere, including southern Florida, California, and Hawaii, although the unusual pods seldom appear even in our specialized markets.

Other names for this legume are Asparagus Pea, Manila Bean, Princess Bean, or Winged Bean; the last name is the most appropriate, perhaps, since it describes the delicious edible pods best. These are borne in profusion on a rampant vine, following showy pale-blue or whitish flowers. The pods measure six to nine inches in length, are usually curving and dark green in color. Each of the four longitudinal angles is set with a conspicuous, toothed, papery ridge, so that when they are sliced transversely, an unusual and attractive shape is obtained.

Typically, these pods are washed, then cut into half-inch slices, and quickly cooked in a bit of boiling salted water. They are served hot, seasoned to taste with butter, salt and freshly ground pepper, and often a touch of soy sauce, Japanese preferred. They can as well be added to soups, or medleys of other vegetables

and meats such as Chop Suey, Sukiyaki, or Mizutaki.

In Southeast Asia, where the Goa Bean is extensively cultivated, the small juvenile tubers are a favored vegetable, prepared much in the fashion of our common potato. The young leaves and fresh sprouts are added as a green to soups, curries, and the like, and in Indonesia the ripe seeds are roasted and eaten with rice, to which they impart a special, pleasant flavor.

GREEN BEAN

Botanically, the Green Bean is referable to *Phaseolus vulgaris* (Legume Family), an exceptionally variable species. It includes plants of which the seed pods are used when green—for example, the Green Bean—as well as dry shell beans like the navy bean, Boston pea bean, and California tree bean.

Probably an indigene of what is now known as Indonesia, the Green Bean has been cultivated since time immemorial. It was known to the ancient Egyptians, and mentioned by Pliny. In our time it is also called by such epithets as String Bean, Snap Bean, French Bean, *haricot vert* (France), *judía verde* (Spain), *habichuela* (Spanish America), *ejote* (Mexico), *vagem* (Brazil), *fagiolino* (Italy), *Grünebohne* (Germany), and *lūbee* (Arabic lands), among many others.

When buying the fresh vegetable, be sure to choose pods which are small, very firm, and obviously of top fresh quality. Snap off the top (stem) end—any longitudinal "strings" which may be present will generally come off the pods automatically—and plunge them into enough boiling salted water to cover. The addition of a bit of grated onion or even a tiny taste of mashed garlic adds attractive extra flavor. Cook only until barely tender—these luscious pods must never be overcooked. Drain thoroughly, and serve without delay, liberally dressed with butter and seasoned to taste with salt and freshly ground pepper.

During their peak season Green Beans are so good prepared in this simplest of fashions that they may be served as a separate, special course.

THE FOLLOWING salad version of green beans makes an appropriate first-course appetizer.

French Green Bean Salad
Serves 4.

1 pound fresh green beans
½ cup peanut or soy oil
¼ cup wine vinegar
¼ teaspoon chervil
salt and freshly ground pepper
¼ cup finely chopped onion
4 slices hard Italian salami, in thin strips
2 hard-cooked egg yolks, sieved
1 tablespoon minced fresh parsley

Trim green beans, removing any strings, but leaving them whole. Cook in boiling salted water until just done—they should retain some crispness of texture. Drain thoroughly and place in a commodious bowl. Prepare a vinaigrette sauce by combining oil, vinegar, chervil, and salt and pepper to taste, and pour this over the green beans while they are still hot, mixing them carefully. Allow to marinate at room temperature for about 30 minutes, then chill for 1 hour. At serving time, drain the string beans, arrange them neatly on individual plates, and sprinkle with onion, salami strips, sieved egg yolks, and parsley.

THIS omelet starring green beans is of Armenian ancestry, and is a good accompaniment to shish kebab. For a light supper it might be served with pan-broiled link sausages and hot rolls.

Armenian Green Bean Omelet
Serves 4 to 6.

1 9-ounce package frozen French-style green beans
4 tablespoons butter
1 tablespoon chopped fresh parsley
4 eggs

Cook green beans according to package directions until just firm-tender. Drain very thoroughly, squeez-

ing out all possible moisture. In a skillet or omelet pan melt 2 tablespoons of the butter. Mix the green beans, parsley, and eggs together, and pour into the pan. Cook over rather low heat until the omelet forms a slight golden-brown crust on the bottom. Place a plate to fit on top of the omelet, and carefully turn the pan over, so the omelet comes out onto the plate. Quickly melt the remaining butter in the pan, and carefully slide in the omelet, to cook on the other side until golden-brown and slightly crusty. Cut into big wedges and serve at once.

HERE we have a hot dish with Hawaiian overtones, prepared quite simply with the excellent canned vegetable, and good with broiled hamburgers or thick pork chops.

Green Beans Aloha
Serves 4 to 6.

1 16-ounce can diagonal-cut green beans
1 8¾-ounce can pineapple chunks
2 tablespoons brown sugar
1 tablespoon cornstarch
½ teaspoon salt
2 tablespoons butter
3 tablespoons cider vinegar

Drain the beans, reserving ⅓ cup of liquid. Drain the pineapple and reserve liquid. Combine the brown sugar, cornstarch, salt, and butter in a medium saucepan. Add the ⅓ cup reserved bean liquid, all of the pineapple liquid, and the vinegar. Bring to the boil, stirring constantly. Cook for 3 minutes, stirring. Add the beans and pineapple chunks, heat through, and serve while nice and hot.

DILLED GREEN BEANS go well with boiled beef, chicken, or shellfish—especially shrimp or lobster.

Dilled Green Beans
Serves 4 to 6.

1 pound fresh green beans
4 tablespoons butter
¼ teaspoon salt
⅛ teaspoon freshly ground black pepper
¼ teaspoon paprika
2 tablespoons chopped dill pickle
1 2-ounce jar julienne-cut pimiento, drained

Trim green beans, removing any strings, but leaving the beans whole. Cook in boiling salted water until just done—they should retain some crispness of texture.

Drain thoroughly. Meanwhile, melt butter in a saucepan, add other ingredients except pimiento, and mix thoroughly to heat through. Add pimiento, pour over hot beans, and serve at once.

I DO NOT ordinarily approve of combining packages of frozen this, canned that, and precooked something else in good cookery, whether of vegetables or other foods. But the era of convenience foods is upon us, and the following dish is best prepared by making good use of them.

Green Bean Casserole
Serves 4 to 6.

> 2 *packages frozen French-style green beans, cooked,*
>   *drained*
> 1 *can French-fried onions*
> 2 *cans condensed cream of mushroom soup*
> ½ *teaspoon freshly ground black pepper*

In a 1-quart casserole, combine half the onions, all of the green beans, the soup, and the pepper, mixing thoroughly but with care. Bake in preheated 350° F. oven for 20 minutes, or until the contents are bubbling merrily. Top with the remaining onions and bake for an additional 5 minutes. Serve without delay.

HERE we have another casserole utilizing the excellent frozen French-cut green beans. This is an especially hearty concoction, ideally offered with chicken, ham, or pork, in various forms.

Jim's Green Bean Casserole
Serves 4 to 6.

> 2 *packages frozen French-style green beans, cooked,*
>   *drained*
> 1½ *cups commercial sour cream*
> ¾ *cup grated sharp Cheddar cheese*
> 2 *tablespoons light brown sugar*
> 1 *tablespoon flour*
> 1 *tablespoon finely chopped onion*
> 1 *teaspoon salt*
> ¼ *teaspoon freshly ground pepper*
> 1 5-*ounce can water chestnuts, drained, chopped*
> 1 4-*ounce can sliced mushrooms, drained*
> 3 *tablespoons chopped pimientos*
> ¾ *cup dry coarse bread crumbs*
> 3 *tablespoons melted butter*

After cooking and draining green beans according to package directions, combine the sour cream, cheese, brown sugar, flour, onion, salt, and pepper. Carefully

stir in the green beans, water chestnuts, mushrooms, and pimientos. Turn mixture into a 1-quart casserole. Mix the bread crumbs with the melted butter, and arrange over the string beans. Bake in preheated 350° F. oven for about 25 minutes, or until the bread crumbs are nicely browned.

A VERY different way of preparing green beans is in the form of a butter-smooth purée. This recipe, from Brussels, is appropriate with virtually any meat or fish.

Green Bean Purée
Serves 6.

> 2 *pounds fresh green beans*
> *butter*
> *salt and freshly ground white pepper*
> *marjoram*
> *rosemary*
> *buttered coarse bread crumbs*

Trim the green beans, remove all strings, and slice them lengthwise, French style. Cook them in lightly salted boiling water, covered, until very tender. Drain thoroughly, and while still hot run through the fine chopper of a food mill. To each cup of the purée, add a goodly chunk of butter (at least 2 tablespoons), salt and white pepper to taste, plus a touch of both marjoram and rosemary (minced fresh leaves, if possible). Whip the purée with a wire whisk, then turn into a buttered, rather shallow baking dish. Top liberally with buttered bread crumbs and place in a 375° F. oven until the top is lightly browned.

JACK BEAN

The Jack Bean (*Canavalia ensiformis*, of the Legume Family) is a husky shrubby or vining plant, perhaps originally from the West Indies, but long cultivated in the warm parts of both Old and New Worlds.

Also called Sword Bean, Horse Bean, or Chickasaw Lima, it is best known as a forage crop. The broad, heavy seed pods may grow to more than a foot long, but when they are small and tender they make a most palatable green vegetable at the table. The large white seeds, each with a conspicuous dark "eye," are enjoyed by many people when prepared in the fashions suggested for the Broad Bean (page 36), after peeling to remove the rather tough skin. These seeds, or beans, should not be eaten unless thoroughly cooked, preferably in a change or two of water. The fully ripe beans are on occasion roasted and ground to make a sort of coffee substitute.

In Japan, the pods of an allied species (*Canavalia obtusifolia*) are eaten to rather considerable extent. Those of a white variety are preserved in salt, and those of a dark, almost black, form are eaten boiled with seasonings. This legume is essentially unknown, it seems, in this country as yet.

KIDNEY BEAN

The dried legume which we in the United States know as Kidney Bean is a distinct variety of *Phaseolus vulgaris,* the species of which the green bean is a member. It is also one of the kinds of red bean, an entity of infinite subtle forms.

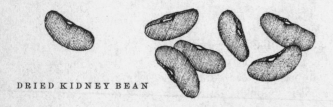

DRIED KIDNEY BEAN

Kidney Beans are extensively used in this country. They are always available in our markets today, either dried or in cans, the latter usually in a slightly sweetened liquid—though the beans are sufficiently sweet by themselves, in my opinion. In specialty Italian stores, the attractive, highly flavorful White Kidney Beans, called canellini, are on sale, as canned imports. Consider substituting these on occasion, or combine the two varieties together.

CANELLINI

Though called "chili," the following dish has only the vaguest resemblance to the famed Mexican or Southwest American specialty of the same name. But it has long been one of my staple recipes. I usually prepare it in at least a double batch, and I find that it develops a special, extra taste when reheated after mellowing overnight, covered, in the refrigerator.

Almost invariably, I serve this Bahamian Chili with heated canned or frozen tamales, Pineapple Cole Slaw

(page 61) and lots of buttered hot crusty Cuban or French bread. A goodly carafe of dry red wine is an admirable accompaniment. No dessert seems necessary after this insidious repast, but some spicy or kosher pickles are perfect along the way.

Bahamian Chili
Serves 6 liberally.

> 4 1-pound cans red kidney beans, undrained
> 2 tablespoons butter
> 2 tablespoons peanut or soy oil
> 2 cups chopped onion
> 1 cup chopped green pepper
> 2 large cloves garlic, mashed
> 1½ pounds lean ground beef
> 1 to 2 teaspoons sugar
> 1 medium bay leaf, crumbled
> ¼ teaspoon ground thyme
> ¼ to ½ teaspoon oregano
> 1 tablespoon or more chili powder
> salt and freshly ground pepper to taste

In a large heavy kettle with cover, heat the butter and oil together, and in the mixture sauté the onion, green pepper, and garlic slowly, until they become soft. Crumble in the ground beef, stirring as needed, and cook until it has browned thoroughly. Add all seasonings (more chili powder if a "hot" dish is desirable), mix thoroughly, cover, and allow to cook over very low heat for 30 minutes. Add the kidney beans with their liquid, mix well, cover again, and simmer over lowest possible heat for at least 1 hour, stirring carefully from time to time.

MY FRIEND and culinary colleague from Cuba, Sra. Benita Robaina, is especially fond of this kidney bean salad, which she delights in offering with such things as her unique version of fried chicken, hot rolls, and fresh limeade.

Benita's Kidney Bean Salad
Serves 4 to 6.

> 1 1-pound can red kidney beans, undrained
> 3 canned whole pimientos, thinly sliced
> ¾ cup coarsely chopped green pepper
> ½ cup coarsely chopped scallions, with tops
> ½ cup peeled diced cucumber
> ½ teaspoon finely chopped garlic
> ¾ cup prepared Italian dressing
> crisp lettuce leaves for base

Combine all ingredients except the lettuce leaves

thoroughly but gently, and allow to chill, uncovered, for at least 1 hour prior to serving—not drained—on crisp lettuce leaves.

CONSIDER the following stalwart medley, a kind of cassoulet with international overtones. Little zucchini, fat knockwurst, and a marvelous series of seasonings combine with the handsome imported canned white kidney beans. The red legumes can be substituted, though with a somewhat different end flavor, of course. Russian pumpernickel is my favorite bread with this, a dish of Danish Pickled Cucumbers (page 100) is an excellent salad, and beer must be recommended as a beverage.

Canellini, My Style
Serves 6.

4 1-*pound cans white kidney beans (canellini), undrained*
½ *pound lean thickly sliced bacon, diced*
2 *cups chopped onion*
½ *cup chopped green pepper*
2 *large cloves garlic, mashed*
4 *small firm zucchini, thinly sliced*
1 8-*ounce can tomato sauce*
½ *teaspoon dry mustard*
2 *teaspoons paprika*
½ *teaspoon black pepper*
3 *knockwurst*

In a large skillet, fry the thick bacon dice until they are rather crisp. Remove dice with slotted spoon and drain on paper towels. Discard all but about 2 tablespoons of the bacon fat, and sauté the onion, green pepper, and garlic, stirring often, until they are almost soft. Remove these with slotted spoon, add the thin slices of unpeeled zucchini to the skillet, and sauté for 4 or 5 minutes, turning once. Remove with slotted spoon, and drain on paper towels. In a large bowl, gently but thoroughly combine the undrained canellini, bacon dice, onion, green pepper, garlic, tomato sauce, dry mustard, paprika, and black pepper. Turn into a 2-quart casserole, and bake in preheated 350° F. oven for 40 minutes. Meanwhile, boil the knockwurst in water for 15 minutes, then drain and cut into thick slices. Gently stir the zucchini and knockwurst slices into the beans, and return to the oven for 15 minutes.

AN ATTRACTIVE and filling combination of canned red kidney beans (or canellini, if preferred), those economical, thin smoked pork chops often found in our supermarkets, and a well-seasoned red-wine sauce is found in the following casserole. Offer it with only the most essential accessories—a suitable salad, bread or rolls, and more of the good wine utilized in its cookery.

Kidney Beans Mirabile
Serves 6.

2 1-*pound cans red kidney beans, drained*
3 *tablespoons butter*
½ *cup chopped onion*
1 *large clove garlic, mashed*
⅓ *cup minced parsley*
1 *pound thin smoked pork chops*
1 8-*ounce can tomato sauce*
1 *cup dry red wine*
1 *teaspoon salt*
½ *teaspoon freshly ground pepper*
¼ *teaspoon basil*
½ *cup thickly sliced stuffed green olives*

In a skillet, sauté the onion and garlic in butter until lightly browned. Add parsley and cook until it wilts. Add pork chops and sauté them until well browned on both sides. Combine with drained beans, tomato sauce, red wine, seasonings, and olives, and turn into a sizable, rather shallow casserole, distributing the chops evenly through the mixture. Bake, uncovered, in preheated 350° F. oven for 30 minutes.

TYPICALLY, I prepare my own version of kidney bean salad a day ahead of time, to mellow, covered, under refrigeration. I like it with a menu which includes a savory meat loaf and a very cheesy batch of cheese and macaroni.

Alex's Kidney Bean Salad
Serves 4 liberally.

1 1-*pound can red kidney beans, undrained*
¼ *cup finely chopped onion*
¼ *cup finely chopped green pepper*
2 *tablespoons finely chopped pimiento*
½ *cup finely chopped celery*
¼ *teaspoon oregano*
½ *teaspoon salt*
2 *teaspoons sugar*
½ *teaspoon freshly ground black pepper*
3 to 5 *drops hot pepper sauce*
½ *cup peanut or soy oil*
⅓ *cup wine vinegar*
crisp lettuce for base

In a large bowl, combine thoroughly and carefully all ingredients except the lettuce leaves. Chill overnight. To serve, drain well and arrange on individual beds of crisp lettuce leaves.

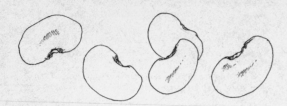

LIMA BEAN

The Lima Bean (*Phaseolus lunatus* var. *macrocarpus*, of the Legume Family) is a very well known vegetable in a great many parts of the world, notably in the tropics. Originating in South America, it was cultivated by the pre-Columbian inhabitants of Peru, and was at an early date introduced into the North American colonies.

As we know it in this country, the Lima is a tall-growing, husky vine or bushy plant, with pods that ripen rather late in the season. These contain a few very large beans—varying in color from palest green or white to red, black, or mottled—which are either very flat and strongly veined (Flat Lima) or plump, lightly veined, and smaller (Potato Lima).

The Lima Bean is a distinct variant of the Sieva or Civet Bean, a smaller, bushier vine with less sizable pods containing small, flat beans—these white, brown or variously mottled—set with strong radiating lines. It has been commonly cultivated in this country since the early eighteenth century, and today is encountered in most tropical lands as well, in differing phases.

The Lima and the Sieva Bean are very rich, starchy legumes, with distinctive flavor and innumerable important uses in the kitchen. The beans are sold in our markets fresh (in season), dried, canned, and frozen.

LIMA Beans are incorporated in a number of excellent soups. Here is an unpretentious, hearty potage, perfect choice for a chilly evening's supper.

Yankee Lima Bean Soup
Serves 4 to 6.

2 cups dried big lima beans
1 large meaty ham bone
2 quarts water
2 cups chopped onion
salt and freshly ground pepper to taste
Cheese Croutons (see recipe below)

Pick over and wash the beans. Using a large heavy kettle with cover, bring the meaty ham bone with the water to a quick boil. Reduce heat to the simmer, add the beans and onion, and cook until the beans are tender. (The quick-cooking modern variety is often done in 20 minutes or so.) Remove about half of the beans with slotted spoon, and mash them thoroughly. Return these to the soup, salt and pepper rather liberally, mix well, and simmer for 10 minutes more. Serve while very hot, garnished with Cheese Croutons, below.

Cheese Croutons
Makes a lot.

6 slices stale white bread
3 tablespoons melted butter
3 tablespoons freshly grated sharp Cheddar cheese

Trim crusts from bread, then cut slices into small cubes. Toss in the melted butter, then roll in the grated cheese. Place in a nonsticking skillet and sauté over low heat, shaking and stirring often, until the little croutons are quite crisp. Use without delay, to sprinkle over servings of the above soup—or consider adding them to your favorite tossed salad of mixed greens.

COOKED lima beans make an excellent salad when chilled in a Vinaigrette Dressing (page 256), or your choice of one of the good commercial salad dressings. A suggestion or two—a creamy blue or Roquefort cheese dressing, or a spicy orange "French" one, and do consider adding a modicum of finely chopped scallion tops before marinating in the refrigerator for an hour or so. Add the drained limas to the dressing while they are still warm for optimum flavorful results.

HERE is a Near Eastern recipe which is served at my house on frequent festive occasions with broiled chicken rubbed with tarragon, or shish kebab made from either lamb or beef.

Lima Beans Arabe
Serves 4 to 6.

2 cups dried big lima beans
1 quart water
3 tablespoons butter
2 cups coarsely chopped onion
2 medium cloves garlic, mashed
½ cup coarsely chopped green pepper
1 8-ounce can tomato sauce
¼ teaspoon ground allspice
2 teaspoons salt
½ teaspoon freshly ground pepper
1 teaspoon grated lemon peel

Pick over and wash the beans. Place in a kettle with the water, bring to a quick boil, then remove from the heat to soak, covered, for 1 hour. Drain off liquid, reserving about ½ cup. In a skillet, melt the butter and sauté the onion, garlic, and green pepper until lightly browned. Stir in the tomato sauce, seasonings, and lemon peel, and simmer over very low heat for about 15 minutes. Combine with partly cooked beans, place in an ovenproof casserole, and bake uncovered in a preheated 325° F. oven until the beans are tender. Add some of the bean liquid if the mixture becomes too dry—it should be a bit soupy when served.

THE FOLLOWING Barbecued Lima Beans are elegant fare. With them, I typically continue the outdoorsy theme and offer an assortment of charcoal-grilled meats—hamburgers, frankfurters, Polish kielbasie, and pork chops.

Barbecued Lima Beans
Serves 4 to 6.

1 cup dried baby lima beans
2 cups water
¼ cup chopped onion
¼ teaspoon minced garlic
¼ cup chopped lean salt pork
2¼ teaspoons prepared mustard
⅛ teaspoon salt
½ teaspoon Worcestershire sauce
½ teaspoon chili powder
½ cup condensed tomato soup
1 tablespoon cider vinegar
1 teaspoon dark-brown sugar
½ cup liquid from beans

Place the dried beans, picked over and washed, and the water in a kettle, cover, and bring to a quick boil. Boil for 2 minutes, remove from the heat and allow to stand for 1 hour, still covered. Then boil the beans again, undrained, until they are just tender, adding water in moderation as needed. Drain off the liquid and reserve it. In a small skillet, cook the onion and garlic with the salt pork until vegetables are lightly browned. Combine contents of the skillet with the cooked beans, plus all other ingredients. Turn into a casserole and bake in preheated 375° F. oven for 25 minutes, or until beans are very tender. Serve without delay.

IN MEXICO I have on several occasions encountered the enterprising use of an especially large variety of lima beans, toasted and spicily seasoned, as superlative hors d'oeuvres with cocktails—or with beer in the picturesque native cantinas.

Toasted Lima Beans
Serves a lot.

2 cups dried big lima beans
1 small bay leaf
2 teaspoons salt
1 large clove garlic, mashed
salt
chili powder

Pick over and rinse beans in cold water. Place in a kettle with fresh water to cover, with the bay leaf, salt, and garlic. Bring to a quick boil, remove from the heat, cover, and allow to stand for 1 hour. Return to heat, and cook, covered, until beans are just barely tender—do not overcook. Drain beans thoroughly, allow to dry, and place in a shallow, lightly greased skillet. Toast the beans, shaking and turning often, over very low heat, until they are slightly browned. Toss with salt and chili powder to taste while hot, and serve at once.

NAVY BEAN

The Navy, Great Northern, and other such beans which are of dried shell-bean type are botanically referred to the species Phaseolus vulgaris—an incredibly variable entity which includes such diverse vegetables as the green bean, the kidney bean, and a host of others.

These dried white (or whitish) beans, which I here perhaps a bit too glibly incorporate under a single category, are of considerable import to the good cook, whether in this country or abroad.

Those self-acknowledged leaders of international cookery, the French, have even adopted these American legumes, calling them haricots blancs sec, and preparing from them a delightful series of kitchen specialties.

To prepare, pick the beans over, discarding any wrinkled or discolored specimens (plus the tiny rocks which for some reason seem to appear in every package), and rinse under cold running water. Do not soak the beans for protracted periods, for this can cause slight fermentation and ruin their delicate flavor. Rather, add the rinsed beans to a quantity of salted water, bring this quickly to the boil, covered, then remove from the heat to soak for about one hour. Then proceed with the recipe.

These white beans are nutritious, tasteful, and extremely adaptable to culinary use. Dishes utilizing them range through a whole gamut of delicacies, domestic and especially foreign—the sources of the latter extending from Spain and Egypt to Japan!

In SPAIN and Portugal, succulent souplike stews are prepared with dried white beans in company with a varied array of other ingredients. Caldo Gallego (pronounced *kahl*-doe gah-*yay*-goe), from the spectacular region of Galicia in northern Spain, is one of these. It is sometimes prepared with garbanzos, but I am partial to the following version.

Caldo Gallego
Serves 6 to 8.

1½ cups dried navy or other white beans (or garbanzos)
¼ pound lean salt pork, diced
1 cup diced cooked ham
2 chorizos (spicy Spanish sausage), sliced
1 cup chopped onion
½ cup chopped celery
½ cup chopped green pepper
½ cup chopped scallions, with tops
2 cups chopped fresh tomatoes
1 to 2 large cloves garlic, mashed
1 meaty ham bone
2 quarts water
salt to taste
¼ teaspoon oregano
3 cups diced raw potatoes
½ pound Swiss chard or spinach

Pick over the beans, rinse them, and place in large heavy kettle with cover. Add water to cover, put lid on pot, bring to a quick boil, then remove from heat to soak for 1 hour. Drain beans into a colander. Using the same kettle, over medium heat, brown the salt-pork dice, then add ham and chorizos, cooking these until lightly browned. Add the onion, celery, green pepper, and scallions, and continue to cook over medium heat, stirring frequently, until the vegetables are limp. Add tomatoes and garlic, mix well, and cook for 5 minutes more. Return the beans to the pot, and add the ham bone, water, salt, and oregano. Cover kettle and bring the *caldo* to the boil, then reduce heat and cook, covered, until the beans are very tender— usually more than 1 hour. Add more water if necessary, but not too much—the stew should be rather thick when served. During the last half hour, add the diced potatoes. During the last 5 minutes, add the Swiss chard or spinach, torn into smallish pieces. Serve while very hot.

A LUSTY Iberian affair that has been transported to the Spanish-speaking populations in the United States is Fabada—from one of the Spanish words for bean, *faba*. There are numberless variants of the recipe, but here is one which is reasonably authentic —and assuredly delicious! Serve it with hot crusty bread, a light green salad, and either beer or good dry red wine, for a memorable meal for ordinary and festive occasions alike.

Fabada
Serves 6 to 8.

1½ cups dried navy or other white beans
2 cups chopped onion
2 large cloves garlic, mashed
¼ pound lean salt pork, diced
1 thick slice ham, in large pieces
½ pound lean bacon, in large pieces
½ pound blood sausage, in large pieces
2 chorizos (spicy Spanish sausage), sliced
2 tablespoons lard
½ teaspoon Annatto (page 16) or ¼ teaspoon
    saffron shreds
salt and pepper to taste
1 small head cabbage, cut into wedges

Pick over and rinse beans under cold water. Place in a commodious kettle with cover, with enough salted water to cover them. Cover, bring quickly to the boil, then remove from the heat, and allow to soak for 1 hour. Add onion, garlic, salt pork, ham, bacon, blood sausage, and chorizos, cover container, and cook over low heat for about 1½ hours, adding a bit of water as needed. Melt the lard in a small saucepan, mix in the annatto (or saffron), add a bit of liquid from the *fabada,* and mix into the big pot. Add salt and pepper to taste, and continue to cook until beans are tender. Add cabbage wedges and cook until just firm-tender. Serve in large bowls, ascertaining that everyone obtains a sample of everything.

Miso (pronounced *mee*-so) is a paste made from fermented rice and soybeans, and is an essential ingredient in a wondrous series of thick Oriental soups. It is available commercially today, usually as a frozen import from Japan, but I prefer to prepare my own *miso,* using dried Navy Beans, as in the following particularly satisfactory potage. If possible, serve this soup in earthenware or stoneware bowls.

Misotaki (Thick Japanese Soup)
Serves 4 liberally.

1 cup dried navy or other white beans
2 tablespoons malt vinegar
1 tablespoon Japanese soy sauce

6 *cups rich chicken stock*

½ *pound cubed lean pork, cut into julienne strips*

2 *small white onions, thinly sliced*

2 *tiny carrots, scraped, thinly sliced*

salt and freshly ground white pepper

½ *to ¾ cup blanched Shirataki (cellophane noodles),*
  (pages 49, 66)

3 *tablespoons minced scallion tops*

Prepare beans as indicated on page 43. Cook until very tender, adding water as needed. Drain beans and mash thoroughly with a fork—do not purée, for the *miso* should be rather coarse. Stir in malt vinegar and soy sauce, and refrigerate, covered, overnight. Next day, bring the rich chicken stock to the boil, add the bits of raw pork, onion and carrot slices, plus salt and white pepper to taste. Cook over high heat for a moment or so, then add enough of the bean paste to thicken the soup to taste. Allow to cook until the meat and vegetables are just barely tender, then stir in the shirataki, which has been blanched in boiling water and drained. Serve the thick soup while very hot, sprinkled with minced scallion tops.

AGAIN a distinctive use for the navy bean, this time in an attractive and remarkably tasteful salad which I first encountered in Egypt. There it was served with roast lamb, rice into which the chef had incorporated plump white raisins and pine nuts, Arab bread, and hot tea with a touch of mint. It was a particularly memorable menu. This bean dish is called *fool mudammas,* and it is pronounced just as it is spelled.

Egyptian Bean Salad
Serves 6.

1½ *cups dried navy or other white beans*

2 *teaspoons salt*

1 *large clove garlic, mashed*

½ *cup light olive oil*

¼ *cup lemon juice*

4 *scallions with tops, thinly sliced*

tiny romaine leaves for base

Prepare beans as indicated (page 43). Cook until just tender, adding water as needed. Drain well and cool. Put the beans in a large bowl and pour over a mixture of the salt, garlic, oil, and lemon juice. Mix carefully but thoroughly. Chill for at least 2 hours, and serve on crisp leaves of romaine or other lettuce, garnished with the thinly sliced scallions.

FOR THOSE of us who appreciate the subtle flavor of the navy bean for itself, here is a very agreeable and simple baked-bean casserole. I find it most enjoyable with steamed brown bread, thick slices of Canadian bacon fried in a bit of butter until nicely browned, and a good tart cole slaw.

Navy Beans Curtis Bay
Serves 4 liberally.

1½ *cups dried navy or other white beans*

1 *cup rich chicken stock*

¾ *cup coarse bread crumbs*

⅓ *cup butter*

Pick over and rinse the beans under cold water. Place in kettle with cover, with enough salted water to cover them. Put on lid, bring quickly to the boil, then remove from heat and allow to soak for 1 hour. Return to heat and cook until beans are just tender. Drain thoroughly and arrange in a rather shallow buttered ovenproof casserole. Pour over the chicken stock, sprinkle with bread crumbs, dot with butter, and bake in preheated 325° F. oven until crumbs are nicely browned and beans are very tender.

PINTO BEAN

The Pinto Bean (a variant of *Phaseolus vulgaris,* of the Legume Family) was first encountered by the Spanish *conquistadores* when they invaded Mexico. It has probably been cultivated since prehistoric times, and is today one of the staple legumes in that country, and indeed in the western portions of the United States as well. The word *pinto* means "paint" in Spanish, which is most appropriate for this speckled, mottled bean.

It is one of the most nutritious of all the legumes, with an especially copious supply of the essential vitamin B-1. With various sorts of red beans, it figures with extraordinary frequency in the daily diets of millions of people in this hemisphere; it has been introduced into parts of Africa and Southeast Asia and has been met with happy acceptance there.

Pinto Beans are often served at my house, especially in these refried beans in the Mexican style. For an unusual appetizer, form the beans into wafer-thin patties and fry until very crisp. Delicious, and especially appropriate with the superb beers—Dos XX or Carta Blanca, for instance—now being commonly imported from that lovely land just below ours.

Frijoles Refritos (Refried Beans)
Serves 4 to 6.

2 cups dried pinto beans
1½ tablespoons salt
½ cup lard
½ cup chopped sharp Cheddar cheese
½ cup grated sharp Cheddar cheese
¼ cup lard

Pick over beans, wash them, and drain. In a large kettle with cover, cook beans in water to cover over low heat. Stir occasionally and add more water as needed; cook until beans are very, very tender—add salt when beans begin to become tender. When they are done, drain and reserve the liquid. Add the ½ cup lard to the beans, and stir thoroughly through while they are hot. Return the liquid a bit at a time, mashing the beans with a fork as this is done. Do not use all of the liquid if the beans become soupy. Add the ½ cup chopped cheese, mix thoroughly, and cook over very low heat until the cheese has melted through the beans. Allow this mixture to cool, preferably overnight, refrigerated. To serve, form the beans into smallish patties, and cook them in the very hot ¼ cup lard until they are well browned on both sides. Sprinkle with grated cheese while hot, to serve with all sorts of Latin dishes.

THE ILLUSTRIOUS pinto bean can also be incorporated in a variety of baked dishes, such as the following one, *frijoles borrachos*, which I like with such things as pork or ham or grilled sausages.

Drunken Beans
Serves 4 to 6 liberally.

2 cups dried pinto beans
¼ pound lean salt pork, diced
1 teaspoon salt
⅛ teaspoon garlic powder
⅛ to ¼ teaspoon oregano
2 tablespoons butter
¾ cup coarse-chopped fresh tomato
¾ cup coarse-chopped green pepper
¾ cup coarse-chopped onion
½ cup liquid from beans
½ cup stale beer

Pick over beans, wash them, and drain. In a large covered kettle, cook beans in water to cover with the salt-pork dice, salt, garlic powder, and oregano, until the beans are just tender, adding water as necessary. Drain the beans, reserving ½ cup of liquid. In the same kettle, melt the butter and sauté the tomato, green pepper, and onion over low heat, stirring often, until vegetables are just barely soft. Add beans, mix well, and simmer uncovered for 10 minutes. Add the reserved bean liquid and simmer for 10 minutes more. Then add the beer, mix well, and simmer over very low heat for 15 minutes. Serve while good and hot.

PINTO BEANS are often utilized in the highly personalized versions of chili which one encounters in our Southwest and in parts of Mexico. Every good cook swears by his or her own special recipe. Here is one, originally from some happy expatriate Yankees residing in Morelia, the old capital of Michoacán State, in Mexico. They traditionally served it, as do I, with tortillas, a cool salad of shredded lettuce and avocado slices, and beer.

Pinto Beans Alegre
Serves 6 to 8.

2 cups dried pinto beans
6 cups water
1 46-ounce can tomato juice
3 large cloves garlic, mashed
4 tablespoons olive oil
2½ cups chopped onion
2 pounds lean ground beef
¾ cup chopped green pepper
4 large stalks celery, thinly sliced
2 6-ounce cans tomato paste
1 to 2 tablespoons chili powder
2 tablespoons salt
½ teaspoon freshly ground black pepper

Pick over beans, wash them, and drain. Place in a heavy kettle with cover, with the water. Cover, bring to the boil, then remove from the heat, and allow to stand, covered, for 1 hour. Add tomato juice and cook slowly, uncovered, while preparing the meat mixture. In a large skillet, sauté the garlic for about 5 minutes, stirring constantly. Add onion, ground beef, green pepper, and celery. Stirring, cook until the meat is well browned and crumbly. Turn this mixture into the bean kettle, add tomato paste, and seasonings, and mix well. Cover and simmer until beans are tender, usually about 2½ hours.

WITH its pleasantly subtle, nutty flavor, the pinto

bean can be substituted for just about every dried bean recipe to be encountered anywhere, from ornate casseroles to chilled salads.

RED BEAN

The Red Bean, alias Red Pea, is known in Spanish-speaking America as *frijol colorado* or *habichuela rosada*. It is a special form of the widespread and amazingly variable botanical species *Phaseolus vulgaris*, many of whose other phases appear elsewhere in this volume under a diversity of names. This one occupies a prominent position in the good cuisine of many lands to the south of ours, particularly Mexico and the West Indies. Its culinary uses are myriad, ranging from thick soups to hearty stews to tasteful medleys with rice and meats.

The flavor of the Red Bean is somewhat like that of the allied kidney bean, though perhaps not quite so pronounced. It can, though, be utilized for every recipe given in this book for the kidney bean.

Red Beans are raised to some degree in this country, notably in our southwestern states. They are increasingly available in our domestic markets, especially those in Cuban or Puerto Rican districts.

THE WONDERFUL cooks of Jamaica frequently commence their multicourse dinners with bowls of piping-hot Red Pea Soup. This is, of course, made with our Red Bean, but when the flavor is as sumptuous as this, who worries about details of nomenclature?

Jamaica Red Pea Soup
Serves 6 to 8.

1 *pound dried red beans (or kidney beans)*
2 *quarts water*
¾ *cup chopped onion*
¼ *pound lean salt pork, diced*
salt to taste
minced hot chili pepper, or Tabasco sauce to taste
Pickapeppa Sauce to taste

Pick over and wash the beans. Place them in a heavy kettle with cover, with the water. Cover and bring to a quick boil. Remove from the heat and allow to soak,

covered, for 1 hour. Add onion and salt-pork dice, and cook the soup over rather low heat, covered, until beans are very tender. Toward end of cooking period, add seasonings to taste—good Jamaican cooks often incline to be rather heavy-handed with their country pepper, which we know as hot chili pepper. Whirl hot soup in electric blender briefly, or force through a coarse sieve—it should retain some degree of texture. Reheat and serve while very hot.

FARTHER southward in the Caribbean islands, in Trinidad, we find the following hearty dish. I like it with a cucumber salad and green beans in some version or other.

Trinidad Red Beans and T'ings
Serves 4.

½ *pound dried red beans (or kidney beans)*
4 *cups water*
salt and pepper
1 *small bay leaf*
4 *cups fresh-cooked hot rice*
¾ *cup coarsely chopped cooked ham*
½ *cup coarsely chopped scallion tops*
salt and freshly ground black pepper

Pick over and wash the beans. Place them in a heavy kettle with cover, with the water, and bring to a quick boil, covered. Remove from heat and allow them to soak for 1 hour. Resume cooking over medium heat, adding salt and pepper to taste, plus the bay leaf, until the beans are tender, adding a tiny bit more water if needed. Drain thoroughly. Lightly combine with hot rice, ham, and scallion tops in a skillet. Season to taste, and quickly heat through, stirring carefully, on top of the stove. Serve while very hot.

SCARLET RUNNER BEAN

The Scarlet Runner Bean (*Phaseolus multiflorus*, of the Legume Family), also known as the Painted Lady Bean because of the multicolored pods and beans, is an elongate, slender vine from Mexico and other warm lands of the Western Hemisphere, long cultivated for its showy scarlet racemes of flowers, and for its edible beans. These are large beans, sometimes almost an inch in length, varying from red, mahogany-brown, or black to white (the last in the cultivated form known as Dutch Case-knife Bean, which also has ornamental white flowers). They are enclosed in pods up to six inches long which are consumed in the manner of green beans when juvenile.

Variants of this bean, or group of beans to be more accurate, have been grown by man since prehistoric times in Mexico and our own Southwest. Dried or more rarely fresh, they are occasionally to be encountered in markets in Arizona, New Mexico, and such areas, where they are valued for their rich, rather nutty flavor.

Scarlet Runner Beans may be cooked in the ways suggested for pinto beans or lima beans elsewhere in this book.

YAM BEAN

Three kinds of Yam Bean (*Pachyrhizus erosus, P. palmatilobus,* and *P. tuberosus,* of the Legume Family) are of more than casual import in the international vegetable world. Known also as Potato Bean, Tuber Bean, and Sincamas, these are climbing plants with lobed, three-parted leaves, rather attractive pealike blue or white blossoms, and tremendous tuberous roots which may attain a length of eight feet and a weight of seventy pounds! They are natives of the tropics, and little known in this country. On rare occasions, they may be found in our larger markets, offered as *ñame,* a name which correctly refers to the true yams (genus *Dioscorea*).

In addition to the ponderous underground tubers, the pendent seed pods—up to eight inches in length and with an odd tuberous thickening near the tips— are used, when small, boiled as a tasty vegetable. They possess a rather positive flavor and are best when simmered in salted water for a longer time than is usually recommended for such things.

In Mexico, particularly in the torrid tropical regions of both coasts, I have partaken of the tubers on several occasions, most often boiled until tender, and heavily seasoned with fiery Salsa Fría (page 185). In certain parts of Central America, again in the hot lowlands, the huge roots are occasionally offered raw—after thinly slicing and after protracted soaking in cold water to which some lime juice or cider vinegar has been added—as a salad, frequently with diced canned pimientos.

YARD-LONG BEAN

Though the Yard-Long Bean (*Vigna sesquipedalis,* of the Legume Family) is most often seen in this country as a horticultural curiosity, in the Asiatic tropics— where the species originates—it is extensively cultivated for its delicious edible pods and beans.

An annual, straggling vine with rather pretty, usually white, flowers, it is remarkable for its slender, elongate seed pods, which may attain a length of four feet, yet a breadth of only a half-inch or so. When these are young and soft in texture, they are popularly eaten as a green vegetable, with a flavor which is accurately designated by the alternate vernacular, Asparagus Bean.

The following Indonesian recipe is frequently offered at an authentic rijstafel.

Yard-Long Beans Javanese
Serves 4.

> 4 cups yard-long bean pods, washed, cut into 2-inch
>   lengths
> 2 tablespoons peanut or soy oil
> 2 teaspoons shrimp (or anchovy) paste
> 1 cup Coconut Milk (page 254)
> 1 to 2 teaspoons Japanese soy sauce
> ¼ teaspoon dark molasses

Using only the young, tender bean pods, trim off ends and wash thoroughly prior to cutting into lengths. In a wok or large skillet, heat the oil, blend in the shrimp paste (or anchovy paste, which is more generally available hereabouts), and the coconut milk. Add the bean pods, soy sauce, and molasses, and bring to a boil over high heat, stirring constantly. Lower heat and simmer until bean pods are tender, but not overcooked.

BEAN SPROUT

The delicious, crisp Bean Sprouts which we can now obtain with such ease, canned or even occasionally fresh, in our American markets are the product of artificial germination of a small round green or golden legume, the Mung or Mungo Bean. Botanists usually refer it to *Phaseolus aureus,* and consider it to have come originally from the tropical parts of Asia. The species has been cultivated by man since ancient times, as far afield as Africa and Greece. The Chinese, in particular, have valued it for millennia, and today it figures with tasteful prominence in Oriental cuisine.

These beans, too, are very important in the Far East in the manufacture of one of the kinds of transparent

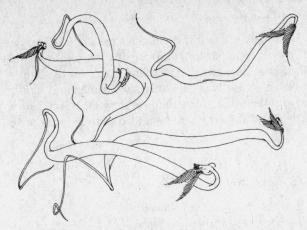

vermicelli, known variously as long rice, cellophane noodles, *sai-fen* (Chinese), and shirataki (Japanese) —but these are also made from other types of beans, from several of the edible seaweeds, and even from the true yams.

The plant which produces the bean which produces the sprout which we consume is a somewhat twining one, clothed with long brown hairs on vegetative parts. The smallish yellow flowers are followed by abundant three-inch cylindrical, vaguely curved pods, each containing upward of a dozen seeds—our beans. These are eaten, fresh or dried, and possess a very pleasant, bland flavor. Mung Beans make an attractive hot table dish boiled in lightly salted water until tender, then mashed or whirled in an electric blender to make a savory purée, this usually seasoned with soy sauce.

To produce Bean Sprouts, the little Mung Beans are induced to germinate, generally between layers of wet cloth or paper in a dark, cool place for a few days. It is not difficult to sprout your own Mung Beans, and you may find the delicacy of the fresh sprouts makes it worth undertaking this process.

Do not, by the way, bother to remove loose hulls or little roots from the sprouted beans, a tedious task often recommended; most of the vitamins and much of the flavor are contained in these often discarded parts.

Bean Sprouts and Chicken
Serves 4.

> 3 *cups fresh mung-bean sprouts*
> 1 *tablespoon peanut or soy oil*
> 1 *cooked chicken breast, slivered*
> 2 *or 3 teaspoons soy sauce*
> ½ *teaspoon sugar*
> ¼ *teaspoon monosodium glutamate*

Rinse the bean sprouts quickly in cool water, and drain thoroughly, shaking out as much moisture as possible. Using a wok or large shallow skillet, over high flame, heat the oil, and add the bean sprouts and slivers of cooked chicken breast. Stir-fry for just a minute or two, adding the soy sauce, sugar, and monosodium glutamate. Serve at once, while the bean sprouts still retain their luscious crisp texture.

THIS salad made with bean sprouts can be made ahead of time, and even eaten a day or so later. Though designed for use with Japanese or other Oriental menus, I have found that it accompanies perfectly such things as sautéed pork or lamb chops, broiled hamburgers, or baked ham.

Nikko Salad
Serves 4.

> 1 1-*pound can bean sprouts, drained*
> 1 *small can water chestnuts, cut into small dice*
> 2 *tablespoons finely chopped scallions, with tops*
> 2 *tablespoons wine vinegar*
> ⅛ *teaspoon powdered ginger*
> 3 *tablespoons Japanese soy sauce*

Drain canned bean sprouts, then rinse under running cold water, and drain thoroughly again. Combine with all other ingredients in a bowl, mixing lightly but well, and chill for at least 1 hour. Drain thoroughly and serve in rather small amounts.

HERE is a somewhat more ornate bean sprout salad that goes well with fried or broiled chicken, shrimp, or lobster.

Bean Sprouts Vinaigrette
Serves 4 to 6.

> 2 1-*pound cans bean sprouts, drained*
> 3 *tablespoons wine vinegar*
> ¾ *cup light salad oil*
> ½ *teaspoon dry mustard*
> 1 *tablespoon Japanese soy sauce*
> 1 *tablespoon sugar*
> 1 *tablespoon finely chopped pimiento*
> 2 *tablespoons drained sweet-pickle relish*
> ½ *cup finely chopped fresh parsley*
> 2 *teaspoons chopped chives*

Thoroughly drain the bean sprouts, rinse under running cold water, then drain thoroughly again. Blend together all other ingredients, mixing them well with a fork. Pour over the bean sprouts, mix well, and chill for at least 1 hour. Drain at last moment and serve, if desired, on a bed of crisp lettuce leaves.

WHETHER fresh or canned, bean sprouts are admirable last-minute additions to soups, such as the following Korean creation, in which subtle flavors and delicate textures blend in fascinating fashion.

Korean Bean Sprout Soup
Serves 6.

2 cups fresh or canned bean sprouts
¾ pound lean stew beef
2 tablespoons peanut or soy oil
½ cup coarsely chopped onion
2 small cloves garlic, mashed or minced
2 teaspoons salt
¼ teaspoon freshly ground black pepper
2 quarts rich beef stock
3 tablespoons Japanese soy sauce
3 scallions, with tops, coarsely chopped
Tabasco sauce to taste

In a deep heavy kettle with cover, heat the oil. Chop the beef into very small dice, and add it to the oil, together with the onion, garlic, salt, and pepper. Over high heat, cook for 5 minutes, stirring constantly. Add the beef stock (preferably fresh) and soy sauce, cover the kettle, reduce heat, and simmer until meat is tender. Add the drained bean sprouts, scallions, and Tabasco sauce to taste, cover again, and simmer for 4 or 5 minutes—the sprouts should still be crisp in texture. Serve piping hot.

IN ORIENTAL restaurants, rare indeed is the menu on which some kind of *foo yung* dish, made with bean sprouts, does not appear. The following version, with rice and vinegar-marinated cucumbers, makes a perfect light supper.

Shrimp Foo Yung
Serves 4.

1 cup canned bean sprouts, drained, rinsed
6 eggs
1½ cups cooked shrimp, chopped
½ cup finely chopped scallions, with tops
¼ cup thinly sliced water chestnuts
½ cup thinly sliced mushrooms, fresh or canned
1 tablespoon Japanese soy sauce

¼ teaspoon black pepper
3 tablespoons peanut or soy oil
Foo Yung Gravy (see recipe below)

Beat eggs with all ingredients except oil and gravy until well blended. In a skillet or omelet pan, heat the oil. Pour in egg mixture and cook until lightly browned on bottom. Carefully turn omelet and lightly brown other side. Serve immediately on warm plates, with Foo Yung Gravy to be added to individual taste.

Foo Yung Gravy
Makes enough for above recipe.

½ cup chicken broth or bouillon
2 tablespoons Japanese soy sauce
½ teaspoon sugar
1 tablespoon cornstarch

In a small saucepan, combine all ingredients. Stirring constantly, bring to the boil. Immediately reduce heat and, still stirring, simmer until sauce is clear. Keep warm and serve as soon as possible.

Note: Soybean sprouts may be substituted in all the foregoing recipes.

A LEGUME related to the mung bean, although as yet rarely encountered in our markets, is the Urd. This is botanically *Phaseolus Mungo*, and differs in technical details from the mung bean, most notably in its oblong, almost black little seeds, these borne in pods with long hairs. It is used in China, Tibet, and certain other parts of eastern Asia as a rather important item of the daily diet, the little legumes usually boiled—sometimes in tea—until tender, then seasoned with salt or soy sauce.

BEET

The Beet, or Beetroot, as we know it in our kitchens is a derivative of a sprawling seaside plant (*Beta vulgaris,* of the Goosefoot Family) extensively distributed from the Mediterranean to the Caspian Sea. The modern Beet thrives particularly in cool countries, and in the cuisines of certain of these, this adaptable and very handsome vegetable appears on the table in some guise at virtually every meal.

There are several different kinds of Beets, including some especially developed for the high sugar content of their tuberous roots, others for their sizable foliage, which is used as a prized potherb, and still others for their leaves in vivid, often iridescent shades of red, green, and yellow, which are planted as spectacular ornamentals in the flower garden.

Oddly enough, Swiss Chard (page 86), alias Sea-Kale Beet, is in actuality a variety of true Beet (one of the so-called Leaf-Beets), with proportionately small, woody roots and large leaves with very broad thickened stalk and midrib.

Fresh Beets are available in leafy bunches in our produce markets, and canned in a variety of forms—whole, sliced, and julienne. They are nutritious vegetables and contain abundant supplies of vitamins—these especially in the tops, which should always be utilized by the good cook.

In buying fresh Beets, choose those with small firm roots and crisp green or reddish-green tops. Always cook the Beetroots unpeeled, with an inch or two of leaf stems still attached. Cutting of the Beet's skin causes the red color to dissolve into the boiling liquid.

Like Beets, I used to thrive in a chilly northern area—the tip of Maine athwart Canada's Province of New Brunswick—before I was happily transported to more tropical climes. At home in Houlton, Maine, my grandmother used to serve us the greens and the little beetroots in the following delectable manner.

Beets and Greens, Maine Style
Serves 4.

2 *big bunches small beets, with fresh leafy tops*
¼ *pound lean salt pork, diced*
butter
salt and freshly ground pepper
cider or wine vinegar (optional)
2 *hard-cooked eggs, finely chopped (optional)*

Cut tops from beetroots, leaving a couple of inches of stalk on roots. Wash roots but do not peel them. Place in a considerable quantity of boiling salted water, cover, and cook over medium heat until they are just tender. Drain, plunge into a kettle of cold water, and slip off the skins, stems, and little apical roots. Drain again and keep warm. Fry the salt-pork dice in a small skillet until crisp; remove pieces from the grease with slotted spoon and reserve them. Thoroughly wash and drain the beet tops. Just prior to serving time, place leafy tops in a large kettle with cover, with a small amount of rapidly boiling salted water. Add the cooked salt pork, cover and cook until the leaves and fleshy stalks become crisp-tender. Drain at once, add warm whole or halved cooked beetroots,

plus a goodly amount of butter, and shake the kettle over the heat for a few moments. Serve at once, seasoned with salt and pepper, and offering vinegar and a dish of chopped eggs on the side for optional—but delicious—accessories.

BORSHCH (or Borscht) is the best known of the soups in which beets figure with prominence. There are dozens of variations—Polish, Ukrainian, Siberian—but here is one which is an almost universal favorite. It is very hearty, and makes an excellent main dish on a wintry evening, accompanied by heated crusty bread and a flagon of good red wine.

Russian Borscht
Serves 4 to 6.

3 *cups finely chopped raw beets*
1 *pound lean stew beef*
2½ *quarts water*
1 *tablespoon salt*
½ *cup coarsely shredded carrots*
2 *cups coarsely chopped onion*
2 *tablespoons tomato paste*
2 *tablespoons wine vinegar*
salt and freshly ground pepper
sour cream

In a large kettle, bring the stew beef, cut into smallish chunks, water, and salt, to a quick boil, covered. Reduce heat and simmer, still covered, until meat falls apart—adding a bit more water if necessary. Add beets, carrots, onion, tomato paste, and vinegar, cover again, and simmer until vegetables are just tender. The soup should be a thick one. Add additional salt, plus freshly ground pepper to taste, and serve while hot with dollops of sour cream.

COOKED beets, chilled, are especially suited to use in various kinds of salads. These range from simplicity to some degree of complexity, as indicated in the recipes below.

Easy Beet Salad
Serves 4.

1 1-*pound can shoestring (julienne) beets, chilled*
1 *cup chilled sour cream*
3 *tablespoons snipped chives*
crisp lettuce leaves for base

Just at serving time, drain the beets thoroughly and arrange them nicely on a bed of crisp lettuce leaves (Romaine is especially apropos here). Top with goodly dollops of sour cream and sprinkle with snipped chives to serve, particularly with hot seafood.

Beet-Herring Zakooska

1 cup chopped canned shoestring (julienne) beets, drained
2 pickled-herring fillets
1 cup chopped tart, peeled apple
¼ cup minced onion
½ teaspoon minced fresh dill (or ¼ teaspoon dried dill weed)
¼ cup finely chopped dill pickle
1 cup sour cream
1 teaspoon cider vinegar
1 tablespoon salad oil
⅛ teaspoon freshly ground pepper

Use herring preserved in a vinegar liquid (not in tomato or mustard sauce). Drain, and cut the fillets into very small dice. Combine thoroughly with all other ingredients, cover, and refrigerate for one hour prior to serving. Do not garnish with parsley or other greenery—this is not approved of by the gourmet *zakooska* fancier! Accompany with firm white and/or dark Russian breads, if possible, and lots of iced curls of butter, as an exceptional hors d'oeuvre.

PICKLED Beets are a pretty and tasty accompaniment to all sorts of hearty things from Finnan Haddie or creamed salmon with peas to roast stuffed chicken. The following recipe is an old-fashioned one, again from northern Maine. Do not discard the pickling liquid after the beets have been consumed! Rather, add to it several shelled hard-cooked eggs and allow these to pickle for a few days in the refrigerator prior to serving, whole or quartered, with meat, fowl, or seafood.

Pickled Beets Houlton
Serves 4.

1 1-pound can or jar tiny whole beets
½ cup cider vinegar
2 tablespoons sugar
½ teaspoon salt
3 or 4 whole cloves
¼ small bay leaf
1 small onion, sliced wafer-thin

Drain beets but reserve their liquid. Place drained beets in small serving bowl. In a small saucepan with cover, combine beet liquid with all of the other ingredients. Bring to a boil, then reduce heat, cover, and simmer for 10 minutes, stirring occasionally. Pour over beets and allow to cool. Refrigerate for at least 2 hours (preferably overnight) before serving.

HERE is an excellent hot beet dish to serve with pork or ham.

Beets in Orange Sauce
Serves 4 to 6.

4 cups cooked, sliced beets
3 tablespoons coarsely grated orange rind
1 cup orange juice
½ teaspoon salt
1 tablespoon cornstarch
⅛ cup butter
freshly ground pepper

Using top of a double boiler, over hot water, combine the orange rind and juice with the salt and cornstarch. Cook, stirring often, until the sauce is thickened. Add the butter and stir until thoroughly blended, then add the beets, heat through, and serve at once, well seasoned with freshly ground pepper.

FOR AN unusual, very handsome vegetable dish with broiled meats, offer the friends at your table a bowl of beets which have been skinned after boiling until tender, then put through a potato ricer, and dressed with butter, with salt and pepper to taste. If desired, sprinkle with finely chopped fresh parsley or crisp watercress leaves.

AND, FINALLY, there is the famous New England specialty with a quaint name and memorable flavor and texture:

Red Flannel Hash
Serves 4.

1½ cups coarsely chopped cooked beets
1½ cups coarsely chopped boiled potatoes
1½ cups coarsely chopped corned beef
⅓ cup minced onion
3 tablespoons butter
½ cup evaporated milk
salt and freshly ground pepper

In a large, heavy skillet, place the beets, potatoes, cooked corned beef (fresh or canned variety, to your choice), and onion, with the butter. Bring up the heat to rather high degree, lightly mix the ingredients in the skillet, and pour the evaporated milk over them. Lower heat and cook, stirring with care now and then, until heated through. When a good brown crust has formed on under surface of the hash, use a slotted spatula to turn it over into several pieces. Continue to cook these until crusty-browned on under surface, and serve the hash while very hot.

BREADFRUIT

The Breadfruit (*Artocarpus communis*) is a part of the daily diet of millions of people in such regions of the world as Polynesia, Micronesia, Jamaica, Brazil, where this nutritious fruit is used in a variety of fashions as a starchy vegetable.

The tree is a very impressive one, with huge lacquered green, deep-lobed leaves, and is often encountered as a prized ornamental in tropical gardens and conservatories. These trees bear their usually roundish, warty or prickly yellowish-green fruits throughout the year, with particularly heavy production during the early summer months. The fruits measure up to about eight inches in length by six inches in diameter, and may weigh as much as ten pounds apiece. There are many different and distinctive varieties of Breadfruit, the most highly prized being completely seedless—though the seeds, if present, are a delicacy when roasted. Whether seedless or not, the Breadfruit is inedible until it is cooked—boiled, steamed, or baked—as a vegetable.

The slightly immature fruit has a flavor and texture much like grainy bread when properly prepared, and is of an attractive ivory-white or vaguely yellowish color. In Hawaii and other islands of Polynesia, a sort of poi—much like that manufactured from taro—is prepared on festive occasions from it.

The species has been cultivated since prehistoric times, and is not today authentically known in the wild state. Its original haunts are presumably Malaysia, and it was transported to the various insular groups of Micronesia and Polynesia by the fantastic migrations of the early peoples. Realizing its unique potentials as a food, the notorious Captain Bligh succeeded in introducing it into Jamaica from Tahiti in 1792. This was Bligh's second such expedition, the first one being the disastrous voyage of the *Bounty*.

Breadfruit is rarely encountered in our mainland United States markets, which is unfortunate, since the handsome big fruits are in abundant supply in Puerto Rico, Hawaii, and other tropical areas that frequently export choice edibles. Canned Breadfruit is to be found in gourmet shops, imported mostly from Jamaica, but in my opinion it is too sweet.

Properly cooked, fresh Breadfruit is an unusually tasty and distinctive substitute for potatoes, rice, or pasta, with high carbohydrate value and rich availability of thiamine and vitamin C.

Baked Breadfruit
Serves 6 to 8.

Choose a soft, ripe breadfruit. (To speed up ripening of breadfruit, remove the stalk and pack the indentation left in the fruit with coarse kosher salt; the fruit will be soft-ripe within a couple of days.) Place breadfruit in a well-greased pan and bake in preheated 350° F. oven for 1 hour, or until a sharp knife plunged into it comes out clean. Cut baked fruit into quarters and remove seeds, if any. Cut or break each quarter into suitable-sized individual portions, and serve them hot with melted butter, salt, and freshly ground pepper to taste, accompanied by wedges of lime, or lemon, or sour orange. If feasible, bake your breadfruit over a good bed of charcoal—it affords it a particular flavor which is superb.

BREADFRUIT Chips are a personal favorite that I first encountered in Jamaica. The chips should be made fresh just at serving time, since they do not store particularly well.

Breadfruit Chips
Makes about 8 dozen chips.

> 1 *green to semiripe breadfruit*
> *heavily salted water*
> *deep fat or oil for frying*

Peel breadfruit, cut it into quarters, and remove all parts of the core. Slice breadfruit lengthwise into wafer-thin pegs and soak for about 1 hour in the heavily salted water. Pat dry on absorbent paper towels and fry, a few at a time, in hot deep fat or oil, until golden-brown. Drain thoroughly. If desired sprinkle with a bit of salt, and serve while nice and hot with beer or cocktails.

A VERY hearty and flavorful soup is made from ripe breadfruit in several of the Caribbean islands. This unusual menu item also includes malanga or taro tubers, and a green papaya.

Breadfruit Soup
Serves 6.

1 *medium-size ripe breadfruit*
1 *large malanga or 1 pound taro tubers*
½ *pound lean stew beef, in small cubes*
2 *tablespoons peanut or soy oil*
3 *quarts water*
2 *or 3 carrots*
1 *medium-size green papaya*
2 *onions*
2 *medium-size ripe tomatoes*
1 *bay leaf*
salt and freshly ground pepper
Tabasco sauce

Peel breadfruit, malanga or taro, carrots, papaya (discard seeds), and onions, and cut into smallish pieces. In a skillet, thoroughly brown the little cubes of beef in the oil. Turn all vegetables, browned beef cubes, diced tomatoes, and bay leaf into a soup kettle and add the water. Bring to a quick boil, reduce heat, cover kettle, and simmer until vegetables and meat are tender. Season to taste with salt and freshly ground pepper and a dash or two of Tabasco sauce during last half-hour or so of cooking. Turn hot soup into an electric blender and whirl briefly, correct seasoning, and serve while very hot.

MAY MOIR, who, like me, likes good food, orchids, and Siamese cats (not necessarily in that order!), has contributed many pleasant things to this book. Here is her Hawaiian Breadfruit Papaiee Pudding, made from the pulp of a perfectly ripe breadfruit.

Breadfruit Papaiee Pudding
Serves 4.

1 *very ripe breadfruit*
1½ *cups Coconut Milk (page 254)*
sugar to taste
salt to taste

Peel very ripe breadfruit, remove core, and mash thoroughly, or put through food mill. Blend in the coconut milk, add sugar and salt to taste, and mix well. Turn into buttered ovenproof casserole and bake in preheated 325° F. oven for about 40 minutes, or until pudding is firm and delicately browned on top.

ONE further use for the breadfruit, one which makes this splendid tree a particular joy to all connoisseur cooks. The leaves, in most forms measuring more than a foot in length, with a breadth of upward of 6 to 10 inches, are startlingly attractive and make the most amazing table mats imaginable! When fresh, their lustrous green color is dazzling, and they can easily be dried—flattened between absorbent sheets of newspaper, with weights to press them down to avoid curling of the margins—and reused time and again.

BRIEF mention must be made here, too, of the Breadnut or *pana de pepita*, a distinctive form of the breadfruit. The huge fruits are covered with thick spines, and inside are comprised mostly of large brownish seeds. After boiling or, preferably, roasting, these seeds are reminiscent of top-quality chestnuts, and are greatly prized in many tropical lands as snacks, or are used in soups or stuffings for roast fowl. Breadnuts are to be found in markets in Hawaii and Puerto Rico, but very rarely reach the United States mainland, unfortunately.

BREADROOT

The Common Breadroot of the United States is botanically known as *Psoralea esculenta,* of the Legume Family. Its genus is known collectively as Scurfy Peas or Scurfpeas, and contains more than a hundred species, several of which are of casual importance as vegetables in various parts of the world.

The Breadroot is a bushy smallish plant that grows in prairie sections of this country and Canada. The Amerindians and early colonists in our Midwest often knew it as *pomme blanche.* The tuberous roots, about the size and shape of small turnips, are often borne in clusters. The various Indian tribes who live in the species' habitat have long cultivated them for their starchy, bland-flavored flesh. The roots are eaten raw or, more commonly, roasted, and when suitably seasoned are quite pleasant. Today the tubers are rarely encountered in our markets, although they are worthy of greater attention.

Several other kinds of Psoraleas have edible tubers, and the leaves of some species are made into refreshing teas.

BROCCOLI

Broccoli is another of our vegetable paradoxes. Technically it is a long-season cauliflower, which is in turn a form of the common cabbage species (*Brassica oleracea* var. *botrytis,* of the Crucifer Family). The Broccoli is, in all probability, the parent of cauliflower, from which it differs principally in its coarser vegetative parts, the usually smaller heads, and in the fact that its condensed flowers with their little stems do not form an edible "curd" at an early date. In England, where Broccoli is very popular, it is often called Winter Cauliflower.

Oddly enough, though Broccoli was valued by the Romans some two thousand years ago, its cultivation in the United States dates only from the 1920s. Then a trial planting was made in California's Santa Clara Valley, and the sizable Italian population of that state quickly made it available in their markets and restaurants, with far-reaching results.

Today, California, and to a lesser degree, Arizona, send Broccoli to all parts of this country by the thousands of carloads each year. When purchasing fresh Broccoli (the frozen kind is also most acceptable), look for a fresh dark-green luster to the flower cluster, and for tightly closed buds. If any open yellow blossoms are present, look further.

To cook Broccoli, place in 1 inch of boiling salted water over medium heat in a kettle with a tight lid. If the stalks are thick, slash them lengthwise or cut the stem in diagonal slices that will cook as quickly as the flowerets. Cook for 8 to 10 minutes, until just crisp-tender. When done, the flower clusters should retain their deep-green color.

Many widely varying flavors and seasonings are compatible with Broccoli: among these are crisp bacon, thinly sliced chicken or ham, pastrami, smoked turkey, capers, chopped nuts, coriander, curry powder, nutmeg, and pimiento.

A seasoned mayonnaise sauce goes equally well with hot or cold Broccoli. Add to 1 cup of homemade or commercial mayonnaise, in order listed: ¼ of a garlic clove, minced, ¼ teaspoon ground coriander, and ⅓ cup of chopped smoked turkey or smoked ham.

Personally, I think there is nothing more luscious than hot Broccoli, cooked until just crisp-tender, served with cider or wine vinegar to taste, and salt and freshly ground pepper, after a goodly dollop of butter has been melted over the rich greenery.

BROCCOLI with sour cream is singularly apropos with pork, roast veal, or as a hot dish to accompany an ornate garnished platter of assorted cold cuts. Did you know that *smetana* means sour cream in Russian?

Broccoli Smetana
Serves 4.

1 *big bunch fresh broccoli*
2 *tablespoons flour*
1 *cup commercial sour cream*
1 *tablespoon "hot" horseradish*
1 *teaspoon cider vinegar*
½ *teaspoon salt*
¼ *teaspoon freshly ground black pepper*

Clean and cook broccoli as suggested on page 55. In a bowl gradually and thoroughly combine the flour with the sour cream (this at room temperature, to avoid curdling when heated). Place this in top of double boiler over boiling water and cook, stirring constantly, until smooth. Add the horseradish, vinegar, salt, and pepper, and mix thoroughly. Pour sauce over hot broccoli and serve at once.

THERE are a number of superlative cream soups made with broccoli. One of my personal favorites is this cold one.

Broccoli Soup Pierrot
Serves 4 to 6.

1 *big bunch fresh broccoli*
1 *cup rich chicken broth or bouillon*
½ *cup finely chopped onion*
1 *can condensed cream of mushroom soup*
3 *tablespoons butter*
½ *pint commercial sour cream*
1 *teaspoon capers, drained*
2 *tablespoons chopped pimiento*

Clean broccoli and cook as suggested on page 55. Drain, reserving ½ cup of the cooking liquid. Place the broccoli, the ½ cup liquid, the chicken broth or bouillon, and the onion, in a saucepan, and bring to the boil. Cook for 3 minutes, stirring constantly, then pour the hot mixture into an electric blender. Add the can of soup, the butter, sour cream, capers, and pimiento, and blend very briefly—tiny bits of green and red should still be fluttering through the medley. Chill thoroughly before serving, accompanied by Melba toast rounds, if desired.

BROCCOLI, fresh and cooked till crisp-tender, then chilled and marinated in a piquant dressing, makes a delectable salad. It is excellent with Italian pasta dishes, and can also form an exciting part of an anti-

pasto. In this recipe, I like to make use of one of the good commercial dried salad-dressing mixes as a time-saver.

Broccoli Ugo
Serves 4.

1 *big bunch fresh broccoli*
1 *package Italian salad-dressing mix, prepared as directed*
2 *tablespoons finely chopped scallion tops*

Clean and cook the broccoli as suggested on page 55. Drain and rinse under running cold water to curtail additional cooking. Prepare the salad-dressing mix according to package directions, preferably using red wine vinegar. Place broccoli pieces in a serving dish, pour the dressing over, sprinkle with the chopped scallion tops, and chill thoroughly prior to serving.

BRUSSELS SPROUTS

According to the botanists, the Brussels Sprout is a distinct phase of the same species of plant (*Brassica oleracea*, of the Crucifer Family) as the cabbage, cauliflower, and kale. Growing erect, with a big apical tuft of coarse crumpled leaves, the stout stem bears quantities of small compact globular buds through most of its length. These, much like miniature cabbage heads, are the "sprouts" which Belgians and just about everybody else in the Western world consume with such pleasure.

The French name for this attractive, highly flavored vegetable is *chou de Bruxelles*, the German *Kohlsprosse*. Both of these countries make considerable use of the Sprouts, which are at their peak for a brief season during the fall and winter months. Today, however, we can enjoy the excellent flash-frozen vegetable throughout the year.

As is the rule for all of these cabbage relatives (and indeed almost all leafy vegetables), Brussels Sprouts must never be overcooked. For some reason, in England, where this vegetable is extremely popular, it is often boiled until gray and mushy.

Brussels Sprouts have been around since the thirteenth century, and it would seem to be about time that everyone learned how to prepare them properly. The flavor and pleasant texture are best retained if

BRUSSELS SPROUTS

the cleaned little sprouts are put into a very small amount of lightly salted water, this boiling rapidly, then cooked in the tightly covered container for about 6 to 8 minutes only. Drain thoroughly, and serve without delay, laved in butter and seasoned with salt, white pepper, and either Cayenne or nutmeg.

When purchasing the fresh vegetable, acquire only those specimens which are vivid green in color, firm to the touch, and unwrinkled. The Sprouts quickly lose their unique flavor after being picked.

Cooked hot Brussels Sprouts may be served with a light cream sauce or a rich cheesy one. They can be arranged, raw, around a roast of beef or veal for a final few moments' cooking in the oven, being basted several times with the rich juices of the meat. They can be made into a purée—a favorite English fashion, which effectively hides the identity of the vegetable, or they can be baked, covered, in a small amount of rich beef or chicken stock until just tender, then garnished with a sprinkling of freshly grated Parmesan or sharp cheese.

HERE is a delicious version of these perky sprouts, which is especially suitable to accompany poultry or veal.

Brussels Sprouts Chez Nous
Serves 6.

4 cups (1 quart) Brussels sprouts
3 tablespoons butter
½ cup small white onions, sliced wafer-thin
⅓ cup rich chicken stock
salt and white pepper to taste

2 teaspoons chopped fresh parsley
1 teaspoon snipped fresh chives

Cook Brussels sprouts in a small amount of rapidly boiling salted water, tightly covered, for about 5 minutes. Drain and keep warm. In a sizable heavy skillet, melt the butter and over low heat sauté the thin onion rings until they are barely soft, stirring often but with care. Add the stock, season rather highly with salt and white pepper, and simmer for 5 minutes. Add the Brussels sprouts, and cook, basting the vegetables constantly, until they are just tender but not overly soft. Serve at once, sprinkled with parsley and chives.

BUCKWHEAT

The Buckwheat (*Fagopyrum esculentum*, of the Buckwheat Family) is an annual grain plant, probably originally from central and western China, but cultivated for centuries in many parts of the globe. The kernels of the seeds are of considerable importance as food; they are most often roasted and ground into a flour, this figuring in such things as pancakes and crisp thin cakes. In the Orient, Buckwheat flour is made into the luscious *soba* noodles which are happily now available as imports from Hong Kong and Japan. These, added to soups or cooked in a light stock, then drained and served as one would spaghetti, are excellent.

Buckwheat Groats, also called Kasha, are the hulled kernels of Buckwheat. This product is commonly used as a breakfast cereal, as a flavorful addition to soups, as a side dish with gravy, and as an ingredient in stuffings for meats.

BURDOCK

The Burdock (*Arctium Lappa,* of the Daisy Family) is very well known to everyone in most temperate parts of this country—as an all too common and despised weed. Anyone who has ever spent an hour or two picking off its wickedly sharp prickled burs will never forget it.

But this objectionable plant also figures prominently in the great cuisines of the Orient, the huge roots being made into a much-favored vegetable condiment. The roots, measuring as much as four feet in length, have a brown to grayish skin and white flesh, this coarse and fibrous. Usually a biennial, with large, broad, vaguely heart-shaped leaves on elongate stalks, the Burdock is cultivated as an annual in Hawaii. The vegetable—the juvenile roots often with foliage attached, the larger ones without leaves—is offered in sizable bunches in Honolulu markets, and may also appear on occasion in Oriental sectors of large cities on the mainland as well. It is most frequently encountered under its Japanese name, *gobo,* but sometimes under its Chinese label, *ngau-pong.*

Through a singularly arduous regime of soaking, cooking, resoaking, and seasoning, Burdock root can be prepared for the table. But it seems far easier to purchase the canned product, *gobo,* imported from Japan. These slender sticks are offered as a condiment with festive repasts—and are endowed with a flavor strange to most Occidental palates, and with a volcanic ''heat'' of disconcerting persistence.

Cabbage

CABBAGE—GREEN, WHITE, AND RED

The Cabbage is one of the innumerable forms of the species *Brassica oleracea* (Crucifer Family), these characterized by a more or less compact head formed by the leaves. Its close relatives include a marvelous roster of vegetables—kale, collards, cauliflower, broc-

coli, and Brussels sprouts. The basic wild plant, appearing on exposed chalk cliffs in England and other parts of Europe, was noted by man at a very early date, apparently, for records of the pre-Christian era remark selected variants of it as having been introduced into gardens.

The cultivation of Cabbage as a vegetable extends today to almost all parts of the globe, for it is an exceedingly adaptable plant which will thrive under even adverse conditions. In this country, for instance, well more than five hundred varieties are offered by commercial seedsmen. And rare indeed is a market anywhere in the world, from Finland to Florida, which does not boast of a proud array of firm Cabbage heads—green, white, or red, conical or round or flattish, the leaves smooth to elegantly puckered and crinkled. The French call it *chou,* the Chinese *yang-pai-ts'ai,* the Germans *Kraut,* the Portuguese *repôlho,* the Greeks *lahano,* and the Italians *verza*—and all of these cuisines count Cabbage as an important ingredient of many inspired culinary creations.

Good cookery with Cabbage covers the entire globe, from old-time Yankee classics to esoteric Asiatic novelties.

In choosing a Cabbage I search for one which is very firm to the touch, with crisp unblemished greenish outermost leaves. A very white head usually means that it is too ripe, and apt to be tough and without flavor, while an overly green one can signify immaturity, with poor cooking characteristics.

CABBAGE soups are justifiably popular. Diverse in content, they are typically very hearty affairs, often made the principal item on the menu of a wintry evening, with hot crusty bread on the side. Here is a perfectly delicious pottage from the Leeward Islands of the Caribbean, including subtle tastes of the tropical edibles which abound there.

Cabbage Soup St. Lucia
Serves 6.

  2 cups finely shredded cabbage
  2 tablespoons peanut or soy oil
  ½ pound raw medium shrimp, shelled, coarsely chopped
  1 teaspoon finely chopped fresh ginger root
  3 tablespoons minced onion
  1 tablespoon minced green pepper
  1½ quarts water
  1½ cups diced raw malanga or taro
  2 teaspoons salt
  ½ teaspoon freshly ground white pepper
  Tabasco sauce to taste
  2 tablespoons finely snipped chives

CHINESE CABBAGE

RED
CABBAGE

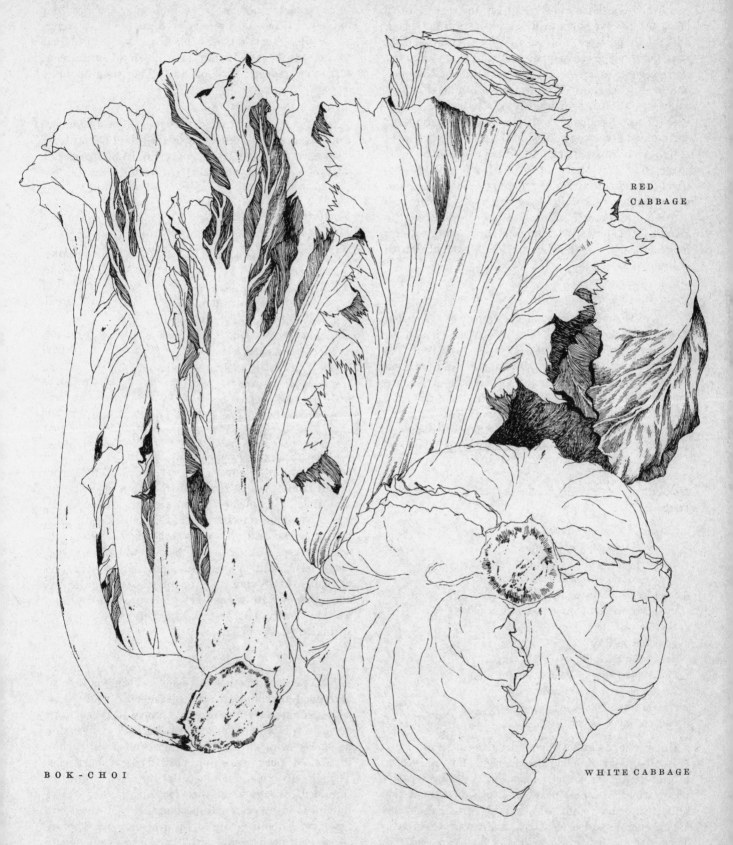

BOK-CHOI

WHITE CABBAGE

In a large heavy soup kettle with cover, heat the oil, and over high flame quickly stir-fry the shrimp for 2 minutes. Remove shrimp pieces with a slotted spoon, add the ginger root, and stir-fry for 2 minutes. Add the onion and green pepper and continue to stir-fry until vegetables are soft. Remove with slotted spoon and add to shrimp. To seasoned oil, add shredded cabbage, and still over high heat, stir-fry for 2 minutes. Remove cabbage and reserve separately from shrimp and other vegetables. Add water to kettle, with malanga or taro, salt and white pepper, reduce heat, cover container, and simmer until vegetable is just barely tender. Return shrimp, ginger root, onion, and green pepper, mix well, and continue to simmer, still covered, for about 15 minutes. Add cabbage, season to taste with Tabasco, and simmer for 5 minutes—not longer! Serve very hot, each portion sprinkled with chives.

ONE of the most famous of the soups which so often grace groaning Russian tables is Shchee. Though essentially a peasant dish, it sometimes appears in elegant ethnic restaurants in this country—and for good reason. I like to serve my own version of Shchee (pronounced just the way it is transliterated from the Cyrillic alphabet) with thick slabs of Russian pumpernickel or black bread, with sweet butter, and fried thick slices of Polish sausage (kielbasie) on the side.

Shchee
Serves 6.

2 1-*pound heads firm cabbage*
2 *quarts strained rich beef stock*
2 *tablespoons butter*
1 *cup coarsely chopped onion*
1 *cup finely chopped carrot*
1 *cup coarsely chopped celery, with some tops*
1½ *teaspoons salt*
1 *medium bay leaf*
1 *teaspoon dried dill weed*
2 *cups quartered peeled potatoes*
2 *tablespoons minced parsley*
freshly ground black pepper to taste
sour cream (optional)

Cut cabbages into wedges, removing core and any hard ribs. Coarsely chop the cabbage, and reserve. In a large kettle with cover, heat the stock, preferably fresh, and the richest possible. In a skillet, melt the butter, and over high heat, stirring often, cook the onion, carrot, and celery until they start to brown. Turn into the hot stock, with salt, bay leaf, and dill weed. Cover kettle and simmer soup for 20 minutes,

then add potatoes, to simmer until they start to become tender. Increase heat and add cabbage and parsley, to cook uncovered for 3 or 4 minutes only. Serve while very hot, with black pepper to be added to individual taste. If desired, a dollop of sour cream can be stirred into each portion of hot soup at table.

HERE is a cabbage salad that is a perfect summertime dish, to be served alongside a grand selection of barbecued meats—chicken, spareribs, hamburgers, hot dogs, *et al.*—from your backyard brazier or pit.

Cabbage Salad Miami
Serves 4 to 6.

5 *cups shredded cabbage*
ice water
1 15½-*ounce can kidney beans*
⅓ *cup finely chopped dill pickles*
¼ *cup finely chopped green pepper*
¼ *cup finely chopped scallions, with tops*
½ *cup mayonnaise*
½ *teaspoon celery seed*
⅛ *teaspoon oregano*
1½ *teaspoons salt*
½ *teaspoon freshly ground black pepper*
½ *teaspoon paprika*

Place cabbage, shredded not too finely, in a bowl with ice water to cover, and refrigerate for 1 hour. Drain kidney beans, reserving their liquid, and combine them with pickles, green pepper, and scallions, mixing well, in another bowl. Chill this for 1 hour, mixing occasionally. In yet another bowl, thoroughly combine some of the reserved bean liquid with mayonnaise, celery seed, oregano, salt, and black pepper, and chill this. At serving time, drain cabbage thoroughly, and combine with kidney bean mixture and dressing, tossing lightly but thoroughly. Offer each portion sprinkled with paprika.

THE FAVORITE method of using cabbage as a salad is in good old cole slaw (Oh, please, not "cold" slaw, as is seen on so many a menu!). Every cook has his or her own special version of this adaptable delicacy, to be offered with all sorts of things from fried shrimp to broiled pork chops or braised beef short ribs. Though many a recipe calls for marinating of shredded cabbage in a sauce for some time, I prefer to chill it in ice water, to be thoroughly drained and tossed with the dressing at the last moment. This insures the superb crispness that a cabbage salad should have.

Imperial Cole Slaw
Serves 6.

4 *cups finely shredded cabbage*
ice water
1 *teaspoon salt*
⅔ *cup mayonnaise*
1 *tablespoon wine vinegar*
¼ *teaspoon dry mustard*
¼ *teaspoon onion juice*
½ *teaspoon sugar*
1 *cup chilled green seedless grapes*
½ *cup slivered toasted almonds*

Place cabbage, shredded with a very sharp knife, in a bowl, add ice water to cover, plus the salt, and refrigerate for 1 hour. Meanwhile, prepare a dressing by combining the mayonnaise, vinegar, dry mustard, onion juice, and sugar, and chill this. At serving time, drain the cabbage thoroughly, add the chilled whole grapes, the slivered almonds, and the dressing. Toss very lightly and serve without delay.

FROM this delectably elegant cole slaw, let us travel on to a far simpler version.

Pineapple Cole Slaw
Serves 4 to 6.

1 *medium head firm cabbage*
ice water
1 *teaspoon salt*
1 *small can crushed pineapple*
½ *cup mayonnaise*
½ *teaspoon celery seed*
¼ *teaspoon freshly ground pepper*

Chop the cabbage into small pieces, removing all coarse parts, but do not shred it. Place in a bowl, add ice water to cover, plus the salt, and refrigerate for 1 hour. In another bowl, thoroughly combine the undrained pineapple with all other ingredients and chill this. At serving time, drain the cabbage thoroughly, mix in the dressing, toss lightly, and offer promptly.

IT IS very important to cook cabbage briefly. That way it retains its marvelous crisp texture and all of its flavor, as well as its essential vitamins and food values. Few vegetables are as utterly dismal as cabbage which has been boiled and boiled until it is a gray, sodden mass.

Here is the simplest recipe imaginable, one which well displays all of the vegetable's best points. It comes from Nixon Smiley, of the *Miami Herald,* who was introduced to it by a notable Guatemalan cook named Maria.

Maria's Cabbage
Serves 4.

2 *small heads firm cabbage*
water
salt
butter
freshly ground pepper

Cut the cabbages into slices ¼ inch in thickness. Pour about 2 quarts of water in a large pot with a tight lid and bring to a rolling boil. Place the cabbage in the water, cover tightly, and bring water to the boil again. Remove pot from the heat, thoroughly drain off the liquid, replace the lid and, still off the heat, allow cabbage to steam for perhaps 5 minutes. The cabbage should still be firm in texture—cooked *al dente,* as one does pasta. Serve very hot, with lots of butter and freshly ground pepper.

NATASHA was a Russian who lived in the apartment under me in Berkeley. She had an oversize refrigerator, full of formula for the babies—and bottles of ice-cold vodka. She was a fantastic cook, and on several festive occasions served the unique omelet described below. It was especially appropriate with boiled beef, accompanied by Horseradish Sauce (page 123).

Cabbage Omelet Natasha
Serves 4 to 6.

1 *medium head firm cabbage*
2 *tablespoons minced onion*
1 *teaspoon lemon juice*
4 *tablespoons butter*
4 *eggs*
½ *cup sour cream*

Shred the cabbage with a sharp knife and parboil it in a very small quantity of salted boiling water for 3 minutes. Drain thoroughly into a colander, pressing out as much moisture as possible. Turn into a bowl and combine with minced onion, lemon juice, and if necessary a pinch of salt. In a good skillet or omelet pan melt half the butter. Lightly beat the eggs, then briskly fold them into the cabbage mixture. Pour into the pan, and over medium heat cook until the omelet forms a light golden-brown undercrust. Place a plate to fit on top of the omelet, and carefully turn it over, so the omelet comes out onto the plate. Melt the remaining butter in the pan, and carefully slide the omelet back in, to cook on the other side until golden-brown and slightly crusty. Cut into wedges and serve at once with liberal dollops of sour cream.

HERE is a typical way with cabbage from the charming old town of Key West. I like it with roast pork, this basted during cooking with lime juice in the Cuban style, boiled new potatoes, and beaten biscuits. Simple fare, but superb!

Cabbage Conch Style
Serves 4.

2 small heads firm cabbage
4 or 5 small white onions, peeled, halved
1 cup diced cooked ham
½ teaspoon salt
½ teaspoon freshly ground black pepper
1 cup water
butter

Quarter the cabbages, removing any coarse ribs and cores, and cook in a big pot, covered, with all other ingredients except the butter, for about 8 minutes, or until the cabbage is done just to the crisp-tender stage. Add butter to taste, mix gently, and serve at once.

THERE are many versions of Colcannon, a robust Irish dish comprised of cabbage and fresh hot mashed potatoes. Consider this one next time you have a good big batch of savory beef stew!

Irish Colcannon
Serves 4 to 6.

2 small heads firm cabbage
2 cups hot freshly mashed potatoes
⅓ cup melted butter
2 tablespoons grated onion
salt and freshly ground pepper to taste
additional butter

Shred the cabbage with a sharp knife and cook it in a very small amount of boiling, lightly salted water, covered, until it is just crisp-tender. Drain thoroughly, pressing out as much moisture as possible. Add to the mashed potatoes, then whip in the melted butter, together with grated onion, and salt and freshly ground pepper to taste, until thoroughly mixed. Place in an ovenproof serving dish, run under preheated broiler to brown lightly, and serve dotted liberally with additional butter.

NOT long ago, a culinary crony who had spent some

years in what is now Tanzania prepared an African dinner for us. It was a repast of myriad courses, occupying some four hours' actual time at table. Among the several surprising and flavorful dishes was the following cabbage creation. The crisp balls were served with a kind of Salsa Fría (page 185), very "hot," which we added to individual taste.

African Cabbage Balls
Serves 6.

1 small firm head cabbage
½ pound calf's liver
2 tablespoons peanut or soy oil
1 cup minced onion
⅓ cup minced green pepper
⅓ cup peeled minced tomato
2 cups cooked rice
¾ teaspoon salt
½ teaspoon freshly ground black pepper
3 tablespoons peanut or soy oil

Shred the cabbage very fine with a sharp knife, discarding all coarse ribs and core. Put the liver through coarse grid of food mill. In a skillet, over rather high flame, heat the oil and, stirring constantly, cook the onion and green pepper until they are slightly browned. Stir in tomato and continue to cook for a moment or so more. Remove skillet from heat and thoroughly stir in cabbage, liver, rice, salt, and black pepper. Allow to cool slightly, then form into compact balls about 1 inch in diameter. Heat the 3 tablespoons oil in a skillet, and fry the cabbage-liver balls until very brown on all sides. Serve while hot, with Salsa Fría or comparable sauce on the side, if desired.

MY ORIENTAL menus are perhaps not always quite as authentic as they might be, but I take great delight in preparing them, and the chosen friends who are invited for periodic participation seem pleased by the results. One side dish over which just about everybody waxes enthusiastic is the following piquant cabbage.

Cabbage Orientale
Serves 4.

1 medium head firm cabbage
4 tablespoons peanut or soy oil
2 scallions with tops, coarsely chopped
½ medium green pepper, coarsely chopped
½ small clove garlic, mashed
3 tablespoons cider vinegar
2 tablespoons sake or dry sherry

2 *tablespoons Japanese soy sauce*
2 *tablespoons sugar*
¼ *teaspoon dried crushed hot chili peppers*
½ *teaspoon salt*
1 *tablespoon cornstarch*
1 *tablespoon warm water*

Cut cabbage into wedges about 1½ inches thick, paring off coarse ribs and core. In a large skillet with cover, quickly sauté the scallions, green pepper, and garlic in the oil over very high heat, stirring constantly, until they begin to brown. Add cabbage wedges, and sauté for 2 minutes, stirring with care to avoid breaking them apart. Add all other ingredients except cornstarch and water, mix well but carefully, lower heat and simmer, covered, for 3 minutes. Add cornstarch mixed with warm water, blend in well, cook until the sauce thickens slightly, and serve at once.

SAVOY cabbage, also known as Milan cabbage, is characterized by splendidly crumpled leaves. These cabbages should be afforded extra-special treatment by the good cook to combine their pleasing appearance with delicious flavor. Here, in my opinion, is just such a recipe. Serve with mashed potatoes or steamed rice, liberally buttered.

Stuffed Savoy Cabbage
Serves 4.

1 *large firm head Savoy cabbage*
¾ *pound ground lean pork*
½ *cup finely chopped onion*
1 *cup coarsely chopped peeled tart apple*
1 *teaspoon salt*
¼ *teaspoon freshly ground pepper*
1 *tablespoon lemon juice*

Pull off spreading outermost leaves from cabbage, rinse and reserve these. Using a sharp knife, carefully hollow out the cabbage head, leaving a firm shell about ¾ inch thick. Thinly shred cabbage removed from interior, first paring off any coarse ribs. In a nonsticking skillet, cook the ground pork, stirring often, until it is lightly browned. Remove pork with slotted spoon and drain off all but about 1 teaspoon of the fat. In same skillet, sauté the onion until soft, then stir in the chopped apple, salt, pepper, and lemon juice. Stir in the shredded cabbage and browned pork, and cook for just 1 or 2 minutes. Remove skillet from heat, allow to cool slightly, then fill cabbage shell with pork-apple mixture. Wrap cabbage tightly in heavy aluminum foil, and set on a rack over a pan of hot water. Bake

in preheated 400° F. oven for 30 minutes. Carefully unwrap stuffed cabbage, and serve set into the reserved raw cabbage leaves.

RED CABBAGE is a handsome form of this vegetable, with a large well-rounded firm head. It is often found in our good produce markets. Finely chopped or shredded, it forms an attractive and flavorful addition, raw, to slaws and other types of salads. When cooking it, be sure to add some lemon juice or vinegar to the liquid so that it will not turn a lurid purple. The red cabbage in cans or jars is often more purple than red, I find.

Here is a famous French version of red cabbage, prepared as it is in Normandy. This is especially appropriate with pork, rabbit, duck, or goose.

Red Cabbage Normande
Serves 4 to 6.

1 *2-pound firm red cabbage*
4 *tablespoons butter*
2 *medium onions, thinly sliced*
4 *large tart apples, peeled, quartered*
1 *or 2 small cloves garlic, minced*
¼ *teaspoon nutmeg*
¼ *teaspoon allspice*
¼ *teaspoon caraway seed*
salt and freshly ground black pepper
1 *teaspoon grated orange zest*
2 *tablespoons light brown sugar*
2 *cups dry red wine*
2 *tablespoons wine vinegar*
¼ *cup water*

Remove core and heavy ribs from cabbage and shred it coarsely. Using a heavy covered saucepan, cook in the butter, stirring once, for 5 minutes. In a large ovenproof casserole with cover, arrange a layer of cabbage, then one of onion slices, then of apple wedges, topping each layer with garlic, spices, salt and pepper to taste, and orange zest. Fill casserole with these layers, sprinkle brown sugar over top, and add wine, wine vinegar, and water. Cover casserole and cook in 375° F. oven until cabbage is tender, adding a bit more red wine if needed. Serve while very hot.

ANOTHER exceptional dish utilizing red cabbage is a classic one from around Limoges, in the province of Limousin, France. This is one of those slow-simmered casseroles which gives off utterly tantalizing aromas as it cooks. Serve it with braised or roast pork for optimum effect.

Red Cabbage, Limoges Style
Serves 4 to 6.

1 2-pound firm red cabbage
¼ pound lean salt pork, diced
1 quart rich beef stock
20 raw peeled chestnuts, coarsely chopped
salt and freshly ground pepper to taste

Remove core and heavy ribs from cabbage, and shred it coarsely. Bring diced salt pork to the boil in a small amount of water, allow to stand for a few minutes, then drain thoroughly. Place the cabbage and salt pork in a large ovenproof casserole with cover, add stock, preferably fresh, and chestnuts, and seasonings to taste. Stir gently, cover, and cook in preheated 375° F. oven until cabbage and chestnuts are tender, usually about 2 hours.

SAUERKRAUT, or kraut, is a special form of cabbage, shredded to varying degrees, and fermented in brine, often with special added seasonings. Its origins are a bit uncertain, but supposedly date back thousands of years to ancient China. Pickled forms of cabbage somewhat similar to sauerkraut are still found in Oriental cuisine, such as the Korean national dish of *kim chee*.

The uses of sauerkraut, whether from the old-time barrel or more modern can or refrigerated pliofilm packet, are literally legion. Though traditionally offered with pork, duck or goose, it adapts admirably to dishes of beef, veal, and lamb, especially of the slow-simmering variety. It also appears in unusual soups, special sandwiches, medleys with other vegetables, and diverse salads. Sauerkraut juice is justly popular with many bon vivants, and it even figures in the production of cakes and an odd but tasty ice cream.

I very much enjoy sauerkraut steamed with top-quality frankfurters or knockwurst, or with baked spareribs, or with pork and/or veal in a savory goulash, or with good old Yankee grilled hamburgers.

And then there is the famous classic *choucroute braisée à l'Alsacienne*, alias Braised Sauerkraut with Meats. Whenever I am fortunate enough to be presented with a precious loaf of fresh sourdough bread by a thoughtful friend coming from San Francisco by plane, a lovely big batch of this sauerkraut masterpiece is habitually created without delay. There are a great many recipes in the culinary literature for this Franco-German marvel; mine is one that has evolved, happily, through many years of *choucroute* consumption. Allow plenty of time to prepare this, and several hours and selected close friends to help eat it.

Braised Sauerkraut with Meats
(*Choucroute Braisée à l'Alsacienne*)
Serves 6 to 8.

2 pounds fresh refrigerated sauerkraut
¼ pound lean salt pork
2 medium cloves garlic, minced
freshly ground black pepper
2 cups dry white wine
1 to 2 cups rich chicken stock
2 medium onions
4 whole cloves
assorted meats (see below)

Drain the fresh sauerkraut and rinse it in a large kettle of cold water. Drain again and squeeze out most of the moisture, but do not crush the kraut. Using your heaviest large Dutch oven or iron kettle with cover, arrange thin slices of the salt pork over bottom and up sides as far as possible to form a sort of erratic lining. Fluff half of the sauerkraut into the kettle, sprinkle with half of the minced garlic, and rather liberally grind some black pepper over it. Top with remaining kraut, garlic, and more black pepper. Gently pour the wine and chicken stock over (this preferably fresh) to bring liquid level to top of sauerkraut. Push the onions, peeled and impaled with the whole cloves, down into the kraut. Cover container tightly, and cook in preheated 325° F. oven, or over low heat on top of the stove, for about 3 hours—most of the liquid should have been absorbed, yet the sauerkraut should retain some firmness of texture. Prepare your choice of meats as outlined below. Serve everyone a goodly portion of the braised sauerkraut, drained, a selection of the hot cooked meats, and a hot boiled potato or two. On the side, offer one or more kinds of fresh firm bread—sourdough, pumpernickel, and rye make a perfect choice. And a selection of mustards—two or three kinds, preferably, including a sharp mustard sauce.

Offer your family and/or guests as many of the meats as you wish: at least a good Polish sausage (kielbasie), a jar of the little imported or domestic cocktail frankfurters, and knockwurst. Slice the kielbasie thick and fry in a little oil until well browned on both sides. In another skillet, do likewise with cocktail wieners. Boil the knockwurst (I like to allow 1 per person), covered, in water until the skins pop open, usually about 20 minutes.

Additional suitable meats for the *choucroute* repast include lean spareribs, cut into small chunks, boiled with onion, celery, a bit of salt, and several peppercorns; pan-browned breakfast sausages; fresh pig's knuckles boiled with an onion and handful of celery leaves until tender; spicy Italian sausage, thin-sliced and fried until almost crisp; fried garlicky Spanish *butifarra* or *longaniza* sausages, if available; sliced roast pork or baked ham; thin fried smoked pork chops; or even, and with authenticity in the Alsatian manner, hunks of roast duck, goose, or pheasant. Prepare each meat in a separate container, so that the flavors do not become overly involved with one another. Keep everything hot, to be served simultaneously with the sauerkraut, atop it in the kettle or Dutch oven, if desired.

BOK-CHOI

Bok-choi (*Brassica chinensis,* of the Crucifer Family) is one of the most widely used "specialty" vegetables of the Chinese in this country. The plant is extensively cultivated from California to Florida, and it appears as an ingredient in many of the soups and stir-fried dishes offered by our Oriental restaurants. Alternate spellings for the vegetable's name include *pak-choi* and *bok-toi,* and it is also known as Pak-choi Cabbage or Chinese Cabbage (page 65) and in Japanese, *hakusai.*

The basal root leaves of Bok-choi have conspicuously thickened, broad, rather rounded stalks—white or greenish for the most part—and sizable broad dark glossy-green blades. The blanched hearts are a great delicacy, often found as special items in Chinese stores. The vegetable is vaguely reminiscent of Swiss chard, which is a form of beet and not even in the same botanical family as Bok-choi. Some of the many forms of Bok-choi bear tuberous roots which are eaten much in the manner of turnips, after boiling and peeling.

The attractive leaf vegetable has a very pleasant flavor and an elegant crispness that is unique. Like all leafy greens, Bok-choi must be used as promptly as possible after picking and must never be overcooked.

Both the thick stalks and the green parts of the leaves are used in cookery. Naturally, the stalks require a bit longer time over heat than the leaf blades.

Cut into bite-size pieces, Bok-choi is a favorite last-minute addition to clear soups with won ton, or it can be quickly stir-fried as in the following fashion. This dish should not be limited to service with Oriental foods—it makes an exciting addition to more ordinary fare such as baked ham or grilled hamburgers.

Bok-choi Stir-Fry
Serves 4.

1 *medium head fresh bok-choi*
2 *teaspoons peanut or soy oil*
1 *teaspoon salt*
1 *tablespoon cider vinegar*
1 *tablespoon sugar*
2 *teaspoons soy sauce*
2 *teaspoons cornstarch*
⅓ *cup hot water*

Rinse bok-choi and strip green blades from fleshy stems of leaves. Diagonally cut stems into bite-size lengths and tear leaves into sizable chunks; keep the two parts separate. In a wok or shallow big skillet, heat the oil, and over high flame stir-fry the stem pieces for about 2 minutes. Meanwhile, thoroughly combine all other ingredients in a bowl. Add the pieces of green leaves to wok or skillet, and at once stir in the hot sauce. Cook, stirring carefully, for just a few seconds, until the sauce has thickened slightly. The bok-choi stems should still be quite crisp. Serve at once.

To this basic recipe, such meats as cooked pork julienne, strips of quick-fried beef, or bits of cooked poultry or shellfish can be added to heat through at end of cooking process.

Bok-choi is frequently dried. It is then known in Chinese as *bok-choi gawn,* and added to soups and stewlike dishes for a unique and delicious flavor.

CHINESE CABBAGE

Chinese Cabbage is known botanically as *Brassica Pe-tsai* (Crucifer Family). This specific epithet is the Chinese name for the plant (*pai-tsai* is a variant). In English it is also called Long Cabbage and Celery Cabbage and, somewhat confusingly, the related Bok-choi (page 65) is also known as Chinese Cabbage.

This attractive vegetable is in good domestic markets today almost throughout the year. Yet many good cooks are unaware of it, and of its extensive culinary uses. The bunch as sold has broad-ribbed whitish-green leaves, these strong-veined and more or less crinkled. The not particularly compact median foliage (the large, coarse outer leaves are typically discarded prior to appearance in our stores) often attains a length of eighteen inches and measures four to six inches or so in breadth.

Originally from China, this pleasant vegetable was cultivated to a limited degree in France as early as the first part of the nineteenth century. Today it is widely grown in Europe and has been known in our own country since about the year 1900.

The flavor of the Chinese Cabbage is reminiscent of the common, firm, round species, but it has a delicate tartness that endears it to Oriental and Occidental cooks alike. *Pe-tsai* may be served in just about every fashion customarily suggested for the round cabbage. It is good in salads, such as the Chinese Cabbage Slaw, below. It is delicious when cooked until firm-tender, then sauced with a smooth Hollandaise or Mornay. It is well suited to inclusion in a good sukiyaki or comparable stir-cooked Oriental medleys. It can even accompany a platter of corned beef in that famous Hibernian dish which is virtually unknown in the Emerald Isle.

I LIKE the following chilled salad with such things as Beef Satés or broiled pork chops.

Chinese Cabbage Slaw
Serves 4.

4 cups thinly sliced inner leaves Chinese cabbage
ice water
1 cup peanut or soy oil — sesame oil
1 clove garlic, mashed
¼ teaspoon freshly ground pepper gr. pepper
(Tabasco)
⅓ to ½ cup wine vinegar bean sprouts
2 tablespoons Japanese soy sauce alfalfa "
2 tablespoons slivered water chestnuts scallions
ginger (cut up)

Place the thinly sliced Chinese cabbage in a bowl, cover with ice water, and refrigerate for at least 1 hour. Meanwhile, combine the remaining ingredients, except the water chestnuts, in a jar with tight-fitting lid, and shake thoroughly to blend. At serving time, thoroughly drain the Chinese cabbage, pat dry with paper towels, and lightly toss with the dressing, sprinkling over the water chestnut slivers at the very last moment.

HERE we have an unusual chilled appetizer in which our handsome vegetable is prominently displayed.

Chinese Cabbage Rolls
Serves 6.

1 bunch Chinese cabbage
2 tablespoons peanut or soy oil
2 medium green peppers
2 tablespoons soy sauce, Japanese preferred
½ tablespoon salt
¼ teaspoon crushed dried red peppers
2 tablespoons malt vinegar
2 tablespoons sugar
dash monosodium glutamate

Separate Chinese cabbage into single leaves. Boil leaves in lightly salted water until just barely tender, usually about 10 minutes, then drain carefully and rinse with running cold water. Cut each leaf crosswise into 2 parts, and when cool roll tightly, then cut each roll into 1-inch lengths. Arrange the cabbage rolls in a shallow serving dish. Seed the green peppers and cut into julienne strips. In a skillet, heat the oil and fry the green peppers over high heat, stirring constantly, for 3 minutes. Add remaining ingredients, mix well, and cook for a minute or 2, then pour over the cabbage rolls. Let stand at room temperature for 30 minutes or so, then chill. Serve cold as a distinctive appetizer.

ORIENTAL soups are justly famed for their subtle flavors. Here is a tasteful recipe in which Chinese cabbage figures. Shirataki are those slippery skinny "cellophane" noodles beloved by Japanese and Chinese. They can be bought, in cans or dried, in almost all specialty food stores.

Pe-tsai Soup
Serves 4 to 6.

1 bunch Chinese cabbage
2 ounces shirataki
½ pound lean ground beef
⅓ cup coarsely chopped scallions with tops
1 egg
¼ teaspoon powdered ginger
1 teaspoon sake or cooking sherry
½ teaspoon salt
6 cups rich chicken stock
2 teaspoons salt

Cut Chinese cabbage into 2-inch lengths, wash, and drain. Soak the shirataki in hot water and drain. Thoroughly combine the ground beef with the chopped scallions, egg, ginger, sake or sherry, and ½ teaspoon salt. Form into tiny balls about the size of a small walnut. In a sizable kettle with cover, heat the stock. Add the meatballs and boil, covered, for 10 minutes. Add the Chinese cabbage and continue to boil, still covered, for 5 minutes more. The vegetable should retain much of its crisp texture. Skim off any froth which forms. Add the shirataki and 2 teaspoons salt, heat through, and serve while very hot.

CACTUS

Though the seedy fruits of a number of different kinds of Cacti are edible, the vegetable utility of these succulent plants is largely restricted to the *nopales* of Mexico and Guatemala (mostly *Nopalea dejecta*). This group is best known for the shrubby species

(*Nopalea cochenillifera*) on which the cochineal insect thrives.

The young growths (not leaves, as they are commonly called, but the specialized fleshy stem sections) of the Nopal Cactus are to be found in virtually every market in Mexico, in many parts of Guatemala, and even on occasion in the large cities of California and New York.

These padlike growths are peeled—cautiously, since they are set with vicious tiny spines—then cut into lengthwise strips or large dice. Cooked in lightly salted water until tender, *nopales* are then doused with various sauces or incorporated into special omelets (usually during Lent), or dipped into a light batter and deep-fried in lard until crisp, or combined with fried bits of pork or spicy sausage (chorizo, usually) and tomatoes. They are also served chilled, in salads with shredded lettuce and/or cubed avocado.

Nopales or the smaller juvenile *nopalitos* are now available in gourmet shops in this country, in cans or jars of varying dimensions. These are to be recommended, since the preparation of the fresh cactus growths can be a rather awkward and potentially painful process.

OUR RECIPE, a complex but authentic one, comes from Mexico's second city, the handsome metropolis which is the capital of Jalisco State. Serve it with rice, some sort of cooked beans, sautéed plantains, tortillas, and beer.

Nopales Guadalajara
Serves 6.

1 *large can* nopales (*or* nopalitos)
4 *tablespoons butter*
¾ *cup finely chopped onion*
1 *medium clove garlic, minced*
½ *cup chopped green pepper*
1 *or more small hot pepper* (*chile*), *chopped*
1 *cold large tortilla, finely chopped*
¼ *teaspoon ground cloves*
2 *cups rich chicken or pork stock*
¼ *pound dried tiny shrimp*
2 *eggs, separated*
1 *cup lard*

Drain the *nopales* or *nopalitos* and cut them into strips or large dice. In a commodious heavy skillet, heat the butter, and sauté the onion, garlic, green pepper, and hot chile pepper to taste (the fresh kind infinitely superior to dried or canned in this instance), plus the tortilla. Cook, stirring frequently, until the vegetables start to soften, then add the cloves and

rich stock. Mix well and simmer over very low heat, stirring often, until the sauce is somewhat thickened. Meanwhile, prepare tiny shrimp cakes: Soak the dried shrimp (available in Mexican and Oriental specialty shops) in a bit of water, drain them, chop coarsely, put into a shallow pan and toast for about 20 minutes in a preheated 300° F. oven, shaking the pan often during this process. Beat the egg whites until they reach a peak, then fold in the lightly beaten yolks, and finally the chopped toasted shrimp. Heat the lard to 370° F. in a heavy pot, drop the shrimp mixture by teaspoons into it, and fry until nicely browned. Drain on paper towels, and add, with the strips or dice of *nopales* to the simmering sauce. Allow to simmer for a couple of minutes, and serve.

CALABAZA

Calabaza (pronounced ka-la-*bah*-za) is one of the myriad forms of cucurbits, a huge and complex group including the squash, pumpkins, and gourds of many lands. This one, also known as the West Indian Pumpkin or Green Pumpkin, is a favorite in Latin America and in recent years has been grown to some considerable extent in our warmer states, notably Florida, to supply the markets in Miami, New York, Chicago, and the like.

The Calabaza is most often picked and sold when rather small, seldom more than eight or ten inches in diameter. Generally round, some forms are conspicuously elongate or even almost pear-shaped, but all have a heavy rind which is white or light yellow closely mottled with rich dark green. The flesh is a vivid orange-yellow, and often slightly fibrous.

The Calabaza possesses a delicious and delicate flavor which approximates that of the North American field or pie pumpkin crossed with a big Hubbard squash, and, indeed, this attractive tropical cucurbit can be utilized in virtually every way recommended for Yankee pumpkins or the larger kinds of squash.

Our Latin-American friends do some wondrous things with Calabazas. A Mexican restaurant in Miami, for example, offers a superb cream soup with a base of this vegetable. Cuban friends serve parboiled chilled slices of it on a base of shredded lettuce, dressed with a piquant oil and vinegar sauce. Calabaza is also good simply cooked until tender, riced or mashed, and served while very hot with butter, salt, a good sprinkling of freshly ground pepper, and a tiny dusting of nutmeg.

THE FOLLOWING luscious fritter has Antillean antecedents. Easily prepared, with much of the work done ahead of cooking time, the fritters are especially suitable with roast pork or pork chops, or with broiled chicken.

Calabaza Fritters
Serves 4 to 6.

3 cups cooked, mashed calabaza
¼ cup minced onion
1 teaspoon baking powder
1 teaspoon salt
⅛ teaspoon freshly ground pepper
2 eggs, beaten well
½ cup melted lard

To prepare the fritters, thoroughly combine the mashed (or riced) calabaza with all ingredients except the melted lard. In a smallish skillet, heat the lard and drop the calabaza mixture carefully into it by heaping tablespoons. Fry the fritters until nicely browned on all sides, a few at a time, removing them with a slotted spoon to drain on absorbent paper towels. Serve as soon as possible, while very hot. If calabazas are not available, fresh or frozen Hubbard squash can be used; the flavor will not be quite the same, though!

DURING a trip to Jamaica, where I had the happy privilege of assisting in adjudication of the Culinary Arts Festival, I came across a truly remarkable display of original dishes utilizing the West Indian pumpkin, as the calabaza is called there. One which particularly excited me is the following prizewinning recipe by Mrs. Norma Lyn, of Black River, in St. Elizabeth Parish.

Jamaica Meat-Stuffed Calabaza
Serves 8 to 10.

1 round calabaza 8 to 10 inches in diameter
2 tablespoons cooking oil
2 pounds lean ground beef
2 cups ground smoked ham
2½ cups finely chopped onion
½ cup finely chopped green pepper
2½ teaspoons salt
2 teaspoons olive oil
2 teaspoons oregano
1 teaspoon vinegar
1 teaspoon ground black pepper
dash of Cayenne pepper
2 large cloves garlic, mashed
¾ cup seedless raisins
⅓ cup chopped stuffed olives
1 8-ounce can tomato sauce
3 eggs, beaten

With a sharp knife, cut a circular top, about 5 inches in diameter, out of the calabaza. Save this for the lid. Scoop out seeds and scrape inside clean. Place calabaza in a large kettle, cover with salted water. Bring water to the boil, then simmer, covered, until pumpkin flesh is almost tender when pierced with a fork—about 30 minutes. The calabaza must still be firm enough to hold its shape well. Carefully remove from hot water, drain well, and dry outside. Sprinkle inside with a little salt. In a large skillet, heat the oil, and add the ground beef, ham, onion, and green pepper. Cook over high heat, stirring, until the meat is browned and crumbly. Remove from heat. Mix together listed ingredients salt through garlic, and add to meat along with raisins, olives, and tomato sauce. Mix well. Cover skillet, and cook over low heat for 15 minutes, stirring occasionally. Remove from heat to cool slightly, then thoroughly mix in the beaten eggs. Fill cooked calabaza with meat stuffing, pressing the stuffing slightly to pack it firmly. Cover loosely with the calabaza lid. Place calabaza in a shallow greased baking pan and bake in a moderate 350° F. oven for 1 hour. Allow to cool for 10 or 15 minutes before slicing to serve.

ANNOTTO Bay is one of the most picturesque of the small port towns on Jamaica's North Coast. Its name is, of course, a variant of Annatto (page 16), that unusual special vegetable seasoning which figures so prominently in much tropical American cookery. One of the particularly notable cooks at Annotto Bay is Mrs. Beryl Donaldson, and here is her superb pudding made with calabaza—which this pleasant lady calls just plain pumpkin.

Cottage Pumpkin Plum Pudding
Serves 12 to 14.

5 cups grated raw calabaza
½ pound (2 sticks) butter
½ pound brown sugar
1 teaspoon vanilla extract
1 teaspoon mixed pie spices
½ teaspoon nutmeg
3 eggs
small piece fresh lime rind
2 cups flour
½ teaspoon salt
4 tablespoons mixed candied fruit
1 tablespoon light Jamaica rum
1 tablespoon cooking sherry
hard sauce

Cream together the butter and brown sugar. Blend

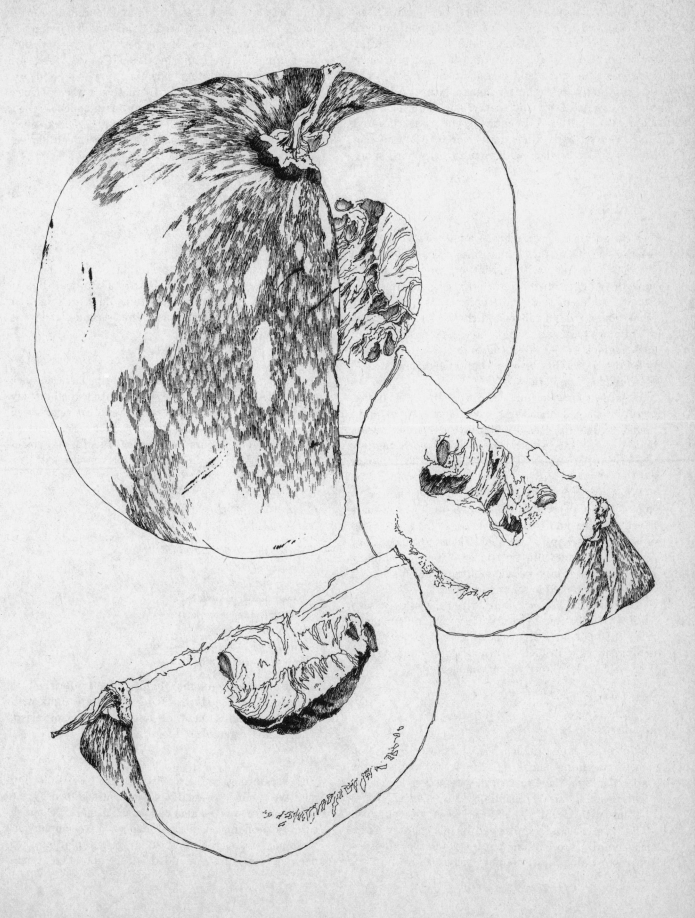

in vanilla extract, mixed pie spices, and nutmeg. Beat eggs well, with the piece of lime rind; pick out and discard this after beating. Blend eggs into butter-sugar mixture. Mix the pumpkin, which has previously been peeled and grated, with the flour and salt, and add gradually to the butter-sugar mixture. Add rum-soaked candied fruit and sherry, and again mix well. Pour into a buttered, lined mold, and steam, covered, until well set and rather dark-colored. Allow to cool, and serve thin wedges with your favorite hard sauce.

CANNA

The rather numerous kinds of Canna (of the genus of the same name, of the Canna Family) have long been justifiably popular with gardeners, for their stateliness, their huge foliage, and masses of complex showy flowers. Indigenous to the tropics of the world, the edible underground tubers and rhizomes of the Canna are of more than casual importance as items of food in such regions as the West Indies and South America, and are on occasion to be encountered in markets in Hawaii and New York.

Usually somewhat purplish in color, these fleshy, irregular-shaped structures vary from two to eight inches in length. Heavily starchy in content, when boiled these tubers have a bland flavor, vaguely reminiscent of Malanga (page 141) or Taro (page 228).

When utilized at the table, after boiling and scraping of any fibrous skin found necessary, the tubers benefit by the addition of such seasonings as grated onion and perhaps a dash of Tabasco sauce. They can also be made into fritters or, after preliminary brief boiling, thinly sliced and fried until crisp in lard or oil, or added to soups and stews.

In Australia, *Canna edulis*, the most widely seen species, is cultivated to some extent, for the flour made from the subterranean parts, this used as a type of arrowroot. It is, in fact, known as Queensland Arrowroot, or Purple Arrowroot, in commerce.

CAPER

The Capers of our kitchen are the flower buds of a somewhat vining shrub (*Capparis spinosa*, of the Caper Family), these pickled in seasoned vinegar. The plant, bearing sizable handsome, short-lived, white blossoms with a central puff of stamens with purplish stalks, is occasionally cultivated in this country as an ornamental. It occurs in nature from the Mediterranean to India, mostly in dry rocky places.

Capers are used as seasoning and condiments in the cuisine of many lands, from France and Germany to Southeast Asia. Those of the best quality—nonesuch or nonpareil—are imported from France; these are smaller than most other varieties, very firm, and perfectly round. They have a distinctive, rather puckery flavor, which is especially pleasant with boiled seafood, poultry, or lamb, as in the following excellent sauce. It also adds delight to such vegetables as cauliflower, potatoes, turnips, and rutabagas.

Caper Butter
Makes ½ cup.

> 1½ to 2 tablespoons drained capers
> ¼ pound (1 stick) butter

In a heavy saucepan, preferably one of the non-sticking variety, cook the butter until it is lightly browned, stirring frequently to avoid scorching. Stir in the capers, simmer for a few seconds, then use without delay.

THEN here is a most interesting dip, flavored with our pickled posy buds, to be served with a good display of crisp raw vegetables—cauliflower flowerets, sliced mushrooms, sliced yellow summer crookneck squash or zucchini, and fingers of tender turnip. It comes from a good friend in Chicago, the nutritionist Mrs. Peter A. Hess.

Caper Vegetable Dip
Makes enough.

> 1 tablespoon capers, drained
> 1 cup mayonnaise
> 2 chopped hard-cooked eggs
> 1 teaspoon dry mustard
> 1 teaspoon anchovy paste
> pinch garlic powder
> 1 tablespoon parsley flakes
> dash of coarsely ground pepper

Mix all ingredients thoroughly together. Refrigerate for several hours before serving as a dip or dunk with a handsome assortment of bite-size pieces of crisp, chilled, raw vegetables.

CAPERS are essential to the success of the following medley, a delicious amalgam sometimes known by the rather unfortunate name of Cuban Hash. Its Spanish title is pronounced peek-ah-*dee*-yo. I accompany it with hot steamed rice, fried or baked plantains or bananas, a salad of shredded lettuce and sliced tomatoes with oil and vinegar dressing, and a side dish of Haitian Black Beans (page 35). Guava shells or paste with cream cheese and crackers is a perfect dessert, and beer is a most acceptable beverage.

Picadillo
Serves 4 to 6.

1 tablespoon capers, drained
¼ cup peanut or soy oil
1 large clove garlic, mashed
2 large onions, finely chopped
1 large green pepper, finely chopped
1½ pounds lean ground beef
1 1-pound can Italian-style tomatoes
¼ teaspoon oregano
salt and pepper to taste
¼ cup chopped stuffed olives
½ cup chopped seedless raisins
1½ tablespoons cider vinegar

In a large skillet with cover, sauté the garlic, onions, and green pepper in the oil until they are soft but not browned. Gradually crumble in the ground beef, stirring it as it browns. Add the can of tomatoes, undrained, breaking up the tomatoes with a fork. Add all other ingredients, not forgetting the essential capers, mix well, cover, and simmer over very low heat for at least 1 hour, stirring occasionally. The mixture should be only moderately moist, and any excess grease should be skimmed off. Serve very hot over or with hot steamed rice.

CARDOON

The Cardoon (*Cynara Cardunculus*) is a tall-growing, thistlelike plant, originally from the southern parts of Europe. It is a close relative of the globe artichoke, but unlike that delicious vegetable, the flower heads are not used. In the Cardoon, the edible portion is the thickened stalk and midrib of the prickly young leaves. These are popular in France and Italy, and to a lesser degree elsewhere in Europe, but are as yet seldom encountered in this country.

The Cardoon is a very adaptable, delicious vegetable, one that should be more widely known and appreciated. Seeds are available from several companies, and the plants can be grown with notable ease in many parts of the United States.

Interestingly, the Cardoon was introduced into Argentina many years ago as a valued garden plant. It quickly became a noxious and ineradicable weed on

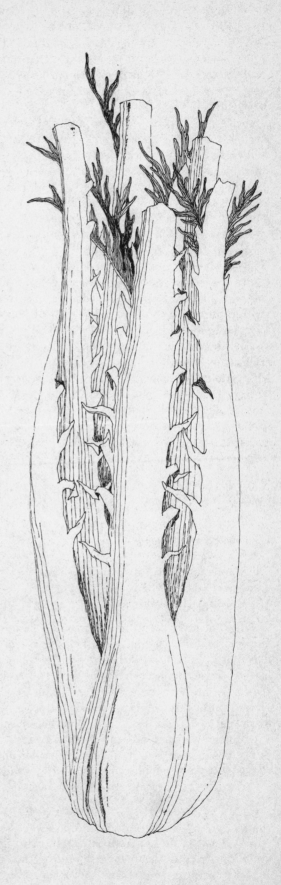

the pampas. However, the huge Italian colonies in Buenos Aires and other cities delight in the vegetable, and beautiful bunches of the palest green, trimmed stalks are found with frequency in the big Argentine produce markets. A recipe of Italian ancestry from Buenos Aires, which makes excellent use of the Cardoon, will be found below.

The best Cardoon leaves are artificially decolored, much as is done with celery. To prepare, the fleshy median leaf stalks are trimmed, cut into lengths two or three inches long, and cooked until just crisply tender in boiling salted water to which a touch of lemon juice has been added to prevent darkening. Properly prepared, the stalks and ribs possess a marvelous texture and a subtle flavor somewhat reminiscent of both celery and artichokes!

After blanching in the salted water, the pieces of Cardoon can be prepared in many delectable ways. They can simply be served chilled, dressed with a light vinaigrette mixture, with freshly ground pepper. Or they can be added to a good green salad, or even, as an unusual ingredient, added at the last minute to vegetable soup. Dressed with a light cream sauce, perhaps with a touch of mixed salad herbs, and served hot with veal, they are memorable. Or dip the blanched, drained, dried sections of Cardoon into a light batter, and deep-fry them until just crisp; serve these very hot, with salt and freshly ground pepper, especially with beef dishes.

Cardoons Milanaise
Serves 4 to 6.

2 pounds bleached young cardoons
½ cup melted butter
⅓ cup freshly grated Fontina or Parmesan cheese
salt and freshly ground pepper
¼ cup chopped fresh parsley

Trim the leafy parts away from the fleshy stalks and ribs of the vegetable. Cut stalks into lengths of 2 or 3 inches and drop them into a big kettle of salted boiling water. Bring back to the boil, and cook until the pieces are just barely tender—do not overcook! Drain thoroughly. Arrange cardoons in a shallow ovenproof dish, pour over the melted butter, sprinkle with the cheese, and salt and freshly ground pepper to taste. Run dish under a preheated broiler until the cheese melts and bubbles. Sprinkle with parsley and serve at once, with veal or pasta with a meaty sauce.

A DELIGHTFUL Italian antipasto is the raw vegetable dunk known as Bagna Cauda, literally, "hot bath." It is distinctly an audience-participation affair, which ideally offers at least four or five kinds of vegetables—including, ideally, our tasty cardoon—from which everyone selects at leisure, for immersion in the heated seasoned liquid. Accompany with slabs of crusty Italian bread, and a good dry red wine—Italian, of course.

Incidentally, specially designed earthenware containers with a heating unit for the Bagna Cauda are available from specialty gourmet shops. During the preparation and use of the liquid, be sure that it does not come to the boil—just simmers merrily. If the event is a particularly festive one, sprinkle a small quantity of minced white Italian truffles over the top of the Bagna prior to use.

Bagna Cauda
Seres 6 to 8.

½ cup butter
½ cup light olive oil
2 to 4 medium cloves garlic, mashed
5 to 10 anchovy fillets, mashed
½ teaspoon freshly ground black pepper
cardoon stalks, trimmed
carrots, tiny, scraped
celery stalks, trimmed
green peppers, trimmed, rinsed of seeds
fennel stalks, trimmed
cherry tomatoes, rinsed
scallions, whole, trimmed

Using an earthenware crock over an alcohol lamp, a chafing dish, or even the top of a double boiler, combine the butter and oil over very low heat, stirring occasionally. Add the garlic and anchovies to taste, plus the black pepper, mix through, and simmer until the anchovies have dissolved—usually about 15 minutes. Present with the various raw vegetables, cut into suitable dimensions, bite-size or otherwise, attractively arranged on platters, from which everyone selects items to be dunked into the "bath," which is kept warm but never boiling.

CARROT

The Carrot (*Daucus Carota*) is a native of the warmer parts of Europe and western Asia, but was used as a food crop in such places as China, Japan, and India as early as the thirteenth century. It is a member of the same botanical assemblage, the Umbelliferae, as the parsnip, fennel, and the delicate Queen Anne's Lace

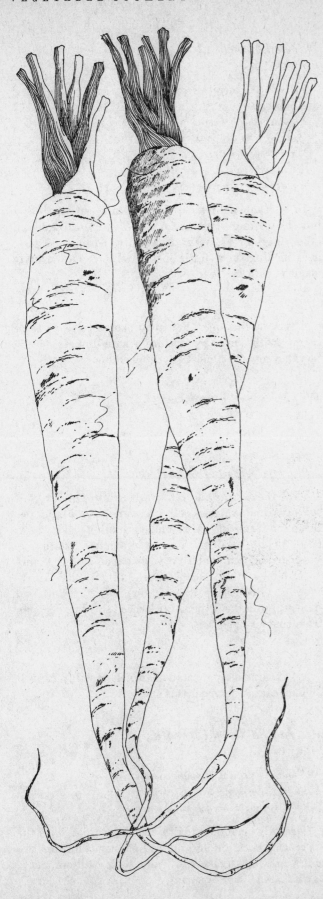

of our flower gardens—and the deadly hemlock. Once regarded as a "bad weed," Carrots are now an extremely popular vegetable in this country, due in part to the development of vastly improved varieties, tremendously increased commercial production, and the influence of European culinary habits. In recent times, tiny "baby" Carrots, just two or three inches long, have been put on sale in many areas. Previously these delectable juveniles were to be had only as canned imports from Belgium, or as inhabitants of choice backyard gardens.

Do not peel fresh carrots—just scrub them thoroughly, and steam them (sliced lengthwise rather than transversely, to retain more of the abundant vitamin supply) until just tender; then rub off the skins under cold running water. They can then be cut into strips or julienne sticks, if desired, for reheating.

The Carrot is an exceptionally adaptable root vegetable, figuring in all sorts of showy dishes from soups to soufflés and cakes.

HERE, for example, is a beautiful rich soup of Spanish ancestry.

Carrot Soup Español
Serves 4.

3 cups diced raw carrot
1 large tomato, peeled, diced
⅓ cup chopped onion
1 small clove garlic, mashed
2 teaspoons peanut or soy oil
6 cups whole milk
salt and freshly ground white pepper
½ cup sour cream

In a heavy saucepan with cover, cook carrot dice in a very little water until they are soft. Drain off any excess moisture and mash carrots until smooth. In a sizable skillet, mash the tomato and quickly sauté it with the onion and garlic in the oil, stirring constantly, until vegetables are soft but not browned. Add the mashed carrots, mix well, then gradually add the milk and heat through, but do not allow to come to the boil. Season to taste and serve hot topped with a goodly dollop of sour cream.

CARROTS cut into tiny slivers and quickly cooked with a minimum of liquid form one of my favorite modes of serving this rich, pretty vegetable. Preparation can be done in advance (it does require quite a bit of attention with a sharp knife), and the julienne refrigerated in tightly wrapped foil until cooking time. This is very good with lamb chops or pot roast of beef.

Carrots Julienne
Serves 4.

1 pound tiny carrots, scraped, cut into very thin slivers
½ cup water
1 teaspoon salt
3 to 4 tablespoons butter
1 to 2 tablespoons minced parsley

Using a saucepan with tight-fitting cover, add the carrot slivers with water and salt. Cook, covered, over rather high heat, shaking the pan occasionally, until the carrots are just tender. Do not overcook them, please. Remove pan from heat, add butter and parsley, shake over heat again, and serve while hot.

For Minted Carrots, which are sheer perfection with roast lamb, or beef in any of its guises, or fowl, substitute about ½ teaspoon shredded fresh mint leaves (or slightly less, if using dried mint) for the parsley called for in preceding recipe. A touch of freshly ground black pepper is advantageous here, too.

FRIED Carrots have long been favored vegetables in Belgium, France, and parts of Italy—and, to some degree, in the Midwest of this country. But these easily prepared, delicately delicious objects are seldom encountered elsewhere. Try them, for instance, with fried chicken or baked pork chops.

Fried Carrots
Serves 4.

1 pound tiny carrots
1 egg
½ cup milk
½ cup dried bread crumbs
deep fat or oil for frying

In a saucepan with tight-fitting cover, cook the carrots in a small amount of lightly salted boiling water for 5 minutes. Drain and plunge into cold water; then rub off skins. Drain thoroughly and pat dry with paper towels. Lightly beat the egg with the milk, and dip the carrots into this. Roll in bread crumbs and carefully lower into hot fat or oil heated to 375° F., to cook until just tender. Drain on absorbent paper towels and serve while nice and hot.

SAUTÉED carrots in a devilishly piquant sauce are a most valuable addition to the menu roster of every inspired cook.

Deviled Carrots
Serves 4.

1 pound tiny carrots, scraped
⅓ cup butter
2 tablespoons brown sugar
1½ teaspoons dry mustard
2 or 3 drops Tabasco sauce
½ teaspoon salt
⅛ teaspoon freshly ground pepper

In a sizable skillet with cover, sauté carrots in hot butter, turning them often, for 5 minutes. Add all other ingredients, mix thoroughly, cover, and cook over medium heat until just barely tender—usually about 10 minutes.

ELEGANT, this one! You may choose to serve these carrots with one of your more ornate dinners, but in fact they go with almost anything edible.

Wine-Glazed Carrots
Serves 4.

1 pound tiny carrots
2 tablespoons butter
2 tablespoons port or muscatel wine

Wash the carrots and plunge them into a quantity of boiling salted water. Cook, uncovered, for 5 minutes. Drain and rub off skins under running cold water. If carrots are at all sizable, cut into halves lengthwise. Wash again, and pat dry with paper towels. Sauté in butter over high heat, stirring often, until lightly browned. Reduce heat, add wine, cover skillet, and simmer until the wine is absorbed, shaking the pan from time to time.

A FAVORITE simple salad in which the tiny canned Belgian carrots figure is this one.

Marinated Tiny Carrots
Serves 4 to 6.

2 7-ounce cans tiny Belgian carrots, drained
⅓ to ½ cup commercial "French" dressing
2 tablespoons minced fresh parsley

Carefully combine the drained tiny carrots with the "French" dressing and minced parsley. Chill for two hours, mixing occasionally and with caution. Serve as a cold appetizer or salad.

PANCAKES made from potatoes, browned well on both sides, are favorite accouterments to many a meat or fowl entrée. Here is a rather unusual variation, in which grated carrots add color and extra flavor. Serve the very hot pancakes with spoons of sour cream, if desired. This is excellent with pot roast.

Carrot-Potato Pancakes
Makes 12 pancakes.

3 *large carrots, scraped, grated*
3 *medium baking potatoes, peeled, grated*
½ *cup minced onion*
⅓ *cup finely chopped fresh parsley*
½ *cup milk*
¼ *cup sifted flour*
3 *eggs, lightly beaten*
1½ *teaspoons salt*
¼ *teaspoon freshly ground pepper*
sour cream (optional)

Combine the carrots, potatoes, onion, and parsley. Combine with all other ingredients except the sour cream, and beat until very well blended. Drop by tablespoonfuls onto a hot, greased griddle, and cook, turning once, until nicely browned on both sides. Serve at once, while very hot, with sour cream on top, if desired.

THE FOLLOWING cake made from carrots is an exceptional one. It is fine-textured, wonderfully moist, and improves as it ages—assuming any remains after the first day.

Bootsie's Carrot Cake
Serves 6 to 8.

3 *cups grated carrots*
2 *cups sugar*
2 *cups self-rising flour*
1½ *cups cooking oil*
4 *eggs*
1 *cup chopped walnuts or pecans*
1 *small can crushed pineapple, drained*
1 *teaspoon vanilla*
1 *teaspoon cinnamon*
Cream Cheese Icing (recipe below)

Grease and flour tube or loaf pan. Sift together the sugar and flour, then beat in the oil and eggs. Stir in the carrots, nuts, pineapple, vanilla, and cinnamon. Bake in preheated 300-325° F. oven for 90 minutes. Let cool in the pan for 45 minutes, then remove and spread with the following icing.

Cream Cheese Icing

1 *8-ounce package cream cheese, softened*
1 *1-pound box powdered sugar*

Thoroughly combine the softened cream cheese and sugar, and spread over the cooled carrot cake.

ENTERPRISING cooks in the northern reaches of Italy prepare, on special occasions, a fabulous torte, in which grated carrots furnish a major flavoring ingredient.

Italian Carrot Torte
Serves 6 to 8.

3 *cups finely grated small carrots*
9 *tablespoons sugar*
4 *eggs, separated*
2 *cups finely grated blanched almonds*
¼ *teaspoon ground allspice*
2 *teaspoons Marsala*
whipped cream or Zabaglione

Thoroughly combine the sugar with the egg yolks, and beat this until it thickens. Stir in the grated (or ground) carrots and almonds, plus the allspice and Marsala. Beat the egg whites until stiff and gently fold these into the mixture. Turn into a liberally buttered 9-inch pie plate and bake in preheated 275° F. oven for 1 hour. Serve while barely warm, each portion topped with whipped cream or zabaglione.

AGAIN using the tiny carrots available in select markets these days, consider the following simple yet fabulously flavorful dish.

Carrots à la Lipolani
Serves 4 to 6.

1½ *pounds tiny new carrots*
1 *10½-ounce can beef consommé*
⅓ *cup melted butter*
1 *teaspoon sugar*
2 *tablespoons minced fresh parsley*

Wash the carrots and plunge them into a liberal quantity of boiling salted water to cook uncovered for 10 minutes. Drain and cover with running cold water to rub off the skins, and trim off both ends. Arrange in a sizable shallow baking dish, overlapping as little as possible. Pour over them the beef consommé and the melted butter, and sprinkle with the sugar. Place in preheated 325° F. oven and cook, uncovered, until the tiny carrots are just tender, usually about 20 minutes. Sprinkle liberally with parsley and serve with the lovely juices in individual side dishes.

FLEMISH Carrots, or *carottes flamandes,* form an elegant sweet casserole that appears on epicurean tables on both sides of the Atlantic. There are several variations of the recipe, but here is the one I prize most highly. Especially appropriate with veal, chicken, or ham.

Flemish Carrots
Serves 6.

  1½ *pounds tiny new carrots*
  ⅓ *cup melted butter*
  2 *teaspoons sugar*
  3 *egg yolks*
  ¼ *cup heavy cream*
  2 *tablespoons minced fresh parsley*

Wash the carrots and plunge them into a liberal quantity of boiling salted water, to cook uncovered for 10 minutes. Drain and cover with running cold water, to rub off the skins, and trim off both ends. Cut lengthwise into very thin slices, and arrange in a large, shallow ovenproof casserole, sprinkling each layer with melted butter and sugar. Place casserole in preheated 325° F. oven, and bake until carrot slices are just barely tender—usually about 20 minutes. Thoroughly beat the egg yolks into the cream, adding the parsley, and top the carrot casserole with this sauce. Return to oven for just a moment, and serve without delay.

CASABANANA

The Casabanana (*Sicana odorifera,* of the Squash Family) is one of the amazing cucurbits, increasingly cultivated by connoisseur gardeners in the warmer parts of this country for its large stout cucumberlike fruits, which are delicious and variously used as a vegetable. From South America, the plant is also known as *curuba, pepino,* and *pepino angolo.*

The vine is a very husky perennial, rather attractive in appearance, and quickly attaining a height in excess of forty feet. The lobed leaves often exceed ten inches in diameter and make a good screen for unsightly fences and the like. Following the pretty yellow flowers, the pendant smooth cylindrical fruits develop. These may reach lengths of two feet, with a diameter of about four inches. As they ripen, they take on a handsome orange-crimson or brownish-red

color and give off a pervading, pleasantly aromatic scent.

The young green fruits are sliced thin and quickly sautéed, as one prepares zucchini. When the fruit is mature, the juicy pulp, from which the numerous black seeds are first removed, is made into a spicy kind of preserve, especially in the West Indies, or it is macerated in water to give a refreshing *horchata,* a kind of punch.

CASSAVA

Cassava, Brazilian Arrowroot, Manioc, Mandioca, Aipim, or Yuca—all refer to the same tropical vegetable, the sizable tuberous roots of a remarkably handsome bushy plant. In this country, until recently, most people have known it only as the source of commercial tapioca. But in the warm countries of the world, *Manihot utilissima* (and closely allied botanical species) is an extremely important source of starch in the diets of countless millions of people.

Originally from Brazil, the Cassava was transported to the Asiatic tropics by the colonizing Portuguese as early as the seventeenth century. Two major kinds are known—"Bitter" and "Sweet" Cassava. Both contain greater or lesser quantities of deadly hydrocyanic (prussic) acid in the juice of the roots. This substance is, fortunately, removed by thorough cooking.

The Cassava plant is an exceptional ornamental, upward of ten feet in height in rich soil, with long-stalked hand-shaped leaves set in ornate array. As such, it is justly prized in choice tropical gardens and in conservatories in more temperate areas. It is a member of the same family as the showy poinsettia and, like that well-known flower, exudes a milky latex when bruised. In fact, commercially important Ceará rubber is derived from another member of Cassava's genus.

Cassava roots are produced in considerable numbers in subterranean bunches somewhat like oversized fleshy brown fingers. In our markets they usually measure eight to ten inches in length, upward of two inches in diameter; often vaguely crooked, the roots frequently possess a more or less prominent apical neck. Their skin is generally an attractive pinkish hue, shading to brown, and is overlaid with an extensive intricate warm brown-colored network of flaky veins. When the skin is pared away, the hard flesh is found to be of a pristine ivory-white shade. It gives off a faint distinctly bitter odor, this indicative of the acid contained in these roots. Cooking completely dispels

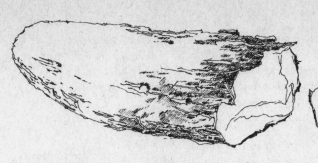

all traces of this dangerous substance—but the roots should not be sampled while raw by the cook.

Basic cooking instructions for Cassava call for thorough peeling, cutting into two-inch lengths, and boiling in lightly salted water for at least one hour. The sections of the tubers split apart into irregular wedges as they become tender, exhibiting a certain number of more or less firm fibers. Toward the end of the cooking process, some extra salt can be added to the pot to good advantage. The texture of the cooked vegetable is vaguely like that of a moist white potato. Its flavor is bland and really not quite like anything else to be found on our tables.

Cassava roots should be used promptly upon their purchase, and to avoid any discoloration of the flesh, should be refrigerated until time of their preparation.

ONE OF the most memorable ways I know of serving Cassava is in an incredible soup-*cum*-addenda, including braised tripe, which is one of the popular country dishes in Nicaragua. Juanita was an exceptionally adept lady in the kitchen at Monte Fresco, where I spent happy days with my hosts, the A. H. Hellers, and their myriad orchids.

Juanita's Mondongo
Serves 6 liberally.

3 *cups peeled, parboiled cassava, cut into sizable chunks*
1½ *pounds fresh tripe*
2½ *quarts salted water*
¾ *cup fresh, raw corn kernels*
2 *small bay leaves*
1 *large clove garlic, peeled, halved*
1 *large onion, coarsely chopped*
1 *tablespoon coarse or kosher salt*
6 to 8 *tablespoons olive oil*
2½ *cups raw, coarsely chopped, peeled tomatoes*
¾ *cup coarsely chopped green pepper*
2 to 5 *hot chili peppers, chopped, or Tabasco sauce to taste*
1 *large partly ripe banana, chopped*
2 *whole cloves*
1 *teaspoon paprika*
¼ to ½ *teaspoon saffron*
¾ *cup parsley sprigs*

Carefully wash the fresh tripe in boiling water and scrape it thoroughly with a knife, discarding the skin that comes off. Place large pieces of the tripe in the salted water, bring to a quick rapid boil, then reduce heat and simmer, covered, for 1 hour, adding the corn kernels (frozen uncooked corn can, of course, be substituted), bay leaves, garlic, onion, and coarse salt during this cooking process. Remove the tripe from the broth with tongs, and allow it to cool enough to handle. Cut tripe into small dice and fry it in part of the olive oil, turning often, until it browns slightly. Return tripe dice to the soup. In the same skillet, adding the rest of the olive oil as needed, sauté the tomatoes, both kinds of peppers (or substitute Tabasco sauce for the hot peppers), and saffron, for 8 minutes. Turn contents of skillet into the soup pot, cover, and simmer for 1 hour more or until tripe is very tender. Add the chunks of cassava 20 minutes before serving, with the sprigs of fresh parsley put in just at the last minute.

BOILED, hot cassava is most often served as a vegetable in the American tropics dressed simply with butter, additional salt if needed, a couple of good grinds from the pepper mill, and a few drops of lime or sour-orange juice. It accompanies all sorts of meals, but to me has always seemed especially appropriate with pork, ham, or chicken.

On occasion, too, one encounters boiled sections of cassava served piping hot with a very robust garlic sauce.

Cuban Garlic Sauce
Makes about ¾ cup.

6 to 8 *large cloves garlic, peeled, minced*
4 *tablespoons butter*
¾ *cup light olive oil*
1 *tablespoon finely chopped parsley*

In a smallish skillet, using 2 tablespoons of the butter and 4 tablespoons of the oil (peanut or soy oil can be substituted, if desired), over medium heat cook the minced garlic, stirring often, until it becomes soft. Add the remainder of the butter and oil as the cooking process continues. Simmer sauce, stirring occasionally, for about 15 minutes, then add parsley, and mix well. Use the sauce while very hot. Store sauce in the refrigerator, in a jar with a tight lid, and use with some discretion.

THE FLOUR made from this root vegetable is an extremely important item in South American cookery, notably that of Brazil, where it appears as *farinha de mandioca*. It is sprinkled, often rather liberally, over all kinds of dishes, from steamed rice to quick-cooked vegetables, as a unique seasoning. Until recently this flour was not generally available in North American markets, but several specialty houses in New York now stock it.

The Indians of tropical northern South America consume quantities of fried or roasted cakes or tortilla-like patties made from this granular flour at almost every meal. The flavor of these is a bit negative for most uses in our own cuisine, but the following recipe, based on Cassava cakes encountered along the Amazon, has been shown to be exciting to our tastes.

Manaus Cassava Cakes
Serves 4 to 6.

1 *pound cassava flour* (farinha de mandioca)
½ *cup crumbled crisp bacon*
½ *cup minced onion*
salt and pepper
warm water
bacon drippings or butter

Thoroughly combine the cassava flour with the bacon and onion, salt and pepper to taste, plus enough warm water to make a rather firm dough. Knead this for about 10 minutes, then pat out into rounds about 4 inches in diameter and ¼ inch thick. Heat the bacon drippings or butter (or a combination of both), and fry the cakes, a few at a time, slowly until they are nicely browned on both sides and rather crisp. Serve at once, or wrap in foil and keep them warm in a low oven. Interesting with cocktails or beer, or to take the place of bread with many a dinner entrée.

FAROFA is toasted cassava flour, and from it an extraordinary array of dishes can be prepared. In Brazil it is made by placing a pound or so of the *farinha de mandioca* in a shallow pan and setting this in a low oven. The flour is stirred often until it takes on a delicate tan color—or perhaps a darker brown, depending on personal predilection. This *farofa* can then be sprinkled over various dishes, from soups to vegetables to meats, to which it imparts a delicate and

delicious flavor. It also figures in such recipes as the following one. I offer this dish, from Surinam, as a special accompaniment to pan-fried steaks which have been marinated in garlic-flavored lime juice.

Genevieve's Cassava
Serves 6.

½ *pound cassava flour, toasted*
2 *tablespoons butter*
3 *eggs, beaten*
1 *tablespoon butter*
1 *tablespoon lard*
2 *tablespoons finely chopped parsley*
½ *cup finely chopped onion*
1 *teaspoon finely chopped garlic*
2 *cups finely chopped peeled, seeded tomatoes*
2 *cups fresh corn kernels, undrained*
2 *cups grated carrots*
salt and hot pepper sauce to taste

Prepare the *farofa* (toasted cassava flour) as indicated above. In a sizable skillet, melt the 2 tablespoons butter, add the beaten eggs, and scramble them until they are firm and in small pieces. Remove from skillet, and keep warm. Melt the butter with the lard, and sauté the parsley, onion, garlic, and tomatoes, stirring often, until they are very soft. Stir in the undrained corn kernels and the grated carrots. Heat through, then stir in the toasted cassava flour. Add the scrambled eggs, mix very thoroughly but with care, season to taste with salt and hot pepper sauce, and heat until the mixture is crumbly and fluffy. Serve while very hot.

AT CHRISTMASTIME, a special cassava pie is served on most tables in Bermuda, that incredible islet set so far into northern latitudes, where coconut palms flourish and such tropic delights as this cassava grow. The pie is an ornate affair requiring a strong arm for grating the fresh root. I must thank the kind people at the Bermuda Chamber of Commerce in Hamilton for furnishing me with this authentic recipe for one of their most renowned culinary creations.

Bermuda Cassava Pie
Serves 6 to 8.

4 *pounds raw cassava roots, peeled, grated*
½ *cup butter, softened*
1½ *cups sugar*
6 *eggs, beaten*
½ *cup all-purpose flour*

1 *teaspoon baking powder*
1 *teaspoon salt*
1½ *teaspoons nutmeg*
½ *teaspoon cinnamon*
½ *teaspoon allspice*
½ *teaspoon ground cloves*
¼ *teaspoon baking soda*
½ *cup brandy*
3-*pound stewing chicken, cut into pieces*
¾ *pound cubed lean pork*
¾ *pound cubed veal*
1 *teaspoon salt*
1 *teaspoon dried parsley flakes*
½ *teaspoon thyme*
2 *teaspoons flour*

To prepare the pie: Cream together the butter and sugar, then beat in the eggs. Sift together the flour, baking powder, salt, nutmeg, cinnamon, allspice, cloves, and baking soda, and gradually mix into the creamed mixture; then add the grated cassava. Mix in the brandy. Place half of this batter in a liberally buttered 13″ × 9″ × 4″ ovenproof casserole or pan, patting it down well. Meanwhile, in a heavy kettle, place the chicken pieces, plus pork, veal, 1 teaspoon salt, parsley flakes, and thyme. Add enough cold water to cover, cover the kettle, and simmer over very low heat for about 1½ hours, or until the chicken falls from the bones and the other meats are tender. Remove meats from broth with slotted spoon. Remove chicken from bones, cube, and combine with the cooked pork and veal. Heat 1 cup of the broth in a saucepan, and blend in the flour. Reserve remainder of the broth. Cook the broth and flour until a thin gravy is obtained. Add this to the chicken, pork, and veal cubes, and place on top of the layer of cassava pie dough. Top with remaining batter. Bake in preheated 350° F. oven, uncovered, for about 3 hours, basting with reserved broth whenever the crust appears to become dry. The pie is done when it comes away from the sides of the pan. Remove pie from oven, cover with a damp cloth, then a dry cloth on top of that. (This keeps the crust from hardening while the pie is cooling.) Serve cut into squares, while warm.

CAULIFLOWER

The Cauliflower is one of those rather freakish vegetables derived from the common cabbage species; in fact, it is known by botanists as a variety of the cabbage (*Brassica oleracea* var. *botrytis,* of the Crucifer Family).

The oddly formed heads, called curds, with compacted flowers and upper stems, are variable in dimensions and color. In this country pristine white curds are the most prized, but in Italy, where the *cavolfiore* is cultivated to a tremendous extent, the small heads are often vivid green or even purple in color. Technically, the Cauliflower and our well-known broccoli intergrade, and there are some odd forms in between, occasionally encountered in gourmet kitchen gardens.

Fresh firm Cauliflowers are today available in our markets almost throughout the year. The frozen vegetable is always on sale, so that cooks of today can enjoy this princess of the Cabbage Family at any time. When purchasing the vegetable, select only very firm heads without brownish bruises or discoloration; the subtending foliage—also edible, by the way, and excellent when chopped and added to soups—should be rich green, never yellowed.

Basic cooking instructions for this nutritious, delicate vegetable call for boiling in a tightly covered container in a small amount of salted water until just tender. Ideally, one should carefully break the Cauliflower head apart into flowerets, slashing any thick stalks lengthwise so all parts cook evenly. Overcooking can be even more disastrous with this lovely edible than with most of the cabbage clan—the pieces should retain considerable firmness of texture. If desired, add a tablespoon of milk, or a teaspoon of lemon juice to the cooking liquid; this assists in retaining the white color so prized by most Americans. Personally, I consider few vegetables as attractive or as flavorful as a whole head of fresh Cauliflower, boiled until just tender, or, if cooked in flowerets, then reassembled (use toothpicks if necessary), and served without delay, anointed with a light cheese sauce. Or serve the vegetable with melted butter, a touch of salt and freshly ground white pepper, and just a tiny dash of freshly ground nutmeg.

Cauliflower is used in many felicitous ways. Cream of cauliflower soup, served hot or chilled with a few snippets of fresh chives, is elegant, yet seldom encountered in this country. Timbales made from the puréed vegetable are fascinating fare, especially with a cheese sauce, to be offered with broiled or baked ham. And the little flowerets, boiled with a bit of lemon juice in the water until just barely tender, are delectable when dipped into a light batter and quick-fried in butter. And raw, the neat pieces are superb with various sorts of piquant dips, while they form an attractive addition to the Bagna Cauda (page 72) or Japanese Tempura (pages 252–53).

For an exceptional one-dish version of the regal Cauliflower, prepare the following recipe. Addition of a hot roll and glass of dry white or rosé wine makes a perfect simple and simply elegant menu.

Stuffed Cauliflower
Serves 4 to 6.

1 *large, firm head cauliflower*
2 *tablespoons butter*
½ *cup finely chopped onion*
2 *cups ground cooked ham*
2 *teaspoons finely chopped pimiento*
4 *cups coarse bread crumbs*
1 *egg*
½ *cup whole milk*
½ *teaspoon salt*
⅛ *teaspoon black pepper*
3 *tablespoons butter*
paprika

Cook trimmed whole cauliflower, stem end down, in a large kettle of boiling salted water for about 15 minutes, until it is slightly tender, yet still compact and firm. Do not dismantle the head for this recipe, please. Drain thoroughly and allow to cool. In a skillet, sauté the onion in the butter until just soft, then mix in the ham, pimiento, and bread crumbs. Beat the egg, add the milk, salt and pepper, and mix thoroughly with the ham mixture. Put the drained cauliflower in an ovenproof dish, without crowding it, and carefully force the stuffing between the flowerets of the vege-

table, arranging any leftover stuffing around its base. Dot liberally with the butter, and bake uncovered in preheated 350° F. oven until the stuffing is set and lightly browned, usually about 20 minutes. Dust lightly with paprika and serve.

WHEN I arrange a lavish antipasto—oftentimes to be served alone with hot crusty Italian bread and a good bottle of Valpolicella Bertani as a special supper—I like to make available a bowl containing the following marinated cauliflower salad. Its origins are in that picturesque town where Romeo and Juliet plighted their troth and all of that.

Cauliflower Salad Verona
Serves 4 to 6.

1 *large head cauliflower*
1 *small can anchovy fillets, drained, chopped*
½ *cup sliced ripe olives*
¼ *cup chopped red onion*
¼ *cup thinly sliced pimiento*
¼ *cup light olive oil*
2 *tablespoons lemon juice*
¼ *teaspoon freshly ground pepper*

Trim the cauliflower and separate into flowerets. Cook the pieces in a small quantity of salted water, with a touch of lemon juice added if desired, until just tender but still firm. Drain thoroughly and allow to cool. Combine all other ingredients, and pour them over cauliflower in a salad bowl. Toss gently and chill for 2 hours prior to serving.

MY FRIEND and colleague, Ed Flickinger, noted South Florida landscape designer and tropical horticulturist, is also an exceptional and inventive amateur chef. He has resided in Japan and has a fine hand with the subtleties of Oriental cuisine, as perceive the following dish, to be served with side bowls of steaming-hot rice and if possible a portion of thinly sliced pickled daikon.

Ed's Cauliflower Beef
Serves 4 or 5.

1 *large head cauliflower*
1 *pound sirloin steak, sliced ⅛-inch thick*
½ *teaspoon salt*
2 *teaspoons Japanese soy sauce*
½ *teaspoon sugar*
5 *tablespoons peanut or soy oil*
½ *cup scallions with tops, cut into ½-inch lengths*
½ *cup thinly sliced onions, made into rings*
½ *teaspoon salt*
2 *tablespoons Japanese soy sauce*
½ *teaspoon sugar*
½ *cup chicken broth or stock*
1 *tablespoon cornstarch, mixed with 1 tablespoon water*

Rinse cauliflower and break into flowerets, slashing diagonally any thick stalks. In a sizable bowl, combine the thin slices of beef with the ½ teaspoon salt, 2 teaspoons soy sauce, and ½ teaspoon sugar. Mix well and marinate at room temperature for 10 minutes. Parboil cauliflower pieces in lightly salted water for 5 minutes and drain thoroughly. Preheat a wok, paellero, or large shallow skillet with cover, and add 3 tablespoons of oil. Over very high heat, quickly stir-fry the marinated beef slices until they are nicely browned—usually 3 or 4 minutes at most. Remove cooking utensil from heat, and with slotted spoon remove the beef. Add the remaining 2 tablespoons of oil and ½ teaspoon salt to the same utensil and, again over high heat, quickly stir-fry the scallions and onion rings, just until they are almost limp. Remove these vegetables with slotted spoon, draining them well, and reserve. Add the flowerets of cauliflower, together with the 2 tablespoons soy sauce and ½ teaspoon sugar. Carefully stir-fry these over high heat, for 1 minute, then add

the chicken broth or stock. Cover and cook over medium heat for about 4 minutes, then remove cauliflower with slotted spoon and reserve. Blend in the cornstarch mixed with the water and continue to cook, uncovered, until the sauce thickens slightly. Return all meat and vegetables to the cooking utensil and toss carefully so that the sauce coats every piece. Cover and heat thoroughly for 2 or 3 minutes—but no longer, or it will be overcooked! Remove from heat and serve immediately with steamed rice.

USING the excellent frozen cauliflower, the modern cook can come up with the following pleasantly flavored and textured casserole—to be served with such diverse meats as a nicely broiled chicken which has been basted with butter and lemon juice, or fried thin pork chops, or grilled patties of seasoned ground beef.

Cauliflower Casserole
Serves 6.

2 *9-ounce packages frozen cauliflower*
¾ *teaspoon salt*
1 *recipe Simple Cheese Sauce (page 254)*
¼ *cup slivered roasted almonds*
1 *3½-ounce can French-fried onions*
½ *teaspoon paprika*
2 *tablespoons finely chopped fresh parsley*

Cook frozen cauliflower according to package directions, but without salt or other seasoning in the water. Drain thoroughly and arrange the flowerets in a buttered 2-quart casserole, sprinkling them with the ¾ teaspoon salt. Prepare the Simple Cheese Sauce. While it is hot, stir in the almonds and half of the French-fried onions. Pour this mixture over the cauliflower. Sprinkle with the paprika, cover the casserole, and bake in preheated 400° F. oven for 15 minutes. Remove the cover, sprinkle with remaining onions and the parsley, and bake for another 5 minutes.

CELERIAC

Celeriac (*Apium graveolens* var. *rapaceum*, of the Carrot Family)—also known as Celery Root, Celery Knob, or Turnip-Rooted Celery—is a special variant of celery which is cultivated for the considerably enlarged root, rather than for the stalks and foliage. It has been grown by man for several centuries, especially in Europe, where it is justly prized. This nutritious, particularly tasteful root vegetable should be far better known in this country.

The root possesses a faint bitterness that can be dispelled by peeling and blanching in salted water to which 2 tablespoons of lemon juice have been added, or by marinating in salted lemon juice. The prepared vegetable is then cut into slices or julienne sticks and added to lusty soups and stews, served with cream or Mornay or Hollandaise sauce, chilled and added to such wonderful things as Salade Niçoise, or chilled and simply dressed with oil and vinegar.

Aficionados who delight in its positive "celery plus celery" flavor merely peel the root, cut it into small cubes, and eat it raw, usually with a bit of coarse salt. Crisp fritters are made from the puréed vegetable, notably in France, and this purée is often combined with mashed potatoes—1 cup of the latter to 2 cups of Celeriac—then offered hot, buttered, with seasonings.

I LIKE Celeriac prepared in the following vaguely plebeian, but exceptionally good, fashion. Dressed with butter to which some snipped fresh chives have been added, it is particularly appropriate with a beautifully broiled chicken.

Celeriac Maison
Serves 4.

2 small celeriac
4 cups rich chicken stock
1 tablespoon lemon juice
⅓ cup melted butter
1 tablespoon minced fresh parsley

Peel celeriac, wash them, and cut into coarse dice. Place in chicken stock, to which lemon juice has been added, and cook over medium heat, uncovered, until just tender. Drain thoroughly and serve while hot with melted butter and parsley.

THE FRENCH, who have so long appreciated this root vegetable, refer to it as *céleri-rave*. *Céleri-rave rémoulade* is one of the classic appetizers of France— and a delectable one to offer here at home, too.

Celeriac Rémoulade
Amply serves 6 to 8.

2 small celeriac
2 tablespoons lemon juice
2 teaspoons salt
4 tablespoons Dijon or Düsseldorf prepared mustard
3 tablespoons boiling water
⅓ cup light olive oil
2 to 3 tablespoons white wine vinegar

salt and freshly ground white pepper
3 tablespoons minced fresh parsley
2 teaspoons snipped fresh chives

Peel celeriac and cut into tiny, even julienne strips about 2 inches long and ⅛ inch thick. Place in a bowl with lemon juice and salt, mix well, and allow to marinate at room temperature for one hour. Prepare a dressing by placing the mustard in a large, warmed bowl, then adding the boiling water a few drops at a time, whipping constantly with a wire whisk or electric mixer at medium speed. Continue to whip, now adding the oil, again a drop or two at a time. The dressing should now be rather thick. Whip in the vinegar, a drop or two at a time, tasting from time to time to determine the amount desired, then season to taste with salt and white pepper. Gently mix in the marinated celeriac sticks, cover, and leave in refrigerator overnight. Turn into an attractive serving dish, sprinkle with the parsley and chives, and serve with suitable crackers and white toast rounds as a piquant hors d'oeuvre.

CELERY

Celery (*Apium graveolens*, of the Carrot Family), which appears in bountiful array in all of our American markets nonstop throughout the year, is a sort of supervegetable. It is one whose every part can—and should—be utilized in good cookery, from the knobby root of a special variety (Celeriac, above) through the crisp fat stalks to the abundant vivid-green foliage.

Celery is known by various vernaculars in differing parts of the globe. For example, in Italian, *sedani;* in Chinese, *chin-t'sai;* in Spanish, *apio;* in French, *céleri;* in German, *Sellerie;* and so on and on.

As a wild plant it grows in boggy areas from Scandinavia to middle Africa, eastward into Russia. Interestingly enough, in this original state it is not fleshy-stalked at all, and scarcely recognizable as relating to our cultivated vegetable.

French gardeners first took up the development of superior forms of this plant during the seventeenth century, and it was first produced in this country by Dutch farmers in Kalamazoo, Michigan, in 1874, according to record. Today Celery is big agricultural business in many of our United States. Florida is one

of the prime producers, especially of the robust unbleached green Pascal variety.

Calorically only 9 calories per cupful, Celery is
notably attractive both to eye and to palate, and it
adapts itself wonderfully to all sorts of dishes.

Consider the two basic ways to make use of the leafy
tops of Celery, for instance. Stew the top portion of
the bunch, leaves and all, and strain the liquid. Store
this in the refrigerator, where it is ready to be mixed
with additional water or milk in sauces, gravies, or
stews. The second way gives you a product which can
be stored on the pantry shelf. Dry the Celery leaves
thoroughly in a very slow oven, then rub through a
sieve to make a powder. Add this powder to fish, meat,
vegetables, or whatever you like, and note the additional and delicious flavor.

Leftover bits of Celery need not be wasted, either:
chop and drop the pieces into boiling potatoes, carrots,
or green beans to add a special, fresh taste.

I like to offer family and friends pieces of Celery
for nibbling on many occasions, to commence the repast. A favorite, very attractive way of preparing
bite-size sections of the stalks is by cutting slashes at
angles along their edges, then chilling them in ice
cubes and water until the pieces curl nicely.

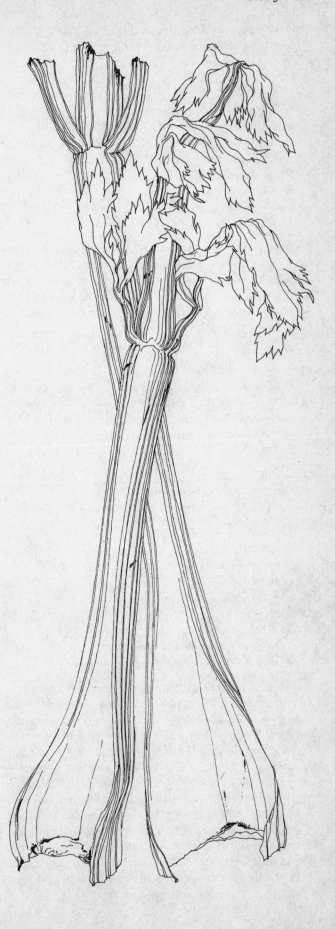

A GOODLY array of crisp Celery stalks (or ribs),
stuffed with various savories, is a happy thing to
present at one's table, I feel. Consider the following:

Stuffed Celery

Place celery stalks in a bowl of ice water, with
added ice cubes, to crisp in the refrigerator for at
least 30 minutes. At the last moment, drain thoroughly, and stuff with a liberal hand using an assortment from the suggestions below. Serve while still
crisp.

Minced shrimp, lobster, or crab, lightly seasoned
with salt and white pepper, and bound into a paste
with a modicum of mayonnaise or Kay's Boiled Salad
Dressing (page 255).

Guacamole (page 24).

Softened cream cheese mixed with finely chopped
stuffed olives, ripe olives, crumbled crisp bacon,
minced pimientos, or what have you.

Softened sharp cheese of almost any sort—consider
Gorgonzola, as a piquant novelty—especially with a
touch of minced fresh parsley.

Chicken or ham salad.

OLD-TIMEY North American Celery Salad seldom
seems to appear on our menus these days, and like so

many recipes that we relished during younger days, this one would seem suitable for reinstatement!

Celery Salad
Serves 4.

4 cups coarsely chopped crisp celery
1 cup coarsely chopped sweet green (or red) pepper
3 tablespoons finely sliced scallion tops
⅓ cup mayonnaise
salt and freshly ground white pepper
2 tablespoons finely chopped fresh parsley
crisp lettuce leaves for base

Lightly toss the celery, sweet pepper (a combination of green and red is attractive and flavorful), scallion tops, mayonnaise (homemade or commercial), and salt and pepper to taste. Chill thoroughly. At serving time, arrange the celery mixture on crisp lettuce leaves, and sprinkle with parsley.

HOMEMADE celery soup is a relative rarity these days, too, since the canned varieties are so readily available and very good for most uses. But consider, pray, this luscious recipe the next time you pine for a pot of something special to spruce up a meal.

Celery Soup Christiane
Serves 4.

1½ cups finely chopped celery, with some tops
5 cups rich chicken stock
⅓ cup grated onion
¼ cup finely chopped fresh parsley
salt and freshly ground white pepper
2 egg yolks
1 cup heavy cream
2 tablespoons finely chopped pimiento
2 tablespoons thinly sliced pitted ripe olives

Using rich fresh or canned chicken stock, bring to the simmer in a heavy saucepan with cover. Add the celery, onion, and parsley, and cook, covered, until the celery is very tender. Turn contents of saucepan into electric blender, and whirl for about 30 seconds at high speed. Correct seasoning with salt and pepper— be rather light-handed here, please! Place blended mixture in top of a double boiler, over hot but not boiling water. In a bowl whip the egg yolks until they are light, then gradually whip the cream into them. Gradually add this mixture to the soup, stirring with a wooden spoon until it thickens. When the soup forms a light film on the spoon, add the pimiento and ripe

olives and serve immediately, very hot, in heated bowls.

A GREAT many of our wonderful vegetables can be braised. Braising is a simple but often neglected form of cookery, which permits the full flavor of the vegetable to be retained.

Consider, for example, Braised Celery, a classic dish. There are many recipes for *céleris braisés,* but these usually include a number of spices that somewhat mask the delicacy of the vegetable itself. Hence I prefer this one, very simple, and ambrosial to the palate.

Braised Celery
Serves 4.

4 bunches tender celery hearts
boiling salted water
3 cups rich chicken stock
salt and freshly ground white pepper
4 tablespoons butter

Trim the young tender celery hearts to uniform length (about 5 inches), reserving the trimmings and foliage for other suggested uses. Carefully rinse out any grit from center of bunch and tie bunches with kitchen string, so they retain their shape during cooking. Plunge the tied bunches into a large kettle of boiling salted water, and cook uncovered for 10 minutes. Remove and drain thoroughly. Place celery in shallow baking dish with cover, pour over the chicken stock (fresh or canned), season rather liberally with salt and white pepper, and dot with butter. Cover and place in preheated 350° F. oven for about 1 hour. Remove cover and return to oven until celery is nicely browned and firm-tender.

IF YOU have made the Grand Tour of Europe, you have doubtless encountered the following celery dish on more than one occasion, especially served to accompany fowl of any sort—from the most elegant of wild pheasant or woodcock to the scrawniest of French chicken! Here at home I have also found it most satisfactory with veal and pork.

Celery au Gratin
Serves 4.

8 to 10 large clean celery stalks, halved lengthwise, cut into 2-inch pieces
boiling salted water
juice of ½ lemon

bouquet garni *of ½ small bay leaf, 5 sprigs fresh parsley,*
  tied in a piece of cheesecloth
3 *cups rich beef stock*
1 *cup hot light cream*
2 *tablespoons cooking sherry*
1½ *cups freshly grated Swiss cheese*
¾ *cup buttered coarse bread crumbs*

Blanch the celery pieces in boiling water to cover for 5 minutes. Drain and rinse at once under running cold water. Place the celery in a sizable saucepan with the lemon juice, *bouquet garni,* and rich beef stock. Cook over very low heat until just crisp-tender (do not overcook!), stirring carefully but often. This usually requires about 20 minutes or so. Drain the liquid from the celery and reduce it over high heat to about ½ cup. Stir in the cream, correct seasoning, and add the sherry. Arrange half the cooked, hot celery pieces in a rather shallow, liberally buttered casserole, and pour half of the liquid over them. Sprinkle with half the grated cheese, then top with the remaining celery pieces and liquid. Sprinkle with the remaining cheese, and top with bread crumbs. Place in preheated 450° F. oven and bake until the topping is nicely browned. Serve immediately.

WALDORF Salad is an old-fashioned array of crisp ingredients, which gets made on many an occasion at my house. It is a sweet salad but one that adapts itself admirably to service with all sorts of things, from a platter of cold cuts to a batch of fabulous fried chicken.

Waldorf Salad
Serves 6.

1 *cup diced tender celery*
1 *cup diced apples, peeled or not*
⅓ *cup halved seedless raisins*
¼ *cup grated carrot*
½ *cup broken walnut or pecan meats*
¾ *cup Kay's Boiled Salad Dressing (page 255) or*
  mayonnaise
crisp lettuce for base

Combine all ingredients except the lettuce, thoroughly but carefully, and chill well. Serve goodly dollops of the salad, dusted with paprika if you are so inclined, on crisp lettuce leaves.

AN EXCELLENT choice with seafood is the following savory celery dish.

Celery Amandine
Serves 4.

4 *cups finely chopped celery*
¼ *pound (1 stick) butter*
2 *tablespoons finely snipped fresh chives*
½ *cup finely chopped scallions, with tops*
½ *small clove garlic, mashed*
1 *cup blanched, slivered almonds*

Using a heavy skillet, melt half the butter, and in it cook the celery over low heat for about 3 minutes, stirring constantly. Add the chives, scallions, and garlic and cook a bit longer, still stirring constantly. The vegetables should retain much of their crisp texture when served. Meanwhile melt the remaining butter in another heavy skillet and in it sauté the almonds until they are nicely browned. To serve, turn celery mixture out onto a warmed platter, and sprinkle over it the almonds in their butter sauce. Consume immediately!

ORIENTAL cooks do marvelous things with celery, cooked quickly until still rather crisp. Prepared à la Asparagus Nipponese (page 22), if desired with the addition of some coarsely chopped water chestnuts, one quickly obtains a simple and admirable addition to any menu.

Then here is a more ornate celery dish, which can form one of the principal menu items for your next Far Eastern dinner fête.

Celery Shrimp Kowloon
Serves 4 to 6.

6 *cups 1-inch diagonal slices celery*
1 *5-ounce can drained water chestnuts, thinly sliced*
1 *can condensed cream of chicken soup*
3 *cups diced cooked shrimp*
4 *tablespoons finely chopped pimiento*
4 *tablespoons butter*
¾ *cup stale bread dice*
¼ *cup toasted slivered almonds*

Cook celery slices in briskly boiling water, with a dash of salt, until they are crisp-tender. Drain at once under running cold water. Drain again, thoroughly. Mix with the water chestnuts, undiluted soup, and pimiento, and turn into a buttered casserole, layering with the shrimp. In a skillet, melt the butter, and sauté the bread dice, stirring frequently, until they are very lightly browned. Add the almonds, mix well, and spread over the celery-shrimp mixture. Bake in preheated 350° F. oven for about 20 minutes, until the topping is very richly browned.

Most smooth-textured foods taste infinitely better with something crisp added. Nothing does this better than the judicious addition of celery. Crunchy Deviled Crab is a prime example. Most recipes call for bread crumbs, butter, and seasonings. But try the following version with crisp, flavorful, nutritious celery, and you will never in the future neglect including this ingredient.

Crunchy Deviled Crab
Serves 4.

1 *cup chopped crisp celery*
1½ *cups drained flaked crabmeat*
2 *tablespoons lime juice*
1 *teaspoon grated onion*
1 *tablespoon finely chopped green pepper*
2 *tablespoons butter*
¼ *cup chopped fresh parsley*
½ *teaspoon dried mustard*
¼ *cup fine bread crumbs*
¼ *cup mayonnaise*
¼ *cup undiluted condensed cream of mushroom soup*
⅛ *teaspoon Worcestershire sauce*
2 *drops Tabasco sauce*
¼ *teaspoon curry powder*
parsley sprigs
lime wedges

Thoroughly combine the crabmeat, lime juice, and grated onion. Refrigerate this. In a skillet, in hot butter, sauté the celery and green pepper for 5 minutes, stirring often. To this, add all remaining ingredients except parsley sprigs and lime wedges, including the crabmeat mixture. Pack into individual seafood baking shells. Sprinkle with the fine bread crumbs, dot with butter, and bake in preheated 350° F. oven until brown, usually about 30 minutes. Serve hot, garnished with parsley sprigs and wedges of fresh lime.

CHARD

In this country, the name Chard is usually applied to a special form of a variety of the common beet (*Beta vulgaris* var. *Cicla,* of the Goosefoot Family), and describes a vegetable with large tuffets of unusually vivid bright green foliage, the midriffs and stalks of which are conspicuously enlarged. It is also known as Swiss Chard or Sea-Kale Beet (not to be confused with Sea Kale, which is *Crambe maritima,* page 209). In other lands, just to confuse things further, Chard is sometimes synonymous with the beets that are grown particularly for their edible, abundant leaves, or even the ornamental beets with showy varicolored foliage.

Bunches of fresh crisp Chard are seen in some produce markets, usually during the autumn months, but it is not one of our commoner vegetables. It is of singularly easy cultivation in the home garden in most areas (though not in South Florida), and seeds of selected variants are readily available from reliable commercial sources.

I habitually cook Chard by rinsing off the bunch, trimming off the leaves from the thickened leaf-stalks (called chards), cutting these into three-inch or so lengths, then quickly blanching them in boiling salted water. I save the leaves to add, coarsely chopped, to minestrone or a similar vegetable soup. The foliage can, of course, be cooked along with the chards, but I find these so attractive that, for aesthetic value alone, I segregate the two parts of the plant. The crisp chards, just barely tender, are served at once with lots of butter, freshly ground pepper, and on occasion a touch of wine vinegar.

This is one vegetable invariably offered at my table as a special course, all by its glorious self!

CHAYOTE

The Chayote (*Sechium edule,* of the Squash Family) is a fabulous vegetable from Mexico and Guatemala; it was cultivated by the Mayas and Aztecs long prior to the discovery of America. It has during the past few years become increasingly available in choice markets throughout this country, through plantings principally in South Florida.

Chayote (pronounced chy-*oh*-tee) is derived from the Mayan *chayotli.* Elsewhere in the American tropics, where the vines have long been planted, it is known as Christophine, Chocho, or, in Portuguese-speaking Brazil, *xuxú.* And European gourmets have appreciated it for decades, and know it, especially from plantings in North Africa, under such names as Vegetable Pear, Custard Marrow, *pepinella,* and *brionne.*

The vine, a rampant perennial one, produces almost throughout the year a prodigious quantity of fruits, which we prize as a superb delicate vegetable. Pendant, normally ice-green, vaguely pear-shaped objects three to six or eight inches in length and several inches broad, they are set with several longitudinal furrows and in some forms are vaguely soft-prickly.

Special, rather rare variants have alabaster white, yellow, and green-mottled fruits.

The Chayote has a unique texture and flavor—crystalline well describes the first; a cross between a cucumber and a zucchini the second.

In purchasing Chayotes, avoid any that are wrinkled or at all soft. The very firm young specimens are by far the most desirable—even their solitary flattish central seed is edible after cooking. This exceptional vegetable is best appreciated when treated in the simplest, most unadorned fashion. Here is a favorite way with fresh juvenile Chayotes:

Chayotes with Butter
Serves 3 to 6.

6 *medium young chayotes*
lightly salted water
butter
freshly ground pepper

Cut the chayotes, unpeeled, into quarters or halves, and steam in a small amount of lightly salted water until just tender—usually about 25 to 30 minutes. Do not overcook. Drain, peel, and while still hot serve with liberal supplies of butter and freshly ground pepper, white or black.

THE quartered or halved young chayotes may also be parboiled, then sautéed gently in butter until brown, with additional butter and freshly ground pepper at table. Europeans frequently cube the vegetable and, after steaming, serve it dressed with a light white or cheese sauce.

IF ONE has a large plot of chayotes, he might consider serving up a batch of the very young sprouting shoots of the vines. Pick off the curly tendrils, and cook the sprouts in salted water until tender, to be served as an unusual and tasteful green. The vine supports a rather large starchy tuberous root which is also utilized in Mexico as a vegetable, being boiled until tender, sliced, then either candied with brown sugar (as Sweet Potato Camote, page 226), or fried in butter or lard.

ONE of the loveliest vacation spots I know is the hostelry at Santa Maria de Ostuma, high in the orchid-hung cool forests of Nicaragua's mountains. The site is a working coffee plantation, and from its rustic buildings one can visit nearby essentially unexcavated ancient pyramids and view some of the most spectacular scenery in this part of Middle America. One of the edible specialties of the establishment is a luscious chayote soup, and I thank Don Leo F. Salazar, the courtly and erudite proprietor, for this recipe.

Chayote Soup Santa Maria
Serves 6.

6 *medium young chayotes*
1 *tablespoon sugar*
2 *quarts rich chicken stock*
1 *cup shredded cooked chicken*
½ *cup thinly sliced scallions, with tops*
1½ *tablespoons salt*
1 *teaspoon freshly ground pepper*
crisp tiny croutons

Cut chayotes into quarters, and steam them in a small amount of water with the sugar for 8 minutes. Drain and peel them, and cut into 1-inch pieces. In a kettle combine the chicken stock, the shredded chicken, scallions, salt, and pepper, and simmer for about 15 minutes. Add the chayote pieces and simmer the soup, covered, until they are firm-tender, usually about 15 or 20 minutes. Serve immediately, garnished with tiny croutons.

STUFFED chayotes appear on many a good Latin table in various fine forms. Here is one of my favorite ways.

Chayotes Stuffed with Beef
Serves 4.

4 *large fresh chayotes*
lightly salted water
2 *tablespoons peanut or soy oil*
¾ *cup finely chopped onion*
1 *large clove garlic, mashed*
1 *pound lean ground beef*
3 *medium tomatoes, peeled, coarsely chopped*
4 to 8 *drops Tabasco sauce*
salt and freshly ground pepper
8 *tablespoons butter*
1½ *cups grated sharp Cheddar cheese*

Halve the chayotes lengthwise and steam them in a small amount of salted water until just tender, then drain. Carefully scoop out the pulp, leaving a thin, firm shell. Chop the pulp finely, allow it to stand in a bowl for a few minutes, then turn into a colander to drain off any excess liquid. In a large deep skillet, heat the oil, and sauté the onion and garlic, stirring often until soft but not browned. Crumble in the lean beef and continue to cook until meat is well browned. Add tomatoes, chayote pulp, Tabasco sauce, and salt and pepper to taste. Mix well, and continue to cook for about 20 minutes over medium heat. Turn mixture into a colander and allow the excess juice to drain off. Lightly fill the chayote shells with the mixture; place any excess in a small ovenproof casserole for baking along with the chayotes. Dot liberally with butter, sprinkle with grated cheese, and bake in preheated 350° F. oven for 15 minutes. Serve without delay.

SHRIMP-stuffed Chayotes are elegant fare, and superb for that special luncheon with tropical overtones. Accompany with a papaya salad, your favorite cool beverage, and hot crisp rolls.

Chayotes Stuffed with Shrimp
Serves 4.

4 *large fresh chayotes*
lightly salted water
2 *tablespoons butter*
¾ *cup finely chopped onion*
2¼ *cups toasted bread crumbs*
oregano to taste
salt and freshly ground pepper to taste
2½ *cups minced cooked shrimp*
¾ *cup toasted bread crumbs*
3 *tablespoons butter*

Halve the chayotes lengthwise and steam them in a small amount of salted water until they are just tender, then drain. Carefully scoop out the pulp, leaving a thin but firm shell. Chop the pulp finely and drain off any excess liquid in a colander. In a large deep skillet, sauté the onion in the 2 tablespoons butter until it is translucent, then add the chayote pulp and the 2¼ cups bread crumbs, plus oregano, salt, and pepper to taste. Simmer over low heat, stirring often, for about 10 minutes. Add the minced shrimp, mix well, and heat through. Fill the chayote shells with the mixture, sprinkle with the ¾ cup bread crumbs, and dot with 3 tablespoons butter. Arrange the stuffed chayotes in a large shallow baking pan and bake in preheated 350° F. oven until the topping is lightly browned. Serve at once.

THE EXTRAORDINARILY good cooks of Brazil make extensive and memorable use of chayotes, which they call *xuxú* or *chuchú* (pronounced shoo-*shoo*). They use a melon-ball cutter to make little balls, which are steamed in just a bit of lightly salted and sugared water. When just firm-tender, the green globes are drained and served hot with butter and freshly ground white pepper, plus the tiniest pinch of ground cinnamon.

JAMAICANS usually call the chayote by the cheerful name of *chocho*. Here is one of Mrs. Morris Cargill's special ways with it as an elegant hot dessert.

Dessert Chayotes Charlottenburgh
Serves 6.

3 *medium-sized young chayotes*
lightly salted water
1 *cup milk*
3 *egg yolks, lightly beaten*
1½ *tablespoons light brown sugar*

¼ *teaspoon salt*
2 *tablespoons halved plumped seedless raisins*
1 *teaspoon dark Jamaica rum*
3 *egg whites*
pinch cream of tartar
2 *tablespoons slivered toasted almonds*

Halve the chayotes lengthwise and steam them in a small amount of lightly salted water until they are just tender, then drain. Carefully scoop out the pulp, leaving a thin but firm shell. Chop the pulp finely, allow it to stand in a bowl for a few minutes, then drain off excess liquid, using a colander. Combine pulp with the milk, beaten yolks, brown sugar, salt, the halved raisins (which have been soaked in warm water till plump, then drained), and the rum. Lightly fill the chayote shells with this mixture. Without delay, whip the egg whites, chilled, with a pinch of cream of tartar, until they form peaks. Place stuffed chayote halves in a shallow pan, top each with meringue mixture, sprinkle with almond slivers, and bake in preheated 325° F. oven until meringue has lightly browned, usually about 12 to 15 minutes. Serve immediately.

CHESTNUT

There are several different kinds of Chestnuts, of the genus *Castanea,* at least three of which are cultivated for their edible nuts, these enclosed in ornate prickly cases and extensively used as vegetables in epicurean cookery. These members of the Oak Family are very important food items in many parts of the world, notably southern Europe, China, and Japan. During the winter months, fresh Chestnuts are available in lustrous-brown piles in our markets, and from them

we can create some of the most richly savory dishes in our repertoire of international cuisine. When the nuts are not in season, they are available canned or variously preserved in containers, frequently with sweetened liquids.

In many big cities in this country, around Christmastime, vendors on the streets offer hot roasted Chestnuts, just as in lands abroad. Whenever I see or smell these glorious hot nuts I think of Naples during the war, when the Italian populace had little edible left to offer us sailors and soldiers except these products of the formerly magnificent and extensive Chestnut forests near the city. Most of the trees were cut down during the conflict to provide firewood and only today are the replanted forests coming back to their original impressive state.

To prepare fresh Chestnuts, with a sharp knife make a cross on the flat side of each nut. Place them in a shallow pan, sprinkle rather liberally with melted butter, and heat in preheated 350°F. oven until the shells curl back, usually about 20 minutes or so, shaking the pan from time to time. Peel off the shells while they are still hot, then place in water to cover, to soak for 5 minutes. The brown inner skin, which can be rather bitter, is then easily removed. The nuts will still be rather firm-textured after the above preliminaries, and usually require some additional cooking—although many of us like them just reheated quickly in melted butter with perhaps a touch of minced parsley and a bit of salt, shaken until coated thoroughly, and served as is.

The following European recipe is perfect with such things as sauerbraten, roast veal, and even good old Yankee meat loaf.

European Chestnuts
Serves 6.

2 *pounds chestnuts, prepared and peeled as directed above*
2 *tablespoons melted butter*
2 *teaspoons sugar*
2 *cups rich beef stock or bouillon*
3 *tablespoons butter*
2 *tablespoons sugar*
1 *tablespoon granulated flour*
½ *cup rich beef stock or bouillon*
salt and freshly ground pepper

Place the prepared, peeled chestnuts in a saucepan, add the 2 tablespoons butter, the 2 teaspoons sugar, and 2 cups beef stock or bouillon. Cover and over low heat simmer until they are tender—usually about 20 minutes. Drain thoroughly. In a smallish skillet, melt the 3 tablespoons butter with the 2 tablespoons sugar, and cook over very low heat until it starts to brown, then sprinkle in the flour, mix well, and blend in the ½ cup beef stock or bouillon. Add the chestnuts, and shake the skillet over low heat until they are well coated, moist, and glossy. Serve hot.

CHESTNUT Purée is a delicious concoction especially appropriate with turkey or duck or other fowl, or with wild game.

Chestnut Purée
Serves 6.

2 pounds chestnuts, prepared and peeled (page 89)
4 tablespoons melted butter
2 teaspoons sugar
2 cups rich beef, veal, or chicken stock
3 tablespoons heavy cream
salt and freshly ground pepper

Place the prepared, peeled chestnuts in a saucepan, add 2 tablespoons melted butter, the sugar, and the rich stock or bouillon. Cover and cook until the chestnuts are very tender, and start to fall apart, usually 30 minutes or so. Drain, and put chestnuts through a potato ricer. While hot, blend in the remaining 2 tablespoons butter, cream, and salt and pepper to taste. Serve hot.

THE ITALIANS, the French, and the Spanish all have succulent soups with chestnuts as a base. The following recipe is very rich and does not go with every menu you may conjure up. So consider it carefully and do enjoy it to its fullest—if necessary an hour or so prior to your dinner. Then take a nap.

Chestnut Soup
Serves 6.

1 pounds chestnuts, prepared and peeled (page 89)
2 cups coarsely chopped carrots
1 cup finely chopped onion
1 cup coarsely chopped scallions, with tops
2 cups finely chopped celery
2 tablespoons light olive oil
2 quarts rich chicken stock or bouillon
½ cup coarsely chopped parsley
2 whole cloves
½ cup light cream
salt and freshly ground pepper

In a heavy deep kettle with cover, cook the carrots,

onion, scallions, and celery in oil (peanut or soy oil can be used), stirring frequently, until they begin to brown. Add the prepared, peeled chestnuts, the chicken stock or bouillon, parsley, and cloves. Cover kettle, and simmer the soup until the chestnuts are very soft, usually an hour or so. Pour the soup while hot into an electric blender, and whirl until it is smooth. Return this purée to the kettle, fold in the cream, and heat through, but do not allow to come to the boil. Season to taste with salt and pepper. Serve while very hot, if desired garnished with a sprinkling of additional parsley.

AND THEN we have an old-time favorite for the holiday season, a good robust chestnut stuffing for turkey, chicken, or other fowl. This will admirably stuff a 10- to 12-pound turkey, and of course should be put into the bird just at roasting time, never in advance.

Savory Chestnut Stuffing
Makes about 12 cups.

2 pounds chestnuts, prepared and peeled (page 89)
½ cup butter
1 cup coarsely chopped onion
1 cup coarsely chopped celery
⅓ cup chopped fresh parsley
½ cup seedless raisins
6 cups stale white bread cubes
3 cups peeled tart apple cubes
1 tablespoon salt
¼ teaspoon freshly ground pepper
½ cup light cream

Place the prepared, peeled chestnuts in enough water to cover and cook them over low heat until they are barely tender. Drain thoroughly and chop coarsely. In a skillet, melt the butter, and in it cook the onion, celery, and parsley, until the onion is soft. Stir in all other ingredients, toss lightly with two forks, and use as stuffing for a turkey or other festive fowl.

CHICORY

Chicory is one of the myriad members of the Daisy Family which is of value to man. This one is known scientifically as *Cichorium Intybus,* and is much confused—both in this country and in its native Mediterranean region—with Endive (page 109) and Escarole (page 110).

It is extensively cultivated for its rather bitter, more or less curly-crisp foliage and for the elongate taproot, both in Europe and in parts of the United States, where the plant occurs as a weed in waste places. In recent times American horticulturists have developed a series of variants which are grown for their showy erect wandlike spikes of sizable blue, purple, or white blossoms, these opening only during sunny hours.

Also known in this country as Succory, this is an exceptionally useful vegetable. The young tender sprouts, in particular, are boiled briefly in two changes of salted water, then served as a potherb with butter and the customary seasonings. The rinsed, chilled leaves of more mature status are popular as salad greens. And the roots of the cultivated Chicory are boiled or braised and served with various sauces, as a pleasant somewhat parsniplike dish. The roots of the wild plant are also of considerable importance as an adulterant of coffee, the bitterness being much relished in such places as New Orleans and other sectors of our Southeast—and, of course, in France, as *chicorée*.

The special kinds of Chicory that are grown for their foliage occur in several attractive color forms— bleached almost white, palest yellow, pink, and rich red. The tightly crisped leaves of some of these, the flatter leaves of others, when combined with other vegetables in salads, making intriguing and distinctly tasteful dishes. Here is one such recipe, which I enjoy offering as a separate course prior to red meat entrées.

Chicory Salad
Serves 4.

1 *bunch fresh chicory*
⅓ *cup light olive oil*
1 to 2 *tablespoons wine vinegar*
¼ *teaspoon salt*
⅛ *teaspoon freshly ground pepper*
¼ *cup finely chopped scallion tops*
½ *cup peeled cucumber dice*
4 *red radishes, thinly sliced*

Very thoroughly wash and drain the chicory. Tear into pieces, pat dry, and chill wrapped in a clean kitchen towel for 1 hour. Prepare a dressing of oil, vinegar, salt, and pepper, and allow to mellow during this period. At serving time, combine chicory and other vegetables, these chilled and the cucumbers drained, pour the dressing over, toss lightly but thoroughly, and offer with pride to your assembled guests.

AFTER complete washing—never soak these leafy vegetables for protracted periods of time—and thorough draining, prepare the following distinctive dish made with fresh chicory. Accompany with side portions of hot linguine or spaghettini dressed with butter, and a goodly flagon of dry white or rosé wine.

Chicory Chicken
Serves 4.

1 *bunch fresh chicory*
boiling salted water
3 *boned, skinned chicken breasts*
salt and freshly ground pepper
4 *tablespoons butter*
1½ *cups rich cream sauce*
½ *cup freshly grated Swiss cheese*

Thoroughly wash and drain the chicory. Shred it and plunge into a considerable quantity of boiling salted water to cook until just barely tender. Drain and rinse under running cold water. Cut the chicken breasts, on the diagonal, into very thin slices. Season these rather liberally with salt and pepper. Melt the butter in a sizable skillet and sauté the chicken slices until they are just golden on both sides. Using, preferably, individual ovenproof baking dishes, arrange portions of the shredded chicory on the bottom, top with sautéed chicken slices, then add your favorite rich cream sauce, and finally sprinkle liberally with freshly grated cheese. Just prior to serving, run under preheated broiler to heat through and melt the cheese.

WHEN BEAUTIFUL, crisp-fresh bunches of chicory are available in our markets, I make extensive use of them as a superb braised vegetable, to accompany just about any imaginable meat dish. The faint bitterness that remains is piquant and refreshing.

Braised Chicory
Serves 4 to 6.

1 *bunch fresh chicory*
boiling salted water
2 *beef bouillon cubes*
2 *cups boiling water*
salt and freshly ground pepper
freshly grated Parmesan cheese (optional)

Thoroughly wash and drain the chicory. Tear into large pieces and blanch in a good quantity of boiling salted water for about 8 minutes. Drain thoroughly and arrange in a shallow ovenproof dish. Combine the beef bouillon cubes with the 2 cups boiling water and pour over the chicory. Season rather liberally with salt and freshly ground pepper. Place in preheated 350° F. oven until chicory is firm-tender, usually about 10 minutes. If desired, sprinkle with freshly grated Parmesan just before serving.

CHINESE SPINACH

The Chinese Spinach (*Amaranthus gangeticus*) is one of a group of related plants of the Amaranth Family which is extensively cultivated in the tropics and subtropics, where it is often prized as a potherb. This one is on occasion seen in Oriental markets in this country, under the Chinese names *yin-choi* or *hon-toi-moi*, or the Japanese name *hiyu*. The seedlings or tender juvenile shoots of the plant are plucked when about six inches long, tied into bunches, and offered for sale.

The smooth stems are set with thin-stalked smallish green leaves. Depending on the variant of the plant, the leaves differ markedly in shape, some being linear, others almost wedge-shaped. When cooked like ordinary spinach—with which this Amaranthus has scant affinity—a tasty green vegetable is obtained. Often called *bhaji* in India and Ceylon, it is much used as an ingredient of the marvelous Vegetable Curries (see pages 251–52) produced by native cooks. In Indonesia, side bowls of lightly steamed, hot Chinese Spinach frequently occupy a place on the formidable Rijstafel, and, on less festive occasions, accompany fish or fowl, with rice.

The true Chinese Spinach is presumably indigenous to India, but it has been cultivated throughout eastern Asia since time immemorial. The Chinese recognize several varieties, including an especially crisp one found in Hawaiian and Californian markets, with white instead of green stems.

The Tampala (*Amaranthus oleraceus* and variants) is grown, especially in India, Ceylon, and Burma, for its edible young stalks and foliage, and for its tiny brown or yellow seeds, these boiled as a vegetable, or, when dried, ground into a flour. This interesting vegetable has recently been introduced into the United States.

A number of forms of both of these species of Amaranthus, with highly colored leaves, are valued for more aesthetic purposes; they are grown by horticulturists in many parts of the world as ornamental plants.

Like all such greens, these amaranths must be cooked for only the briefest of periods. They quickly boil down into a mushy mass, and become quite inedible. But washed, shaken dry, and steamed with some butter in a covered container in just their own juices for a very few minutes, they retain a pleasant firm texture and offer a delightful flavor vaguely akin to spinach with a touch of horseradish added. The taste of the different forms, incidentally, varies to considerable extent, some being rather "hot," while others are notable for their blandness.

If the seedlings or shoots are very long, they can be coarsely chopped or cut into lengths of suitable dimensions. Here is a rapid-fire recipe that happily utilizes Chinese Spinach (or Tampala) in this form.

Chinese Spinach Nuuanu
Serves 4.

2 *large bunches Chinese spinach or tampala*
2 *teaspoons peanut or soy oil*
½ *pound lean ground beef*
1 *small clove garlic, mashed*
½ *cup finely chopped onion*
2 *teaspoons Japanese soy sauce*

Thoroughly wash, but do not soak, the Chinese spinach (or tampala), removing roots and cutting into 3-inch lengths. Shake off as much moisture as possible. In a wok or large shallow skillet, over high heat, stir-fry the ground beef, garlic, and onion in the oil until the meat just turns color. Add the Chinese spinach (or tampala) and soy sauce, and continue to stir-fry until it wilts and becomes just slightly tender —usually just a couple of minutes. Serve at once, with individual bowls of hot rice on the side.

In Jamaica and certain other islands of the West Indies, this plant is known as Callaloo or Callilu. These names can also apply to the young leaves of certain aroids, such as Taro (page 228). One of the finest of the many superb soups found on good tables from Manchioneal to Montego Bay is the following one made from Callaloo.

Callaloo Soup
Serves 4 to 6.

2 *large bunches fresh callaloo*
2 *quarts salted water*
¼ *pound diced lean salt pork*
½ *cup coarse-chopped onion*
1 *tablespoon cooking sherry*
Pickapeppa Sauce to taste

Trim off blemished leaves and coarse stems from callaloo. Rinse, then place in soup kettle with 1 quart of the salted water. Bring to a quick boil, cook for 10 minutes, then drain. Bring second quart of water to the boil, add the blanched callaloo, coarsely chopped, with the salt pork and onion. Cover kettle and cook over medium heat for 20 minutes more. Add cooking sherry and a rather liberal dollop of Pickapeppa Sauce. Turn hot soup into electric blender and whirl until smooth. Return to kettle, heat thoroughly, correct seasoning, and serve while very hot, with croutons if desired.

CHINESE Spinach, or Tampala, or Callaloo can be used as a filler for some savory patties or small hot turnovers in the Jamaican style, the vegetable being coarsely chopped, cooked until just barely tender, then seasoned with sautéed onion and, generally, a rather liberal dose of minced hot chili pepper—Jamaican country pepper. Hot to the tongue, but delicious!

CONSIDER, for example, the following famous salad dressing. It was created at the Palace Hotel in San Francisco in 1915 to honor George Arliss, who was appearing in that city in a play entitled *The Green Goddess*. The sauce is most often used over a hearty array of crisp bits of Romaine and cooked, chilled lobster, crab, shrimp, or chicken.

Green Goddess Dressing
Makes about 3½ cups.

⅓ cup finely snipped fresh chives
6 anchovy fillets
1 medium scallion, with top
¼ cup minced fresh parsley
1 tablespoon dried tarragon
⅛ teaspoon garlic powder
3 cups mayonnaise
¼ cup wine vinegar

Chop the anchovies and scallion together until they are very finely minced. Turn into a bowl, add the chives, parsley, tarragon, and garlic powder, and stir in the mayonnaise and vinegar, mixing well. Allow to stand for at least 1 hour prior to use with green salads, or a mixture of greens and cooked chilled seafood or fowl.

CHIVE

Chive or Chives, also spelled Cive (*Allium Schoenoprasum*, of the Lily Family) is a dwarf onion relative, well known for the delicate seasoning ability of its slim hollow green leaves. Widely cultivated in this country (it is native to certain of our northern states, and also to Europe), its tuffets of growth—seldom exceeding six inches in height—and profuse tight heads of filmy violet-colored flowers are sufficiently attractive to appear in many gardens as an ornamental. It possesses the delightful facility of rapid recovery from snipping of the vaguely pungent foliage, and thus is among the most utilitarian of herbaceous vegetables.

Few good cooks, here or abroad, could manage without a pot or garden planting of Chives from which to take fresh cuttings with a kitchen shears. One can also obtain these snippets in flash-frozen and dried form in our stores today, but I do not believe these entirely equal the fresh vegetable.

Chives—known in French as *ciboulette* or *civette*—are widely added to green salads, they are sprinkled with abandon on servings of hearty soups or a hot quiche, and they are very often blended with such foods as cottage and cream cheese, scrambled eggs, and sauces for seafood and poultry.

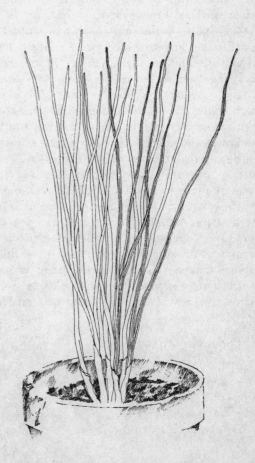

AND THEN, also with chives, this luscious sauce, eminently suited to use over sautéed or broiled chicken, shrimp or lobster, or frogs' legs.

Chive Sauce
Makes about ½ cup.

⅓ cup finely snipped fresh chives
6 tablespoons butter
1 teaspoon Bon Appétit powder
2 teaspoons minced fresh parsley
¼ teaspoon dried tarragon
3 tablespoons dry white wine

Melt the butter, stir in chives and all other ingredients in order given, and simmer for just a moment. Serve at once over hot sautéed or broiled fowl, seafood, or frogs' legs.

CHRYSANTHEMUM

There are a great many different kinds of Chrysanthemums known to science. They are extremely popular in gardens throughout the world for their splendid, typically profuse daisylike or compound flowers. Some species are cultivated commercially for their essential oils and resins, which are incorporated into many popular insecticides.

The Garland Chrysanthemum (*Chrysanthemum coronarium*), a native of the Mediterranean region with attractive cut foliage and later on pretty white flowers, has long been prized by Oriental cooks, especially in its seedling stage, six inches tall or so, as a special vegetable. Everyone is familiar with the pleasant pungent scent of 'Mum flowers and foliage, and this is precisely the flavor of these unique greens when offered at table. In the past, the vegetable has been found primarily in Oriental markets in this country, but nowadays seeds (sometimes under the Japanese name *shimizu*) are available from many domestic sources, and due to their ready growth the plants are increasingly seen in kitchen gardens.

Chrysanthemum Greens
Serves 4.

1 large bunch garland chrysanthemum
2 teaspoons peanut or soy oil
1 teaspoon salt
½ cup water

Thoroughly wash the garland chrysanthemum, trim off the roots, and cut the leafy tops into 2-inch lengths. In a kettle, heat the oil with the salt and water, and when it comes to the boil, add the vegetable. Cook, stirring occasionally, over medium heat, until the greens are tender. Drain, add pepper if desired, and serve while very hot.

COSTMARY or Mint-Geranium is another member of this genus (*Chrysanthemum Balsamita*), a native of western Asia, whose foliage is used to flavor various kinds of ale and comparable beverages. The pickled flower heads of a couple of other species are eaten as a very powerfully flavored condiment in the Orient, notably in Japan. Boiled flower heads of *Chrysanthemum sinense* are eaten in Japan, and to a lesser degree in Taiwan, and the leaves of the same plant are shredded for a pungent seasoning in bowls of hot rice. In our North American cuisine, gourmet gardeners on occasion add a leaf or two, or more often a few flower petals, as a delectably different flavorful garnish to clear soups or to salads.

CHUFA

The Chufa (*Cyperus esculentus,* of the Sedge Family) is a weedy plant, springing up especially in sandy fields—usually after previous cultivation of the soil—in almost all parts of the warm countries of the world. It has been grown by man, often rather casually, since very early times, but is today rarely encountered in commercial food markets, at least in this country. In Africa, however, Chufas are common items, and in tropical areas in this hemisphere with large Negro populations, small backyard plots of the plants are often encountered.

The grassy foliage of the Chufa tops stout stems, these to three feet in height. Each growth is in time furnished with intricate brownish-red or straw-red bunches of bracted flower-clusters.

The edible portions are the subterranean tuberous rootstocks, which are also variously called Chufo, Chewfer, Earth Almond, and Yellow Nut Grass. They are eaten raw or are briefly parboiled, then lightly roasted and salted, to be consumed much as peanuts. They possess a pleasant nutty flavor and crisp texture. In Cuba and elsewhere in the Antilles, this plant is known as *cebollín,* and from ancient times a flour has been prepared from the tubers, this still used to some extent in native cookery. Also, the juice is expressed from the tubers and made into a refreshing, justly popular beverage known as *horchata de chufas.*

Several additional species of the large genus *Cy-*

perus are cultivated in various parts of the world, primarily in the tropics, for their edible rootstocks, or are gathered from the wild for use in aboriginal cookery.

COLEUS

Coleus is a sizable genus of the Mint Family, especially numerous in the tropics of Africa and Indonesia. Many horticulturally evolved Coleus with showy multicolored big soft leaves have long been grown as prized ornamentals in our gardens and greenhouses, and it is not generally known that the group is also of importance abroad as a vegetable.

The most important of the edible Coleus is the Hausa Potato (*Coleus rotundifolius*), a perennial plant widespread from Nigeria to Java. In many of the countries over this gigantic range it has long been extensively cultivated for the smallish round tubers which are produced in great profusion. These are virtually unknown in our American markets, but appear on occasion in such cities as Paris, somewhat as culinary curios. The flavor of these "potatoes" is rather pleasant, a bit spicy, and the texture is moist and grainy.

In Indonesia several other kinds of Coleus are cultivated, not only for the subterranean tubers which the plants bear, but also for the edible juvenile shoots with their accompanying leaves. These are added to quick-cooked vegetable mixtures as an interesting green vegetable—even though they may be vivid purple in color!

COLLARD

Collard is of special importance in this country in our Southern states, where this variant of kale (*Brassica oleracea* var. *acephala*, of the Crucifer Family) is frequently cultivated for the rather coarse, somewhat strong-flavored green foliage. Actually there seem to be several different kinds of plants sold in our markets under the name of Collards or Collard Greens, all of them large heavy leaves with somewhat cabbagelike flavor.

The best known of the forms of the authentic vegetable is the one called Georgia Collard, a husky plant upward of four feet tall, with a great loose mass of foliage near its apex. The youngest leaves, picked when fresh and bright green in color, set with small midribs, and with no obvious wilting are naturally the most desirable.

Collards can be cooked in many fashions. They are perhaps most often finely chopped and boiled in salted water until just tender, then served with butter or bacon fat and seasonings. They are also tasty when, after they are cooked and drained, they are dotted with butter, sprinkled liberally with freshly grated sharp Cheddar or Swiss cheese, then run into the oven until the cheese melts. Like kale, these greens are frequently cooked with pork or ham, the flavors being notably compatible. And some of my Negro friends who are exceptional Southern cooks delight in serving a good batch of Collards with such regional delights as pan-fried fish (sprinkling the vegetable with some of the seasoned fat in which the fish has been fried) and hushpuppies.

If good fresh Collards are not available, they may be found in cans and even in flash-frozen packets.

ONE OF my favorite restaurants in the picturesque old city of Tampa is Las Novedades, where host Manuel Garcia makes available to his patrons an array of splendid dishes, including the following exceptional soup.

Collard Greens Soup
Serves 6.

> 1 *pound fresh young collards, or 1 No. 2 can*
> ½ *pound ham bone*
> 2 *chorizos (spicy Spanish sausages), sliced*
> ¼ *pound white bacon, sliced*
> 1 *No. 2 can Great Northern beans*
> 1 *small minced onion*
> 1 *small minced green pepper*
> 1 *tablespoon bacon fat*
> 4 *medium potatoes, peeled, quartered*
> *salt and freshly ground pepper*

In a sizable kettle with cover, to 1 quart water, add the hambone, chorizos, and the white bacon. Cover and bring to the boil. Reduce heat and simmer, still covered, for about 45 minutes. If fresh collards are being used, rinse and drain them thoroughly, then shred with a sharp knife; simply drain the canned kind. Add collards and drained beans to the soup, cover again, and simmer for 30 minutes more. In a skillet, sauté the onion and green pepper in the bacon fat until they are soft. Turn contents of skillet into the soup, with the potatoes. Season rather heavily with salt and pepper, and simmer, still covered, until potatoes are tender.

BRAZILIAN cooks make extensive culinary use of collards. The elegant national dish of that glorious land, Feijoada Completa (page 35), is, in fact, traditionally accompanied by the following simple version of these tasty greens. Kale is occasionally substituted, if good fresh collards are unavailable.

Collards Brazilian
Serves 4.

   5 cups shredded raw collards
   boiling salted water
   4 tablespoons diced lean salt pork
   salt and pepper to taste

Rinse the collards, drain them well, and shred them with a sharp knife. Bring a good quantity of salted water to a rolling boil, add the shredded collards, mix, then remove from heat and drain very thoroughly without delay. Meanwhile, in a skillet, fry the salt-pork dice until rather crisp. Add the drained, blanched collards, and stir-fry over high heat until the vegetable is tender. Serve without delay, seasoned to taste with salt and freshly ground pepper.

COLTSFOOT

The Coltsfoot is a coarse large perennial plant of the Daisy Family (Compositae), known to botanists as *Petasites japonicus*. Growing mostly in perpetually damp areas of rich soil in Japan—principally the Russian-held island of Sakhalin—specimens as tall as a man are not infrequent. The roundish or kidney-shaped leaves may measure four feet across and are supported on stout stalks; the stalks are sold as a popular vegetable in Oriental markets.

In this country, fresh Coltsfoot, known in Chinese as *foon-dung*, in Japanese as *fuki*, is encountered largely in California and Hawaii, where it is often called Butterbur. The stalks, green or pinkish-green, and measuring one to three feet in length, usually are offered in bunches of a dozen or so, with parts of the felt-textured leaves attached. The smaller stalks are available as well in cans, these imported from Japan, and can be found in specialty markets throughout this country.

The leaf stalks are usually parboiled, then peeled, simmered in a stock with seasonings, and drained for serving. They can be utilized as well in quick-cooked, stir-fried vegetable mélanges in the Oriental fashion,

to which bits of meat can be added if desired. The flavor is rather acid, and the texture when the vegetable is properly prepared (never overcooked) is pleasantly crisp. The Chinese in particular pickle pieces of the stalks of the Coltsfoot in a soy sauce-sugar mixture, to be used as a condiment. The little buds of the pretty, generally purplish-white flowers are used as a condiment, too, often fresh but sometimes preserved in a light brine. These have a puckery but refreshing flavor.

Coltsfoot Stalks
Serves 6.

   1 bunch coltsfoot stalks
   salted boiling water
   2 cups rich chicken or beef stock
   ¼ cup soy sauce
   1 to 2 tablespoons sugar
   butter
   freshly ground white pepper

Cut the coltsfoot stalks into 2-inch lengths and add them to the salted boiling water. Boil for about 5 minutes. Drain thoroughly and peel the stalk sections. Arrange these in a shallow pan, add the rich stock, soy sauce, and sugar, cover, and cook over low heat until the stalks are just barely tender yet still retain some crisp texture—usually about 15 minutes. Serve while hot, with butter and white pepper.

CORIANDER

Though Coriander (*Coriandrum sativum*, of the Carrot Family) is known primarily for its little seedlike fruits—these used as seasoning and flavoring in such things as pastries, confections, and liquors—the weedy plant occupies a special place in the cuisine of China and Mexico. In English, the vegetable is known as Chinese Parsley or Mexican Parsley, in Spanish as *cilantro* or *culantro*, in Chinese as *yuen-sai*, in Japanese as *koyendoro*.

The sawtoothed green leaves, dull, dark green above, lighter underneath, are borne on short stalks attached to a round stem growing up to three feet in height. Originally from southern Europe, Coriander is today cultivated throughout the world. The seedlings of the leafy part of the plant are most often seen in domestic markets tied into small bunches of greenery. When

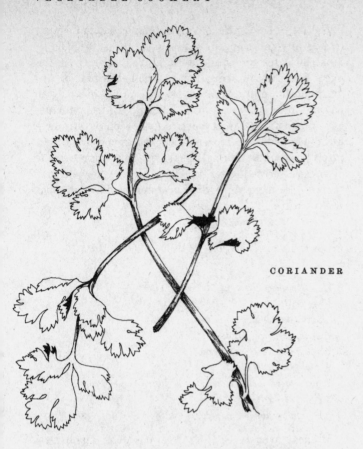

CORIANDER

bruised, the foliage gives off a pervading scent, one that flavors many a Latin and Oriental dish. Such tropical stews as Ajiaco Criollo, described elsewhere in this volume, can be seasoned with Coriander—in moderation, if you please.

CORN

Corn is one of those widely used vegetables that we eat, in some form, with great frequency—in many homes almost every day—yet about whose precise origins even learned botanists are rather unsure.

There are infinite numbers of different kinds of Corn or Maize (most often called simply *Zea Mays,* scientifically), in cultivation throughout the world today. But Maize has never been found anywhere in a truly wild state. It is now generally considered that the plant—or plants, rather—that we know today are derived from ancient hybridization, presumably in Mexico, between a grass called *teosinte,* and an as yet unknown grass.

Columbus first found Corn, as we know it, in Cuba, and took it back with him to Europe. Today it appears in various forms commonly on tables in lands outside of this hemisphere—cornmeal is especially prized

in parts of Italy and Rumania—but our good old Yankee corn on the cob is often relegated to the status of hog fodder on the Continent.

The inhabitants of Mexico still make the greatest use of Corn of any peoples, the thin ground-corn pancakes known as tortillas appearing at virtually every meal in some form or other. Tortillas are prepared from masa, a sort of dough made by soaking and boiling corn kernels in lime water, then grinding them over and over again until a very fine meal is obtained. Dried masa, in packages, is now available here, and in almost every supermarket in this country we can now buy canned or frozen tortillas, ready to heat through or toast in a bit of lard or oil.

Mexican Corn Tostadas are technically a kind of ornate appetizer, made with a base of these toasted corn pancakes. But I like to serve them as a light entrée in the following version, with a salad of Tomatoes Oregano (page 232) and chilled beer.

Corn Tostadas
Serves 4.

8 canned or frozen tortillas
½ cup corn or peanut oil
1 pound lean ground beef
salt and pepper
1 large can commercial taco sauce
1 cup finely chopped onion
1 cup finely chopped firm-ripe tomato
1½ cups shredded lettuce
1½ cups shredded sharp Cheddar cheese

In a skillet over rather high flame, heat the oil and place the tortillas in it one at a time, turning them once and removing them to drain on paper towels almost immediately; prolonged frying makes them overly brittle. Keep fried tortillas warm in a very low oven until ready to assemble the tostadas. Drain off all but about a tablespoon of the oil, and sauté the ground beef until it is well browned and crumbly. Season to taste with salt and pepper.

To assemble the tostadas: Place 4 warm fried tortillas on a cooky sheet, top each with part of the ground beef, drizzle over part of the taco sauce, then sprinkle with onion, tomato, lettuce, and cheese. Top each with second tortilla, and repeat with other ingredients, ending with cheese. Run under preheated broiler until the cheese has just melted, and serve immediately.

SWEET corn kernels, particularly those of the young green ears, are epicurean food in many parts of tropical America. Once while I was exploring the breath-takingly beautiful Mountain Pine Ridge of British Honduras, my Maya hosts served the following luscious version of fried corn to accompany a spit-roasted wild turkey.

Maya Fried Corn
Serves 4.

2 cups fresh or frozen corn kernels
2 tablespoons butter
½ cup minced onion
¼ cup minced green pepper
½ teaspoon salt
¼ teaspoon freshly ground pepper
hot pepper sauce
3 tablespoons evaporated milk

Melt the butter over rather high flame in a medium skillet and add all ingredients except the evaporated milk. Sauté, stirring often, until the corn is nicely but lightly browned. Stir in the milk and serve while hot. Offer hot pepper sauce on the side—the Indians use a potent amount of it!

CORN fritters are popular food in our Southern states. I enjoy these with fried or fricasseed chicken, broiled ham slices, or pan-fried fish. If fresh or frozen corn kernels are not available, a big can of unadorned niblets can well be used in this recipe, thoroughly drained, of course.

Southern Corn Fritters
Makes about 16.

2 cups fresh or frozen corn kernels
1 cup sifted all-purpose flour
1 teaspoon baking powder
1½ teaspoons salt
2 eggs, beaten well
¼ cup milk
1 tablespoon melted butter
lard for deep frying

Sift together the flour, baking powder, and salt. In another bowl, thoroughly combine the eggs with the milk, then stir this into the flour mixture. Mix in the melted butter and corn kernels. Heat lard to 365° F. and drop tablespoons of the corn batter into it. Fry fritters until lightly brown, turning once, usually 3 to 5 minutes. Drain thoroughly on absorbent paper towels, and serve while very hot.

GREEN Corn Soufflé is an adaptable, and satisfying dish. Many cooks shun soufflés, since these, in general, must be eaten the minute they are taken from the oven. But the following dish can be held even for upward of 30 minutes in a low warming oven after baking and yet retain its delicacy. In this recipe, absolutely fresh sweet corn on the cob is strongly recommended; the frozen uncooked kernels are definitely a second choice. Be sure to keep your ears of corn refrigerated after picking, for the kernels lose their subtle flavor with disconcerting rapidity at room temperature.

Green Corn Soufflé
Serves 4.

1 cup fresh corn kernels (from 2 ears)
1 cup milk
3 tablespoons biscuit mix
⅓ teaspoon prepared mustard
⅛ teaspoon chili powder
½ teaspoon salt
1 cup grated medium-sharp Cheddar cheese
3 eggs, separated
⅛ teaspoon baking powder

Preheat oven to 350° F. Combine small amount of biscuit mix with milk. Then add the rest to make a paste. Add the mustard, chili powder, and salt. Heat the mixture in a heavy saucepan over medium heat, and add the cheese. Cut the raw corn kernels from the ears and scrape the corn milk with a knife from the cob. Add to the sauce mixture. Separate eggs, put the yolks into a 1-quart mixing bowl, and beat lightly. Add a small amount of the hot mixture to the yolks, then mix in all of it. In another bowl, beat the egg whites with the baking powder until they form a soft peak. Fold into the corn mixture. Put an ungreased 1½-quart casserole in a pan of warm water and pour the mixture into the casserole. Run the tip of a knife around the mixture about 1 inch from the edge. Place in hot oven and set timer for 55 minutes. When soufflé is ready to serve, the point of a knife inserted in the center will come out clean.

CORN SALAD

Corn Salad (*Valerianella olitoria*, of the Valerian Family) is an autumn-sprouting annual plant, gathered in great quantities in the springtime, especially in fields of corn and other grains. The spoon-shaped or round leaves grow in compact rosettes and are of a pleasant firm texture and somewhat lettucelike flavor. One of its other common names, in fact, is Lamb's Lettuce. The French know it as *mâche*.

This attractive salad vegetable is extensively cultivated in Europe, and large vivid-green bunches of it—individual leaves tied together, or a special variety that forms a rather firm globular head—are often found in produce stalls in France, Holland, and Germany. A distinctive kind, Italian Corn Salad, has longer, paler, slightly hairy leaves, and, as its name implies, is found particularly in Italy. Though all these forms of Corn Salad have been introduced into this country, they are relatively rare in our markets, except in cities with extensive Italian or French populations.

Prepare as Lettuce (pages 134–37). The greens can also be quick-cooked in the manner suggested for Spinach (pages 215–16). A favorite way to use this tasty leaf vegetable is with wafer-thin slices of cooked, chilled tiny beets and thin slices of the stalks of a celery heart, all dressed with a light Vinaigrette Dressing (page 256).

CRESS

Several kinds of plants of the Cabbage (Crucifer) Family, with variously pungent foliage, are categorized in this country under the name of Cress. There are four or five of these more or less cultivated here for use as vegetables, plus others similarly utilized that occur as wild plants. The Watercress is of such considerable importance in contemporary vegetable cookery that it is taken up separately (page 240).

The Garden Cress (*Lepidium sativum*), also known as Pepper-Grass, is a widespread weedy plant of the temperate parts of the globe, long grown in dooryard gardens as a pleasant salad vegetable. When quickly rinsed and chilled after being patted dry with absorbent towels, Garden Cress makes a refreshing addition to salads with lettuce and other greens. The flavor, like that of most of these varied Cresses, is slightly bitter and "hot."

Several other kinds of *Lepidium* are used as vegetables in differing parts of the world—the *maca* (*Lepidium Meyenii*) of the high mountains of Peru and Bolivia, cultivated as a potherb, is the most prominent of these. This would make an exciting addition to the roster of such vegetables in our own country. Others of this genus produce tiny seeds that are used as a seasoning in the manner of black pepper.

Two kinds of Winter Cress are grown for their rather sizable, pungent leaves and edible clusters of small yellow flowers. One is the Common Winter Cress

(*Barbarea vulgaris*), a weedy species of Europe and Asia and parts of North America, also known as Yellow Rocket and Upland Cress. The flavor of the foliage, when eaten raw in salads, is reminiscent of that of Watercress; when cooked, it is much like delicate mustard greens. The Early Winter Cress, also called Bell Isle Cress or Scurvy Grass, is *Barbarea praecox*, again European, but naturalized in fields of our northern states. Its culinary uses are much like those of the Common Winter Cress.

The Cuckoo Flower (*Cardamine pratensis*) is a pretty slender plant of our flower gardens, with rather showy bunches of white or rose blossoms. Its attractive divided stem leaves and larger basal ones are sometimes chopped and sprinkled on salads. The foliage of this plant is very hot and should be used with some discretion. Other representatives of this genus found elsewhere also have more or less frequently utilized edible leaves.

Mention should be made here, too, of a Cress of another plant family, occasionally found in select produce markets in this country. This is the Pará Cress or Brazil Cress (*Spilanthes oleracea*, of the Daisy Family), a widespread weedy plant with somewhat brownish juvenile stems and leaves. These are pungent, and either added to salads or boiled as a spicy potherb.

CUCUMBER

The Cucumber (*Cucumis sativus,* of the Squash-Gourd Family) is one of man's very old vegetables. It appears in the Old Testament, was relished as a culinary treasure by the Caesars of Rome, and was cultivated in ancient China perhaps three millennia ago. This plant is a cucurbit, a member of the same affinity as the squashes, pumpkins, and gourds, and interestingly enough its genus, *Cucumis,* contains our fine and varied edible melons as well.

Originally from southern Asia, the Cucumber—*concombre* in French, *pepino* in Spanish, *Gurcke* in German—exists today in numerous varieties and is extensively cultivated in almost all parts of the world. Special kinds are raised in tremendous quantities for pickling. The raw vegetable (actually a fruit) is a great favorite in salads, and cooked Cucumbers have long ranked high with epicures.

When purchasing Cucumbers, be sure they are very firm to the touch. The majority to be found in our domestic markets are covered with a preservative coating of wax. They should be peeled prior to use, though it is not absolutely essential; the wax merely adds an extra toughness to the rind. When using Cucumbers

in salad, it is often desirable to cut them lengthwise into halves or quarters, then, using a sharp spoon, to scoop out the seeds and their surrounding pulp. The remaining flesh is firmer and less juicy, and when added to the greens of the salad bowl, does not appreciably reduce their crispness. The vegetable is often deeply scored longitudinally with a sharp fork or knife point, then sliced and crisped in ice water until time for using.

PRONOUNCED rah-*ee*-ta, the following Cucumber dish is served as a condiment with curries, especially those from India. It also makes an interesting accompaniment to roast lamb or shish kebab.

Cucumber Raita

2 *medium-size, firm cucumbers, peeled, sliced wafer-thin*
1 *pint yoghurt*
1 *small red onion, grated*
¾ *teaspoon salt*
¼ *teaspoon Cayenne pepper*
⅛ *teaspoon cinnamon*
dash ground cloves

Beat the yoghurt, then add all other ingredients, and mix thoroughly. Chill and serve cold as a condiment.

A FAVORED Scandinavian version of cucumbers is the following, which often appears in smorgasbord.

Danish Pickled Cucumbers
Serves 6 to 8.

4 *large firm cucumbers, peeled, sliced wafer-thin*
2 *tablespoons salt*
2 *cups cider vinegar*
1⅓ *cups sugar*
½ *teaspoon black pepper*
2 *tablespoons minced fresh parsley*

Spread the cucumber slices on one or more plates, sprinkle them with salt, and let them stand at room temperature for 1 hour. Drain off all of the liquid possible, lightly squeezing the slices with your hands. Combine all other ingredients in a saucepan, bring to a boil, remove from the heat, and allow to cool. Pour this marinade over the drained cucumber slices, mix carefully but well, allow to stand at room temperature for 2 hours, then chill and drain before serving.

A SIMPLE, pretty, and exceptionally flavorful hors d'oeuvre combines crisped cucumber slices with imported herring in sour cream, served on those utilitarian little party rye slices now available in every good market.

Cucumber Herring Canapés
Makes about 24 canapés.

1 *large firm cucumber*
1 *loaf (8 ounces) party rye bread*
2 *to 3 tablespoons softened butter*
1 *12-ounce jar herring in sour cream*
2 *teaspoons salt*
3 *cups ice water*
paprika

Wash the cucumber, score the rind with the tines of a sharp fork, and cut crosswise into very thin slices. Place in a bowl, add salt, and ice water to cover—add a couple of ice cubes, if you wish. Let stand for 30 minutes, until the cucumber slices are crisp. Drain them on absorbent paper towels and pat dry. Spread the rye slices liberally with softened butter. Overlap 2 slices of cucumber on each slice of bread. Top with one large or two small pieces of herring, undrained. Sprinkle with paprika and serve without delay.

HERE are three memorable salads, from Brazil,

Italy, and Malaysia, in which cucumbers are prominent.

Brazilian Cucumber Salad
Serves 4.

1 *large firm cucumber, peeled, diced*
1 *or 2 teaspoons lemon juice*
salt and freshly ground black pepper

Place small dice of cucumber in an attractive serving bowl. Add lemon juice to taste—do not overdo here!—plus a rather goodly amount of salt and several grinds of pepper. Chill for 1 hour and serve, drained.

Cucumbers Italian Style
Serves 4.

2 *large firm cucumbers*
2 *tablespoons salt*
1 *8-ounce bottle Italian dressing*
2 *tablespoons lemon juice*
2 *teaspoons chopped drained capers*
2 *teaspoons minced pimiento*
crisp lettuce leaves for base

Wash the cucumbers and, unless they are waxed and the covering is too hard, do not peel them. Cut into fingers about 2 inches long by ¼ inch thick. Arrange, not overlapping, on 1 or more shallow plates, and sprinkle with the salt. Allow to stand for 2 hours at room temperature, draining off the moisture that forms and turning the cucumber pieces often. Pat the cucumber fingers as dry as possible with paper towels, then arrange them in a shallow serving dish. In the meantime, combine the bottled Italian dressing (or make your own, if you wish) with the lemon juice, capers, and pimiento. Pour over the cucumbers and refrigerate for at least 1 hour. Serve, undrained, on crisp lettuce leaves.

Salad Tengku
Serves 6 to 8 liberally.

2 *large firm cucumbers, unpeeled, sliced thin*
4 *large stalks celery, sliced thin*
2 *large cans pineapple chunks, drained*
1 *pint commercial sour cream*
½ *teaspoon dried dill weed*
¼ *teaspoon white pepper*
paprika

In a large bowl, combine all ingredients except the paprika, and mix thoroughly but with care. Chill for 1 hour, then serve in small individual bowls, lightly dusted with paprika.

FAVORITE recipes for cooked cucumbers include this French one, which is simplicity itself.

French Boiled Cucumbers
Serves 4.

3 *large firm cucumbers*
salted boiling water
melted butter
salt and fresh-ground pepper

Use unwaxed cucumbers if available, and wash but do not peel them. Cut into slices 1 inch thick and cook in the rapidly boiling water until just crisp-tender. Do not overcook. Drain thoroughly and serve while hot dressed with melted butter, salt and freshly ground pepper added to individual taste.

Once boiled, these chunks of cucumber can be anointed with various sauces, too, such as a light white sauce, a delicate cheese sauce, or heavy cream just heated through.

BAKED cucumbers stuffed with seafood or leftover beef or pork roast make a superb light main dish! Serve them accompanied by a salad of thinly sliced tomatoes vinaigrette, crusty bread, and possibly a glass of rosé wine.

Baked Stuffed Cucumbers
Serves 4.

4 *large firm cucumbers*
¾ *cup coarsely chopped cooked fish, shellfish, or roast meat*
1 *cup light white sauce*
1 *coarsely chopped hard-cooked egg*
1 *teaspoon finely chopped parsley*
1 *teaspoon finely chopped scallions*
salt and pepper to taste
buttered coarse bread crumbs

Wash cucumbers and cut them lengthwise into halves. Do not peel. Using a sharp spoon, scoop out the seeds and discard. Lightly combine all other ingredients except the bread crumbs and heap mixture into cucumber halves. Sprinkle with bread crumbs and place close together in a shallow ovenproof dish. Bake in preheated 375° F. oven for about 20 minutes and serve while very hot.

For warm summery days, consider the lovely chilled soup described below.

Cold Cucumber Soup
Serves 4.

¾ *cup peeled, diced firm cucumber*
1 *cup rich chicken broth*
1 *can frozen cream of potato soup*
½ *cup commercial sour cream*
6 *stuffed olives, sliced wafer-thin*
paprika

In a kettle over low flame, heat the chicken broth and cream of potato soup, stirring occasionally, until soup is completely thawed and blended. Remove from heat and blend in sour cream and diced cucumber. Chill overnight. Serve very cold, garnished with olive slices and a dusting of paprika.

CURRY VEGETABLES
(Curry-Leaf, Lemon Grass, Honda-para Tree)

Under this rather arbitrary category are lumped several plants whose vegetative parts are used in cookery. These are of importance particularly in India, Ceylon, and Indonesia, and are only casually encountered in this country as yet. But since the plants, two trees and a grass, are now being cultivated in select gardens in Florida, California, and other warm areas, and the delightful and distinctive curries and vegetable dishes of the Asiatic tropics are increasingly popular in American kitchens, brief mention of these seems appropriate here. Others are taken up on page 113 of this book, under the entry Flowers, Edible.

Of primary importance to me is the Curry-Leaf (*Murraya Koenigii,* of the Citrus Family) of Ceylon, where it is known as *karapincha* or *karavempu.* This is a very handsome small tree, with aromatic pungent leaves that are added to curries, soups (e.g., mulligatawny), and rice as a flavoring. It was introduced years ago into South Florida, and on rare occasions is found in our local markets. I wish it were more available, for it is a fascinating and unusual vegetable!

Lemon Grass (*Cymbopogon citratus,* of the Grass Family) has thickened leaf-stalk bases. This part is pickled as a condiment and also added—with discretion, since its lemony flavor is very pronounced—to curries and certain soups in many parts of the Asiatic tropics, and in some areas of the Americas as well. The grass is cultivated for lemon oil and for use in perfumery.

The spectacular Honda-para Tree of tropical Asia (*Dillenia indica,* of the Dillenia Family), with large impressed-veined leaves, showy white flowers, and round green-scaled fruits up to five inches in diameter, is often seen in the warmer parts of Florida, in Hawaii, and in Puerto Rico as a prized ornamental. The fruits are used in making jellies and as a refreshing beverage, but also figure as an integral ingredient, coarsely chopped, in some excellent vegetable curries which on occasion appear in those areas where they are available to connoisseur chefs.

There are literally dozens of additional plants that could be taken up in this interesting vegetable category. Indigenous plants, in whatever part of the world, have long been incorporated into good regional cookery. Even if these are not available on any particular commercial basis, they are well worthy of more than casual consideration by the experimental modern cook.

DANDELION

The Dandelion is at once one of the most objectionable of dooryard weeds, in many parts of the world, and the delight of the epicure! It is a member of the prodigious Daisy Family, *Taraxacum officinale,* which, though originally a native of Europe and Asia, has become naturalized in almost all portions of the temperate zones.

Although rather an "old-fashioned" vegetable, we find today—especially during the early spring months—big bunches of fresh Dandelion greens in good markets, these derived from cultivated plots planted with forms of the original species which have been improved by man. The vernacular name, parenthetically, comes from the French *dent de lion,* "lion's tooth," which refers to the generally prominent teeth on the leaves. Interestingly, the French word for Dandelion is *pissenlit,* just to be perverse!

The best Dandelion leaves are the youngest ones, which are the most tender. As the leaf-rosettes mature, the foliage develops a fibrous character which is almost impossible to overcome even through prolonged cooking. Long cooking also removes the vitamins from the leaves, and much of the pleasingly bitter flavor.

These leaves are usually small in the wild forms, but in some selected variants now developed in France, they are of considerable dimensions and notable flavor. The roots and rhizome are dried and are used medicinally under the name "taraxacum," and in some European countries the roots are roasted and ground as an odd substitute for coffee.

Juvenile Dandelions are eaten, after careful and

rapid washing, raw in salads, with just a light vinaigrette dressing. They are also made into refreshing
soups, popular in parts of Europe and in the Orient;
boiled or steamed in various fashions as a savory potherb; and incorporated into such culinary delights as
fritters, omelets, and even a piquant quiche. And of
course we must not forget the ever-popular wine made
from this adaptable, delectable weed.

Dandelion Soup Chinoise
Serves 4.

> 2 *bunches dandelion greens*
> 6 *cups strained rich chicken stock*
> 2 *teaspoons peanut or soy oil*
> ½ *pound lean pork, slivered*
> ½ *cup cooked, drained Shirataki (cellophane noodles)*
> *(pages 49, 66)*
> 1 *to 2 tablespoons soy sauce*

Trim off any coarse parts at the base of the dandelion leaves, wash leaves well, and pat dry. Coarsely
chop the greens, and add them to the chicken stock in
a kettle, cover, and let simmer. Heat the oil in a small
skillet and sauté the pork slivers, stirring often, until
they are well browned. Remove pork with slotted
spoon and add to the soup, again covering. When the
dandelions are just tender yet still retain some slight
firmness of texture, add the shirataki and soy sauce.
Heat through and serve while very hot.

A FAVORITE way with dandelions is found in the
following old-timey recipe. Serve the greens with boiled
potatoes and thick slices of Canadian bacon sautéed
in a bit of butter until slightly crisp at the edges.

Dandelions Yankee Style
Serves 4.

> 2 *bunches dandelion greens*
> *salted boiling water*
> ¼ *pound lean salt pork, diced*
> ½ *cup coarsely chopped onion*

Trim off any coarse parts at the base of the dandelion leaves, wash leaves well, and tear into sizable
pieces if necessary. In a commodious kettle with
cover, bring about ½ cup of salted water to the boil.
Add the greens, the salt-pork dice, and the chopped
onion, cover, and cook over rather high heat, stirring
occasionally, until the dandelions are tender, but not
overly so. Drain and serve while hot with butter and
seasonings to individual taste. If desired, vinegar can
be offered on the side.

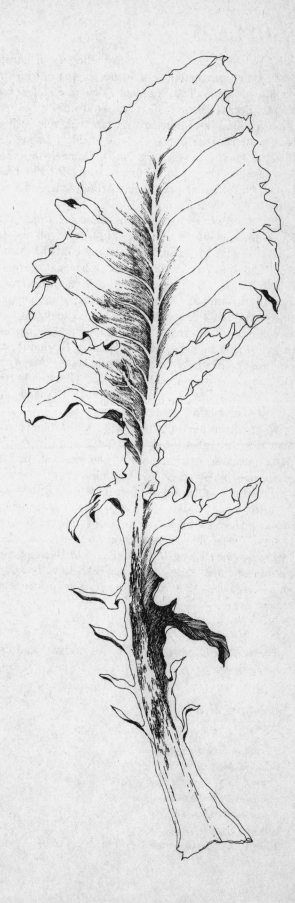

EGGPLANT

Certain vegetables have, through the years, gained positions of particular prominence in the cuisines of certain countries. The Eggplant (*Solanum Melongina*, of the Potato-Tomato Family) is definitely one of these. We find this highly utilitarian vegetable—which is, of course, actually a fruit—very widely favored in the cookery of Near Eastern lands, France, Italy, and Greece. It also comes to the fore in India, the Far East, Indonesia (where it presumably originated, eons ago), and the American tropics.

Because of its tropical origin, commercial plantings of Eggplant—an attractive, big-leaved plant—are most extensive in warm areas; in the United States it is grown especially in Florida and other states around the Gulf Coast. There are selected horticultural variants to be found in markets today, including elongate "serpent"-fruited, dwarf, and white-skinned.

Well-known alternate vernaculars for this interesting vegetable include Guinea Squash (England), *aubergine* (France), *batinjan* (Arabic lands), *berenjena* (Spanish-speaking areas), *berinjela* (Portugal, Brazil), *ai-kwa* (China), *nanbu-naga nasu* (Japan), and *terong* (Indonesia).

When choosing Eggplant (the vegetable is now available throughout the year) for most culinary purposes purchase two or more of the smallest, firmest, most unwrinkled ones you can find, rather than a single large one. If you are fortunate enough to reside in an area that boasts some good Oriental gardeners, acquire from them a batch of the delectable little "baby" vegetables, measuring only two or three inches in overall length. No matter how these are prepared—and the Eggplant is an exceptionally adaptable vegetable—they are a superlative gastronomic experience.

To COMMENCE with, consider this unusual and delicious hors d'oeuvre.

Eggplant Maria
Serves quite a lot.

2 small or 1 medium eggplants
salt and pepper
flour
oil or lard for deep-frying
1 cup mashed potato
salt and pepper
1 large clove garlic, mashed
wine vinegar
olive oil

Peel eggplants and slice into long fingers. Season with salt and pepper, roll in flour, then deep-fry until fingers are nicely crisp. Drain on absorbent paper towels. In an attractive serving bowl, combine the mashed potato with salt and pepper to taste, the garlic, and enough wine vinegar and olive oil to make a mixture of easy dip consistency. Serve with the crisp eggplant sticks.

FOR A very hearty vegetable casserole, I recommend highly the following, which evolved some years back in my own kitchen. Like most culinary accomplishments, it owes certain of its basic origins to a dish from elsewhere—in this case Lebanon. Hence I have named it for the fabled ancient city of Baalbek. The recipe initially appeared in the pages of *Gourmet*.

Eggplant Baalbek
Serves 6.

2 small eggplants, peeled, cut into ½-inch cubes
2 medium onions, chopped
½ medium green pepper, chopped
⅛ teaspoon garlic powder
3 tablespoons olive oil
2 medium tomatoes, diced
2 teaspoons salt
1 teaspoon black pepper
1 8-ounce can tomato sauce
1 cup grated sharp cheese
1 egg, beaten
½ cup whole milk
¼ cup minced fresh parsley
2 tablespoons butter

In a large skillet, sauté the onions and green pepper in oil with garlic powder for 5 minutes, stirring constantly. Lower heat and add eggplant cubes, simmer for 10 minutes, stirring often. Add tomatoes, salt, and pepper, and simmer for 5 minutes more, stirring occasionally. Add tomato sauce, and mix well. Butter a 2-quart casserole and place the vegetable mixture in it. Mix together the cheese, egg, milk, and parsley, and pour it over the eggplant mixture. Dot with butter and bake in a preheated 350° F. oven for 30 minutes.

ONE of my favorite easy and showy entrées for a special dinner party is the following recipe from the banks of the Bosporus. With it I like to serve a rice pilaf or risotto and a fresh spinach salad, plus coffee

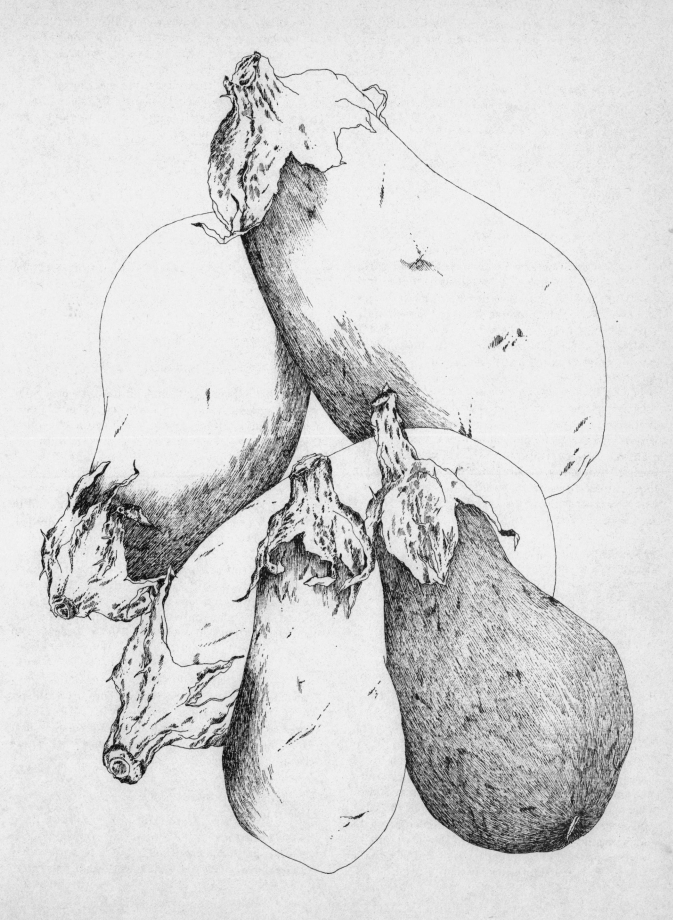

and a very light dessert, such as a fruit sherbet. A bottle of dry red wine makes an admirable accompaniment to the meal.

Turkish Eggplant Skewers
Serves 4 to 6.

2 *small eggplants, unpeeled, in big cubes*
1½ *pounds beef or lamb, in big cubes*
2 *semi-ripe large tomatoes, cut into wedges*
½ *cup lemon juice*
½ *cup light olive oil*
⅛ *teaspoon garlic powder*

Using bamboo or metal skewers, thread alternating cubes of eggplant, meat, and tomato onto 10 or 12 10-inch skewers. Combine lemon juice, oil, and garlic powder, and allow to stand for about 1 hour before use. Brush the liquid on the skewered meat and vegetables as they broil, preferably over charcoal, until meat is done to your individual taste; it should, ideally, be rather rare for best results. Season with salt and freshly ground pepper if desired.

GREEK cookery makes marvelous and extensive use of the eggplant. I like this salad in particular. Try it with almost any lamb dish, or with the Turkish Eggplant Skewers described above—for a very eggplanty repast. It also makes a very different ingredient for that antipasto to serve on special occasions—and you will find that it keeps well, refrigerated, for several days, too.

Eggplant Salad Piraeus
Serves 4 to 6.

2 *medium eggplants*
1 *large clove garlic, peeled*
¼ *cup light olive oil*
½ *teaspoon salt*
⅛ *teaspoon freshly ground pepper*
1 *large firm tomato, unpeeled, diced*
2 *tablespoons minced parsley*
2 *tablespoons minced onion*
½ to ¾ *teaspoon oregano*
2 *tablespoons white wine vinegar*

Bake eggplants, unpeeled, in 350° F. oven for 1 hour. Cool, peel, and dice. Rub a bowl, preferably wooden, with the cut clove of garlic, and discard garlic after use. Put olive oil, salt, and pepper in the bowl, and combine thoroughly. Combine eggplant, tomato, parsley, onion, and oregano in the salad bowl, mixing well but gently. Pour vinegar over all and mix again. Chill for at least 1 hour before serving.

EGGPLANT stuffed with a succulent mixture of ground beef, parsley, mint, and other good things creates an exceptionally tasty dish, one which is found in various forms throughout the Near and Middle Eastern countries. It is virtually a meal in one dish, and can be happily accompanied by Cucumber Raita (page 100). If the small eggplants are available, use them in this recipe, please.

Stuffed Eggplant à la Paul
Serves 6 to 8.

6 *small eggplants*
salt and black pepper
¾ *cup finely chopped onion*
½ *cup olive oil*
2 *pounds lean ground beef*
2 *tablespoons minced fresh parsley*
1 *teaspoon crushed dried mint leaves*
1 *28-ounce can Italian-style tomatoes*
1 *4-ounce can mushroom stems and pieces, drained, chopped*
½ *cup freshly grated Parmesan cheese*

Trim stems from eggplants and halve them lengthwise. Scoop out the pulp, to leave a shell about ½ inch thick. Sprinkle rather liberally with salt and pepper. Chop the eggplant pulp and combine it with the onion; sauté in olive oil until just soft but not browned (usually about 15 minutes), stirring often. Remove vegetables from skillet with slotted spoon and reserve them. Add the ground beef to remaining oil in skillet and cook until meat becomes faintly browned. Return cooked eggplant pulp and onion, plus parsley, mint, tomatoes (these broken up), and mushrooms. Season with salt and pepper. Place eggplant shells in a baking dish and fill each one with the meat-vegetable mixture. Pour any remaining mixture in pan around the eggplant halves. Sprinkle the grated cheese over all, and bake in preheated 350° F. oven for 40 minutes.

INDONESIANS are inordinately fond of eggplant, which they call *terong*. The following dish can be served as is, with rice and a salad on the side, or it can form one of the myriad parts of the elaborate Rijstafel (rice table).

Eggplant Padang
Serves 4 to 6.

4 *small eggplants*
2 *tablespoons peanut or soy oil*
1 *large onion, sliced thin*

1 *small clove garlic, sliced thin*
1 *cup diced cooked shrimp*
¼ *cup warm water*
½ *teaspoon salt*
⅛ *teaspoon fresh-ground black pepper*
dash or two Tabasco sauce

Cut washed, unpeeled eggplants into ½-inch cubes. Heat oil in a heavy skillet with cover and sauté onion and garlic slices for 2 minutes, stirring often and with care. Add all other ingredients, mix well, cover, and cook over low heat for 10 minutes. Serve at room temperature.

CHICKEN and eggplant? It may sound a bit unusual, but I hope you will try this luscious concoction. With a light salad and simple dessert and a bottle of chilled dry white wine, it forms a pleasing meal.

Chicken-Eggplant Casserole
Serves 4 to 6.

2 *small eggplants, peeled, diced*
3-*pound broiler-fryer chicken, disjointed*
1 *teaspoon salt*
¼ *teaspoon freshly ground pepper*
4 *tablespoons butter*
1 *teaspoon salt*
¼ *teaspoon freshly ground pepper*
⅓ *cup flour*
4 *tablespoons olive oil*
1 *cup chopped onions*
⅛ *teaspoon garlic powder*
⅛ *teaspoon ground thyme*
2 *cups rich chicken broth or bouillon*
½ *cup sliced stuffed green olives*

Season the chicken with salt and pepper, then brown in the melted butter in a large ovenproof casserole. After chicken pieces are browned (in this case, use the giblets for something else), cover and simmer over very low heat for 20 minutes. Season the diced eggplant with salt and pepper, then dip into the flour, reserving any of latter remaining. In another heavy skillet, brown the eggplant cubes in the oil. Remove these with a slotted spoon. Add onions and garlic powder (or equivalent of fresh chopped or mashed garlic) to oil in skillet, and cook over medium heat for 5 or 6 minutes, stirring often. Carefully stir in the reserved flour plus the thyme, and blend so that no lumps remain. Add the chicken broth or bouillon, and continue to stir over higher heat until the mixture comes just to the boil. Remove from the heat and add the cooked eggplant dice and sliced olives. Pour over

the chicken in the casserole and bake in a preheated 375° F. oven, uncovered, for 30 minutes, or until chicken is tender.

EGGPLANT Parmigiana is a standby in many Italian restaurants, but all too frequently I have found it to be rather bland for my taste. The following recipe, however, easily solves that problem.

Eggplant Parmigiana Eduardo
Serves 4 to 6.

2 *small eggplants*
salt and pepper
flour
¼ *pound (1 stick) butter*
Rigatoni Speziale Sauce (recipe below)
½ *cup freshly grated Parmesan or Romano cheese*
¼ *pound mozzarella cheese, thin-sliced*

Wash eggplant, and slice crosswise into ¼-inch-thick slices. Dredge in salt and pepper combined with flour. In a large heavy skillet, sauté the eggplant slices in the melted butter until nicely browned on both sides. Remove carefully with slotted spatula and drain on paper towels. Butter a shallow baking dish or casserole of at least 2-quart capacity. In this, alternate slices of sautéed eggplant with Rigatoni Speziale Sauce and sprinkling of grated Parmesan or Romano. Top casserole with a layer of sauce, then grated Parmesan or Romano, and finally slices of mozzarella. Bake casserole in preheated 350° F. oven for 30 minutes, or until eggplant is tender and mozzarella has melted. Serve at once.

Rigatoni Speziale Sauce
Serves 6.

3 *tablespoons butter*
2 *tablespoons light olive oil*
2 *large onions, coarsely chopped*
1 *medium green pepper, coarsely chopped*
1 *large clove garlic, minced or mashed*
3 *large stalks celery, coarsely chopped*
1½ *pounds lean ground beef*
1 6-*ounce can tomato paste*
1 8-*ounce can tomato sauce*
1 1-*pound can Italian-style tomatoes*
½ *teaspoon salt*
½ *teaspoon black pepper*
½ *teaspoon oregano*
¼ *teaspoon mixed herbs*
3 *tablespoons minced fresh parsley*
1 *tablespoon sugar*

In a large heavy skillet, slowly sauté the onions, green pepper, garlic, and celery in the butter and oil until all are limp but not browned. Remove cooked vegetables with slotted spoon, crumble in the beef, and cook, stirring often, until it is browned. Return the cooked vegetables to the skillet and mix well. Combine the tomato paste with an equal amount of warm water, mix well, and gradually stir into the skillet. Gradually add the tomato sauce and the canned tomatoes with their juice, breaking them up with a fork plus seasonings, parsley, and sugar. Mix thoroughly, and simmer over very low heat for at least 1 hour, stirring often.

This sauce is better when reheated a second day, and it freezes very well, too!

RATATOUILLE (pronounced rat-ah-*too*-ee) is a classic version of eggplant, along with other ingredients, from southern France. This recipe is one I have enjoyed in the past in Marseilles, and I suspect you will wish to add it to your regular roster of vegetable dishes, to be served either hot or cold, with almost everything from chicken or duck to beef or lamb.

Ratatouille
Serves 4 to 6.

2 *cups peeled eggplant, in ½-inch cubes*
2 *cups yellow crookneck summer squash, in ½-inch cubes*
1½ *teaspoons salt*
3 *large cloves garlic, mashed or minced*
⅓ *cup olive oil*
½ *teaspoon oregano*
3 *medium onions, thinly sliced*
2 *medium green peppers, cut into thin strips*
½ *teaspoon dried marjoram*
4 *medium firm-ripe tomatoes, peeled, thinly sliced*
¼ *teaspoon dill seeds*

Butter a 2½-quart casserole and cover bottom with cubes of unpeeled squash. Sprinkle with ⅓ of the salt, garlic, and oil. Make second layer with eggplant cubes, repeat with sprinkle of ⅓ more of salt, garlic, and oil, adding the oregano. Make third layer of onion slices, then fourth layer with green pepper strips. Sprinkle with remaining salt, garlic, and oil, and add marjoram. Cover casserole and bake in preheated 350° F. oven for about 45 minutes. Add layer of tomato slices, sprinkle with dill seeds, and bake uncovered at same temperature for 10 minutes. Serve hot or chilled.

EGGPLANT figures prominently in many dishes in the American tropics. Here is an unusual fritter which I like to serve with pork especially, though it does very well with almost any other meat from lamb to beef or fowl.

Eggplant Fritters Mayagüez
Makes about 1 dozen.

3 *small eggplants, peeled, sliced*
½ *cup flour*
½ *teaspoon salt*
⅛ *teaspoon nutmeg*
¼ *cup freshly grated Parmesan cheese*
3 *tablespoons butter*
⅔ *cup fine cracker crumbs*
2 *eggs*
¼ *teaspoon salt*
⅛ *teaspoon freshly ground pepper*
1 *pound (2 cups) lard*

Peel eggplant and boil in heavily salted water just to cover for 30 minutes. Drain thoroughly and place in a large bowl. Mash eggplant. Add the flour, the ½ teaspoon salt, nutmeg, and Parmesan, mixing well. Melt the butter in a skillet, and add the eggplant mixture. Cook over low heat for 5 minutes, stirring constantly. Remove from heat and allow to cool. Take tablespoonfuls of eggplant mixture, form into balls, and roll them in the cracker crumbs. Roll fritters in eggs which are just broken with a fork but not beaten, to which you have added the ¼ teaspoon salt and the black pepper. Roll again in cracker crumbs. Heat the lard (do not use anything else for this recipe!) to 380° F., and fry fritters 2 or 3 at a time until just golden brown. Drain on absorbent paper towels and serve while nice and hot.

NEXT time you have a bang-up curry dinner, consider offering the participants the following excellent dish.

Eggplant Curry Guru
Serves 4.

3 *cups peeled, diced eggplant*
2 *teaspoons salt*
4 *tablespoons butter*
1 *cup minced onion*
1 *medium clove garlic, minced*
½ *teaspoon ground turmeric*
⅛ *teaspoon ground cumin*
⅛ *to ¼ teaspoon crushed dried red peppers*
⅓ *cup chopped pimientos*

In a skillet with cover, sauté the salted eggplant in

the butter until it is just barely tender. Remove eggplant with slotted spoon and keep warm. Add the onion and seasonings and cook, stirring often, until the onion is just golden, yet still retains some texture. Return the eggplant to the skillet, add the pimientos, mix well, and heat through. Serve hot or at room temperature.

ENDIVE

In Endive we encounter one of those extraordinary examples of nomenclatural confusion that abound in the plants man utilizes as vegetables. Botanically, Endive is *Cichorium Endivia*, an annual or perennial species of the diverse and important Daisy Family, probably originally from India, where it has long been cultivated.

In this country, one is apt to encounter the somewhat open curled leaf bunches of Chicory (another member of the same genus; see page 90) sold as Endive or Curly Endive. Then we have Endive Hearts, alias Belgian Endive, which are usually the artificially bleached centers of our present plant—but which may instead be those of chicory! And finally, to compound the muddle, we encounter Escarole, scientifically the same thing as Endive, of which it is a broad-leaved variety (see page 110).

In recent times past, Leafy Endive was a favorite kitchen-garden vegetable in some parts of our Northeastern states. When the attractive full plants approached maturity, the frilly outer leaves were tied up to enclose the heart, which thereupon became blanched to a wonderful pristine white color and possessed a notable delicacy of flavor. The outer greens, still rather bitter, were either dispensed to the chickens or rabbits or cooked for the human fans of the vegetable.

True Leafy Endive is occasionally to be found in markets today and is an excellent salad green, with a pleasant pungency reminiscent of good dandelions. It is often mixed with other, less positively flavored examples of edible greenery in tossed salads. I also like it coarsely chopped and plunged into boiling salted water (after thorough rinsing to remove sand), to cook until just barely tender, then served with butter, salt and freshly ground pepper, and perhaps a light sprinkling of grated Parmesan cheese.

Compact Endive Hearts (sometimes sold simply, and again confusingly, as Endives!) are today to be encountered in many of our good produce markets. They are imported, by and large, from Belgium, and are generally rather expensive. When the budget permits their purchase, be sure that the hearts are firm, palest yellow-and-white in color, and without blemish. Keep them tightly wrapped in wax paper or foil under refrigeration until preparation, and utilize them as quickly as possible.

IN MANY establishments, a salad of rinsed, chilled, raw Endive Hearts with a vinaigrette dressing is considered the absolute acme of *haute cuisine*. Those who object to the bitterness of the uncooked vegetable may find Endive Hearts palatable when simmered in stock,

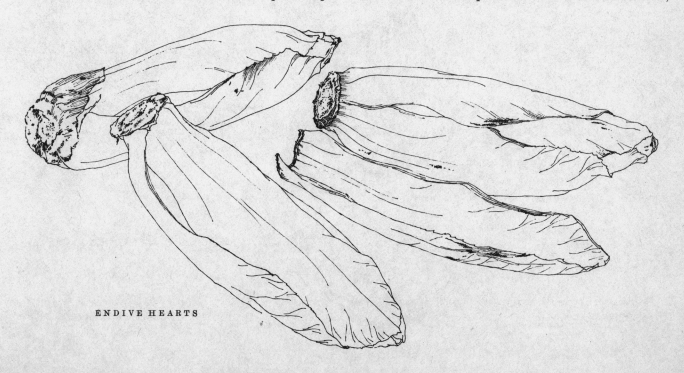

ENDIVE HEARTS

a favorite French method. The result is excellent with poultry or veal.

Endive Hearts Françoise
Serves 4.

8 *firm fresh endive hearts*
⅓ *cup butter*
½ *teaspoon salt*
½ *cup rich chicken stock*

Rinse the endive hearts, discarding any wilted leaves. Place in a heavy saucepan with cover, preferably an enamelware or earthenware one, dot with butter, sprinkle with salt, and pour the rich stock over. Cover and bring quickly to the boil. Reduce heat and continue to cook for about 30 minutes, or until the hearts are tender.

Beef stock may also be used for this recipe with, of course, different final results. On especially festive occasions, the cooked endive hearts are dressed with such sauces as Mornay or Béchamel.

ESCAROLE

Interestingly enough, Escarole and Endive are one and the same plant (*Cichorium Endivia*, of the Daisy Family). However, since their uses in our kitchens are rather different, I consider them separately here.

Escarole is actually a broad-leaved variety of Endive, which is today increasingly cultivated in the United States for sale in our produce markets as a handsome green for salads and specialized cookery. The bunches are usually somewhat flattened, composed of abundant broad, curly-edged green leaves that shade into a more or less bright yellow center and have a faintly bitter flavor and firm texture.

When using this vegetable, be certain to rinse out, very thoroughly, bits of grit which invariably seem to lurk deep inside the bunch. I have never yet encountered a completely clean specimen of Escarole, even in our most elegant stores. Artificially blanched bunches of the vegetable are sometimes found for sale in such establishments and are well worth acquiring.

Do not allow the Escarole leaves to soak for more than thirty minutes or so—flavor can be leached out in this fashion. For better effect, wash them under cold running water.

To use in a salad, tear into bite-size pieces, discarding any coarse midribs, wash thoroughly, pat dry, and roll up in a clean kitchen towel to chill for at least 1 hour. After removing from the refrigerator, serve without delay, dressed with your favorite oil-and-vinegar mixture.

This vegetable, chopped and boiled in lightly salted water until tender, is made into an interesting soufflé

or timbale. Or in this state it can be dressed with butter and suitable seasonings as a fine hot dish. Or the entire bunches, cleaned and drained, can be braised in the manner suggested for Celery (page 84), and perhaps anointed with a light cream sauce or even a cheese sauce.

AND THEN, consider if you will, a perfectly wonderful Escarole soup. This soup, from the glorious Lake District of northern Italy, is appropriate to commence many a menu, though I find it especially desirable when followed by veal in some form.

Escarole Soup Lake Como
Serves 4 to 6 liberally.

1 *large bunch escarole*
¾ *cup diced salt pork*
1½ *cups chopped onions*
2 *tablespoons flour*
2 *teaspoons salt*
½ *teaspoon freshly ground pepper*
2 *quarts rich chicken stock*
½ *cup raw rice, Italian preferred*
2 *cups crisp croutons*

In a skillet, cook the salt-pork dice until lightly browned. Add the onions and cook them, stirring often, until they are soft but not browned. Thoroughly mix in the flour, blending until smooth. Meanwhile bring the rich chicken stock (fresh preferred) to the boil. Turn in the onions and salt pork from the skillet, and add the rice (the short-grain or round variety imported from Italy is preferable here, if only for authenticity). Reduce heat, cover, and simmer until the rice is tender. Wash the escarole very thoroughly, shred it, and add to the soup for the last 5 minutes' cooking time. Serve without delay (the vegetable should retain considerable texture), each portion topped with crisp croutons.

FENNEL

Two kinds of Fennel occupy a special place in our kitchens. The Common Fennel (*Foeniculum vulgare*, of the Carrot Family), originally from southern Europe, is grown for its feathery leaves—these used as a

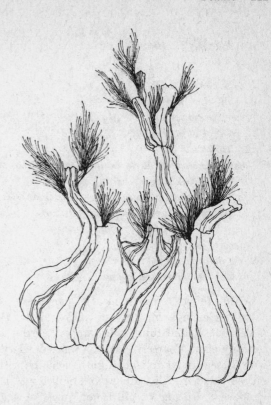

seasoning with such things as beans, lentils, and rice, and for its very aromatic seeds, which are incorporated into such diverse things as apple pie, eggplant, cabbage and its myriad relations, and peas.

The Florence, Roman, or Sweet Fennel (*Foeniculum vulgare* var. *dulce*) is a very distinctive vegetable, one more important to our notice at this point. It is extremely popular in Italy, somewhat so elsewhere around the Mediterranean, and is today increasingly found in our larger American markets.

This Florence Fennel is a member of the same amazingly diverse family as carrot, parsnip, and parsley. Like many of its relatives, it has attractive, highly dissected leaves; in this species the leaves surmount conspicuously thickened stalks that form a bulblike structure. This bulb is borne above the ground, and sometimes measures three to six inches in overall length. The foliage is commonly chopped and sprinkled in green salads, and the thick stalks form an attractive and unusual vegetable that can be served in a number of different tasty fashions. Vaguely like celery in texture and appearance, it possesses a definite flavor of anise.

FROM Naples to Sicily, in particular, *finocchio* is served with great frequency. Italians from these regions are particularly fond of it when chilled in salads, either raw or briefly blanched. Here is one such, very hearty and very flavorful.

Fennel Salad Cassio
Serves 4 to 6.

1 *large bunch fennel*
2 *small celery hearts*
½ *small green pepper, coarsely chopped*
12 *artichoke hearts in olive oil, drained*
12 *pitted black olives*
1 *small can anchovy fillets, drained, coarsely chopped*
2 *or 3 hard-cooked eggs, coarsely chopped*
4 *to 8 slices hard Italian salami, cut into thin strips*
½ *cup coarsely chopped scallions, with tops*
¼ *cup light olive oil*
½ *lemon, juiced*
2 *to 3 tablespoons red wine vinegar*
salt and freshly ground pepper

Wash fennel, remove leafy portions (coarsely chopping enough of these to afford about 1½ to 2 tablespoons), and thinly slice stalks lengthwise, then coarsely chop. Coarsely chop the washed celery hearts with some of their foliage. Lightly combine with listed ingredients through scallions and chill for 30 minutes. Prepare a dressing of oil, lemon juice, vinegar, plus salt and pepper to taste. At serving time, pour this over salad, toss lightly but thoroughly, and serve at once.

OR THE fennel stalks are pulled apart from the bulb, washed, peeled if deemed necessary, and cut into sizable slices, usually transversely. These sections are cooked in lightly salted boiling water for just long enough to make them somewhat tender, yet still crisp, and are thoroughly drained. Drained and chilled, these flavorful bits are combined with coarsely chopped lettuce and diced tomatoes and with some of the fresh feathery leaves, chopped, and are served with a good hearty oil-and-vinegar dressing.

Still another favored combination is chilled cooked (or raw) fennel with tomato wedges, crisped chicory, and pitted ripe olives—these customarily sliced—dressed with a garlicky vinaigrette mixture, to which a modicum of chopped fennel foliage has been added.

The blanched fennel stalks, drained and still hot from the pot, can be served with heated light olive oil or butter, or a combination of both, plus salt and pepper to taste. A pinch of dry mustard stirred into the sauce adds a pleasant touch.

Braised fennel is a fortuitous version of this vegetable, notably appropriate with pasta or risotto dishes, and such divergent meats as roast veal, meat balls, or broiled chicken. Prepare as for Braised Celery (page 84), and if desired add a light cream sauce to heat through prior to serving.

The finely chopped leaves of fennel can be added to butter for snails and to fish, and are often added to a court-bouillon for seafood.

Then there is a famous Provençal dish, *grillade au fenouil*, wherein a suitable fish, usually a sea bass or mullet, is cleaned, rubbed with light olive oil, and laid on an oven rack. A sizable bunch of dried fennel stalks is placed in a pan underneath it, and the fish is broiled, turning as necessary. When the fish flakes easily, the fennel stalks are removed to a heatproof serving dish, the fish laid upon them, and warmed brandy or Armagnac poured over all. This is set afire, and as the fennel burns it gives a particular flavor to the fish, which is thereupon devoured without delay.

TRADITIONALLY served on St. Joseph's Day in Italy is the following dish, in which *finocchio* figures prominently.

Fennel with Spaghetti
Serves 6.

1 *large bunch fennel with tops, finely chopped*
½ *teaspoon fennel seed*
4 *tablespoons olive oil*
¾ *cup chopped onion*
2 *cloves garlic, chopped*
2 *6-ounce cans anchovy fillets in oil*
1 *6-ounce can tomato paste*
1 *8-ounce can tomato sauce*
4 *cups water*
2 *tablespoons pine nuts* (pignoli)
2 *tablespoons seedless raisins*
¼ *teaspoon oregano*
¼ *teaspoon freshly ground pepper*
2 *cups hot toasted coarse bread crumbs*
1 *pound spaghetti, cooked* al dente

In the oil, sauté the onion and garlic, stirring often, until they are lightly browned. Coarsely chop the undrained anchovies and stir them into the oil and vegetables. Gradually add the tomato paste and tomato sauce, plus the water. Mix well, cover, and simmer for 15 minutes. Then add the chopped fennel, fennel seed, pine nuts, raisins, oregano, and pepper, mix well, cover again, and simmer over very low heat for about 1 hour—the sauce should be rather smooth. At serving time, lightly toss the hot drained spaghetti with half the fennel sauce and half the hot toasted bread crumbs. Offer remaining bread crumbs and sauce, each in a separate dish, to be added to individual taste.

FERNS

Of the many thousands of ferns known to man, a number are used as vegetables. Apparently without exception these are uncultivated, and their availability in markets therefore depends upon their collection from the moist forests in which these stately, ancient plants thrive.

Since the mature fronds of most ferns with edible properties are very coarse and fibrous in texture, for culinary purposes we pay attention to the young "sprouting" leaves, usually known by their French name of crosier. In this country, the best known of these is the aptly named Fiddlehead, the crosier of the handsome Ostrich Fern (*Matteuccia Struthiopteris*), widespread in the eastern United States, Europe, and parts of temperate Asia. These are particularly abundant in the region I come from, Houlton, Maine—which can well lay claim to being the "Fiddlehead Capital of the World." The tightly curled sprouts are picked, reverently, when about two inches long, during the earliest springtime, then rinsed and plunged into a quantity of boiling salted water. When tender (the time varies with the degree of development of the crosier), they are served at once—always as a special, separate course—with butter, salt and pepper to taste, and if desired a touch of cider vinegar. So prepared, this extraordinary delicacy retains its pleasantly crunchy texture and all of its flavor, which has been called "a happy combination of artichokes, asparagus, and mushrooms," but which to all of us aficionados tastes like nothing in the world but fabulous Fiddleheads.

Non-purists have in recent years made these fern sprouts available in cans, and I must recommend these if the fresh creature is unobtainable. And others advocate sautéing the crosiers, after an initial brief blanching in salted boiling water, in butter, with lemon juice and seasonings to be added to taste. And still others even go so far as to urge dipping them into a batter for deep-frying. Fortunately, the freshly plucked Fiddleheads are sometimes to be found these days in select Northern markets during their brief season of perfection, and they can of course be prepared in any manner one wishes.

In some of our Northern states, other kinds of fern crosiers appear in small quantities in select shops, also generally during the early spring months. These include the juvenile growths of the Bracken Fern or Brake (*Pteridium aquilinum*), found virtually everywhere in the temperate zones, and to be found in markets in Hawaii and California under its Chinese name of *kuet* or its Japanese one of *warabi*. These are rather strong-flavored, heavy-textured ferns, which usually require two changes of cooking water to make them palatable. They can be baked, after initial blanching, in a cream sauce, the casserole sprinkled with a delicate cheese, if desired.

The Osmunda Ferns, also widespread in the northern hemisphere, are justly popular in Japan and to a lesser degree in our Northern states, the very young crosiers being scraped of their heavy furry covering, then cooked until tender, to be served with butter and suitable seasonings. The small, compact sprouts are imported in cans from Japan, under the name of *zenmai*, and are well worthy of trial.

In different parts of the globe, the very young fronds of several other kinds of Ferns are eaten. In the tropics, where spectacular large tree ferns often abound in montane areas, the huge crosiers sometimes figure in the indigenous diet. These, sometimes eight inches in length, are scraped of their copious scaly covering—the scales are much like sawdust and have the same texture and flavor—and split lengthwise, then cut into suitable sections. In most cases, cooking in two changes of salted water is suggested, and rather protracted boiling is necessary to make them tender. These still usually retain a slight bitterness, which I have found refreshing—I even accentuate it by judicious addition of a few drops of lime juice, with the seasoned butter sauce that customarily accompanies them. These parboiled sections of giant tree-fern crosiers can also be added to soups or simmered, in the Hawaiian style, in a rich beef stock, with the addition of 1 tablespoon sugar, and touch of soy sauce.

FLOWERS, EDIBLE

The flowers of several kinds of plants are eaten as vegetables. We might think of Pumpkin or other Squash blossoms (page 191), delectable when quickly fried, or Nasturtium blooms (page 156) sprinkled over a summertime salad. But there are dozens of others, mostly of regional importance, and of decidedly various flavors.

In our American Southwest, for instance, a casual delicacy is the quick-sautéed flowers of several kinds of native Yuccas, or Spanish Bayonets (of the Lily Family, and not to be confused with *yuca*, the Tapioca plant, page 76). I have enjoyed these Yuccas on several occasions while botanizing and eating my way through Mexico, where these spectacular plants abound in great variety. Often the floral buds contain the tiny grub of a specialized wasp which has deposited her egg there (and conveniently pollinated the *Yucca* flower), so that one has the rather grim prospect of eating both meat and vegetable in one and the same bite. The rinsed petals of certain of these showy blossoms are also added to raw salads, usually dressed with a vinaigrette sauce.

In India, Ceylon, and other parts of the globe where curries are integral parts of the daily diet, certain specialized plant parts are commonly incorporated into these dishes. Elsewhere in this volume, under the category Curry Vegetables (page 102), I have mentioned several of these.

Consider, too, the Indian Butter-Tree, also known as the *illipi* or *mahwa* or *mee* (*Bassia latifolia* and *B. longifolia*, of the Sapote Family), whose fleshy white petals are eaten fresh or, more frequently, dried, in tremendous quantities. In India alone, for instance, it is estimated that annually some 25,000 *tons* of these blossoms are gathered for such unique culinary attention.

The widely cultivated tropical Red Silk-Cotton Tree (*Bombax malabaricum*, of the Kapok Family) has magnificent heavy flowers several inches across of an incredible vivid scarlet hue. The fleshy calyxes are avidly collected after the petals have fallen and are added to quick-cooked curries and such things. The petals, too, are edible, and on several occasions I have relished them here in South Florida, from neighbors' trees, quick-fried in butter after dipping in a very light batter.

Several of the glorious and myriad species of Coral Trees or Immortelles (genus *Erythrina*, of the Legume Family) have flowers with heavy, orange or scarlet petals that are eaten after being dipped in batter, then crisp-fried in butter. (Please note that the flowers of other members of this genus are *not* edible!)

And then we have the extraordinary Agati (*Agati* or *Sesbania grandiflora*, again of the Legume Family). This delightful small spreading tree bears, in its season, a grand profusion of hanging, proportionately huge fleshy flowers, white or reddish in color, the petals of which are delicious when quickly sautéed in butter, preferably with a seasoning of one or two of the tiniest new leaves. Long cultivated in India and Ceylon, where it is known by the euphonious name of *katuru-murunga*, it has been grown in increasing numbers in recent years in Florida, Hawaii, and other warm parts of this country as a prized ornamental. The flavor is relatively bland, but to offer to guests the sautéed flowers hot from the wok or skillet or to sprinkle some of the fresh petals into a bowl of hot clear broth at the last moment is a most pleasant culinary triumph.

GARBANZO

The Garbanzo or Chick-Pea (*Cicer arietinum,* of the Legume Family) is a widely cultivated legume of notable prominence in the excellent cuisine of such areas as the Mediterranean, Asia, and in Mexico and many other parts of Spanish-speaking America. It has been grown since the times of antiquity. The fresh peas are eaten raw as they come from the pod, or are roasted, while the dried ones appear in a wide array of recipes, from hearty soups and stews to salads and even, in sugary syrups, as confections. Ground, they form a flour of some importance, and with prior toasting the ground peas are a sort of substitute for coffee.

There are several distinct varieties, with white, black, and even red peas. The white ones are those most commonly encountered in this country, these usually dried or cooked and canned. In many lands the Garbanzo is probably the most important protein food, hence its cultivation in these days of population explosion is being augmented to a marked degree.

For the average recipe the inexpensive canned Garbanzos are perhaps to be preferred. The dried ones require very lengthy cooking—literally hours and hours in most instances.

To commence with, here is an unusual hors d'oeuvre utilizing these nutty-flavored peas; it comes from Italy, where the legumes are known as *ceci.* The appetizer is pronounced chay-chee-*lee*-na.

Cecilina
Makes a lot.

1 1-*pound can garbanzos*
3 *tablespoons butter*
1 *cup minced onion*

2 *tablespoons minced parsley*
3 *tablespoons coarsely chopped pine nuts* (pignoli)
½ *teaspoon oregano*
few drops Tabasco sauce
2 *tablespoons toasted sesame seeds*

Drain the garbanzos and rinse well under running cold water, then drain thoroughly again. Purée peas in blender or food mill. Melt butter in a smallish skillet and cook onion until transparent. Add onion to purée with all other ingredients except sesame seeds. Mix well, turn into a serving bowl, cover, and chill. Sprinkle with toasted sesame seeds before serving as an appetizer dip with corn chips or pieces of crisp fried tortillas.

IN THE Arab lands, Garbanzos are known as *hommos* or *hummus.* They are very important in the marvelous cuisines of such countries as Syria and Lebanon and Egypt, where one of the special delights made with this lusty legume is the smooth paste called *hommos tahini.* I often offer this in my time-consuming but tasty homemade version with cocktails, accompanied by the crisp sesame-seed crackers and the good puffy Arab bread now available in many of our markets. There is, incidentally, a very good commercial form of this garbanzo dip in choice stores now, imported from Syria.

Garbanzo Dip
Makes a lot.

1 *pound dried garbanzos*
2 *medium or large cloves garlic, mashed*
¼ *cup lemon juice*
¼ *cup light olive or salad oil*
¼ *cup warm water*
1 *tablespoon chopped parsley*

Rinse and pick over the garbanzos and place them in a large heavy kettle with cover, in water to cover. Bring to the boil, covered, then remove from heat and allow to stand for 1 hour. Return to the heat and cook over moderate heat until very tender, with the garlic (add more if you are a genuine fan!), adding more water as needed. This usually requires 3 or 4 hours' cooking time. When garbanzos are very tender, pick off all hulls, discarding these. Drain thoroughly, add lemon juice, oil, and warm water, and make into a coarse or fine purée in the electric blender. Correct seasoning and serve at room temperature or very slightly chilled, sprinkled with parsley, and if desired with a bit more oil whipped in at the last moment.

A WONDROUS variety of attractive salads can be prepared with the garbanzo. This one, from the northern part of Brazil, is good with such things as broiled steak or pan-fried pork chops. *Luz* means "light" in Portuguese, and I think it is an appropriate epithet here.

Garbanzo Salad Luz
Serves 4 to 6.

1 1-*pound can garbanzos, drained*
⅛ *teaspoon garlic powder*
¼ *cup chopped scallions, with tops*
½ *cup chopped firm-ripe tomato*
¼ *cup minced fresh parsley*
4 *tablespoons light olive oil*
1 *tablespoon wine vinegar*
½ *teaspoon salt*
⅛ *teaspoon freshly ground black pepper*

Combine all ingredients carefully but thoroughly, and marinate for 2 hours at room temperature, stirring often. Then chill for 1 hour before serving.

GARBANZOS combined with such edible delights as avocado and fresh spinach create a stalwart salad, often served at my house at luncheon with a platter of sliced cold roast beef or roast lamb.

Garbanzo Salad Ranchero
Serves 6 to 8.

1 1-*pound can garbanzos*
5 *tablespoons wine vinegar*
¼ *cup salad oil*
½ *teaspoon salt*
¼ *teaspoon paprika*
¼ *teaspoon oregano*
dash Tabasco sauce
dash garlic powder
¼ *cup minced onion*
1 *large bunch fresh spinach*
2 *to 3 cups chilled, cubed avocado*
salt and freshly ground pepper to taste

Drain the can of garbanzos. Place in a saucepan with the vinegar, oil, seasonings, and minced onion. Bring just to the boil, then pour into a large salad bowl and chill for at least 1 hour. Thoroughly wash and drain the spinach, trim off coarse stems, and tear the leaves into big pieces. Pat them dry and chill, wrapped in an impeccably clean towel. At the last minute add the spinach and avocado to the chilled bean mixture and toss lightly but thoroughly. Season

to taste with salt and freshly ground pepper, and
serve without delay.

MARTA is an old and good friend, long resident in
Tegucigalpa, the interesting capital of Honduras, who
is famous for her superb, robust Garbanzo Soup. It is
decidedly a meal in one, to be accompanied by such a
salad as Tomatoes Oregano (page 232), lots of hot
crusty bread, and chilled beer. Consider guava shells
with cubes of cream cheese for a perfect and authentic
dessert.

Marta's Garbanzo Soup
Serves 4 to 6.

2 1-*pound can garbanzos*
2 *small bay leaves*
2 *tablespoons minced fresh parsley*
¾ *cup coarsely chopped onion*
2 *whole cloves*
1½ *cups coarsely chopped onion*
2 *tablespoons light olive oil, Spanish preferred*
2 *cups diced cooked ham*
4 *hard-cooked egg yolks, mashed*
1½ *cups diced raw potato*
1 *teaspoon salt*
½ *teaspoon freshly ground black pepper*
½ *teaspoon chili powder*
⅛ *teaspoon oregano*

In a large heavy kettle with cover, combine undrained cans of garbanzos, with 1 can of water, bay
leaves, parsley, the ¾ cup chopped onion, and the
cloves, and bring to a quick boil. Cover and cook over
medium heat until the garbanzos are very tender,
usually about 30 minutes. In a skillet, sauté the 1½
cups chopped onion in the oil, stirring often, until they
are rather brown. Using a slotted spoon, remove about
half of the garbanzos from the soup kettle and mash
them thoroughly with a fork. Return these to the
kettle, together with the sautéed onions, plus all other
ingredients. Mix thoroughly, cover the kettle again,
and simmer until the potatoes are tender. Serve while
nice and hot.

HERE is another soup, this one a special favorite in
the area stretching from Veracruz to Yucatán. It is
frequently served to precede an entrée of fish or shellfish—ocean-fresh, varied, and delicious in this part of
Mexico—usually with rice and plantains on the side.
Again, beer is the perfect beverage—especially if you
can obtain one of the superb Yucatecan varieties.

Sopa de Campeche
Serves 4 to 6.

2 1-*pound cans garbanzos*
½ *pound lean pork, cubed*
olive oil
¾ *cup chopped onion*
2 *cloves garlic, minced*
1 *can beef consommé*
3 *cups water*
salt and freshly ground pepper
¼ *teaspoon oregano*
tomato wedges

Using a large heavy skillet, sauté the pork cubes in
just a touch of the oil, turning them frequently, until
they are very well browned. Remove with slotted
spoon. Add a bit of olive oil to the pork fat remaining
in the skillet, enough to sauté the onion and garlic
until they are lightly browned. Remove vegetables
with slotted spoon. If necessary add a bit more oil to
the skillet, and in it cook the garbanzos (drained, with
liquid reserved for later use) for about 10 minutes—
the peas should be slightly browned. In a large soup
kettle with cover, combine the pork cubes, onion,
garlic, garbanzos, beef consommé, water, reserved
liquid from garbanzos, liberal amounts of salt and
pepper, plus oregano. Cover, bring to a quick boil,
then reduce heat and simmer for 1 hour, or until meat
is very tender. To serve, place a tomato wedge in each
bowl, and pour the very hot soup over it.

THE NATIONAL dish of Spain is called Olla Podrida
(pronounced *oh*-yah poe-*dree*-da). It is a delectable
assemblage, a sort of boiled dinner, Latin style, with
garbanzos. There exist, as one would expect, dozens of
different recipes for this dish. Here is an authentic
one, which offers a complete meal in one—soup, meat
course, and assortment of vegetables. Accompany this
extravagant repast with good quantities of hot crusty
bread, perhaps a green salad, and a husky red wine.

Olla Podrida
Serves 6 to 8.

2 1-*pound cans garbanzos*
3-*pound stewing chicken, cut into serving pieces*
2½ *quarts water*
salt and freshly ground pepper
1 *large onion, quartered*
2 *large stalks celery, chopped*
3 *tablespoons Spanish olive oil*
1 *pound stew beef, cubed*

1 *pound lamb, cubed*
1½ *cups coarsely chopped onion*
2 *to 3 cloves garlic, minced*
1 *cup chopped green pepper*
½ *teaspoon Annatto (page 16)*
1 *pound smoked ham, cubed*
4 *chorizos (spicy Spanish sausages), sliced*
6 *medium potatoes, peeled, quartered*
½ *small Calabaza (page 67), peeled, in big slices*
12 *small carrots, scraped*
1 *pound fresh string beans, cut into 2-inch lengths*
1 *small firm head cabbage, cut into wedges*
1 *package frozen artichoke hearts, defrosted*

Using your biggest heavy kettle with cover, place the pieces of chicken in cold water, add salt and pepper to taste, the quartered peeled onion, and the celery stalks. Cover kettle and cook over medium heat, skimming off any froth, for 20 minutes. Meanwhile, in a large skillet heat the oil (please use the light Spanish olive oil here), and brown the beef and lamb cubes thoroughly. Remove these with slotted spoon. To the skillet add the onion, garlic, green pepper, and annatto. Cook these, stirring often, until soft and starting to brown. Turn contents of skillet, plus browned beef and lamb, ham, chorizos, and drained garbanzos, into the kettle with the chicken. Mix through, cover again, and cook over low heat for 1 hour. The garbanzos and meats should be very tender when done. Add the potatoes, calabaza (or Hubbard squash, in a pinch), and carrots for last half-hour of cooking. Add string beans, cabbage, and artichoke hearts for last 15 minutes of cooking. To serve, drain off the stock and offer this in soup bowls as a first course, the meats and vegetables, arranged separately, as the entrée.

GARLIC

The Garlic (*Allium sativum*, of the Lily Family) is a close ally of the onion but, as is well known, is a far more potent vegetable. Indigenous to southern Europe, it has been cultivated for centuries for the complex bulb, this made up of several parts or bulbils, commonly called cloves. The skins of these little segments are variously white or dull purplish or tinged with rose.

Though Garlic is cultivated in this country, notably in several of our Southern states, much of the supply found in our markets is imported from Italy or Spain. And even though it figures with singular prominence in the cuisine of those lands, in others—England, for example—it is a distinct rarity, even disliked. I, for one, could not conduct my kitchen in proper fashion

without a ready supply of the fragrant Garlic. I prefer the fresh bulbs, but also keep on hand the excellent commercial garlic powder and garlic salt, both of which are very convenient for certain dishes.

When peeling the cloves, one's hands become impregnated with the pervading, persistent odor. This is easily removed by scrubbing the hands with salt, then washing with liberal quantities of soapy water. I personally do not object in the slightest to the perfume of Garlic, but others may be a bit more fastidious.

There are many tales of the miraculous curative powers of this subterranean lily ally. Hung around the neck, it supposedly wards off the evil eye and head colds. Added in liberal amounts to all items of the diet, it thwarts high blood pressure and asthma, and when eaten raw it is said to cure just about every ill known to man. I have not been able to obtain any serious medical opinion that any of these hypotheses are of more than vague psychological value.

In this volume I categorize Garlic cloves by dimensions. A "large" clove is approximately the size of an unshelled almond (a *large* almond, that is), a "small" clove is about as big as the shelled nut; and a "medium" clove is in betwixt. The cloves will keep, unpeeled, for several months, but the supply should be replaced after that.

Important vernaculars for this vital seasoning vegetable include *ail* (French), *ajo* (Spanish), and *aglio* (Italian).

For the avid Garlic fan, consider the following unique cocktail snack. Cooking the Garlic effectively removes most of the strong flavor, leaving only a nut-like delicacy that many of us find marvelously insidious.

Mexican Garlic

peeled garlic cloves
light olive oil
coarse salt

Peel a considerable number of unblemished garlic cloves. Heat a proportionately large amount of oil and sauté the garlic, turning often, until rather well browned. Drain on paper towels, sprinkle liberally with coarse salt, and serve while warm for nibbling with beer and cocktails. Save the scented oil for use in future cookery.

Though onion soup is commonplace in this country nowadays, the various forms of garlic soup so popular in Mexico, Spain, Portugal, and Italy are seldom encountered. A favorite version of this remarkably subtle delicacy is the following one from the southern part of Italy's "boot."

Italian Garlic Soup
Serves 6 to 8.

8 large cloves garlic, peeled
1 tablespoon olive oil
2 quarts strained chicken broth
salt and freshly ground pepper
pinch thyme
pinch rosemary
½ cup light cream
3 egg yolks, beaten
thick slices Italian bread, toasted
¼ cup freshly grated Parmesan cheese

Mash the garlic and sauté it in the oil until light brown. Meanwhile heat the broth in a suitable kettle with cover. Add the garlic and oil, plus the seasonings. Cover and simmer for 1 hour; then strain, and return to the heat. Add the cream to the egg yolks, then add a bit of the hot broth, and combine thoroughly. Return this to the kettle of broth. Simmer for 5 minutes more, then pour over slices of toast sprinkled with cheese in individual bowls.

Aïoli, from Provence in France, is gaining in popularity in the United States as a special cold sauce to be served with an assortment of diverse edibles—from boiled beef, salt codfish, or cooked snails to chilled boiled shrimp, and such vegetables as artichokes, chilled blanched green beans, raw or cooked cauliflower, cooked tiny new potatoes, crisp-tender carrots, and on and on. One of the most delightful dinner parties I have attended in recent times was, in fact, a very impressive array of such foods, beautifully displayed, with the Aïoli sauce offered in individual bowls, into which each one of us dipped our choice of meats and vegetables. A fine well-chilled rosé wine accompanied this, as did an abundant supply of hot crusty French bread.

It is the sort of festive affair that can readily be emulated at home, as involved as one cares to make it. Unless you are positive of the tastes of your guests, I would suggest using only 2 or 3 large cloves of garlic in the sauce.

Aïoli
Makes about 1¼ cups.

2 to 6 large cloves garlic, peeled
2 egg yolks
1 teaspoon salt
¼ teaspoon freshly ground black pepper
1 cup peanut or soy oil
1 or 2 teaspoons wine vinegar

Thoroughly crush the garlic cloves to paste in a mortar. Turn into a smallish bowl with the egg yolks, salt, and black pepper. Using a whisk or electric mixer at medium speed, beat until thick and lemon-colored. Add ¼ cup of the oil, a drop at a time, continuing to beat after each addition, until thickened. Gradually add half of the wine vinegar, then the remainder of the oil, very slowly, beating all the time. The sauce should be thick, but if desired it can be made a little thinner by adding the rest of the vinegar, gradually. Chill before using.

Another fragrant garlicky sauce is this one from Barcelona, that fantastic city in northeastern Spain. It is especially well suited to service with fowl and seafood. Use a garlic press to simplify preparation.

Sauce Catalane
Makes about 1½ cups.

6 to 12 large cloves garlic, mashed
3 tablespoons diced lean salt pork
½ cup finely chopped onion
1 tablespoon flour
⅓ cup dry white wine

1 *whole lemon, unpeeled, thinly sliced*
⅓ *cup coarsely ground blanched almonds*

In a heavy skillet or saucepan, fry the salt pork until rather crisp, stirring often. Add garlic and onion, and cook, stirring occasionally, until vegetables are soft. Sprinkle with the flour and continue to cook, stirring constantly, for 2 or 3 minutes. Add the wine, mix well, and simmer over low heat for 30 minutes. Stir in ground almonds (perferably done with mortar and pestle), and simmer for 5 minutes more.

PERFECT fresh shrimp broiled over a bed of garlic cloves are a delicacy here in South Florida. The lady who came up with this superlative creation resides in Miami Springs and has long been noted for her inventive cuisine. I like Braised Celery (page 84) as an accompaniment, with either buttered rice or hot crusty French bread.

Carrie's Garlic Shrimp
Serves 4 to 6.

20 *to 25 medium garlic cloves, peeled and sliced*
1 *pound sliced fat bacon, slices cut in half lengthwise*
2 *pounds raw medium shrimp, shelled*

Wrap 1 narrow bacon slice around each shrimp and fasten with cocktail picks. Put garlic slices in shallow broiler pan and set the wrapped shrimp directly on them. Broil about 5 inches from the heat source on one side until the bacon is crisp. Turn shrimp and broil other side. Serve shrimp in all their delicate garlicness at once.

IN MOST homes in southern Italy, garlic appears in almost every main dish set on the table. Sometimes its use is overwhelming to the non-addict, but good culinary sense will produce happy results. Here, for example, is a recipe I found during a trip to Naples, which in its original form was far too strong for my palate. With some judicious cutting down of quantities of garlic and tomatoes, I now count it a most enjoyable dish that still retains the savory garlic taste.

Just for the record, the original recipe called for 40 cloves of garlic—and you could taste every one of them.

Macaroni with Garlic
Serves 4.

10 *large cloves garlic*
4 *tablespoons olive oil*

1 *tablespoon fresh, chopped basil or 1 teaspoon dried*
⅓ *cup coarsely chopped parsley*
2 *tablespoons flour*
½ *teaspoon salt*
¼ *teaspoon black pepper*
1 *8-ounce can tomato sauce*
1 *pound straight macaroni, cooked, drained*
½ *cup freshly grated Romano cheese*

Peel the garlic cloves and sauté them in the oil with the basil and parsley until they are well browned. Mash the garlic with a fork, stir in the flour, salt, and pepper, and continue to cook for 5 minutes over medium heat, stirring often. Add the tomato sauce and simmer, uncovered, over low heat for 30 minutes. Prepare macaroni (or ziti or rigatoni or almost any other pasta you wish) according to package directions, drain, and arrange on a heated platter. Pour the garlic sauce over, sprinkle with cheese, and serve at once.

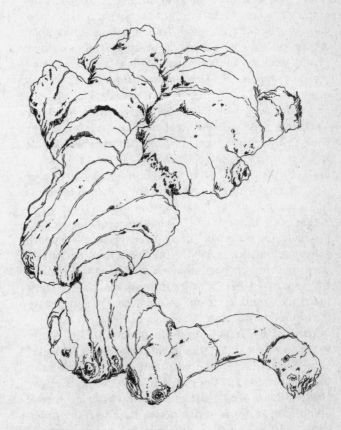

GINGER

There are several thousand kinds of plants in the fascinating family Zingiberaceae, which we know collectively as the Gingers. Of these, a considerable number are tropical plants long grown as valued ornamentals in greenhouse and garden throughout the world, while a couple of dozen are of importance in our international kitchens. Most of these latter, such as Turmeric (*Curcuma longa*) and Cardamom (*Elettaria Cardamomum*), are used primarily as spices. But there are others that decidedly figure in vegetable cookery.

The best known of these Gingers throughout the world is *Zingiber officinale,* the source of culinary Ginger Root. Originally an indigene of India, it is today cultivated for commercial purposes in that country, though in far greater quantities in such widely separated lands as Jamaica, Hawaii, and the Fiji Islands, much of the fresh "root" arriving in our markets today from the Pacific area.

The Ginger Root plant itself is not as attractive as most of its cultivated relations, but I grow my own specimens for cooking purposes, and if you live in a sufficiently equable climate (or have a greenhouse), you can do the same. Obtain some of the knobby dull-brown "roots" (actually a rhizome or specialized underground stem) from your market or Oriental food store and plant them, sprout side up, in a rich moist soil or in a pot with good drainage, in a sunny spot, where the plants will be protected from excessive winds and low temperatures. And do be certain that you have true edible Ginger Root, for there are many other kinds of these plants, superficially like this one in appearance, which are definitely not to be eaten.

To use fresh Ginger Root as it comes from your dooryard or direct from the store, simply slice off just what you require and chop it finely or grate the spicy flesh. Do not peel the root. A hunk of fresh Ginger Root about an inch long and a couple of inches across will give you about 3 tablespoons of finely chopped ginger and more than 1 tablespoon of the grated product. Use a garlic press to express the superb juice from a slice or two of the fresh root, if desired. Store the unused portion of Ginger Root wrapped in foil in your freezer. It will retain its sharpness almost indefinitely and is, in my opinion, always superior to the ground powder for good cookery.

Much of the fresh Ginger Root found in our American markets is older than it might be—and considerably "hotter" than the very delicate pale-pink baby root. When one has the plants in the garden or under glass, it is an easy matter to dig up a front sprout (the plant grows in a distinctive back-to-front direction), and thereby to obtain this superb juvenile rhizome growth.

The slender, spearlike vegetative shoots of the common ginger plant, when just a few inches tall, are severed from the rhizome (which sprouts again), and eaten, either after marinating in sweetened vinegar and oil or candied. These shoots are highly prized in China and Japan and on rare occasions can be found canned in our own specialty shops.

In addition to the fresh root, Ginger is available in several other forms in many of our big markets. The canned fresh variety, dried, pickled, candied (crystallized or preserved), and ground (powdered) root all have a place in the complete kitchen. But because nowadays the fresh rhizomes are so generally available at modest cost, I advocate that they be utilized in the majority of recipes. Many of my Oriental colleagues, in fact, state unequivocally that if the fresh root is not available, no kind of ginger should be substituted for it at all!

NAMASU is a favorite sort of marinated salad in Japan. It varies as to the exact combination of ingredients but it always contains a good touch of freshly grated ginger root. If desired, thin slices of canned abalone can be added to the mixture. And if perchance the Japanese rice vinegar is not available, distilled white vinegar can be used.

Namasu
Serves 6 to 8.

1 *or* 2 *teaspoons grated fresh ginger root*
3 *cups thinly sliced cucumber*
1 *teaspoon salt*
2 *cups thinly sliced scraped young carrots*
1½ *cups thinly sliced small white onions*
2 *tablespoons light-brown sugar*
½ *cup Japanese rice vinegar or distilled white vinegar*
½ *teaspoon monosodium glutamate*
½ *cup thinly sliced canned abalone (optional)*

Prepare the ginger root as above. Peel cucumbers just partially, leaving thin longitudinal strips of green prior to slicing. Arrange cucumber slices on plates and sprinkle with salt. Allow to stand for 30 minutes, drain off liquid, and pat dry. Place in a bowl with carrot and onion slices (and abalone slices if desired). Combine in a saucepan the brown sugar, vinegar, and monosodium glutamate, and bring to a boil. Pour this hot marinade over the vegetables and allow them to stand until cool. Then refrigerate, covered, overnight. Serve small amounts of this, drained, as a salad or relish with fish, fowl, or meat of almost any kind.

HERE is a lovely dish that effectively combines fresh ginger root with duck. The actual cooking time is very brief, so prepare all ingredients in advance and refrigerate them until ready to marinate. I customarily offer this as one of the major items in a multicourse Oriental feast, accompanied by hot rice, Nikko Salad (page 49), and thinly sliced pickled daikon.

Chinese Ginger Duck
Serves 4 liberally.

1 *teaspoon finely chopped fresh ginger root*
3 *cups finely chopped raw duck meat*
2 *tablespoons Japanese soy sauce*
2 *tablespoons sake*
1 *tablespoon cornstarch*
½ *teaspoon salt*
⅓ *cup coarsely chopped scallions, with tops*
2 *tablespoons peanut or soy oil*

Carefully but thoroughly toss together all ingredients except the oil, and allow them to stand for 30 minutes at room temperature. Then, in a wok, a paellero, or a large shallow skillet, heat the oil over high flame and in it stir-fry the mixture for about 4 minutes—not longer! Serve immediately.

ONE OF my favorite ways with good lean pork spareribs is the following gingery delight, to be served as a hot appetizer or as one of the principal courses in a Polynesian repast. The recipe originated on the glorious "Garden Isle" of Kauai, in Hawaii, but through the years its contents have been subtly altered. If the Chinese Five Spices Powder is not available, do not try to substitute anything else, please; just make the dish without it.

Kauai Ginger Spareribs
Serves 6 to 8.

1 *or 2 teaspoons grated fresh ginger root*
2 *pounds small lean spareribs*
½ *cup Japanese soy sauce*
½ *cup tomato ketchup*
¼ *cup sake or cooking sherry*
¾ *cup dark brown sugar*
1 *teaspoon salt*
¼ *teaspoon monosodium glutamate*
1 *large clove garlic, mashed*
¼ *teaspoon Chinese Five Spices Powder*
"hot" Chinese mustard
duk (plum) sauce

Have your butcher crack the spareribs across the middle. Cut the little ribs apart into individual finger-size sections and arrange these in a large shallow bak-

ing pan. In a saucepan, combine the ginger root with all other listed ingredients except the Chinese mustard and duk sauce. Bring to the boil, stirring constantly, then remove from the heat and pour over the spareribs. Marinate these at room temperature, turning ribs several times, for at least 3 hours. About 1 hour before serving time, place ribs in preheated 350° F. oven and bake, basting with marinade and turning ribs occasionally, until tender, usually about 45 minutes. Serve warm with side dishes, for dipping, of "hot" Chinese mustard (dry mustard made into a thin smooth paste with a bit of stale beer), and commercial duk sauce.

As I MENTIONED, many other kinds of ginger are used in other parts of the world, particularly in the Orient, Malaysia, and Indonesia, where these handsome plants abound. There the fleshy rhizomes, young leaf shoots, leaves, and even flowers are included in the indigenous cuisines, and the usually very aromatic seeds are often eaten as spices. About the only one of these which has reached our shores as yet is Mioga ginger (*Zingiber Mioga,* of the Ginger Family), a Japanese plant which is rather extensively cultivated in Japan, infrequently in Hawaii. The subterranean rhizomes are the source of Japanese ginger root, which has a positive bergamot-like flavor. The leafy stems grow three feet tall or so, and the erect flower spikes, arising separately from the same underground rhizome, are topped by a conical group of close-fitting dark-purple bracts, from which the fugacious white, yellow, or buff-colored flowers emerge. These flower heads—*mioga* in Japanese, *keong-fa* in Chinese—are utilized to impart a special flavor to special soups.

GRAPE LEAVES

The fresh tender leaves of the Grape (*Vitis* species, of the Grape or Vine Family) are enjoyed by countless millions of good cooks in many parts of the world. In this country, they are most likely to be encountered, stuffed in some fashion, at a Greek or Syrian or Lebanese restaurant.

As a vegetable, these pretty leaves of the vine have a special firmness of texture—even after cooking—and a uniqueness of flavor that I like. When I can get the tiny burgeoning leaves from grape-growing pals hereabouts, I like to make immediate use of them—they do not retain their vitality long after picking, like all such fragile edibles. Finely shredded, they add an indefinable touch to vinaigrette-dressed green salads. Some chopped bits of leaf added to a clear Japanese soup made with Dashi (page 210) are enticing to my palate. And—also finely chopped—they make an unusual addition to a puffy omelet, or blended into a thin batter for crisp fritters—the latter to be served with sour cream, if desired.

STUFFED Grape Leaves are a bit of trouble to prepare, but are certainly well worth the effort. (If you are disinclined to do your own, then please consider the tasty little ones, generally filled with seasoned rice and packed in oil, which are available in jars imported from Greece.) If fresh grape leaves are available, they are, naturally, to be preferred, but the imported jars of grape leaves, packed in brine, are a satisfactory substitute. There are many ways to stuff the Grape Leaves, but here is my personal favorite.

Stuffed Grape Leaves
Serves 4 to 6.

1 1-quart jar grape leaves
½ pound ground lamb
2½ to 3 cups cooked rice
1 large clove garlic, mashed
⅓ cup grated onion
¼ to ½ teaspoon cinnamon
salt and freshly ground pepper to taste
4 tablespoons butter
2 cups rich chicken stock
lemon or lime wedges

Drain grape leaves and rinse them in cold water. Drain thoroughly and pat dry with paper towels, spreading leaves out flat, glossy sides down, on a commodious working surface. Thoroughly combine the lamb, rice, garlic, onion, cinnamon, and salt and pepper to taste. Place a heaping teaspoon of the filling on center of each grape leaf and fold up, from the sides first, then rolling from the stem end. In a heavy skillet with cover, melt the butter over low heat. Arrange the grape-leaf rolls close together, folded sides down, in the skillet. Pour over them the rich chicken stock, preferably freshly made, and weight down the rolls with a plate to keep them from coming apart during cooking. Cover skillet and simmer the grape-leaf rolls over low heat for 1½ hours. Serve hot or at room temperature, with lemon or lime wedges on the side.

GROUNDNUT

The Groundnut, Potato Bean, or Wild Bean (*Apios tuberosa,* of the prodigious Legume Family) and a native North American plant, is an old-time vegetable, long relished by the Amerindians, yet today seldom encountered save in specialized garden plots. It is a scrambling, rather short vine with pinnate foliage and bunches of oddly attractive, fragrant, chocolate-brown pealike flowers, which produces strings of edible, mostly pear-shaped little tubers from the root.

Some connoisseur culinary gardeners grow the plant in their yards and take special pleasure in serving a goodly batch of the firm tubers, either boiled or roasted, and dressed with butter and suitable seasonings. These possess a delectable nutty flavor, and when properly prepared are of a pleasantly firm texture. I have a friend in Georgia who from time to time sends me a nice little packet of these tubers. I find them particularly acceptable with thin steaks marinated in Cuban style for a while in lime juice, then pan-broiled.

It is indeed unfortunate that Groundnuts are not available on any extensive commercial scale in the United States, as they must be counted among our finest indigenous tuberous vegetables. The dry tubers are available from some seedsmen, and since the range of the species is very extensive—from Virginia southward to Florida and Texas—perhaps some enterprising cooks will plant patches of them in the future.

An interesting additional species of this genus (*Apios Priceana*) from Kentucky has been described as having showy pale-rose flowers and a solitary tuberous root up to seven inches in diameter. This root is edible, but the plant seems to be a contemporary rarity. Yet another member of the group (*Apios Fortunei*) is cultivated in Japan for its egg-shaped little tubers, these reputedly much like our native kind in flavor and texture.

Groundnut as a vernacular name is also applied in many places to the peanut (*Arachis hypogaea*), which is, of course, a totally distinct plant.

HOP

The Hop (*Humulus Lupulus,* of the Nettle Family) is best known for its use in the production of beer, a beverage of more than passing interest and import to almost all of us. The bitter substance utilized to flavor the brew is found, oddly enough, in the tiny glandular hairs that cloak the straw-yellow, catkinlike pistillate inflorescences. The Hop is an attractive vine, extensively cultivated in parts of the United States, as well as in such lands as Germany, England, and even in South America and Australia.

The portion of the Hop plant utilized in vegetable cookery is called the Hop Shoot, or, in French, *jet de houblon.* It is actually the branched bunch of staminate (male) flowers, and the whole tender tip is consumed, this snapped off as one does fresh asparagus. This—or these, rather, since a serving requires a considerable number of these *jets*—is cooked, after thorough preliminary rinsing, in salted water to which some lemon juice has been added.

Hop Shoots are variously served with butter, light cream, or in meat gravy. In Belgium, where this esoteric vegetable is greatly enjoyed, the Hop Shoots are served with poached eggs arranged in a circle and with croutons fried in butter after having been cut into the shape of a comb. I have no idea why.

HORSERADISH

The Horseradish (*Armoracia rusticana,* of the Cabbage Family) is a weedy plant with a thickened elongate root which is of great importance as a "hot" condiment in many countries, including our own. Originally from Europe and parts of Western Asia, it has been naturalized in parts of the United States, becoming a noxious weed in moist areas.

The commercial production of Horseradish is big business here, upward of 18 millions of pounds of roots being processed annually. From these husky roots, packers prepare a variety of sauces, a dehydrated powder, and a powerful and powerfully good vinegar. The grated root is also combined with mustard and is incorporated into various other culinary condiments, such as pickles, to which it imparts its remarkable sinus-clearing properties. Incidentally, Horseradish experts assure us that their product promotes the appetite and aids in digestion, hence those of us who adore it can feel secure when we eat it with everything from roast beef or shellfish to many vegetables. Of course, you can buy the fresh root and grate it yourself. (See also Wasabi, page 238.)

THERE are infinite subtle—and not so subtle—variations of basic Horseradish Sauce. Several excellent commercial ones are available in our markets now, but here is a homemade version I highly recommend to be served especially with boiled meats, such as tongue or beef.

Horseradish Sauce

   freshly grated or prepared horseradish, to taste
   3 tablespoons butter
   3 tablespoons flour
   1½ cups rich beef bouillon

Melt the butter in a saucepan, add the flour gradually, and blend thoroughly, using a wire whisk. In another saucepan heat the beef bouillon to the boiling and add this hot liquid all at once to the butter-flour roux. Stir briskly with the whisk until the mixture is very smooth and somewhat thickened. Season to taste with horseradish, being rather generous. Serve warm with boiled meats.

WITH roast pork or broiled pork chops, consider the following savory accompaniment. As with all such recipes, the prepared horseradish marked "Hot!" with an exclamation point should be utilized if the freshly grated root is not available.

Horseradish Applesauce

Using canned or fresh applesauce, stir in horseradish to taste. Mix thoroughly and chill until ready to use—with pork in particular.

HORSERADISH TREE

The Horseradish Tree (*Moringa oleifera,* of the Moringa Family) is a pretty tree, seldom as tall as twenty-five feet. The tree is also known by such regional vernaculars as *karamungay* (Philippines), and *murunga* or *murunga-kai* (Ceylon). It is originally from India but is now naturalized in such areas as the West Indies and casually cultivated in warm lands throughout the world. Virtually all parts of the plant are utilized by man, principally in the Asiatic tropics from Ceylon to the Philippines.

The coarse roots of the tree are ground as a somewhat inferior substitute for horseradish; the graceful feathery leaves lend a pungent seasoning to vegetable curries and to pickles; the attractive little fragrant flowers are also added to curries; and the hanging pods, strong-ribbed, usually grayish, and up to four feet long, are adapted to several culinary uses. When young, only a few inches in length, the pods are cooked much as string beans, or are coarsely chopped and added to curries and vegetable-meat mixtures. Their flavor is singularly pleasant, somewhat like a spicy potato! As these pods age, they become heavier in texture and are sliced before cooking, or boiled till tender, then sliced, to be served with soy sauce and such seasonings. They are sometimes called Drumsticks.

The valuable ben oil expressed from the seeds of the Horseradish Tree, is used in cosmetics and by makers of fine machinery, such as watches and clocks.

Although this exceptionally interesting tree has been cultivated in the warm parts of Florida and California, and in Hawaii, Puerto Rico, and the Virgin Islands for many years and is not uncommon, its pleasantly "bitey" edible parts are rarely encountered in our markets.

HORSERADISH Tree leaves and pods do turn up occasionally on produce stands in Hawaii. Here is an unusually interesting stew with *karamungay* leaves, from Mrs. L. W. Hurum of Honolulu, who mentions that these leaves are "very rich in vitamins."

Horseradish Tree-Chicken Stew
Serves 4 liberally.

  2 *cups horseradish tree* (karamungay) *leaves*
  1 *13¾-ounce can chicken broth*
  1 *tablespoon finely chopped onion*
  2 *teaspoons finely chopped garlic*
  1 *1-inch piece ginger root, finely chopped*
  1 *3-pound frying chicken, cut into pieces*
  1 *4-ounce can mushroom stems and pieces*
  lemon wedges

In a kettle with cover, heat the chicken broth, then add onion, garlic, ginger root, and chicken pieces. Simmer, covered, until tender, usually 30 minutes or so. Then add the mushrooms, and bring mixture to the boil. Add the rinsed tender *karamungay* leaves, mix through, and cook for 5 minutes. Accompany the stew with lemon wedges and individual bowls of hot rice. If desired, chutney and chopped salted peanuts can be offered on the side.

HUSK TOMATO

There are several kinds of Husk Tomato (genus *Physalis*, of the Potato-Tomato Family) which are raised to some extent for their small edible fruits, both in the United States and elsewhere. These are attractive plants (there are perhaps seventy-five different species in the group), mostly annuals a foot or so tall, with toothed leaves and pendulous, papery, often vivid orange or red structures that contain the fruits. Because of this showy calyx enclosing the fruit, the common name of Chinese Lantern Plant has been given to some of these tomato relatives.

The fruit, used most often as a vegetable in our

cookery, is generally smaller than a cherry tomato, and somewhat reminiscent of it in flavor, though usually a bit more tart, and in some forms it is slightly sticky in texture. In this country, Husk Tomatoes are usually wild plants of waste places, but on occasion they are cultivated—several select kinds are available from seedsmen, and they are by and large very easily grown. They are most often to be found in markets during the autumn months, frequently under the alternate names of Ground Cherry, Strawberry Tomato, or Cape Gooseberry.

These Husk Tomatoes vary in color, depending upon the variety, from vivid yellow or greenish-orange to rich red. Their culinary uses are considerable, and they are increasingly prized by epicure gardeners.

Most of the available sorts can be eaten raw as is, or added whole or halved to salads. A highly flavored, very pleasant sauce can be prepared from them, much as one would make a tomato sauce, and it can be served to advantage especially with roast red meats. The *tomatillo*—"little tomato"—of Mexico (*Physalis ixocarpa*) is very popular there, and to a degree in our own Southwestern states, being used in the production of a variety of heavily spiced "chili sauces."

ONE OF the most delectable preserves that I know is made with the common little yellow Husk Tomato (*Physalis pubescens*).

Husk Tomato Preserves
Fills about 4 jelly glasses.

  2 *pounds cleaned ripe husk tomatoes*
  1½ *cups sugar*
  1 *lemon, juiced, the peel grated*
  1 *cup water*

Pick off all bits of papery husk from the little berries, trim off any blemishes, and rinse them well. In a large heavy kettle with cover, combine the husk tomatoes with all other ingredients, and cook over very low heat, covered, stirring often, until the mixture is reasonably soft but not soupy—usually about 1 hour. Be careful that this does not scorch during cooking. Place in hot sterilized glasses or jars and top with paraffin or lid. Allow to mellow for a couple of weeks prior to use.

SEVERAL kinds of these valuable, interesting plants are grown in Europe, notably France, where they are known as *alkékenges*, and are used to make jams, jellies, and even candies, the whole berries being dipped in caramel or fondant. These esoteric and delicious imports are occasionally to be found in specialty shops in this country.

THE CAPE GOOSEBERRY (*Physalis peruviana*), one variety of husk tomatoes, has been cultivated for more than two centuries in such diverse areas as the Peruvian Andes, South Africa, Indonesia, and Australia, as well as in some of our Deep South states. The yellow fruits are again made into a pleasantly pungent preserve, are eaten raw in salads, and even made into pie and pudding. I have served the following distinctive quiche-like pie on a number of occasions as an accompaniment to steaks and roast beef or pork. The pie is nice when reheated.

Husk Tomato Pie
Serves 6.

> 1 *pound cleaned ripe husk tomatoes, thinly sliced*
> 2 *unbaked 9-inch pastry shells*
> 4 *eggs*
> *salt and pepper*
> ¼ *teaspoon dried basil*
> 1½ *cups light cream*
> 2 *cups grated Swiss cheese*
> 2 *tablespoons finely snipped chives*

Partially bake the pastry shells and allow them to

cool slightly prior to use. Beat the eggs with salt and pepper to taste, plus basil, then fold in the sliced husk tomatoes, cream, cheese, and chives. Pour the mixture into the pastry shells and bake in preheated 350° F. oven for about 40 minutes, or until pie is set and nicely browned. Cut into wedges to serve while very hot.

JAKFRUIT

The Jakfruit (*Artocarpus integra*) is a close relative of the Breadfruit, and like it is a member of the same family as the India-rubber tree and the commercial fig. A huge, handsome tree, it is set with unlobed leaves usually about six inches in length. When in fruit, a prolific specimen can provide a fantastic aspect, for the fruits—perhaps the largest of any plant known—are borne directly on the trunk and larger, older branches. Oval to oblong in shape, and set with six-sided green or brownish fleshy spines in tight array, they weigh from ten to more than one hundred pounds apiece.

The Jakfruit (Jackfruit and Jaca are other names) is highly prized in many parts of the Asiatic tropics, notably Ceylon and certain of the Indonesian islands. It was introduced early to Brazil and is widely used in good cookery there as well. South Florida boasts of a number of mature producing trees, but the fruits are rarities in our mainland markets as yet.

The somewhat fibrous pulp has a rubberlike juice when immature, and preparation of a green Jakfruit affords the enterprising chef the interesting prospect of being literally stuck finger to finger. (Lighter fluid will remove this latex, with considerable staunch scrubbing.) This juvenile Jakfruit flesh is utilized as a vegetable in curries, and is more often cut into sizable chunks and parboiled, then baked, when it has somewhat the texture of moist yet firm bread, with a rather positive and slightly unusual flavor. When ripe, the flesh is made into a delicate sherbet, this widely enjoyed in equatorial Brazil and a few other countries in that part of the world.

The large seeds are surrounded by slick coverings containing a variously sweet or acid juice with a strong bananalike odor. Despite this, the coverings and their attendant liquid are sometimes incorporated into ornate tropical fruit salads. As in breadfruit, the seeds are, when roasted, somewhat reminiscent of chestnuts.

THIS Brazilian pudding is a distinctive novelty, somewhat like a gelatin made by combining oranges with a positive sort of melon.

Jakfruit Pudding
Serves 6.

6 cups jakfruit pulp, plus juicy wrappings of seeds
3 cups milk
⅓ cup sugar
1 teaspoon salt

Bring the jakfruit pulp, juice, and seed envelopes to a boil in the milk, then stir in the sugar and salt. Boil, stirring often, for about 20 minutes. Allow to stand for 5 minutes, then strain the mixture. Pour into an attractive serving dish, allow to cool, then refrigerate until very chilled and firm in texture.

JAPANESE ARTICHOKE

Japanese Artichoke (*Stachys Sieboldii*, of the Mint Family) is a most distinctive plant, today cultivated by connoisseurs in this country, in Europe, and in the Orient, for the abundant white tubers produced just under the ground's surface. It is also known as Chinese Artichoke (the species is indigenous both to China and Japan), *chorogi* (Japanese), *crosne du Japon* (French), and Knotroot.

These tubers, two or three inches long, and conspicuously knotted throughout their length, are pristine white when fresh, quickly becoming brownish and rather soft after being dug. Only the very firm, fresh tubers should be cooked. They are uncommon in domestic markets at this time, though the plant is very easily grown almost everywhere, and its spikes of pretty pale-red blossoms are attractive in the home garden.

The tubers of Japanese Artichoke are somewhat reminiscent of those of Jerusalem Artichoke, with which it has no botanical affinity—and are similarly used. They are very tasty if scrubbed, sliced, and eaten raw—perhaps just with salt, or with a light vinaigrette dressing. Or they can be blanched in boiling salted water, then braised in butter until just barely tender (do not permit them to brown, though!). Or, they may be boiled until firm-tender, then served with a cream or Mornay sauce, or added to a roast of veal or beef to heat through in the meat's juices, or even made into a rich purée.

THEN consider the following excellent croquettes, prepared in the French manner, and especially well suited to service with fowl or veal.

Japanese Artichoke Croquettes
Serves 4.

1 pound firm Japanese artichokes
1 quart rich chicken broth
2 eggs, beaten well
pinch freshly ground white pepper
2 cups fine bread crumbs
hot fat for deep frying
salt

Gently scrub the Japanese artichokes to remove any grit or dark pieces of skin. Then cook them in the chicken broth, only until firm-tender. If desired, cut the tubers in half—or pare them into balls, an authentic though wasteful process. Dip them into the beaten egg, to which the white pepper has been added, then roll in bread crumbs. Carefully lower them, a couple at a time, into deep fat heated to 380° F., and fry for 5 minutes. Drain, sprinkle liberally with salt, and serve without delay.

JAPANESE PEPPER LEAF

The Japanese Pepper Leaf (*Zanthoxylum piperatum*, of the Citrus Family) is also called Japanese Prickly Ash and *sanshō*. A shrubby small thorny tree of Japan, Korea, and parts of China, it is of considerable importance in Oriental *haute cuisine*. It is commonly cultivated, especially in Japan, for the production of a sort of black pepper substitute.

The fresh, pretty, pinnate leaves are used as a rather hot garnish in soups, and for this purpose are also dried and powdered for use as a pungent condiment with many foods—broiled or baked seafood, for example. This Pepper Leaf is imported by specialty shops in this country and is indeed worth a special search.

Interestingly, too, both the inner bark of the tree—the wood of which is highly prized for its vivid yellow color and exceptional heaviness—and the seeds are pickled, after cooking, for a popular, powerful seasoning product.

JERUSALEM ARTICHOKE

The Jerusalem Artichoke is neither from Palestine nor is its affinity with the better-known globe arti-

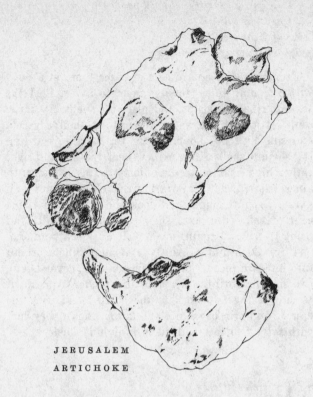

JERUSALEM
ARTICHOKE

lected vegetables. Properly prepared—never over-cooked!—it occupies a unique place in fine international cuisine, however. Favorite uses are in salads, dressed with oil and vinegar, made either from the peeled raw or lightly boiled tubers, whole or sliced; as a last-minute addition, in raw slices, as a garnish to clear soups; pared, quartered, and slowly sautéed in butter until just barely tender; boiled till tender, then puréed and dressed simply with butter, salt, and fresh-ground white pepper; or even parboiled until crisp-tender, then dipped in a very light batter and deep-fried.

CREAMED Jerusalem Artichokes are to be encountered with some frequency on menus in a few French restaurants in this country. The following savory version is perfection with seafood or veal.

Creamed Jerusalem Artichokes
Serves 4.

> 1½ pounds Jerusalem artichokes
> boiling salted water
> 2 teaspoons lemon juice
> 1 cup light white sauce
> 2 or 3 drops Tabasco sauce
> 3 tablespoons minced fresh parsley

Wash and peel or scrape the tubers, and cook them in the boiling salted water, to which lemon juice has been added, until just tender—do not overcook them! Meanwhile, prepare the light white sauce and stir in Tabasco sauce and parsley at last moment. Drain Jerusalem artichokes thoroughly and pour the hot sauce over them. Serve at once.

choke at all close. The plant is a species of sunflower (*Helianthus tuberosus*) which is native to the United States, and about the only relationship with the globe artichoke which it possesses is that it is placed in the same botanical assemblage—the Daisy Family.

The underground clustered whitish 2-inch tubers are the edible portion of this plant. They were greatly prized by the American Indians who in fact cultivated them at the time of the Pilgrims. Jerusalem Artichokes were introduced into France early in the seventeenth century—where they were called *artichauts du Canada,* a name now largely replaced by *topinambour*—but until the era of the famed gastronome Parmentier, the vegetable was little appreciated on the Continent.

Jerusalem Artichokes are most often seen in domestic markets in late winter. Then their crisp texture and very delicate flavor—somewhat reminiscent of true globe artichokes or perhaps of water chestnuts—are at peak development. When purchased, the tubers should be very firm in texture, with no wrinkling of the skin. The culinary gardener in almost all parts of this country can easily raise a suitable plot of this interesting vegetable, bushy and a couple of feet tall, seed being available from a number of commercial plantsmen.

Scrub and scrape or peel the little tubers, and serve them either raw (if so, chilled) or cooked in lightly salted water until crisp-tender.

The Jerusalem Artichoke is among our more neg-

JESUITS' NUT

The Jesuits' Nut (*Trapa bicornis* or *T. natans,* of the Evening Primrose Family) is a remarkably pretty aquatic plant, also known as Water Caltrops, and mistakenly and confusingly as Water Chestnut (page 238), to which it is not related. The plant, widely cultivated in this country as a prized pool or aquarium specimen for its floating, handsomely marked leaves, has strange fruits that are proportionately huge, measuring as much as three inches across the prominent brown or ebony-colored points, these reminiscent of the horns of a bullock.

A native of China, the plant has for centuries been cultivated in the Far East under the Chinese name of *ling-kok,* or the Japanese *hishimomi.* Each fruit contains a solitary big white kernel which is prized as a flavorful delicacy in many ornate Oriental dishes. The fruits are boiled for an hour or so in hot water, then the kernels are removed, to be eaten while still warm. In such areas as Hawaii and California, which boast of extensive Oriental populations, fresh Jesuits' Nuts are frequently available in the markets in September. They are a special edible delight for the celebration of the Chinese Full Moon Festival of that time of year.

In other parts of the United States we can find the boiled nuts in tins or jars, in a honey or sugar sauce. The Jesuits' Nut is also found, presumably naturalized, in Lake Maggiore, in northern Italy, where its kernels, eaten after boiling, are highly prized.

Related to the Jesuits' Nut is the Singhara Nut of India (*Trapa bispinosa*), which is today imported into this country in small quantities. The nuts, boiled and salted, are sizable and reminiscent of the delicious macadamias from Hawaii and California.

JICAMA

The Jicama, pronounced hee-*kah*-ma, is a large woody vine (*Exogonium bracteatum*, of the Morning-Glory Family), common in many parts of Mexico. Also called *bejuco blanco*—"white vine," because of the profuse showy white flowers—it is cultivated there, particularly along the Pacific coast, for the large tuberous roots which are eaten raw or prepared in various fashions. These are somewhat reminiscent of sweet potatoes, a closely allied plant, in fact, but their flavor is less sweet and their texture a bit more fibrous.

Jicama tubers are increasingly offered for sale in produce markets in California and on occasion have made their way as well to specialty shops in our large Eastern cities.

This is an unusually interesting "new" vegetable (it has been grown in its native land for centuries!), which can be treated in all manners suggested for Sweet Potato (page 224). I have enjoyed it in particular in the Mexican coastal town of Manzanillo in the following creation.

Jicama-Shrimp Soup
Serves 4 to 6.

3 *cups coarsely diced peeled jicama tubers*
2 *tablespoons lime juice*
1 *pound raw medium shrimp*
2 *quarts water*
2 *tablespoons light olive oil*
½ *cup finely chopped onion*
⅓ *cup finely chopped sweet green chile pepper*

3 *tablespoons coarsely chopped parsley*
2 *teaspoons salt*
½ *cup light cream*
Salsa Fría (*page 185*) *to taste*

Prepare the jicama dice and place them in a bowl with the lime juice, tossing them to cover. Peel the shrimp, rinse the shells, and place the shells in a large soup kettle with the water. Bring to the boil, covered, and simmer for 1 hour. Strain the stock, discarding the shrimp shells. In a skillet, heat the oil, and over rather high heat sauté the onion, stirring often, until almost soft. Add the sweet green chile pepper and parsley, stir through, and cook for 2 minutes. Turn contents of skillet into shrimp stock, add salt, and bring to the boil again, covered. Reduce heat and simmer for 30 minutes. Add the shrimp, whole or cut into bite-size pieces, and the jicama dice, cover again, and simmer until the jicama is just tender. Add about ½ cup of the hot stock to the bowl, blend with the cream, and stir back into the kettle. Serve very hot, with *salsa fría* to be added to individual taste.

KALE

Kale is a rather coarse leafy vegetable which today in the United States, enjoys somewhat limited commercial production. It is, however, very tasty when properly prepared and offers an important source of calcium plus a wide array of vitamins.

Kale, or Borecole, is actually a sort of nonheading cabbage, botanically placed in the huge, complex Crucifer Family and known by the scientific name of *Brassica oleracea* var. *acephala*. Some collards—Georgia collards, for example—are a kind of Kale; other types of so-called Kales—Sea Kale (page 209) and Indian Kale—have little or no relationship to the Kale discussed here.

Two principal varieties of Kale are grown in the United States—Scotch, which has crumpled, very curled, rather prickly grayish-green leaves, and Blue or Siberian, not as crumpled nor as curled as the Scotch, and of a handsome blue-green color. Both varieties are grown commercially in several parts of this country—during the winter in the South, at other seasons in chillier Northern states, because Kale delights in rather low temperatures.

Kale has long been cultivated in Europe, and was probably introduced into this hemisphere in the late 1600s. In relatively recent years a series of spectacular ornamental Kales has been developed, principally in Japan, where their compact rosettes of ornately crisped varicolored leaves are utilized in choice flower gardens.

Purchase Kale in your produce market when the leaves are very firm and show no signs of yellowing. If possible, use the greens the same day, since like many such vegetables, this one quickly loses its flavor and nutritional value after being picked.

Tear or cut the crisp leaves from their thickened heavy stalks, discarding the stalks, which are generally too fibrous to be good eating. Quickly wash the vegetable in cool water—prolonged soaking must be avoided. Thoroughly drain it, and then continue with one of the suggested recipes, as described below.

Since good fresh Kale possesses a unique texture of firmness (but not toughness) when cooked just to the proper degree, and a delicious flavor—a very slight bitterness which is most refreshing—I favor the simplest possible method of preparation, namely:

Boiled Kale
Serves 4.

1 *large bunch fresh kale*
4 *strips lean bacon, diced*
⅓ *cup coarsely chopped onion*
¾ *cup salted water*

Prepare kale as recommended above. Fry the bacon dice in a small skillet with the onion, until latter is soft. Bring salted water to a quick boil in a kettle with cover and add the torn-up kale. Turn in the bacon and onion, cover the kettle, and cook over rather high heat until the vegetable is just tender, adding a bit more water if necessary. Drain off any excess moisture and serve without delay, with butter, seasonings to taste (a tiny touch of nutmeg is a fancy and welcome addition), and if desired a drop or two of lemon juice or wine vinegar.

Boiled kale, drained and hot, can be topped with a light cream sauce or a delicate cheese sauce, if desired. The plain cooked vegetable is, too, frequently served with sausage in various forms, this typically fried until done to taste, and added to the kale, with a bit of its grease, for a moment or so prior to serving at table.

The Chinese cultivate to a considerable degree a form of kale with relatively flat uncurled foliage called *kai-lan-choi;* it is found in many Oriental markets in this country. Often the bunches of the vegetable are set with pretty spikes of yellow or white flowers, which are consumed along with the greens. The following recipe can be prepared with the crisp-leaved Scotch or blue varieties, as well as the flat kale.

Oriental Kale with Fish
Serves 4.

1 *large bunch fresh kale*
1½ *teaspoons peanut or soy oil*
1 *small slice fresh ginger root*
½ *teaspoon salt*
½ *pound finely sliced, firm-textured fish*
½ *cup water*

Prepare kale as suggested on page 129. Using a large wok or shallow skillet, heat the oil over high flame and stir-fry the ginger root, salt, and finely sliced fish for about 30 seconds. Add the kale, plus the water, and continue to stir-fry for about 3 minutes, or until the vegetable is done to taste. It should, in this dish, retain considerable texture. Serve at once.

GOOD cooks of Italian antecedents are very fond of kale. Here is an Italian recipe I enjoy with such disparate dishes as roast veal and spaghetti with meatballs.

Italian Breaded Kale
Serves 4.

1 *large bunch fresh kale*
¾ *cup salted water*
¼ *cup light olive oil*
1 *medium clove garlic, mashed*
¾ *cup coarse bread crumbs*
2 to 3 *tablespoons freshly grated Parmesan or Romano cheese*

Prepare kale as indicated on page 129. Bring salted water to a quick boil in kettle with cover and place vegetable in it. Cover and cook over medium to high flame until kale is just tender. Then add the oil, garlic, bread crumbs, and cheese, stir lightly, and continue to cook for about 3 or 4 minutes. Drain off any excess moisture and serve at once.

KOHLRABI

Kohlrabi is one of the extraordinarily diverse close relatives of the common cabbage, known by botanists as *Brassica oleracea* var. *Caulo-Rapa*. It has been aptly described as much like a turnip growing on a cabbage root, though the flavor is more delicate and more subtle than either of those vegetables.

This is a handsome vegetable and a splendid one for extensive use in the kitchen. It is very easily cultivated, even by the novice gardener, in almost any part of this country and appears with increasing frequency at virtually all seasons in our better produce markets.

The stalked foliage can be boiled, preferably in a change of water, and offered as a rather pungent green vegetable with butter and seasonings. And the succulent stem of the Kohlrabi, usually white, prettily flushed with purple, can be boiled in salted water, to be mashed or riced with a modicum of cream and butter; it can be cubed and incorporated into stews with bland meats; the parboiled vegetable can be thinly-sliced and lightly sautéed in butter; the raw stems can be stuffed with ground beef or veal and baked; the entire structure can be cut apart into wedges and put back together with cocktail picks, to offer chilled with sour cream dip as an appetizer; choice bits of it can be utilized in the marvelous Bagna Cauda (page 72); cubes or thin slices can be incorporated in sukiyaki or tempura; and on and on.

THE GREEK custom of serving crisp-cooked vegetables with a sauce of egg yolks and lemon juice is a felicitous one, excellent for our versatile Kohlrabi.

Kohlrabi Avgolemono
Serves 4 to 6.

1 *pound kohlrabi*
3 *tablespoons butter*
3 *egg yolks, beaten*
2 *tablespoons lemon juice*

Trim the kohlrabi, discarding the leaves or using them for soup. Cut the vegetable into slices about ¼ inch thick and boil them, covered, in a small quantity of salted water for 10 minutes. Reserve about 2 tablespoons of the cooking liquid. Drain and pat the slices dry with paper towels. Melt the butter in a skillet and over rather high heat sauté the slices until nicely browned on both sides. In a small saucepan, over low heat, heat the beaten egg yolks with the reserved cooking stock, and gradually beat in the lemon juice. Pour this into the skillet with the kohlrabi slices and heat through, to serve without delay.

KUDZU

The Kudzu (*Pueraria hirsuta,* of the Legume Family) is a remarkable vine, indigenous to China and Japan, which has long been casually cultivated in the subtropics and tropics of both hemispheres for its edible, often gigantic tuberous roots. Variously tapering or fantastically branched, these can attain an overall diameter of six or eight feet and a tremendous weight. The skin is straw-colored to light brown, while the firm fibrous flesh is white.

Only the small roots are used as table vegetables, principally by persons of Oriental ancestry in the United States in Hawaii and California. The roots are boiled in salted water until tender, peeled, then usually mashed for serving. The flavor of the Kudzu (known in Chinese as *fan-kot*) is very positive, somewhat bitter, and generally not too acceptable to the Occidental palate.

In this country, the Kudzu is often planted as a vine for pergolas and arbors, where it can be quite overwhelming—from a single established root, vegetative growth in a single season can exceed fifty feet!

In the Orient, a high-quality starch is derived from the tuberous roots, and from the coverings that cloak them is made *ko* or *ko*-hemp, a good, thin, very strong fiber.

Another kind of Kudzu (*Pueraria tuberosa*, of India) is a rarely seen, ornamental, fast-growing bluish-flowered big vine which has been introduced into warmer parts of the United States. It produces huge tuberous roots that are eaten in the Asiatic tropics as a starchy vegetable after protracted cooking to remove the acrid resin they contain.

LEEK

The Leek (*Allium Porrum,* of the Lily Family) has been cultivated in the Mediterranean and North Afri-

can regions since prehistoric times. In the *haute cuisine* of France it is an essential ingredient as a flavoring for all sorts of masterpieces, and this lovely sleek onion relative—somewhat like an overgrown scallion, but with larger foliage and relatively undeveloped subterranean bulbous thickening—is also extensively grown for the kitchen in lands from Wales to Egypt.

Leeks have long been relative rarities in many markets in the United States; until recently they were imported—and expensive. But cultivation of the vegetable in the home garden is easily accomplished in most parts of this country, and commercial plantings have made it more generally available today.

Leeks should be washed thoroughly before using, to remove all traces of grit and sand. If very gritty, they may have to be split lengthwise to facilitate cleaning. Because the flavor of the Leek, in all parts, is rather a positive one, the vegetable is most often blanched lightly in boiling water prior to use. But it is this same flavor that endears the Leek to good cooks everywhere.

Favorite ways of treating this superb vegetable include the one suggested for Scallions à la Grecque (page 208); boiled in salted water till just tender, then chilled and topped with chopped hard-cooked eggs, minced parsley, and salt and pepper, with a light vinaigrette dressing to be added to individual taste at table; incorporated into a rich quiche-like tart; or added to a rich Belgian potato soup of justifiable fame.

And then we have the following delightful soup from Scotland, hearty as one would anticipate. Some of my antecedents came from Ayr, and when I was quite young, Cock-a-Leekie Soup graced our table on many a chill Maine evening. Some of the authentic recipes for this soup call for the addition of dried prunes toward the end of the simmering, but I find this a thoroughly unfortunate suggestion.

Cock-a-Leekie Soup
Serves 6.

8 to 10 *leeks, thickly sliced*
1 *large fat stewing chicken*
2 *quarts water*
½ *cup coarsely chopped celery, with leaves*
¼ *cup coarsely chopped parsley*
1 *medium bay leaf*
salt and freshly ground pepper

Place the cleaned chicken, with its giblets, in the water in a large soup kettle with cover. Add celery, parsley, bay leaf, plus goodly quantities of salt and pepper, and bring to a quick boil, covered. Reduce heat and cook over very low flame until the chicken falls from the bone. Skim off fat and strain the soup. Coarsely chop the chicken meat and giblets and return these, with the leeks, to the strained broth. Simmer, covered, for about 30 minutes, until the leeks are tender, correct seasoning, and serve while very hot.

LENTIL

The Lentil (*Lens esculenta* or *Ervum Lens*—it depends on the botanical authority—of the Legume Family) is one of man's most ancient foods, having been cultivated since prehistoric times in the eastern Mediterranean region, and in India. The optical lens, upon its invention, was named for this bean, because of the marked similarity in shape. The seeds of the small, shrubby plant are used in a tremendous array of dishes, from savory highly nutritious soups and stews, to pies, the famous Indian Dhal (page 133), and as a flour utilized by millions of people.

There are two distinctive varieties, one (the common French kind) brownish, yellowish, or grayish, the other (Egyptian or Syrian) reddish or orange-red. Those who speak French know the legume as *lentille,* in Spanish it is *lenteja,* in Portuguese *lentilha,* in German *Linse,* and in Arabic *addis.*

FEW SOUPS are as completely satisfying as the following robust German one. Serve it with thick slabs of

pumpernickel, Danish Pickled Cucumbers (page 100), and beer or coffee for a wonderful wintry-eve repast.

German Lentil Soup
Serves 6 liberally.

1½ *cups dried lentils*
1 *pound knockwurst, cut into 1-inch pieces*
3 *medium potatoes, peeled, diced*
2 *large stalks celery, diced*
2 *large onions, diced*
1 *quart chicken broth or bouillon*
1 *quart water*
3 *tablespoons flour*
salt and freshly ground pepper to taste

Soak the lentils in cold water for 2 hours. Drain thoroughly. In a large heavy kettle with cover, combine the lentils, knockwurst (or smoked sausage, or frankfurters, if desired), potatoes, celery, and onion. Add the chicken broth (or bouillon) and water; you may wish to add a bit more liquid later on, for a somewhat thinner soup. Cover and cook over very low heat for about 1 hour, or until the vegetables are quite soft. In a small heavy skillet, brown the flour, being careful that it does not scorch. Stir this vigorously into the soup, mashing out any lumps. Simmer, uncovered, for 5 minutes more. Season to taste and serve while very hot.

ONE OF my Syrian friends introduced me to the following Syrian Lentil Soup, again a very hearty affair. He offered it, in small bowls, to precede a luscious feast of shish kebab, a salad of fresh spinach, and warm Arab bread. Use the pretty red lentils for this recipe, if available.

Syrian Lentil Soup
Serves 4 to 6.

1 *cup dried red lentils*
1 *meaty lamb bone*
2 *quarts water*
3 *tablespoons light olive oil*
1½ *cups chopped onion*
¾ *cup chopped green pepper*
3 *cups diced fresh tomatoes*
¼ *teaspoon marjoram*
salt and freshly ground pepper

Using a large kettle with cover, bring the lamb bone (uncooked or left over from a roast) to the boil in the water. Skim off any scum that forms, and add the lentils which have been picked over and rinsed in cold water. Cover kettle and cook over medium heat while preparing the vegetable seasonings. In a skillet, heat the oil, and sauté the onion and green pepper, stirring often, until they are lightly browned. Stir in the tomatoes, add marjoram, plus salt and pepper to taste (be rather liberal), and simmer the sauce for about 15 minutes over low heat. Turn sauce into the soup, mix through, and continue to cook until lentils are very tender. Serve with each portion a bit of the meat from the lamb bone along with the lentils.

LENTIL salads of several varieties are to be encountered in Europe, notably in Germany, Austria, and Czechoslovakia. Here is an especially tasty recipe which at my house is typically served to accompany a fine wiener schnitzel or schnitzel à la Holstein.

Lentil Salad
Serves 6 liberally.

2 *cups dried lentils*
1½ *quarts water*
2 *medium bay leaves*
1 *large onion, stuck with 4 whole cloves*
1 *teaspoon salt*
¼ *teaspoon salt*
¼ *teaspoon freshly ground pepper*
½ *teaspoon dry mustard*
½ *teaspoon paprika*
6 *scallions with tops, finely chopped*
½ *cup finely chopped dill pickles*
3 *tablespoons wine vinegar*
4 *tablespoons peanut or soy oil*
4 *or 5 medium potatoes, boiled, thinly sliced*
2 *cups shredded lettuce*
2 *tablespoons minced fresh parsley*
1 *teaspoon minced chervil*

Pick over and rinse the lentils in cold water. Place in a kettle with the 1½ quarts water, bay leaves, clove-impaled onion, plus 1 teaspoon salt. Cover container and bring to a quick boil. Remove from heat and allow to stand for 1 hour. Then cook until the lentils are just barely tender, usually only 5 minutes or so. Drain lentils, discarding bay leaves and onion. Prepare a dressing by combining ingredients listed from the ¼ teaspoon salt through the oil. Arrange individual servings of thinly sliced potatoes on the lettuce, topping these with liberal scoops of the drained lentils, and pouring the dressing over. Chill salads, and at serving time sprinkle with parsley and chervil.

THE GOOD cooks of Mexico have created a unique vegetable combination of lentils and sautéed slices of ripe plantains, to be served especially with pork or chicken. I first encountered this delicacy during a botanizing expedition to the attractive tropic city of Manzanillo.

Lentils Manzanillo
Serves 6.

1 *cup dried red lentils*
1 *quart water*
1 *tablespoon salt*
1 *small bay leaf*
3 *tablespoons butter*
½ *cup chopped onion*
¼ *cup chopped green pepper*
¼ *teaspoon freshly ground pepper*
2 *tablespoons butter*
1 *large ripe plantain, thickly sliced*

Pick over and rinse lentils in cold water. Cook, covered, in water with the 1 teaspoon salt and bay leaf until tender. Drain thoroughly. Meanwhile, melt the 3 tablespoons butter, and sauté the onion and green pepper until soft, stirring often. Add salt and pepper. In another skillet melt the 2 tablespoons butter, and sauté the ripe plantain slices until nicely browned. Lightly combine hot lentils, onions and green pepper with the plantain slices, and serve without delay.

TRAVELERS to India, or visitors to Indian restaurants in this country, will without a doubt have already encountered Dhal, for this is one of the favorite Indian fashions of utilizing the lentil. Typically, ghee—clarified butter—is used here, but pretty much the same effect is obtained with plain ordinary butter. Serve the Dhal either hot as a side dish with curries, or chilled as a very interesting condiment with all sorts of beef and lamb recipes.

Dhal
Serves 4 to 6.

2 *cups dried lentils*
3 *cups water*
¼ *to ¾ teaspoon crushed dried red (chili) peppers*
2 *teaspoons salt*
¼ *teaspoon ground turmeric*
4 *tablespoons butter (or ghee)*
1 *cup chopped onion*
1 *medium clove garlic, mashed*

Pick over and rinse lentils in cold water. Drain and place in kettle with cover, with the 3 cups water, dried red (chili) peppers, salt, and turmeric. Cover and cook over very low heat until the lentils are soft and the water is largely absorbed, stirring often. Correct seasoning—the lentils should be rather spicy. Melt the butter (or ghee) in a small skillet, and sauté the onion and garlic until they are just golden, stirring occasionally. Thoroughly drain the lentils, and pour the onion-garlic mixture over them. Serve hot or chilled.

ONE OF the most distinctive ways I know of with lentils—and one of the most pleasing to the palate—is the following recipe for fritters. These are served, of all things, as a dessert, especially to terminate a repast of baked ham, butter-browned thick slices of cooked boniato or regular sweet potato, and my old pet, Pineapple Cole Slaw (page 61). Use the easy canned lentils for this dish.

Lentil Fritters
Serves 4 to 6.

2 large cans lentils, drained
⅓ cup grated onion
½ cup walnut pieces
⅓ cup grated carrot
1 egg, lightly beaten
¼ teaspoon marjoram
lard or light oil for deep frying
confectioners' sugar

Run the canned lentils, onion, walnuts, and carrots through coarse grid of a food mill. Thoroughly blend in the egg and marjoram. Form into compact balls about an inch in diameter. Lower into lard (preferably) or a light oil which has been heated to 370° F. Fry, a few at a time, until well browned, drain on absorbent paper towels, and while hot dust with confectioners' sugar. Serve while hot.

LETTUCE

Lettuce as we know it has been cultivated for well more than two thousand years. Botanists call the basic plant *Lactuca sativa,* and because of its structure place it in the Daisy Family. It is not known in the wild, but presumably comes from another species indigenous to Asia.

Modern Lettuces occur in almost overwhelming variants, scarcely a year passing without the commercial availability of new, improved kinds. The leaves we consume in such tremendous quantities are the enlarged root leaves, those adorning the flowering stem usually being much more coarse and of different form.

In this country, we find several basic kinds of Lettuce, including Head, Leaf, Iceberg, Romaine, and the like. Within each of these categories we find countless subtle variations, ranging from soft and buttery in texture to firm and crisp. Due to contemporary production methods, a marvelous array of Lettuces is usually available in our markets every day of the year.

Americans most often use Lettuce in salads; it is, in fact, by far our most important salad green. Bibb, Boston, and Iceberg are particularly well suited to salads, either as is or in combination with other greens and, very often, cucumbers and tomatoes.

European cooks make far more extensive culinary use of this plant than we do—in soups, in special dishes with special sauces, braised, baked, stewed, and stuffed. The French call it *laitue,* the Spaniards *lechuga,* the Portuguese *alface,* the Germans *Kopf,* and everybody does wonderful things with it.

Using one of the compact head lettuces, such as Iceberg, I prepare, on very special occasions, the following, to offer with chicken, pot roast, and other foods. This is an easy and elegant dish. Some cooks make this in the oven, but I always do it atop the stove with felicitous results.

Braised Lettuce
Serves 4.

4 firm heads lettuce, quartered
2 thick slices lean bacon, diced
½ cup sliced carrots
½ cup coarsely chopped onion
1 tablespoon finely chopped parsley
salt and pepper to taste
2 cups rich beef stock
2 tablespoons butter

In a large heavy ovenproof casserole, fry the bacon dice over high heat on top of the stove, stirring frequently, until rather soft. Add carrots, onion, and parsley, and continue to cook for about 5 minutes, stirring often. Season rather liberally, then add the lettuce quarters. Reduce heat to medium degree, cover the casserole, and, still on top of the stove, cook for 15 minutes, basting the lettuce once with the juices. Pour in the rich beef stock, fresh or canned, and continue to cook, basting every 10 minutes or so, until the lettuce is completely wilted and very tender, usually almost an hour. Remove lettuce to a heated platter and

at once raise heat under the casserole to reduce the braising liquid to about 1 cup. Stir in the butter and pour sauce over the lettuce, to serve at once.

LETTUCE soup in its multitudinous forms quite often makes an appearance from good European kitchens. Here is a superb French chiffonade of lettuce, to be served chilled.

Iced Lettuce Soup
Serves 4.

    1 large firm head lettuce
    4 cups rich chicken stock
    1 tablespoon finely snipped chives
    salt and freshly ground white pepper
    1 cup light cream
    1 tablespoon finely chopped fresh parsley

Cut lettuce into quarters, discard any core part or heavy veins, and cut into very fine strips with a sharp knife. In a saucepan, heat the stock and add the lettuce chiffonade. Cover the container and simmer for 5 minutes, then remove from heat, add chives, season to taste, and blend in the cream. Allow to cool, then refrigerate for several hours, covered, to serve very cold, with garnish of parsley.

So OFTEN we have lettuce salad just as a salad, with a favorite dressing—vinaigrette, Thousand Island, American "French," or something created by the chef of the house. The good cooks in many parts of Pennsylvania prepare the following superb lettuce salad.

Pennsylvania Dutch Wilted Lettuce Salad
Serves 4.

    1 large or 2 small heads compact head lettuce
    4 slices lean bacon, diced
    2 tablespoons cider vinegar
    ½ cup heavy cream
    ⅛ to ¼ teaspoon dry mustard

Sauté the bacon dice until crisp. Drain off all but a tablespoon or so of the bacon fat. Add the vinegar and cook for a minute, stirring constantly. Stir in the heavy cream and dry mustard, mix well, and heat through (do not boil), stirring constantly. Pour this hot dressing over the lettuce, which has been torn into bite-size pieces. Serve at once while the greens are nicely wilted.

ONE of my favorite lettuce salads is a stuffed lettuce. The first time I encountered this fabulous dish was in Laguna Beach, California, where I was invited to a luncheon by the then-leading señora of the local social whirl. Her luncheons were extraordinary affairs, oftentimes with six and seven courses, hot and cold running butlers, and regular appearance by the Hollywood stars in temporary residence in the community. I recollect little of the menus, and have forgotten most of the antics that accompanied the hours-long feasts, but even today, with much more tranquility, I serve Laguna Stuffed Lettuce for my own coterie of friends. Iceberg lettuce is practically obligatory here.

Laguna Stuffed Lettuce
Serves 6.

    1 large firm head iceberg lettuce
    1 3-ounce package cream cheese, softened
    1 2¼-ounce can deviled ham
    ½ cup finely chopped celery hearts
    2 tablespoons minced green pepper
    1 tablespoon minced pimiento
    3 tablespoons mayonnaise
    ½ teaspoon salt
    ¼ teaspoon freshly ground pepper

From a very firm head of lettuce, thoroughly chilled, remove the core with a very sharp knife and hollow out about ⅔ of the middle. Use this lettuce for other things. Thoroughly blend together all other ingredients, and carefully stuff the hollowed-out lettuce. Wrap the stuffed lettuce in aluminum foil and chill for 2 hours. Cut into six pieces and serve without delay.

IT SEEMS almost heretical to do anything more to the glorious leaf lettuces—Bibb and the like—than to offer them, beautifully chilled and patted dry, with your favorite lightest of oil-and-vinegar dressings. But here, if you will, is one salad in which the superbly tender foliage is wilted with a heated sauce. Since this must be eaten without a second's delay, I very much recommend serving it as a special, separate course.

Leaf Lettuce Lisbôa
Serves 4.

    4 heads leaf lettuce
    ½ cup melted butter
    1 teaspoon lemon juice
    1 tablespoon Madeira
    ½ teaspoon salt

Rinse the lettuces and shake them as dry as possible, keeping them whole but discarding any blemished outside leaves. Arrange each lettuce, opening it up slightly, on a salad plate. Heat the other ingredients in a saucepan, stirring until well blended and hot but not boiling, and pour this over the lettuce. Consume at once.

USING leaf lettuce, which they call *sheng-ts'ai*, the talented Chinese cooks prepare an extremely attractive, quickly stir-fried dish. Though usually served with Oriental meat creations, I have found this to be most compatible with more prosaic American food, such as steaks and lamb chops.

Chinese Fried Lettuce
Serves 4.

4 *heads leaf lettuce*
6 *tablespoons peanut or soy oil*
1 *small clove garlic, mashed*
2 *teaspoons soy sauce, Japanese preferred*
¼ *teaspoon monosodium glutamate*

Thoroughly rinse lettuce leaves, tear them into large chunks, and pat dry with absorbent towels. In a wok or large shallow skillet, over high flame, heat the oil, and in it quickly cook the garlic, stirring constantly, until lightly browned. Add the lettuce, sprinkle with soy sauce and monosodium glutamate, and stir-fry for just 1 minute. Serve immediately.

THE SPLENDORS of Brazilian cuisine, as I have mentioned elsewhere, are as yet little appreciated outside of that land—which is regrettable. An excellent example of the heights to which this inspired cookery reaches is found in this *brasileiro* version of a hot lettuce casserole. I find it a perfect dish with poultry of any variety, from duck or chicken to guinea fowl or turkey.

Brazilian Lettuce
Serves 4.

2 *medium heads iceberg lettuce*
3 *quarts water*
1 *tablespoon salt*
1 *cup yoghurt*
½ *teaspoon salt*
⅛ *teaspoon freshly ground pepper*
⅛ *teaspoon ground nutmeg*
2 *hard-cooked eggs, coarsely chopped*
½ *cup thinly sliced peeled cucumber*

2 *tablespoons fine bread crumbs*
4 *teaspoons butter*

Cut out thick ribs from outside of lettuce heads, and wash heads thoroughly. In a large kettle with cover, bring water with salt to rapid boil. Plunge lettuce heads into water, cover, and boil for 8 minutes over high heat. Drain and plunge into a kettle of cold water, then drain again, very thoroughly, pressing out all possible moisture. With a very sharp knife, cut lettuce leaves into very thin strips. Arrange lettuce in a well-buttered shallow baking dish. Thoroughly combine the yoghurt with the salt, pepper, nutmeg, and chopped eggs, and place on top of lettuce. Arrange cucumber slices over casserole, then sprinkle with bread crumbs, and dot with butter. Bake in preheated 400° F. oven until topping is browned, usually about 10 minutes. Serve without delay, cutting down through varied layers for each portion.

USING head or leaf lettuce, cook 1 head or bunch per person in chicken stock, covered, for 10 minutes. Then drain thoroughly and force through a coarse sieve. Serve this in individual ramekins, mixed with smallish quantities of a light Simple Cheese Sauce (page 254), well seasoned, to be run under broiler at last moment to brown lightly prior to serving at table.

ROMAINE

ROMAINE is a well-known variant of the common lettuce (*Lactuca sativa* var. *romana*). Up to two feet tall, it forms a cylindrical or conical vegetable of crisp oblong leaves with broad median ribs. The outermost foliage is a rich green color, but because of the generally compact structure of the bunch, the inner ones are bleached to a pretty whitish-green hue.

Also known as Cos Lettuce, this flavorful green is most often used in salads, notably the renowned Caesar Salad (see below). But the vegetable can also be braised or stewed and served with a sauce such as cream, Mornay, or Hollandaise. If the outer leaves of the bunch are being utilized, it may be necessary to strip out their somewhat tough large midribs.

As is so often the case with famous dishes, fifty different chefs and/or restaurateurs claim to have invented Caesar Salad. In trying to track down the origin of this culinary delight, I found that *Sunset* magazine in March 1945 published a recipe for it, having "discovered the salad in a small Coronado (California) restaurant." It is also described in two cookbooks published a year or so thereafter. However,

Sr. Alex Cardini, of Cardini's Restaurant in Mexico City, affirms that he invented the original Caesar Salad in 1926, naming it after his brother. Whoever Caesar was, and whenever this assortment of ingredients occurred to him, we should all be grateful.

If one prepares all of the ingredients in advance and tosses them in proper sequence at table—which is obligatory with this showpiece, anyway—then Caesar Salad is no more complicated than many more commonly served mixtures of greenery. Try this elegant salad with a good hot quiche, a bottle of chilled white or rosé wine, and in the company of some favorite friends.

Most recipes for Caesar Salad call for chopped anchovies, but I list them as optional, since I feel they seriously detract from the delicacy of the medley. And please use a raw egg, unless your system just absolutely rebels at the thought.

Caesar Salad
Serves 3 to 6.

1 *large head, or 2 small heads Romaine lettuce*
1 *large clove garlic, mashed*
¼ *cup light olive oil*
⅓ *cup peanut or soy oil*

2 *cups tiny stale bread cubes*
½ *teaspoon salt*
freshly ground black pepper
1 *raw egg*
2 *tablespoons fresh lemon juice*
4 *to 8 anchovy fillets, chopped (optional)*
½ *cup freshly grated Fontina or Parmesan cheese*

Wash the Romaine, tear into good-size hunks, and pat dry in a clean kitchen towel. Refrigerate, wrapped in a fresh towel, until ready to use and until well chilled. Crush the garlic in a small bowl, add the two kinds of oil, and let stand at room temperature for at least 1 hour. Using several tablespoons of the garlic oil, brown the stale bread cubes. If essential, cook the egg in boiling water for exactly 1 minute, then remove it with a slotted spoon and cool under running cold water. Allow to cool, unshelled, until ready to use.

With your guests seated at table, serve the crisp chilled Romaine in your biggest salad bowl. Sprinkle with the salt, then liberally grind over the black pepper. Discard any obvious bits of garlic and pour the remaining garlic oil over the salad. Lightly toss until every piece is well coated. Then break in the raw (or barely coddled) egg, add the lemon juice, and again toss lightly but thoroughly. Add the chopped anchovies (if you must) and the grated cheese, and toss once more. Finally add the crisp croutons, toss very gently, and consume without appreciable delay.

LILY

Estimates of the number of botanical species of Lilies, genus *Lilium* (of, logically enough, the Lily Family), range from about one hundred to more than five hundred. These frequently spectacular plants are widely utilized in flower gardens throughout the temperate world.

As vegetables, a number of different kinds of Lilies are extensively cultivated—in China, Japan, Taiwan, parts of Southeast Asia, and even portions of the USSR—for their bulbs, which are edible. These are often pickled or otherwise preserved prior to use, and when available in our domestic markets—generally in cans—may be an interesting culinary experience for the adventuresome epicure.

I have tried the bulbs of several species of *Lilium* on a number of occasions, and I cannot state with truthfulness that I have enjoyed them particularly. Their texture is all right, but the very dominant flavor seems quite alien to my palate—and, as a rule, I will eat and enjoy just about anything. Perhaps you will like these exotics, however.

In any case, Lily bulbs are utilized in Oriental cookery in a variety of ways, chilled as appetizers, in soups, and in stir-fry medleys with other vegetables and such foods as shrimp, pork, and chicken.

Highly valued in Chinese cookery, and available in specialty food shops in this country are Golden Needles, the dried flower buds of the spectacular Tiger Lily (*Lilium tigrinum*), or in some cases, of one of the closely allied Oriental species. These are customarily offered for sale by the ounce or pound in a pressed block, gilded in color.

To utilize Golden Needles, one cuts off the needed amount and soaks it in a bit of hot water until soft—usually for an hour or so. If necessary, the firm bits of stem are trimmed off the buds prior to their being added to the recipe. The softened buds are customarily cut into small lengths, though this is not obligatory.

The flavor of these buds is a very distinctive one and at first try may prove a bit odd to the Occidental taste. In Chinese, they are known by the euphonious name of *gum-jum*.

Golden Needles Chicken
Serves 4 to 6.

1 *dozen dried golden needles*
4 *large dried black Oriental mushrooms*
1 *broiler-fryer chicken, disjointed*
3 *tablespoons peanut or soy oil*
1 *tablespoon Japanese soy sauce*
2 *tablespoons sake or dry sherry*
1 *teaspoon minced fresh ginger root*
3 *canned water chestnuts, finely chopped*
1½ *cups rich chicken broth*
2 *scallions, thinly sliced*

Soak dried golden needles and dried black Oriental mushrooms (both available in specialty food shops) in hot water to cover for about an hour, in separate containers. Drain thoroughly, discarding liquid, rinse under running cold water, and squeeze almost dry. Cut the golden needles into bits about 1 inch in length, and thinly slice the mushrooms, discarding any bits which are still woody. In a large skillet with cover, heat the oil and in it thoroughly brown the disjointed chicken, a couple of pieces at a time. Add the soy sauce, sake (or sherry), and ginger root. Add the golden needles, mushrooms, water chestnuts, and chicken broth, mix through, cover the skillet, and simmer over low heat until the chicken is tender. Stir in scallion slices for last 2 or 3 minutes of cooking. Serve with individual bowls of steamed rice.

LOTUS

Two kinds of Lotus are known to science; these are of the genus *Nelumbo* (often spelled *Nelumbium*, of

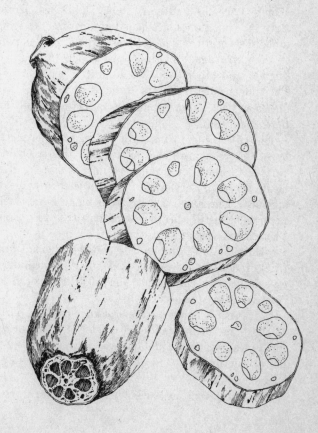

the Water-Lily Family) and known since prehistoric times for their magnificent foliage, their immense showy blossoms, and for their extensive culinary use.

In this country the American Lotus (*Nelumbo lutea*), native in the Eastern United States southward to Florida and westward to Texas, has long been prized by the Indians as an important food plant. The entire plant is edible, from juvenile leaves (these boiled) to large starchy subterranean (or submarine, I suppose) rhizomes to flower petals and large seeds. The seeds, in particular, are unique delicacies when roasted, having a remarkable nutlike flavor and crunchy texture. On occasion they can be found in specialty shops, particularly in regions boasting of sizable wild colonies of the plants. Alternate vernaculars for this extraordinary plant include Water Chinquapin (or Chinkapin), Water-Nut, Duck Acorn, and Nelumbo.

The Oriental, East Indian, or Sacred Lotus (*Nelumbo nucifera*) extends in nature from the Caspian Sea to Japan, and southward to northern Australia. Though often called, in horticulture, the Egyptian Lotus, that plant is in actuality a completely different thing, of the allied genus *Nymphaea*. There are many spectacular forms in common cultivation as ornamentals throughout the world, with flowers often a foot in diameter, and glorious stalked leaves which in themselves justify the cultivation of this aquatic.

Even more than its Western relative, this Lotus is of importance as a culinary item. The leaves, particularly the young ones, are boiled and utilized as a vegetable in several parts of the Eastern world. The petals of the extravagant blossoms are added to clear consommés and other soups as decorative garnishments. The stamens of the flowers are used, especially in such places as Laos and Vietnam, to impart a special savor to teas and tisanes.

The ripe seeds (often with the vaguely bitter embryo removed) are dried or roasted, then pickled in various fashions, or ground to make a starchy Lotus meal. When preserved in a rich sweetened soy sauce mixture, then ground, these seeds make Lotus jam, a favorite filling of select Oriental pastries and desserts. The canned seeds are available in Chinese markets in the United States and can be added—in small quantities, it should be emphasized—to stir-fried dishes, especially with chicken or pork. Their flavor is distinctive, to say the least.

Lotus root is doubtless the best known edible portion of the plant in international cuisine. Called *lin-ngau* in Chinese, *hasunone* in Japanese, this is an extraordinary structure when one encounters it fresh in specialized shops.

The Lotus root, as a whole, may measure upwards of four feet in length, with a diameter of more than three inches. It is divided into segments resembling links of fat sausage, usually reddish-brown outside and white to buff-orange within. A cross-section of each segment discloses ten perforations of two sizes, the smaller alternating with the larger.

It is a productive aquatic crop, in great demand, large quantities being shipped especially from Hawaii to supply Oriental populations from San Francisco and Los Angeles to New York. The fresh root is usually harvested from July to November, but is available at other seasons sliced and preserved in various ways, usually in a sweet sauce to which soy sauce and often rice wine have been added.

These roots, typically quartered lengthwise, then thin-sliced transversely, are important to many kinds of Chinese cookery in a variety of stir-fry medleys, particularly with pork or beef.

AND THEN we have the following stalwart soup.

Lotus Root Soup
Serves 4.

2 *medium segments lotus root*
1 *pound lean pork, thinly sliced*
1 *teaspoon cornstarch*
1 *tablespoon soy sauce*
¼ to ½ *teaspoon freshly ground pepper*
1 *quart water*
1 *teaspoon salt*

Cut off and discard ends of each joint of lotus-root segments or links. Wash and scrape the skin. Cut roots lengthwise into halves, then cut crosswise into ½-inch lengths and wash thoroughly again. Combine the pork slices with the cornstarch and soy sauce. Bring the water and salt to the boil, add the pork mixture and the lotus root, cover, and cook over low heat until the vegetable is tender.

LUFFA GOURD

The Luffa Gourd (*Luffa acutangula*, and also *L. cylindrica*, of the Squash Family) should be pronounced *loo*-fah. Alias Dishcloth Gourd, Dishrag Gourd, or Towel Gourd, this interesting plant is well known to many people in this country for its nonculinary uses. The mature gourds are soaked in water until the flesh rots away, then the filamentous coarse skeleton is utilized as a scrubbing instrument in the kitchen or in the bath—hence yet another vernacular, Vegetable Sponge.

But in their more juvenile state, these interesting cucurbits are frequently purveyed in choice markets as an unusual and delicious vegetable. Cultivated to some extent in Hawaii and California, they appear on occasion in stores in certain of our larger cities elsewhere, and are commonplace in many tropical lands. The edible forms are found under their Chinese names of *see-kwa, sua-kwa,* or *sin-kwa,* the Japanese *hechima,* or as Vegetable Gourd, Sponge Gourd, Rag Gourd, or even Chinese Okra.

Like most other members of its alliance, this is a rampant, coarse vine. Originally from the tropical parts of Asia and Africa, the Luffas have been cultivated in virtually all warm parts of the globe for centuries. In this country they are extensively grown as unusual and valuable annuals, the seeds being available from many commercial seedsmen.

When found in food stores, the vegetable measures up to two feet in length, with a maximum diameter of about two inches. With green, somewhat wrinkled skin, Luffa Gourds are narrower at the stem end than at the enlarged apex, often slightly curved, and are set with a number of prominent longitudinal ridges. The flesh of the immature vegetable is white and somewhat spongy. It has a flavor rather reminiscent of cucumber, a vague relative, although its texture is not as firm, as a rule.

The young vegetables are justifiably popular in such things as chop suey or as savory additions to stir-fry meat medleys, and the like. The very young gourds are often sliced and dried, for use as a special and highly prized ingredient in Chinese soups, or are eaten fresh, cooked as one would yellow crookneck squash.

MALANGA

Although Taro, genus *Colocasia* (see page 228), is grown to some extent in the United States and in the warmer lands of this hemisphere, the root vegetables of the group—the aroids, or members of the Arum Family (Aracae)—encountered with greatest frequency in this part of the world belong to a completely distinct assemblage. These plants are to be encountered under a bewildering variety of names—Malanga, *malangüilla, tanier, tannia, taya, belembe, yautía, tiquisque, quequisque,* and *otó,* among others. Botanists relegate all of them to two, or possibly more, species of one genus of aroids, *Xanthosoma.* Malanga is probably the most widely used vernacular epithet, and will serve our present purposes.

In markets in our large North American cities, and almost everywhere in tropical America, we encounter Malanga in two forms—as a root vegetable in the shape of tuberlike corms, and sometimes in flat-roundish offsets from these corms. The stem-shaped corms can measure a foot in length, with a diameter of three inches, while the offsets (or cormlets, to be technical) attain an expanse of three inches and an almost comparable thickness. As with taro, the young leaves of these aroids are also sold as edibles, gathered into bunches of potherbs. Malanga leaves are most likely to be found in markets during the rainy season, when these bog-dwelling plants reach their full flush of growth.

Malanga roots are usually covered with a dark dull-brown or yellowish-brown rough, thickened skin, and often have somewhat pronounced annular rings toward the apex.

Basic preparation calls for peeling and cutting the roots into lengths of two inches or so and boiling in lightly salted water until almost tender. The flesh varies in color from ivory-white to distinctly yellowish, depending upon the variety. In both texture and flavor, it is reminiscent of a mealy but slightly moist white potato. Like the allied taro, Malangas contain more starch than white potatoes and are, as well, a rather good source of thiamine. After the initial parboiling, the Malanga roots can be prepared in virtually every way suggested for our Irish White Potato (pages 187–91). The recipes for Taro (page 228) apply equally well to this vegetable.

Boiled (or steamed) Malangas, cooked until very tender, lend themselves admirably to being riced or mashed. They are then dressed with a modicum of cream and good quantities of butter, and offered at table with salt and fresh-ground pepper. The raw vegetable is generally highly acrid, because of the presence of microscopic needle-like crystals of calcium oxalate, but thorough cooking removes all traces of this characteristic, and well-prepared Malangas are preferred by many good cooks to the finest white potatoes from Maine or Idaho. Some selected forms to be encountered particularly in the West Indies produce copious numbers of the potato-shaped offsets, with fibrous skin, which are notably delicate in flavor and quite as attractive as tiny new potatoes of more northern climes.

I have relished the very juvenile foliage on many occasions, in towns around the perimeter of the Gulf of Mexico's southern part, and along the Caribbean coast further along. The plants are trimmed of any overly heavy stems or midribs, much as one would treat spinach, then washed thoroughly to remove all particles of soil. The leaves are steamed in a small amount of salted water, covered, over high heat, until

they just wilt yet still retain some texture. Served drained, while very hot, with butter and salt and fresh-ground pepper to taste, these greens in the opinion of many of us far excel even the finest varieties of common spinach.

ONE OF my personal favorites among Malanga dishes is the following, which I acquired during an orchid-hunting trip to Nicaragua's picturesque Caribbean port of Bluefields. I first had it served with thin-filleted pan-fried fish, flapping-fresh from the palm-fringed lagoon, with wedges of fresh lime and the omnipresent black beans and rice. In Bluefields we partook of Victoria beer, and I find that a good beer here at home is a perfect beverage when I repeat this repast. Cubes of guava paste and cream cheese with unsalted puffy Cuban crackers create a most enjoyable finale to what I consider a delectable tropical meal.

Malanga Bluefields
Serves 6.

1 *pound malangas*
3 *tablespoons butter*
¼ *teaspoon freshly ground pepper*
1 *teaspoon salt*
1 *tablespoon cornstarch*
2 *teaspoons brown sugar*
2 *egg yolks*
lard or light oil for frying

Peel, wash, and cut malangas into 2-inch lengths (or cut roundish offsets in half). Bring a quantity of lightly salted water to a rolling boil, and cook the vegetable until tender. Drain thoroughly and mash or put through potato ricer. Thoroughly blend in butter, pepper, salt, cornstarch, brown sugar, and egg yolks, in that order. When slightly cooled, form into walnut-size balls. Heat enough lard or light oil (peanut oil, for example) to 375° F. so that about 3 inches of oil is available. Lower the balls, a few at a time, into this hot liquid, and fry until golden brown, usually 5 minutes or so. Remove with slotted spoon and drain on absorbent paper towels. Serve while very hot.

AJIACO (pronounced ah-hee-*ah*-ko) is a sort of generic name for a series of stews or thick soups, popular in a great many parts of Latin America. Each country has its own special version, these differing markedly in precise ingredients—notably the various tropical vegetables included.

The following delicious concoction is Cuban in origin, was introduced into my home by the illustrious Sra. Benita Robaina, and in its authentic form contains malanga, *ñame, yuca,* boniato, calabaza, and *plátano.* If necessary, the *ñame* or *yuca* could be omitted, I suppose. Serve in commodious bowls, with crusty hot Cuban or French bread, hot rice, and a light salad of shredded lettuce and sliced avocado. Beer is a perfect beverage here.

Ajiaco Criollo
Serves 6 to 8 liberally.

2 *medium malangas*
2 *medium* ñames
1 *rather large* yuca
2 *or 3 medium boniatos*
1 *large green plantain* (plátano)
2 *to 4 medium potatoes*
1 *large piece calabaza*
1 *meaty ham bone*
2 *quarts water*
½ *pound* tasajo (*shredded beef*)
1 *pound cubed lean pork*
2 *teaspoons salt*
2 *tablespoons lard*
3 *or 4 cloves garlic, mashed*
1½ *cups chopped onion*
1 *large green pepper, coarsely chopped*
1 *8-ounce can tomato sauce*

Peel all the vegetables, malanga through calabaza, and cut them into large chunks. Using your largest heavy pot with cover, place the meaty ham bone in the 2 quarts water. Bring to a quick boil, skim off any froth, then add the *tasajo* (or use stew beef simmered in a small amount of water until it can be shredded), pork cubes, and salt. Parboil the malanga, *ñame,* and *yuca* separately, until each is almost tender. Then add the drained chunks to the Ajiaco, and continue to cook over low heat, the container covered. For last 20 minutes or so of cooking, add the pieces of boniato, plantain, potato, and calabaza. The vegetables should retain some character when the dish is finished, and not have cooked down to an indeterminate mush. Meanwhile, prepare a *sofrito* by melting the lard in a skillet and sautéing the garlic, onion, and green pepper, stirring often, over rather high heat for 15 minutes. Add the tomato sauce, mix through, and turn this into the Ajiaco when the malanga, *ñame,* and *yuca* are added. Add salt if necessary (black pepper is not authentically used in this recipe) and serve so that everyone gets a sample of everything.

AMONG the innumerable culinary delights at Charlottenburgh, the splendid home of the Morris Cargills in Jamaica, is the special version of hearty fritters which Lovie, the principal cook of the estate, has perfected. She usually makes these from malanga, which she calls by its native name of *tannia.* On occasion, she alternates with coco tubers, alias taro or dasheen, to give a subtly different species of fritter. Although they are most often served piping hot with just about any kind of meat, I found these fat delicacies superlative eating at room temperature, with cold duck (stuffed with big chunks of onion and basted during roasting with orange juice) on a memorable picnic at Hardwar Gap, in the beautiful Blue Mountains above Kingston.

Lovie's Tannia Fritters
Makes about 12.

1 *cup finely grated raw malanga or taro*
1 *tablespoon flour*
½ *teaspoon salt*
½ *teaspoon baking powder*
1 *or 2 teaspoons finely snipped chives*
freshly ground black pepper to taste
deep fat for frying

Wash and peel the malanga or taro, wash again and grate finely to make 1 cup. Thoroughly combine with all other ingredients except the deep fat, beating well. Heat fat until it smokes, and drop the mixture into it by spoonfuls. Fry until golden brown, drain on absorbent paper towels, and serve either hot or at room temperature.

MATRIMONY-VINE

The Matrimony-vine (*Lycium chinense,* of the Potato-Tomato Family, Solanaceae), is a rather sprawling, vinelike shrub with spiny stems, set with smooth, dark or bright-green leaves that are utilized principally in soups as an interesting vegetable. Growing to as much as six feet tall and across, the plant is cultivated to some degree in temperate parts of the United States as a garden ornamental, because of its purplish flowers followed by abundant showy scarlet fruits, which hang from the arching or semi-erect branches.

Originally from China and probably other parts of eastern Asia, the Matrimony-vine is seldom encountered in this country as a culinary item outside of

Oriental produce markets in California and Hawaii. Bunches of the young growths of the plant, cut into lengths twenty or so inches long, are encountered on occasion, and can be utilized to good advantage in soups such as those described under Basella (Malabar Nightshade) (page 33) and Chinese Mustard (page 154).

The flavor of Matrimony-vine is rather delicate, yet with a pleasant spicy touch.

Melons

A great many different kinds of Melons have been developed through the centuries in various parts of the globe. These, of diverse appearance and botanical identity, appear in the cuisine of almost every nation. All are members of the large Cucurbit Family, which also contains such things as squash, pumpkin, and cucumber.

Oftentimes the cook in this country thinks of Melons solely as fruits, for use in desserts, salads, pickles, or condiments. But there are several distinct Melons which are used primarily, some exclusively, in various cooked forms, as unique and attractive vegetables.

BITTER MELON

Two representatives of the genus *Momordica,* of the Squash Family, are of some importance as vegetables in various parts of the world. The better known of these is the so-called Bitter Melon or Balsam Pear (*Momordica Charantia*), an inhabitant of the tropical parts of Asia and Africa which has become naturalized in the Antilles in this hemisphere. It is grown in many North American gardens as an annual ornamental vine, and its seeds—as of its relative, the Balsam Apple (*Momordica Balsamina,* of similar geographic dissemination)—are available from a number of domestic sources.

The vines are graceful, with pretty lobed leaves of a particularly vivid green hue, inch-wide yellow flowers, and fruits of extraordinary characteristics. Bitter Melon fruits are especially prized as vegetables by good Oriental cooks and often are found in specialty produce markets. Six to ten inches long and up to almost three inches in diameter, they taper at each end and are covered with blunt smooth warts. In their

immature condition, while green, they are picked for culinary use. When ripe, they become bright yellow to vivid orange, and they split open, the three sections recurring from the apex to disclose the pulpy pith and numbers of showy bright-red-covered patterned white to brown seeds.

These red arils around the seeds are edible, and I considered them a particular delight as a child in Central Florida, where the plant is even today found to considerable extent in old gardens. The seeds themselves should never be eaten, we were told, and subsequently one of my more experimental pals found to his dismay that they are a violent purgative.

The unopened greenish-yellow or dark-green fruits of the Bitter Melon are boiled whole, or cut into sections and stir-fried; they are vaguely reminiscent of a bland squash, but with a decided degree of sourness. The young foliage makes a good potherb, steamed after rinsing and dressed with butter, possibly a touch of vinegar, and seasonings. And the mature vegetables, without the seeds, can be sliced and sautéed in butter or a light oil until just barely tender. In this form they are often incorporated into curries in such places as India and Ceylon.

The fruits of the Balsam Apple, which are fatter than those of the true Bitter Melon and rarely grow longer than three inches, vary from smooth to somewhat warty. When mature, they become a splendid waxen orange shade which makes a well-grown vine a delight in the garden. As a vegetable, this cucurbit is used like its more popular relative, the Bitter Melon

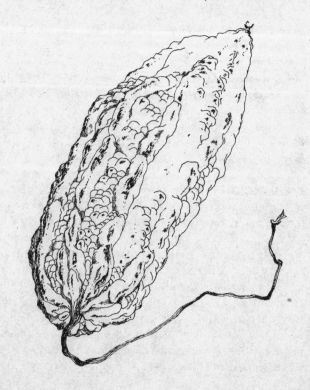

(alias *fu-qua, fooh-quar,* or *foo-gwa* in Chinese, *tsuru-reishi* in Japanese).

Bitter Melon's distinctive flavor is, I suppose, strictly an acquired taste. I find it cool, somewhat like that of bitter candy mints, and especially refreshing during warm summer weather. The vegetable is an important ingredient of special soups, is stuffed in a variety of ways, and frequently is found in medleys with meats, notably with beef. In those fascinating Oriental markets in our larger cities, Bitter Melons are also available in cans, as well as dried, these generally imported.

IN KOREA, soups known by the unusual name of *kook* are served at almost every meal including breakfast. Typically, a big heavy brass soup-bowlful is served to each person—no small portions in soup-loving Seoul. The following version is one utilizing the basic Korean *kook* with Bitter Melon.

Bitter Melon Soup, Korean
Serves 4 to 6.

> 2 *medium bitter melons*
> *salted boiling water*
> ½ *pound lean beef, thinly sliced*
> ½ *teaspoon mashed garlic*
> 3 *scallions, with tops, finely chopped*
> 1 *teaspoon Toasted Ground Sesame Seeds (recipe below)*
> 1 *to* 2 *tablespoons soy sauce*
> 1 *to* 2 *tablespoons peanut or soy oil*
> 6 *to* 7 *cups water*
> *salt and freshly ground pepper to taste*
> 1 *teaspoon monosodium glutamate*

Cut bitter melons into halves lengthwise, scoop out pulp and seeds and discard these. Wash melon shells and cut into ⅛-inch slices. Cook in boiling water for 3 minutes, then drain. Chop the thin slices of beef into coarse dice, using a very sharp knife or cleaver. Thoroughly combine with the mashed garlic, scallions, sesame seeds, and soy sauce. In a heavy soup kettle with cover, heat the oil, add the meat mixture, and stir-fry until the meat is browned to taste. Add the water, bring to the boil, then cover kettle, lower heat and simmer for 15 minutes. Add the bitter melon, cover again, and simmer until it is firm-tender. Add salt and pepper to taste, plus monosodium glutamate, and serve the soup while very hot.

Toasted Ground Sesame Seeds

> 1 *cup white sesame seeds*
> 1 *teaspoon salt*

Place sesame seeds in a heavy ungreased skillet, preferably a seasoned cast-iron one. Cook over medium heat, shaking and stirring constantly, until seeds are nicely and evenly browned. Remove from heat and sprinkle with salt. Thoroughly mash in a mortar with pestle. Use as needed (as in above Korean *kook*), storing leftovers in dry jar with tight-fitting lid.

Next time you become inspired to prepare an elegant multi-course Oriental repast at home (an increasingly popular habit with enterprising amateur chefs in these parts), acquire a couple of bitter melons for the following handsome, tasty dish as one of the items on the menu.

Stuffed Bitter Melon
Serves 4.

> 2 *large bitter melons*
> ½ *pound ground lean pork*
> 2 *teaspoons tiny dried shrimp*
> 3 *soda crackers*
> ½ *teaspoon cold water*
> *salt and pepper to taste*
> 1 *to* 2 *teaspoons soy sauce*
> 1 *to* 2 *teaspoons minced scallions*
> 1½ *teaspoons peanut or soy oil*

Cut the bitter melons crosswise into 2-inch lengths, scoop out and discard pulp and seeds. Run the ground pork through fine grid of a meat grinder. Cook, stirring often, in 1 teaspoon oil, until rather well done. Wash and drain the dried shrimp and run these through the meat grinder. Combine the pork and shrimp, and run again through the grinder. Briefly soak the crackers in the cold water, then combine with the salt and pepper, soy sauce, and scallions. Chop fine and add to the meat mixture. Stuff the sections of bitter melon with this. Bring oil to high heat in a wok or a large shallow skillet and brown both sides of the melon sections in the oil, turning them with a spatula. Add a little water to the skillet, lower heat, and cook stuffed bitter melon for about 12 minutes, or until firm-tender. Serve without delay, pouring some of the gravy over each portion.

Bitter melons, as well as the perky little balsam apples, are cultivated commercially to some degree in the United States today, especially in Hawaii and California. In both states I have found the following version of good old chop suey in the homes of friends of Far Eastern extraction, and occasionally in good Chinese eateries.

Bitter Melon Chop Suey
Serves 4.

> 2 medium bitter melons
> salted boiling water
> ½ pound lean beef, thinly sliced
> 1 teaspoon cornstarch
> 1½ teaspoons peanut or soy oil
> ¼ teaspoon salt
> 1 to 2 teaspoons soy sauce
> 1 thin slice ginger root

Cut bitter melons into lengthwise halves, scoop out and discard pulp and seeds. Wash melon shells and cut into ⅛-inch slices. Plunge into boiling water to cook for 5 minutes, then drain thoroughly. Combine the thin slices of lean beef with the cornstarch. Using a wok or shallow skillet, heat the oil over high flame, then add the salt, soy sauce, and thin slice of ginger root. Stir-fry for a moment, then add the beef and stir-fry for 1 minute longer. Remove meat with slotted spoon. Add the sliced bitter melon and stir-fry for 1 minute, then return the cooked beef, add a small amount of water to make a gravy, cook 30 seconds or so, and serve at once.

ORIENTAL PICKLING MELON

The Oriental Pickling Melon (*Cucumis conomon,* of the Squash Family) is a close relative of the common cucumber. A native of China and Japan, it is today to be found with some frequency in Oriental markets in this country's larger cities, the fresh vegetables usually appearing in March and April. The Oriental Pickling Melon is oblong and cylindrical, eight to twelve inches long and up to three and a half inches in diameter, with a smooth white or pale yellowish-green skin and white flesh.

When these melons are mature—but not old—they are added to fish soups, such as the one below. More commonly, they are pickled after having been allowed to ripen on the vine. The pickles, known as *yuet-kwa* in Chinese and *shiro-uri* in Japanese, are eaten chilled, as a crisp condiment. Or they are added to thinly sliced beef or pork mixtures, for steaming in a soy-sauce-seasoned dish until meat and melon are just tender.

Oriental Pickling Melon Soup
Serves 4.

> 2 large Oriental pickling melons
> salted boiling water
> 1 quart (4 cups) rich fish stock, strained
> 2 tablespoons Japanese soy sauce
> 1 teaspoon sugar
> 1 tablespoon cornstarch
> 2 to 4 tablespoons finely chopped scallion tops

Peel melons and cut into halves lengthwise. Scoop out and discard seeds. Cut halves transversely into ½-inch lengths and boil in the salted boiling water for 5 minutes. Drain, discarding water. Bring 2 cups of the rich fish stock to the boil, with the soy sauce and sugar, then thoroughly blend in the cornstarch. Heat the remainder of the stock in a kettle to the boil, add the pieces of melon, then stir in the seasoned stock mixture. Cook, covered, until the melon is just tender, and serve while very hot, garnished with the scallion tops.

WATERMELON

The Watermelon (*Citrullus vulgaris*) is one of the diverse squash-pumpkin clan. Originally from the dry parts of southern Africa, it was cultivated by the ancient Egyptians and at a very early date introduced into India and China. In the warm parts of Europe, it was popular hundreds of years ago, and by 1629 it was well known in this country in Massachusetts.

Today Watermelon is one of the best known of those cucurbits that can be utilized both as a vegetable and as a fruit. Its cultivated varieties here, encountered principally in the warmer states, are numerous, and, especially during the summertime, large and small specimens are to be found in every market. In recent years, seedless forms have been developed by our busy American agricultural breeders; but these are frowned upon by many of us who delight in the summer pastime of taking chilled Watermelons on a picnic, cut into huge wedges and consumed with much dripping of pink juice and spitting out of the ebony seeds.

In China there are a great many selected variants, called West Melons, since they were developed primarily in the western reaches of that land. These are raised to some degree in the United States, and can be bought in Oriental produce markets. Traditional Chinese homes often invite favored guests to special

festive "eating parties," at which these notable delicacies, properly iced, are served—*just* Watermelons and nothing else. Then there are other forms raised primarily for their crunchy seeds, the flesh being of strictly secondary importance to the connoisseur.

The Preserving Watermelon, a round, mottled vegetable with hard white flesh, inedible when raw, is often known in the United States as Citron, although this name is more accurately applied to a large lemonlike fruit (*Citrus Medica*) from a shrubby little tree of the Mediterranean region. The thick flesh of both is candied and extensively used as a confection and in such things as fruit cakes.

WE MOST often enjoy Watermelon fresh, as a fruit, but the rind of the finer varieties available in this country adapts itself excellently to vegetable cookery. Here is a very tasty recipe of Chinese origin that could be a memorable addition to your next homemade Oriental repast.

Braised Watermelon Rind
Serves 4 to 6.

10 *cups cut-up watermelon rind*
½ *cup peanut or soy oil*
1 *cup diced lean pork*

2 *cups sliced fresh mushrooms*
4 *scallions with tops, cut into 1-inch diagonal lengths*
2 *cups cooked crabmeat*
2 *tablespoons soy sauce*

Pare off green outer peel of melon and the pink flesh, using only the white or green-white rind. Cut this into bite-size pieces. In a wok or large shallow skillet, heat the oil and in it stir-fry the pork dice until they are nicely browned. Remove meat with slotted spoon and keep warm. Add to the pan the mushrooms, scallions, crabmeat, and watermelon pieces and stir-fry over very high flame until the melon chunks are just barely tender, yet still retain considerable texture. Add the soy sauce and serve immediately, with small bowls of hot steamed rice on the side.

WINTER MELON

The Winter Melon (*Benincasa hispida*—with *B. cerifera* an important synonym—of the Squash Family) is a fascinating cucurbit of unusual appearance and exceptional culinary uses. A large soft-hairy vine produces huge oblong fruit a foot or more long and often eight inches thick, sometimes weighing up to forty pounds. This is cooked in a variety of ways as a vegetable, principally in the Orient.

Green in color, this fruit-vegetable is rather heavily coated with a white wax substance, giving to it a most distinctive and attractive appearance. The flesh of the melon is thick, firm, and white, and encloses a quantity of pith and small seeds. It is renowned for its wonderful keeping quality when fully mature—from six to twelve months, provided the heavy rind is not broken!

Rarely encountered outside of Chinese specialty markets in this country, the Winter Melon should be more widely grown and appreciated by the connoisseur culinary gardener. Some of the alternate vernacular names for it—Ash Melon (or Ash Pumpkin), White Gourd, Wax Gourd, and Chinese Preserving Melon—are amply indicative of its appearance and primary use in the kitchen. Additional common names that have been applied to this cucurbit include *doan-gwa, dung-kwa,* and *tung-kua,* and *zit-kwa* when immature (Chinese), *tōgan* or *togwa* (Japanese), and *calabaza china* (Spanish-speaking America).

The rind of the semiripe or ripe Winter Melon is very popular in sweet pickles or preserves (sometimes available in cans from Hong Kong), and can also be prepared in the fashions described below.

In Japan—and to some degree in Japanese colonies in our large cities—the juvenile fruits of the Winter Melon are eaten as a sort of condiment vegetable, lightly steamed and flavored with a modicum of soy sauce, particularly with seafood. And in India and some parts of tropical Africa, the fruit is eaten when immature, thinly sliced or coarsely chopped, with rice and in vegetable curries.

To prepare the Winter Melon for any of its diverse uses, wash and scrub off the waxy bloom. If the outside rind seems overly hard, pare away just the outermost layer and discard it. The seeds, incidentally, can be eaten after roasting, but their definite bitterness is an acquired taste.

HERE IS a favorite stir-fry dish in which Winter Melon enjoys a prominent position. In it, the unique texture and flavor of this cucurbit come through very well.

Winter Melon Gourmet
Serves 4 to 6.

> 1 *winter melon, about 6 pounds*
> 2 *tablespoons peanut or soy oil*
> ½ *pound lean pork, cut into slivers*
> 1½ *cups coarsely chopped scallions, with tops*
> 1 *tablespoon soy sauce, Japanese preferred*

Wash the melon and scrub off all the wax. Peel off

the outermost part of rind if this is overly hard. Discard pith and, if desired, roast the seeds of the vegetable after washing in several changes of water. Cut the flesh into chunks about 2 inches square and allow them to drain on absorbent paper towels for about 30 minutes. In a wok or shallow sizable skillet, heat the oil and stir-fry the pork slivers over high heat. Add the pieces of winter melon and continue to stir-fry until the vegetable starts to become tender. Add scallions and soy sauce and continue to stir-fry for about 2 or 3 minutes—all the vegetables should still retain some crispness of texture when served.

WINTER Melon Soup is a fabulous concoction—and a famous one—offered on occasion by good Oriental restaurants in this country. Its precise ingredients are variable, but the following recipe is both authentic and tasty. Sometimes the entire melon is parboiled, hollowed out, and filled with the soup mixture, but this version is far easier—the management of the entire vegetable as a "serving dish" can be complicated. A special repast, the soup is customarily served as an entrée, with bowls of hot rice alongside.

Winter Melon Soup
Serves 6.

> 1 *winter melon, about 6 pounds*
> *salted boiling water*
> 1½ *cups thinly sliced raw chicken breast*
> 1½ *cups slivered cooked ham*
> 2 *tablespoons cornstarch*
> ½ *teaspoon freshly ground pepper*
> 2 *tablespoons peanut or soy oil*
> 2 *thin small slices ginger root*
> 1 *small clove garlic, mashed*
> ½ *cup thinly sliced bamboo shoot*
> 1 *cup coarsely chopped raw shelled shrimp*
> 8 *cups rich chicken stock*
> 1 *cup scallions, with tops, cut into ½-inch diagonal lengths*
> 2 *to 3 teaspoons sake or dry sherry*
> *soy sauce to taste*

Scrub and wash off the waxy covering of melon and cut it in half crosswise. Scoop out pulp and seeds. (Dry and roast the seeds, if desired, for use at another time.) Cut melon into slices about 1 inch thick, then wash again to remove all soft pulp. Place these slices in a good quantity of salted boiling water and cook for 5 minutes. Drain. Thoroughly combine the thin slices of chicken breast and ham slivers with cornstarch and pepper. In a large heavy soup kettle with cover, heat the oil, add the thin slices of ginger root and the garlic, and stir-fry over rather high heat for 2 minutes. Add the seasoned chicken and ham, and stir-fry for 3 minutes more. Add bamboo shoot, shrimp, and chicken stock, and bring to the boil. Add the rounds of melon, lower heat to simmer, cover the kettle, and simmer for about 30 minutes, or until melon is just tender—do not overcook. Add the scallions, sake or sherry, and soy sauce to taste, for the final 2 minutes of cooking. Carefully remove the slices of melon and place in each commodious soup plate or shallow bowl. Add soup. Serve while very hot, with accompanying side bowls of hot rice.

STEAMED Winter Melon is another popular version of preparation, rather old-fashioned but still to be encountered in select Chinese restaurants in such places as New York, San Francisco, and Honolulu.

Steamed Winter Melon
Serves 4.

1 *small tender winter melon (weight under 3 pounds)*
½ *pound thinly sliced ham*
soy sauce to taste
freshly ground pepper to taste

Scrub and wash off waxy covering of melon, and cut crosswise into 2-inch pieces. Wash thoroughly, and sandwich pieces of ham, by making vertical slits in melon, into each section. Place on rack in a large kettle with cover, over boiling water, cover and steam until the melon is tender, usually about an hour. Season melon sections to taste with soy sauce and pepper, serving while very hot.

MILLET

A number of different kinds of grains—the seeds of several distinct species of grasses—are categorized as Millet. Cultivated by man since prehistoric times in various parts of the globe, they are very seldom encountered as culinary items in this country. In southern Europe, Africa, and parts of Asia, however, several of the Millets are widely used for food.

The grains, of varying dimensions and colors, are typically hulled, then ground to be roasted, added to milk for a kind of gruel, formed into cakes for frying, or fermented to make a potent native beer. North Americans usually encounter the various Millets only in fodder for stock or in birdseed mixtures.

MITSUBA

The Mitsuba (*Cryptotaenia canadensis*, of the Carrot Family) is vaguely reminiscent of green celery, although the hollow yellow-green stalks are not as plump as celery stalks. The plant, as seen in bunches in Oriental markets, seldom exceeds eight or ten inches in length.

A native of Canada and certain of the northern reaches of this country, where it is known as Honewort, this unusual plant has long been cultivated in Japan, and to a lesser degree by Japanese colonies in Hawaii and California.

The rather spindly roots are blanched briefly in salted water, then cut into julienne strips and quickly fried in a little light oil. The stalks and foliage are cut into suitable lengths and added to clear soups for their distinctive flavor—or they are plunged into boiling water for a moment, then served lightly dressed with soy sauce.

MUGWORT

Mugwort (*Artemisia vulgaris*, of the Daisy Family) is a rather pretty plant with often purplish stems, dissected leaves which are white-cottony underneath and green above, and erect bunches of yellowish flowers. Grown extensively as an ornamental in flower gardens throughout the temperate zones, this native of the northern parts of North America and Europe also figures as a seasoning vegetable in Oriental cookery. In Chinese it is called *ngaai*, in Japanese, *yomogi*.

The seedlings or branches from more mature specimens appear in markets in bunches about a foot long. All parts of the plant give off a very positive scent that is somewhat alien to many Western palates but beloved by Orientals.

The following recipe for festival rice cakes, or *mochi*, is a rather involved one. I think it is far easier for the average interested reader of this volume to purchase the prepared little cakes—available particularly during Chinese New Year—and add them to Misotaki (page 44) or a clear chicken broth. The recipe is quoted from Chung and Ripperton's invaluable work on the use of Oriental vegetables in Hawaii.

Mugwort Rice Cakes (Mochi)

"Select young leaves and tender twigs of the plant; wash them well; boil in a little water until they are tender. Then steam with rice [glutinous rice is most often used here—A.D.H.]. When the vegetable-rice mixture is thoroughly cooked, place it in a mortar and mash. Then form the mass into balls and fill the center of each with *an*, a mixture of sugar and beans. [*An* (pronounced ahn) is prepared by soaking 1 pound Adzuki Beans (page 33) for 24 hours.] Drain, add fresh water sufficient to cover, and let come to a boil. Drain again, and add more fresh water and let come to a boil, repeating this process four times to remove any bitter taste from the beans. After the final draining, mash the beans. Then add to them sufficient water to permit washing out and removal of the finer particles, when strained through cheese-cloth. Add sugar to the strained mass and cook slowly until it has the consistency of mashed potatoes."

MUSHROOM

There are countless thousands of different kinds of fungi, the vast aggregation of flowerless plants that includes our edible Mushrooms. This fantastic assemblage also contains the deadly poisonous creatures known as toadstools, which are sometimes disastrous to the casual gourmet who fancies himself an authority when plucking apparently edible Mushrooms from the wild forests and fields where they grow. A mycologist friend has stated that only the expert should eat Mushrooms collected in the wild. But since even this authority has occasionally become ill from eating forest specimens, it would seem wise for all of us to restrict our Mushroom hunting to the shelves and baskets of our neighborhood markets.

In this country, commercial Mushroom raising is big business. The "Mushroom center" of Kennett Square, Pennsylvania, near the fabulous Longwood Gardens, supplies astronomical quantities of these fruits of the soil to the entire nation throughout the year. More than twenty million pounds are produced annually—indeed a lot of edible fungi! These are principally of the species *Agaricus bisporus*, a plant also raised commercially in Europe.

Only a small percentage of the known Mushrooms are edible, but there are so many species known to science that this list of culinary desiderata includes several hundred distinct kinds. Today, happily for the epicure, a number of the superb European Mushrooms—Chanterelles, Cèpes, Morels, and the fantastic French and Italian Truffles—are available in our domestic markets, dried, in cans, or on rare occasions in our big cities, fresh, as expensive imports. And the varied delectable dried black Mushrooms of the Orient are increasingly to be had in some of our specialty shops.

Mushrooms, whatever their type, and whether fresh, canned, dried, or frozen, are to my way of thinking absolutely essential to good cookery. When one considers the rich flavor they impart to dishes in which they are incorporated, then their cost is distinctly within the reach of even the most budget-conscious homemaker.

When utilizing fresh Mushrooms which by chance need cleansing, quickly rinse them under running cold water, and pat dry with paper towels. Never soak them—and do make use of them as rapidly as possible. Though some recipes call for huge Mushrooms, up to four inches across the cap, I have a decided personal predilection for the medium-size ones, seldom in excess of 1½ inches across. Their texture seems more pleasant, with none of that faint woody pithiness oftentimes encountered in their larger brethren.

In your market, choose fresh Mushrooms which are absolutely without brownish bruises or blemishes, and which have not opened to expose the brown gills to any appreciable degree.

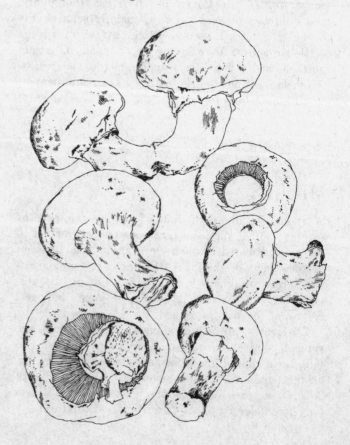

Never overcook fresh Mushrooms. These are ephemeral creations, of brief life span. Cooking for just a few minutes is guaranteed to retain flavor, nutritional value, and the unique consistency they possess. Handle them with care and use them judiciously, and Mushrooms will add gustatory delight to almost anything imaginable.

To COMMENCE with, here is an extraordinary appetizer combining raw Mushrooms with a piquant cocktail sauce.

Raw Mushroom Cocktail
Serves 4.

8 to 12 *fresh button mushrooms*
1 *cup commercial chili sauce*
⅓ *cup tomato ketchup*
2 *tablespoons lime juice*
1 *teaspoon prepared "hot" horseradish*
2 to 3 *drops Tabasco sauce*
salt and freshly ground pepper to taste
2 *cups finely chopped celery hearts*
2 *cups shredded lettuce*

Clean the mushroom buttons and refrigerate them until ready to use—do not cut until the last moment, to avoid discoloration. Prepare a sauce by thoroughly combining listed ingredients from chili sauce through salt and black pepper to taste; chill this for at least 1 hour prior to use. Lightly combine the chilled chopped celery and shredded lettuce, and divide it among 4 chilled cocktail bowls. Just at serving time, thinly slice the chilled mushrooms through cap and stem, and arrange these on the bed of celery and lettuce. Top with liberal dollops of the cocktail sauce, and present at the table immediately.

HERE is another version of raw mushrooms which I very much enjoy. It is true gourmet fare, especially appropriate with such dishes as *coq au vin*, roast veal, or *saltimbocca*.

Raw Mushroom Salad
Serves 4.

1 *pound small fresh mushrooms*
2 to 3 *heads Bibb or butter lettuce, small innermost leaves only*
light oil and wine vinegar
salt and freshly ground pepper

Using clean, fresh white mushrooms, slice through caps and stems to about ⅛-inch thickness. Tear washed, dried, chilled little lettuce leaves into bite-size pieces. Gently toss the mushrooms with lettuce, dress without delay with oil and vinegar to taste, and season with salt and freshly ground pepper.

HERE is a delicious chilled salad that combines the inexpensive canned mushrooms with tender baby lima beans in a spicy sort of marinade-sauce. I find it very appropriate with stews, meat or seafood casseroles, and such things. It is well-nigh perfection, too, for a meatless meal. Serve individual helpings on crisp lettuce leaves, if you wish.

Mushroom-Lima Salad
Serves 4 to 6.

1 *large can sliced mushrooms*
1 *package frozen baby lima beans*
¼ *cup finely chopped onion*
1 *teaspoon dried parsley flakes*
¼ *teaspoon oregano*
⅓ *cup wine vinegar*
3 *tablespoons salad oil*
⅛ *teaspoon garlic powder*
½ *teaspoon salt*
¼ *teaspoon freshly ground pepper*
¼ *teaspoon celery salt*

Cook lima beans according to package directions until just firm-tender. Drain, rinse under running cold water, and drain thoroughly again. Toss together the limas, drained mushroom slices, onion, parsley flakes, and oregano. Combine all other ingredients in a jar with cover and shake until thoroughly mixed. Pour sauce over mushroom-lima mixture, toss carefully but thoroughly, and chill for 2 hours prior to serving.

A VERY French way of utilizing mushrooms is as Duxelles, a sort of essence of mushroom that can be used as a basis for a quick mushroom sauce, as a superior flavoring for all sorts of things from scalloped potatoes to crisp-cooked green vegetables—spinach, broccoli, and the like—or as a prime ingredient in a memorable stuffing for fowl or chops. I like Duxelles, too, heated quickly, and spread over crisp toast rounds or those lovely cassava lace cakes now available in our specialty shops, as a delicate hors d'oeuvre.

There are many versions of Duxelles, including those anointed rather pointedly with garlic or thickened with flour or cornstarch. But I prefer the simplest possible form, which brings forward the unique mushroomy flavor.

Duxelles

1 *pound fresh mushrooms*
⅛ *to ¼ pound butter*

Chop the mushrooms very fine. Melt the butter in a medium-size, heavy skillet (I use lots of butter, but you may prefer a somewhat drier mixture, especially for use in stuffing), and over rather low heat sauté the mushroom mince, stirring often but gently, until it turns dark—usually about 12 minutes. Use while hot, or allow to cool, and store in a tightly covered jar. It will keep, refrigerated, for weeks, or it can be frozen without impairing the delectable flavor in any degree.

ONE OF my pet fashions with mushrooms, to be offered as a snack or appetizer—and a very rich one, indeed—is this easy cheesy casserole. Serve the hot dish with little party rye or pumpernickel slices. Beer is a perfect accompanying beverage. Genuine Fontina cheese is rather hard to locate in this country, but Parmesan can be substituted to afford an approximate result.

Mushrooms Fontina
Serves 4.

1 *pound fresh small or medium-size mushrooms*
¼ *pound (1 stick) butter*
salt and freshly ground pepper
2 *cups freshly grated Fontina (or Parmesan) cheese*

Clean the mushrooms and slice them thin through caps and stems. Melt the butter in a large skillet and sauté the mushroom slices until they are nicely browned, turning them often but with care. Do not overcook, and do not crowd them too much in the skillet. Remove from the heat and season to taste with salt and freshly ground pepper. Using a smallish oven-proof casserole with cover, arrange a layer of the mushrooms with butter sauce, then a good sprinkling of the Fontina (or Parmesan) cheese, then more mushrooms, then more cheese, and so on, finishing the topping with cheese. The casserole can be refrigerated for up to two days now, if desired. Just prior to serving, set covered casserole into preheated 375° F. oven and bake for about 10 minutes, or until the cheese has thoroughly melted.

STUFFED mushrooms occur in a variety of versions, to be offered as superb hors d'oeuvres or on occasion to accompany the meat course. The recipe was given me ages ago by a good culinary crony in California.

Mushrooms Contra Costa
Serves 6.

12 *medium-size fresh mushrooms*
fresh lemon juice
2 *tablespoons butter*
2 *tablespoons grated Swiss cheese*
¼ *cup fine bread crumbs*
2 *tablespoons minced fresh parsley*
½ *clove garlic, mashed*
1 *tablespoon grated onion*
salt and freshly ground pepper
2 *to 4 tablespoons cooking sherry*

Rinse mushrooms and remove stems, leaving caps intact. Sprinkle a few drops of lemon juice on each cap. Prepare stuffing as follows: Mince the mushroom stems very fine and sauté in butter until cooked but still slightly firm. Combine these with all other ingredients listed except the sherry, mixing thoroughly. Add enough sherry just to moisten the mixture. Pile stuffing liberally into mushroom caps, sprinkle with additional bread crumbs, and dot with butter. Bake in 350° F. oven for 15 minutes or until topping is nicely browned. Serve while very hot.

FIRM, medium-sized mushrooms stuffed with crab-meat make a marvelous hot hors d'oeuvre or main dish with little effort.

Mushrooms Stuffed with Crab
Serves 6 to 10.

2 *dozen medium mushroom caps*
3 *tablespoons butter*
1 *tablespoon flour*
1 *tablespoon melted butter*
½ *cup light cream*
1 *cup cooked, flaked crabmeat*
1 *tablespoon sherry*
dash celery salt
dash Cayenne pepper
salt and white pepper to taste
snipped fresh chives

In a large skillet, sauté the mushroom caps (use the stems to flavor something else, or make Duxelles out of them—recipe above) in the 3 tablespoons butter for 2 minutes, turning them once. Meanwhile, in a saucepan, blend the flour into the melted butter. Gradually stir in the cream, and cook sauce slowly, stirring constantly, until it thickens. Add the crabmeat, sherry, celery salt, Cayenne, and salt and white pepper to taste. Combine thoroughly. Stuff the sautéed mushroom caps with the crab mixture. Sprinkle with the snipped chives and serve while warm.

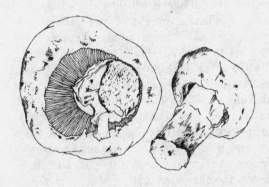

HERE is a lovely Spanish mushroom dish, a subtly spicy marinated affair—heavenly with almost any meat course imaginable. Prepare enough to have leftovers.

Mushrooms Marinated Sevilla
Serves 4 to 6.

> 1 *pound fresh medium-size mushrooms*
> 2 *lemons, juiced*
> 4 *tablespoons light olive oil*
> *salt and freshly ground pepper*

Slice mushrooms rather thin lengthwise through caps and stems. Arrange slices in an attractive dish, pour lemon juice and oil over, and season lightly with salt and pepper. Marinate, refrigerated, for 2 hours, carefully turning the mushroom slices once during the process. Remove from refrigerator 30 minutes prior to serving.

A MUSHROOM Soufflé, to me, seems just about the peak of culinary hauteur. Though many of us are a bit wary of attempting soufflés, this one is rather easy and highly recommended. It demands a special position in the menu, of course. Try it with poultry or, if used as an entrée, with delicate cucumber or watercress sandwiches.

Mushroom Soufflé
Serves 6.

> 1½ *pounds fresh medium-size mushrooms*
> 6 *tablespoons butter*
> 6 *eggs, separated*
> 4 *tablespoons flour*
> 1½ *cups light cream*
> *salt and pepper*
> *dash nutmeg*

Put mushrooms, peeled if desired, through finest blade of food chopper, or mince by hand. Cook over very low heat in butter for 8 to 10 minutes, stirring often. Meanwhile, beat the egg yolks until they are foamy. Remove mushrooms from the heat and stir in the beaten egg yolks. In another saucepan, over low heat, blend the flour and cream thoroughly together. Turn into top of a double boiler and continue to cook until mixture thickens. Add the mushroom mixture, salt and pepper to taste, and nutmeg. Continue to cook, stirring from the bottom of the container, until the mixture coats a wooden spoon. Remove from heat, allow to cool a bit, then fold in the egg whites, these beaten until stiff but not dry. Pour into 6 liberally buttered individual soufflé dishes. Set these into a pan of hot water, and bake in preheated 350° F. oven for 30 minutes or until the soufflés are done to perfection. Serve without a moment's delay!

MAKING use of the lovely imported European mushrooms known as morels (other types of morels occur in this country), we can create an elaborate yet not too difficult vegetable dish to accompany roast or broiled meats.

Morels and Artichokes
Serves 6.

> 1 *cup canned morels, drained, or* ½ *cup dried, soaked,*
>   *then drained*
> 1 *14-ounce can artichoke hearts, drained*
> 3 *tablespoons butter*
> 3 *tablespoons flour*
> 1 *cup milk*
> ¼ *cup light cream*
> ¼ *teaspoon salt*
> 2 *tablespoons freshly grated Parmesan cheese*

Arrange drained artichoke hearts upright in bake-and-serve dish or individual dishes. Fill centers with mushrooms. Melt butter, stir in the flour, then add the milk and cream. Stir until almost boiling, simmer for

2 minutes over reduced heat, and add the salt. Spoon sauce over filled artichoke hearts, sprinkle with grated Parmesan, and bake in preheated 350° F. oven for 15 minutes.

WITH imported chanterelles, cèpes, or morels, clam chowder can easily be made into an exciting and tastefully novel soup-stew, as follows.

Mushroom-Clam Stew
Serves 3 or 4.

> ½ cup drained canned chanterelles, cèpes, or morels
> 1 7-ounce can minced clams
> 1 8-ounce bottle clam juice
> ½ cup light cream
> ¾ cup milk
> 1 tablespoon butter
> few chopped fresh celery leaves

Drain liquid from minced clams into a saucepan, add bottled clam juice, light cream, and milk. Bring just to the boil. Add clams and mushrooms. Let heat for 4 minutes without boiling. Serve while very hot, with butter and celery leaves on top.

HERE we have a superb French veal dish incorporating these exotic, delectable, imported mushrooms now so happily available in our own country. Ideally, this should be served with plain boiled rice and a light green salad. A good bottle of dry white or rosé wine, suitably chilled, is an auspicious accompaniment, too.

French Veal Mushroom Ragoût
Serves 3 or 4.

> 1 cup drained morels, chanterelles, or cèpes
> 1 pound veal, cut into cubes for stew
> 1 teaspoon salt
> 1 tablespoon cornstarch
> 2 egg yolks
> ⅓ cup heavy cream

Place veal in a sizable skillet with cover, add 1¾ cups cold water, and bring slowly to the boil. Add salt, cover, and simmer for 1¼ hours. Add mushrooms and heat through for 5 minutes. Mix the cornstarch with 1½ tablespoons cold water and stir into the simmering stew. Stir egg yolks with cream, add some of the hot broth from stew, then return all to the skillet. Cook for 1 minute, without boiling. Serve with or over hot rice.

Mustard

For our purposes, Mustard applies to the leafy portions of several kinds of rather coarse cabbage relatives (genus *Brassica,* of the Crucifer Family) which are used more or less extensively as greens. When allowed to go to seed, commercial table mustard and mustard oil are made from the seeds of several of the varied species—the foliage of which is also edible.

The flavor of Mustard greens is a distinctive one, rather strong, and not beloved by all epicures. I am personally very fond of an occasional batch of them, crisp and vivid green with no yellowing nor blemish, as prepared in the fashion recommended on page 129 for boiled Kale, an allied plant. The big bunches of greens are frequently available in our supermarkets, notably in the South and West, where several of these plants have run wild to become rather noxious weeds. Mustard greens are even available in cans and flash-frozen packets these days, so a lot of other Americans must share my opinion of them!

CHINESE MUSTARD

Chinese Mustard is a coarse-growing leafy annual of the Crucifer Family, known botanically as *Brassica juncea.* Among its many alternate vernaculars, the best known are Leaf-Mustard Cabbage, Broad-Leaved Mustard, Brown Mustard, Indian Mustard, *kai-choi* (Chinese), and *ogarashi* (Japanese).

The basal leaves, with swollen and often curving stalks, are typically large, though those averaging six to twelve inches long are most preferable for use in the kitchen. Highly variable in shape, they are usually dark green in color, and have a characteristic crumpled surface. In some forms, a pronounced white powdery bloom occurs on the stalks.

Seedlings and leaves, with their stalks, of immature specimens are sold in Oriental markets. They are used as potherbs in various dishes—stir-fried medleys of vegetables with pork or fowl or seafood, or in soups, or simply steamed until just tender, then dressed with butter and appropriate seasonings. The small, round, reddish-brown-to-black seeds are ground to make an oil which is used to some degree in Asia, both for cooking and medicinally.

The term Chinese Mustard—at least in casual parlance among North Americans—also signifies powdered English mustard combined with a tiny bit of water or stale beer to form a very "hot" condiment widely appreciated as an accessory to Oriental delicacies.

Chinese Mustard Soup
Serves 4.

1 *bunch Chinese mustard*
1 *pound lean pork, slivered*
1 *teaspoon cornstarch*
1 *to 2 teaspoons soy sauce*
freshly ground white pepper
1½ *teaspoons peanut or soy oil*
1 *small slice fresh ginger root*
1 *tablespoon dried tiny shrimp*
1½ *quarts water*

Thoroughly wash the Chinese mustard and cut or tear into 2-inch lengths, discarding all obviously tough portions. Stir the pork slivers into the cornstarch with the soy sauce and season rather liberally with white pepper (black pepper can be used if desired). Heat the oil in a heavy sizable pot with cover and cook the ginger root for a minute or two, stirring it around. Add the pork mixture and the tiny shelled shrimp and stir-fry for about 2 minutes. Add the water, cover the kettle, and cook over medium heat for 15 minutes.

Next add the Chinese mustard, cover pot again, and cook until the vegetable has just reached the firm-tender stage. Serve while very hot, offering additional soy sauce on the side.

TUBEROUS-ROOTED CHINESE MUSTARD

Another of the diverse Brassicas which has long found considerable popularity in the Orient is the Tuberous-Rooted Chinese Mustard (*Brassica napiformis,* of the Crucifer Family). Presumably originally from China, it was introduced into this country as long ago as 1889, yet today is seldom encountered outside of specialized Oriental markets.

The thin, bluish, rather sparse foliage of the plant is irregularly toothed along the edges, and the expanded part is set on an elongate, slender stalk. The tuberous root, sometimes four inches in diameter, is very reminiscent of the common turnip—a related species. White or purplish-skinned, these Chinese Mustard tubers have a sweet, rather moist, firm flesh that makes them appropriate to use in soups and stir-fried dishes.

POTHERB MUSTARD

The multitudinous kinds of edible plants referred to the genus *Brassica,* of the Crucifer Family, are even today confusing both to botanist and cook. An example is the present one, which is usually known in this country as Potherb Mustard or as Potherb-Mustard Cabbage, and which appears to be referable scientifically to *Brassica japonica.*

Originally from Japan, it was introduced into California in the nineteenth century, and has to some extent become naturalized in places there. The greens have been sold in San Francisco markets as California Pepper-Grass.

As a green vegetable, it is very popular with those of Japanese ancestry, who refer to it as *midsuna* (the commonest Chinese vernacular is *sui-choi*). It is cultivated today both in our West and in Hawaii, the soft, thin, deeply cut leaves, arranged on slender white stalks, being gathered into bunches for sale. The seedlings have the finest flavor, vaguely reminiscent of Swiss chard but with a bit more pungency.

Though incorporated into many stir-fry medleys utilizing such meats as pork, shrimp, or lobster, the full savor of Potherb Mustard can best be appreciated if it is treated in the manner suggested for boiled Spinach (page 215).

NASTURTIUM

In this country, our showy garden Nasturtiums are not Nasturtiums at all! They are, rather, members of the genus *Tropaeolum,* a group of mostly vining plants with showy, often very intricate flowers, natives of the cooler areas of Chile and Peru. The true botanical genus *Nasturtium* once applied to certain plants of the Crucifer Family, including the Horseradish and Watercress, but the name is now generally out of scientific vogue.

Several of the wild Andean species of *Tropaeolum,* notably the Tuber Nasturtium or Ysaño (*T. tuberosum*), produce irregular, somewhat pear-shaped tubers up to three inches in length. These are eaten to some extent in their native habitat, and the plants have in fact been cultivated for that purpose since pre-Columbian times in Bolivia and Peru. The Ysaño has also been introduced into Europe, where it is raised to modest degree by connoisseurs of the tubers. These are boiled, usually after being dried for a month or so, to be served with butter and customary seasonings. They possess a positive, somewhat acrid flavor that is alien to most North American palates.

The leaves of the common Flowering Nasturtium (*Tropaeolum majus* and variants) are picked to be added, judiciously, to springtime salads. Both buds and the juvenile seed pods are added to vinegars for flavoring, or pickled, to be used much as capers. And the rinsed petals of the fresh blossoms—vivid yellow, orange, or scarlet in color—are sprinkled atop elegant salads on occasion, imparting a crisp flavor that must be sampled to be appreciated!

NETTLE

Two botanically—and structurally—different plants used as vegetables are in cultivation under the name Nettle. The best known of these is a true Nettle, of the genus *Urtica,* abundantly furnished on its sizable leaves and young shoots with wickedly stinging hairs. Because of its pleasant spinachlike, slightly bitter flavor, the Nettle has long been utilized in Scotland, parts of France, and other European lands as a potherb, purée, or in hearty soups. It was introduced into this country by immigrants, and it quickly spread to become a pestiferous weed, particularly in parts of New England. The stinging hairs, ineffective after cooking, make the use of sturdy gloves and considerable caution essential in picking and preparing this interesting vegetable for the table.

The second of these plants is the Dead Nettle, or White Nettle, *Lamium maculatum,* of the Mint (not Nettle) Family. This is a diffuse fuzzy plant with pretty white to purple-red flowers, and no stinging hairs. It is cultivated occasionally as an ornamental in Northern gardens, and the connoisseur will enjoy its tender young growths, quickly steamed till just tender, then dressed with butter and seasonings. Either of these Nettles is sometimes served with a poached egg atop each portion.

Or they can be made into the following interesting soup.

Nettle Soup
Serves 4.

3 cups coarsely chopped young nettle growths, leaves and stems
1 quart rich mutton or beef stock, strained
⅓ cup pearl barley
salt and freshly ground pepper
2 hard-cooked egg yolks, sieved

Bring the stock to the boil in a heavy kettle with cover. Add the barley and simmer over medium heat, covered, until barley is almost tender. Add the nettles and continue to cook, still covered, until they are tender yet still retain a bit of texture. Season to taste, and serve each hot bowlful with a sprinkling of sieved egg yolk.

NEW ZEALAND SPINACH

On occasion, in choice markets in the United States— notably in Hawaii and Southern California—one can find bunches of a fleshy potherb known as New Zealand Spinach. This plant (*Tetragonia expansa*) has no particular affinity with true spinach, belonging to the odd family Aizoaceae, the Fig-Marigolds, the incredible succulent South African species of which are highly popular with collectors of cacti and other such inhabitants of the driest deserts.

In the tropics, this fleshy annual is cultivated fairly extensively, supplanting true spinach during the hot summer months. A single plant, though seldom a foot in height, may spread over a diameter of some six feet. The somewhat triangular leaves, in some forms slightly fuzzy, and the thick stems are edible. The flavor and texture of this New Zealand vegetable is much like that of true spinach, though the old growths may be a bit coarser and tougher.

New Zealand Spinach is best cooked while very young and firm. Wash the greens thoroughly, drain them, then tear into sizable sections. Steam these in a small amount of salted water until just tender, and serve with liberal quantities of butter and seasonings to taste.

OATS

The cultivated kinds of Oats (*Avena sativa,* of the Grass Family) have been grown since prehistoric times, authentic records being extant of plantings by the ancient Lake Dwellers of Europe. They are grown today to an extensive degree in many temperate-zone lands.

Numerous variants of this grain exist, some of special importance as fodder, others made into Rolled Oats and similar products that appear on many a table at breakfast, or at other meals as cakes, biscuits, and cookies.

Here is a special Rolled Oats stuffing for that big holiday turkey, one which is served at my house regularly every year, either at Thanksgiving or Christmas time. It was originated by some of my Scottish ancestors in eastern Canada. It is, incidentally, also marvelous as a stuffing for thick pork chops or a pork roast.

Oatmeal Stuffing
For a 12-pound turkey.

1 1-*pound box rolled oats* (*not quick-cooking type*)
¼ *pound* (1 *stick*) *butter*
1½ *cups finely chopped onion*
1 *cup finely sliced celery*
1 *cup chopped green celery leaves*
1 *teaspoon Bell's Poultry Seasoning*
2 *tablespoons salt*
½ *teaspoon black pepper*

Using a large heavy skillet with cover, melt the butter. Add the rolled oats and cook over medium heat, stirring often, until the oats are of an even brown color. Add onion, celery, celery leaves, and seasonings, plus a small amount of water—about ¼ cup should suffice. Mix well, cover the skillet and steam until the vegetables are tender but not soft, adding a bit more water if necessary, and stirring frequently. This is a crumbly stuffing and should only be moist enough to barely hold together. When stuffing the bird—at the last moment prior to roasting, of course—do not pack it too tightly, for best results.

OKRA

Okra is the angular seed pod of a kind of Hibiscus (*H. esculentus,* of the Mallow Family); it follows a

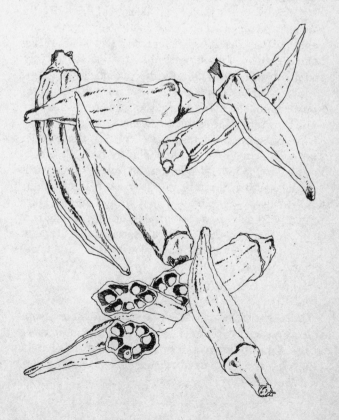

rather attractive yellow flower with a rich red center. Originally from the Asiatic tropics, the plant was early cultivated in Africa, from whence it was introduced into the West Indies and into this country. Alternate names for the vegetable are Ladies' Fingers, Gumbo, *gombo* or *gombaut* (French), *quingombó* (Spanish), *quiabó* (Brazilian), and *bay-mee* or *bamia* (Arabic).

This is a favorite vegetable particularly in the Southern United States, where it is an essential ingredient of many savory stews—these often called gumbos, in fact. As an addition to soups, it acts as a thickening agent, a characteristic which also calls for its use in ketchups and like products.

The fresh vegetable (actually a fruit), when cut and cooked, often has a somewhat mucilaginous texture that is objectionable to many persons. For years I could not abide Okra—except in gumbos—but I now have acquired a definite fondness for it, when properly prepared, as described below.

The juvenile pods are often dried for use during the unproductive winter months. Nowadays we also find the vegetable in several canned forms and in flash-frozen packets. The last are especially well suited for use in the modern kitchen, I have found, since the freezing process seems to cut down on the quantity of gluey juice.

Even the seeds of Okra are used, these when mature being roasted and ground as a palatable substitute for coffee.

According to friends far more experienced with Okra than I, pains should be taken to obtain only the youngest possible pods. These should be very firm and unblemished. The stems should be broken off, rather than cut, the vegetable washed and dried thoroughly, and then refrigerated until the last moment before cooking. For most recipes a brief blanching of the prepared pods in boiling salted water is recommended. This "firms up" the texture, it seems.

Connoisseurs insist that there are few things finer than a big batch of Okra, first slightly parboiled, then drained well, and fried in butter, to be eaten while very hot, with salt and pepper to taste. A light tomato or a cream sauce can be added to advantage. Okra prepared thusly is an admirable accompaniment to poultry, fish and shellfish of all sorts, and red meats. Oftentimes it is automatically served with either rice or hominy grits.

OKRA FRITTERS are an old standby in many noteworthy kitchens in our deep South. They most often enjoy a position on a menu with fried chicken or pan-fried fish, customarily alongside hot steamed rice.

Okra Fritters
Serves 4.

1 pound small okra, halved lengthwise
½ cup flour
½ teaspoon salt
⅛ teaspoon freshly ground black pepper
1 cup flour
½ teaspoon salt
1 teaspoon baking powder
2 tablespoons olive oil
¾ cup milk
1 egg, beaten well
deep fat or oil for frying
½ to ¾ cup melted butter
1 small clove garlic, mashed
Tabasco sauce to taste

Prepare the little okra pods, and dust them lightly with a mixture of the ½ cup flour, salt, and pepper. Refrigerate for 1 hour. Then dip one into a batter made from the 1 cup flour, salt, baking powder, olive oil, milk, and egg. Fry this trial pod in deep fat or oil heated to 370° F., to test the batter consistency. It should be thick enough to cling, yet thin enough to form only a very light, crisp crust when fried. Correct batter, if necessary, by addition of either flour or water. Fry the okra, as per the sample pod. Drain and serve at once, with dip dishes of hot melted butter with garlic and Tabasco sauce.

ONE OF my favorite ways with okra is in a heady gumbo in the Creole style. This beautiful blend of seafood and ham must be simmered very slowly for a considerable period, then served—in small quantities, since it is very rich—with hot rice. A light green salad, some crusty warm bread, and a good bottle of favorite wine combine to create a truly memorable repast.

Creole Gumbo Alejandro
Serves 6 to 10.

2½ cups sliced okra
¾ cup chopped onion
¾ cup chopped green pepper
4 tablespoons peanut or soy oil
2 tablespoons flour
1 teaspoon salt
2 bay leaves
2 tablespoons chopped fresh parsley
¼ teaspoon dried thyme
1 8-ounce can tomato sauce
3 cups raw shelled shrimp, cut into bite-size pieces
1 pint small oysters, with liquor

1 *cup diced cooked ham*
4 *cups rich fish stock*
6 *cups hot water*

In a large heavy kettle with cover, cook the okra (frozen is easiest here), onion, and green pepper in the oil over medium heat until the vegetables are soft and beginning to brown, stirring frequently. Sprinkle with the flour and salt, mix well, and cook for 5 minutes more. Add all other ingredients, mix thoroughly, and cook, covered, over very low heat for at least 4 hours, stirring often and being certain that the gumbo does not stick to the bottom, or scorch. The gumbo should be thick and dark-colored when served—with steamed rice on the side. To reheat, use the top of a double boiler.

In the Spanish-speaking lands southward from ours, okra is known by the melodious name *quingombó* (pronounced keen-gom-*bow*). A specialty dish in the Antilles is *quingombós guisados,* a hearty stew.

West Indian Okra Stew
Serves 4.

1 *pound small okra, quartered*
boiling salted water
2 *tablespoons lard*
¼ *teaspoon Annatto (page 16)*
1 *tablespoon diced lean salt pork*
⅓ *cup diced cooked ham*
½ *cup chopped onion*
⅓ *cup chopped green pepper*
2 *tablespoons tomato paste*
3 *leaves fresh coriander (optional)*
3 *cups hot water*
1 *cup diced cooked shrimp*
1 *teaspoon salt*
2 *cups diced raw potatoes or malanga*

Snap the stems off the okra pods, quarter them, and plunge into boiling salted water. When water returns to the boil, drain okra at once. In a heavy kettle or large skillet with cover, melt the lard over rather high heat, mix in the annatto, add the salt pork and ham, and cook, stirring constantly, for 3 minutes. Add okra, plus all other ingredients, mix thoroughly, and bring to a quick boil. Reduce heat to medium, cover, and cook for 30 minutes. Uncover and continue to cook, stirring often, until the mixture is thickened. Serve with or over hot steamed rice, with fried plantains or bananas on the side.

The Brazilians value the okra, which they call *quiabó* (pronounced kee-ah-*bow*), in their cuisine. During the war, I was in that lovely land many times, and there I learned to enjoy this interesting *ensalada de quiabó*. It is well suited for serving with fowl or pork.

Okra Salad Brasil
Serves 6 to 8.

1½ *pounds small okra, halved lengthwise*
⅓ *cup light olive oil*
⅓ *cup peanut or soy oil*
3 *tablespoons wine vinegar*
½ *teaspoon salt*
½ *teaspoon dried tarragon*
2 *teaspoons minced chives*
2 *teaspoons minced fresh parsley*
2 *or 3 drops Tabasco sauce*

Cook the smallest okra pods available, prepared as indicated on page 158, in lightly salted water until just tender. Drain at once and allow to cool. Then refrigerate for at least 1 hour. Make a dressing of all other ingredients and pour over the nicely arranged chilled okra at serving time.

Then we have a delicious hot version of okra, to be served with such things as roast pork or broiled ham slice. It originates in New Orleans, that picturesque city where okra enjoys a prominent spot in the renowned cuisine.

Okra Pontchartrain
Serves 4.

2 *cups sliced small okra*
2 *tablespoons butter*
½ *cup finely chopped onion*
½ *cup finely chopped green pepper*
1 *cup chopped peeled fresh tomatoes*
½ *teasoon sugar*
⅛ *teaspoon oregano*
salt and black pepper to taste

In a sizable skillet with cover, sauté the onion and green pepper in the butter until they are tender but not browned. Add the okra slices and cook for 5 minutes, stirring frequently but with care. Add the tomatoes (please use fresh ones for this), sugar, and oregano. Cover and simmer for 20 minutes, adding a tiny bit of water if absolutely necessary. The mixture should be rather dry. Season to taste with salt and pepper, mix well, and serve while very hot.

OLIVE

The Olive is one of those edibles that is a fruit and a vegetable at the same time. The splendid smallish tree (*Olea europaea,* of the botanical family Oleaceae) that bears this fruit-vegetable is one of the most important plants known in many parts of the world, especially from the Mediterranean region to India where the species is native. In this country it is cultivated particularly in California, and to a lesser degree in Arizona and New Mexico. In its wild form it is a tremendously long-lived tree, some specimens said to date from the days of Christ.

As would be imagined, the original Olive has evolved into a large number of variants. The fruits of some of these are especially important; these are the common green, brown, or black Olives found on our market shelves in great array, in jars or cans. Often pitted and stuffed with an imaginative range of ingredients, from pimientos to anchovy fillets and blanched almonds, they are also preserved in various seasoned brines that give them added flavor. All these Olives have been subjected to an intricate process of curing, for few things are as incredibly inedible as an Olive in its original state.

Olive oil—utilized by millions throughout the world for cooking, as a medicine, as a lubricant, and in the manufacture of such items as soap—is expressed from the fruits of special varieties. The oil imported from Italy, Spain, and Portugal is valued in our domestic cookery. A sort of minced stuffed green Olive "butter" is available from domestic and foreign sources, this an attractive and tasteful spread for sandwiches and canapes.

Through the ages, tomes have been written on the utility of this remarkable fruit-vegetable. For our purposes, consider the following selection of recipes, which make good use of both green and ripe olives.

I habitually offer bowls of well-chilled green and ripe Olives in variety—never neglecting the puckery, wrinkled, oily black Greek or Italian ones—for nibbling with preprandial libations. On especially festive occasions the following delectable hors d'oeuvre comes into use, too.

Olive-Cheese Nuggets
Makes 24 appetizers.

> 2 *dozen large stuffed green olives*
> 1 *cup grated sharp Cheddar cheese*
> ¼ *cup softened butter*
> ¾ *cup sifted all-purpose flour*
> ½ *teaspoon paprika*

Thoroughly blend together the cheese and the butter. Mix in the flour and paprika, using your hands to form into a dough. Form the dough around the stuffed olives in a thin layer, and be sure that it sticks to them. Place on an ungreased cooky sheet and bake in preheated 400° F. oven until the dough is golden in color, usually about 15 minutes. Serve either while hot or at room temperature.

THE FIRST time I encountered this distinctive soup prepared from olives, I must admit I did not consider it an immediate success. But there is a delicate insidiousness about it, I have discovered, and I now serve it often. I like to garnish it with cheese croutons.

Southwestern Olive Soup
Serves 3 or 4.

> 1 4-*ounce can minced ripe olives*
> 1 *small clove garlic, peeled*
> 1½ *cups rich chicken broth, strained*
> 1 *egg*
> ½ *cup heavy cream*
> *salt and pepper*

In a saucepan with cover, combine the minced ripe olives, whole clove of garlic, and strained chicken broth. Cover and simmer for 15 minutes, then remove and discard garlic clove. Lightly beat the egg and combine it with the cream, then add this to the soup. Heat, stirring frequently, for 7 minutes, but do not allow it to boil. Season to taste with salt and pepper, and serve hot—or chill for a marvelous variation!

MAIN dishes in which the elusive flavor of the olive figures are myriad. One of which I am especially fond is this Latin specialty, a favorite at the Nejapa Country Club in Managua, where I have spent memorable hours with my orchidological colleague, A. H. Heller, and his charming wife. Serve it with rice, a tomato-and-lettuce salad, and hot crusty bread.

Nicaraguan Olive Chicken
Serves 4.

¾ *cup small pitted Spanish green olives*
⅓ *cup olive oil*
3 *tablespoons butter*
2 *fryer-broiler chickens, disjointed*
1 *cup diced, cooked ham*
1 *cup dry white vermouth*
1½ *teaspoons paprika*
1 *teaspoon salt*
¼ *teaspoon freshly ground pepper*

In a large heavy skillet with cover, combine the olive oil and butter, and in it sauté the chicken pieces, a few at a time, turning often, until they are very well browned. Remove pieces with tongs as they are done and keep warm. Add the ham dice (they should be about ½ inch thick for optimum results) to the skillet and sauté until lightly brown; remove with slotted spoon, and keep warm with the chicken. Add the vermouth to pan and deglaze the pan by cooking over rather high heat and stirring constantly, scraping up all of the encrusted bits of meat. Return the chicken and ham, and add all other ingredients. Cover and cook over low heat until the chicken is tender.

HERE is a very pretty entrée salad combining our superb ripe olives from California with canned white tuna (albacore) and tomatoes.

Olive-Tomato-Tuna Salad
Serves 4.

½ *cup ripe olives, cut into large chunks*
1 *7-ounce can white tuna (albacore), drained*
1 *cup chopped celery*
2 *tablespoons finely chopped scallion tops*
⅓ *cup mayonnaise*
1 *tablespoon lemon juice, or ¾ tablespoon lime juice*
4 *large firm-ripe tomatoes*
Romaine leaves for base
pitted whole ripe olives for garnish

Combine chunks of olive carefully (do not mash) with the flaked drained tuna, celery, and scallion tops. Blend the mayonnaise with the lemon (or lime) juice, and toss lightly with the olive-tuna mixture. Cut tomatoes partway through into 6 wedges, and spread open on crisp, chilled leaves of Romaine (or other lettuce, to your choice). Pile the olive-tuna mixture in the opened tomato wedges and garnish with pitted ripe olives.

ONION

Probably originally from western Asia, the Onion (*Allium Cepa*, of the Lily Family) has been cultivated by man since prehistoric times. The Babylonians and the ancient Egyptians ate these bulbous plants, and the flavorful hollow leaves as well, and the Romans and Greeks were fond of them, utilizing them in their often ornate culinary endeavors.

Through the history of the Onion, a considerable number of distinctive varieties have been developed. Though more than two billion pounds of fresh, mature Onions (primarily of the yellow varieties, with pungent flavor) are raised annually in this country alone, we import quantities of selected types—sweet red Italian and delicate big Bermudas being the most prominent. Our own markets also afford us tiny white Onions, far more delicate for cooking than their larger yellow brothers.

The bulbs of this very adaptable liliaceous plant, raw or cooked, dehydrated or desiccated or frozen, are used by the good modern cook just about every day. They figure in items of the menu ranging all the way from elegant hors d'oeuvres to subtle tortes. French Onion soup is famed throughout the world. Onion salads have their staunch fans everywhere. Varied stews would be far blander without the attention of the Onion. And with no thick, juicy slices of sweet Onions, our hamburgers would be pallid imitations of themselves.

Here are some of the delightful, ever delicious ways in which the Onion makes itself known at my house.

To COMMENCE a menu with little hot pies filled with an Onion mixture may seem a bit strange at first thought. But after you taste them, I venture that these savory tartlets will be marked favorites from your kitchen. The recipe is akin to the grand *pissaladière* of southern France, a kind of onion quiche.

Little Onion Pies
Makes about 24 little pies.

> 3 cups diced onion
> pastry shells
> 1 egg yolk
> 2 tablespoons warm water
> 3 tablespoons butter
> 4 slices lean bacon
> 1½ cups grated Swiss cheese
> 4 eggs
> 2 cups light cream
> ¾ teaspoon salt
> ⅛ teaspoon black pepper
> dash nutmeg
> dash Cayenne pepper

Use your favorite pastry recipe to make small shells (or buy frozen patty shells) and carefully place in tartlet or shallow muffin pans. Mix together the 1 egg yolk and 2 tablespoons of warm water; before adding the filling to the little pies, use a pastry brush to coat each shell with this—it keeps them from becoming soggy. Preheat the oven to 400° F.

Filling for the pastry shells: In a shallow skillet sauté the onion in butter until it is just golden but not browned. Remove onion with slotted spoon and keep warm. In another skillet, fry the bacon until crisp, then drain, and crumble it on paper towels to drain further. Combine the onions and bacon, and place about 2 teaspoons of mixture into each pastry shell. Sprinkle a heaping teaspoon of grated cheese into each shell. Beat eggs, then beat in the cream, salt, black pepper, nutmeg, and Cayenne. Pour about 1 tablespoonful of this mixture into each shell. Bake in preheated 400° F. oven for 8 minutes, then reduce heat to 350° F. and bake about 5 minutes more, until the filling becomes puffy and golden brown on top. Serve immediately as delectable hot appetizers or as a truly different main dish!

ONIONS Monaco (or Monégasque) are likewise favorites at the preprandial hour hereabouts, to be offered with tissue-thin slices of prosciutto, coarse-textured bread, and perhaps cubes of Münster or Jack cheese which have been marinated in a good port wine overnight.

Onions Monaco
Serves 6 to 8.

> 1 pound tiny white onions
> 1½ cups water
> ½ cup white wine vinegar
> 3 tablespoons light olive oil
> 3 tablespoons tomato paste
> 2 tablespoons chopped fresh parsley
> 1 medium bay leaf
> ⅛ teaspoon dried thyme
> 2 teaspoons salt
> ½ teaspoon freshly ground pepper
> 1 tablespoon sugar
> ⅓ cup halved seedless raisins

Peel the little white onions, of uniform size if possible, and place them in a medium saucepan with cover. Add all other ingredients, cover, and cook over low heat until the onions are just tender, but still retain some chewy texture. Arrange the onions in an attractive flat serving dish, pour the sauce over them, and chill for at least 2 hours prior to serving, with cocktail picks, as an unusual hors d'oeuvre.

To ACCOMPANY roasts or broiled meats, consider Baked Onions. Just baked, with no frippery—the easiest recipe in the world. This is a version of preparing onions of Italian origin, I believe, which seems little known in this country.

Baked Onions

Allow 1 or 2 firm sizable onions per person. Do not peel them; do not do anything to them. Just set them on the rack of a 300° or 325° F. oven, and bake until they are tender when poked with a sharp fork or toothpick. Allow to stand out of the heat for a moment, then easily slip off the jackets. Serve hot with butter, salt, and freshly ground pepper, and, if desired, just the smallest pinch of nutmeg or cinnamon. Or serve cold with salt and pepper and a few drops of lemon juice.

AT THANKSGIVING or Christmas time in the United States, along with the turkey or the goose, most of us serve, as part of the trimmings, onions in a rich cream sauce. These are good, but they get a bit wearisome year after year. Therefore, at my table, the following Festive Onions appear—and not just at holiday time, either! The casserole is a fine addition to fowl, seafood, pork, or ham, of any variety or version.

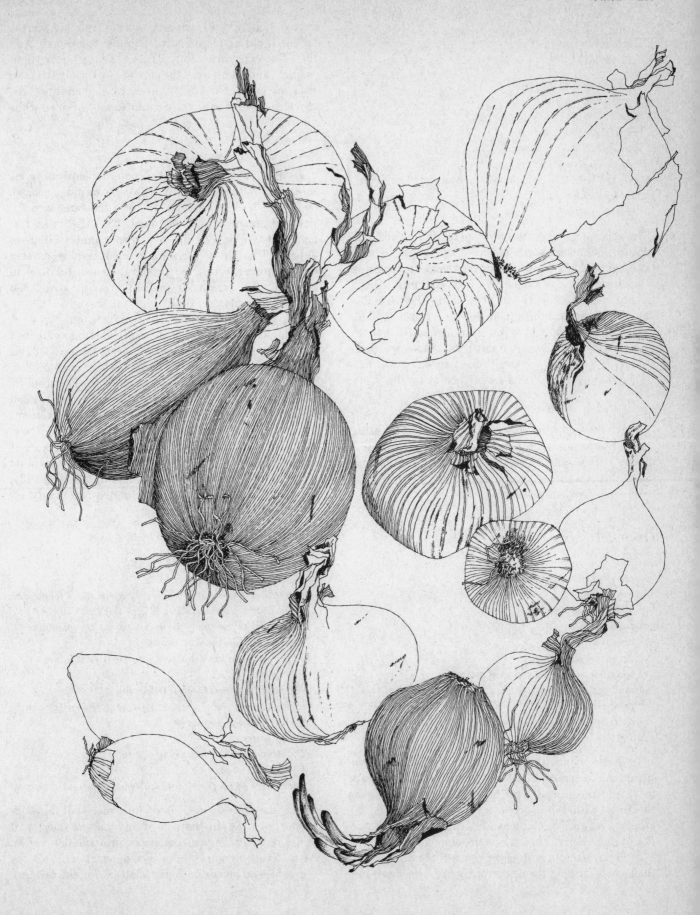

Festive Onions
Serves 4 to 6.

  2 *pounds tiny white onions*
  ½ *cup cider vinegar*
  ¼ *cup peanut or soy oil*
  ½ *cup dry white wine*
  ¼ *cup white wine vinegar*
  1½ *teaspoons salt*
  ¼ *teaspoon freshly ground white pepper*
  2 *tablespoons sugar*
  ½ *small bay leaf*

In a large kettle with cover, place the onions, unskinned, in enough water to cover them, together with the ½ cup of cider vinegar. Cover the kettle, bring to a boil, and allow to simmer for 5 to 7 minutes. Drain the onions and allow them to cool. Skin the parboiled onions and arrange them in an ovenproof dish. Add all other ingredients, and bake in a preheated 400° F. oven for about an hour, or until the onions are fork-tender. If possible, prepare this casserole in advance, refrigerate overnight, and reheat just at serving time.

SERVE the following interesting onion medley, using tiny white onions of uniform dimension, at your next dinner with a veal roast—or beef or lamb, for that matter. It is a rather special concoction, which I offer happily on frequent occasions.

Onions Denise
Serves 4 to 6.

  1 *pound small white onions*
  1 *cup water*
  1 *tablespoon brown sugar*
  1 *teaspoon salt*
  ¼ *teaspoon paprika*
  ⅛ *teaspoon black pepper*
  2 *tablespoons slivered blanched almonds*
  4 *tablespoons butter*
  2 *tablespoons flour*
  1 *teaspoon Worcestershire sauce*
  2 *to 4 drops Tabasco sauce*

In a saucepan with cover combine the water, brown sugar, salt, paprika, and black pepper, and bring to a boil. Add the peeled little onions and combine them carefully with the sauce. Cover and simmer for 30 minutes, or until the onions are tender. Drain off the liquid and reserve this. Place the onions in a greased 1½-quart casserole with cover. Brown the almonds in the butter, stirring them constantly. Add the flour and

brown lightly, still stirring constantly. Stir in the onion liquid and cook until slightly thickened. Add the Worcestershire and Tabasco sauces, mix thoroughly, and pour over the onions. Cover tightly and bake in preheated 375° F. oven for 20 minutes. Remove cover and bake for 5 minutes more. Serve while very hot.

IN THE superb cuisine of Japan, an impressive assortment of fresh vegetables is very rapidly cooked, over high heat, with meat, to form the famous Sukiyaki (pronounced skee-*yah*-kee). This dish was formerly better known in our own country than in Japan! Though it necessitates considerable cutting and chopping, all of the preparation can be done in advance, the various ingredients refrigerated, then cooked in an electric skillet right at the table.

Sukiyaki typically makes use of top-quality beef, but the adventuresome chef substitutes bits of boned chicken, peeled raw shrimp, or even lobster. Onions figure prominently in the array—when crisp-cooked, they are particularly pleasant laved with the succulent juices around them in the dish. The following version of this Japanese showpiece makes use of the excellent imported canned *sukiyaki-no-tomo*, a mixture of several essential ingredients, now available in many of our good markets. Serve the Sukiyaki with individual bowls of hot rice, tiny bits of Nikko Salad (page 49), and sliced pickled daikon. Beer or tea are highly acceptable beverages.

Yokosuka Sukiyaki
Serves 4 liberally.

  8 *to 10 small white onions, peeled, thinly sliced lengthwise*
  1½ *pounds top sirloin, sliced ⅛ inch thick*
  1 *can* sukiyaki-no-tomo *(imported sukiyaki vegetables)*
  1½ *cups thin diagonal slices celery*
  8 *to 10 scallions with tops, cut into diagonal 1½-inch lengths*
  ½ *pound fresh mushrooms, thinly sliced*
  ½ *pound fresh snow peas, or 1 package frozen (optional)*
  ¼ *cup Japanese soy sauce*
  ½ *cup water*
  2 *tablespoons sake or cooking sherry*
  4 *teaspoons sugar*
  small piece of beef suet or 2 tablespoons peanut or soy oil

Cut the thin slices of beef into pieces of bite-size proportions. Drain the can of *sukiyaki-no-tomo*, and if desired cut the bamboo shoots into smaller pieces. Attractively arrange the pieces of meat with all the vegetables on one or more big platters for the advance delectation of your guests. Refrigerate until cooking time, if desired. In a small saucepan, combine the soy sauce, water, sake or cooking sherry, and sugar, and bring to a quick boil, stirring to dissolve the sugar. Remove from heat at once. Use electric skillet at the table and preheat to 260° F. Seat your guests, display the beauteous platters of edibles, and be sure the other items of the menu will be ready within about 8 to 10 minutes. Melt a smallish piece of beef suet in the electric skillet or heat about 2 tablespoons peanut or soy oil. Add half of the meat pieces and quickly stir them around, turning them carefully. A moment later, add half of the sauce from the saucepan, plus half of all the vegetables except the snow peas, if these are being used. Add the celery a few seconds before the others, and cook the meat-vegetable mixture, uncovered, for about 5 minutes. Turn ingredients with a spatula, add snow peas, and cook for 2 or 3 minutes more— no longer! The vegetables will be crisp-textured and delicious. Serve each person a portion of the hot, fresh Sukiyaki preferably in smallish Oriental bowls (which better retain the heat of the mixture than would a plate), accompanied by rice and whatever else you are serving. When this first batch of Sukiyaki has been consumed, cook the remainder and serve again, with fresh hot rice and replenished hot tea or cold beer. Ideally, chopsticks should be used to eat this fare.

THE MANY fine cooks in Mexico are justifiably famous for their superb soups. Their *sopa de cebollas* (onion soup) is not so well known elsewhere as the French variety, but it is marvelously flavorful.

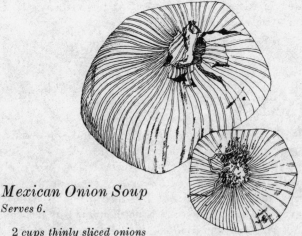

Mexican Onion Soup
Serves 6.

2 *cups thinly sliced onions*
2 *tablespoons butter*
1 *tablespoon peanut or soy oil*
2 *egg yolks, beaten*
½ *teaspoon dry mustard*
3 *cups scalded whole milk*

3 *cups boiling rich chicken stock*
⅓ *cup coarsely grated Swiss cheese*
½ *teaspon chopped fresh coriander (cilantro), or pinch of dried*
salt and freshly ground pepper

In a heavy kettle, heat the butter and oil, and sauté the onion rings, stirring often, until they begin to brown slightly. Remove from heat and blend in the egg yolks and dry mustard, then gradually add the milk, stirring after each addition. Blend in the chicken stock (fresh, preferably), and add the cheese and coriander. Heat through, stirring often, but do not allow to boil. Season to taste, and serve while very hot.

BEAUTIFUL big round or ovoid onions are superlative when stuffed and baked until flavorful and tender. Here is one of my favorite ways, a main dish from central Florida, to be accompanied by a crisp green salad with vinaigrette dressing, and perhaps cornmeal sticks or muffins.

Stuffed Onions Orlando
Serves 4 to 6.

8 *large onions*
½ *pound country pork sausage*
½ *cup coarsely chopped fresh tomatoes*
1 *tablespoon minced green pepper*
1 *tablespoon minced fresh parsley*
1 *small clove garlic, mashed*
1 *teaspoon salt*
¼ *teaspoon freshly ground black pepper*
½ *cup coarse bread crumbs*
butter

Plunge the onions, unpeeled, into lightly salted boiling water and cook for 10 minutes. Remove with slotted spoon, allow to cool slightly, and peel. Using a sharp knife or grapefruit knife, scoop out centers of the onions, leaving a firm shell of several layers. Coarsely chop the onion centers. In a skillet, sauté the sausage meat, stirring often, until it is rather dry, draining off fat. Add chopped onion, tomatoes, green pepper, parsley, garlic, and salt and black pepper. Mix through and cook over very low heat for 10 minutes, stirring often. Stuff the onion shells with this mixture, top each one with bread crumbs, dot liberally with butter, and set in a shallow ovenproof pan. Bake in preheated 400° F. oven for about 30 minutes, or until the onions are very tender when tested.

FARTHER south, in the spectacular volcano-studded

republic of Nicaragua, I have on several occasions enjoyed a handsome salad in which rings of sweet onions are used with tropical fruits and peanuts. I offer this distinctive creation with roast pork or sautéed lamb chops or broiled chicken halves.

Nicaraguan Onion-Fruit Salad
Serves 4.

2 *large sweet onions, sliced wafer-thin and separated into rings*
1 *cup fresh pineapple cubes, undrained*
1 *cup papaya cubes, undrained*
1 *cup orange sections, undrained*
½ *cup mayonnaise*
shredded lettuce
⅓ *cup coarsely chopped salted peanuts*

Lightly combine the onion rings, pineapple and papaya cubes, and orange sections, these seeded and trimmed of all membrane, with the mayonnaise (homemade, preferably). Chill for 1 hour, and serve portions on shredded lettuce, sprinkled at the last moment with the chopped salted peanuts.

THE EGYPTIAN Onion, or Tree Onion, is a special variant of the common kind (*Allium Cepa* var. *bulbellifera*), occasionally cultivated by gourmet gardeners in this and other countries. The vegetative parts are much reminiscent of the normal onion, but the inflorescences bear a tight tuft of diminutive bulblets in place of flowers.

If planted, these little bulblets—buttons, they are often termed—quickly form a miniature onion bulb, which can be pulled and eaten. But as they are, perched oddly up above the parent specimen, they have a special place in the connoisseur's kitchen. Varying in color from red or purplish-red to white, they can be added, peeled and whole, to mixed green salads, to which they impart a delicate and characteristic flavor.

Or they can be pickled, as below, and offered at table as a pretty condiment.

Pickled Egyptian Onions

40 *Egyptian onion bulblets*
1½ *cups light olive oil*
1½ *cups white wine vinegar*
1 *tablespoon sugar*
3 *whole cloves*
1 *small bay leaf*
2 *teaspoons salt*
½ *teaspoon freshly ground white pepper*

Peel the tiny bulblets and place in heavy saucepan with all other ingredients. Cover the pot and cook over very low heat, stirring occasionally, until the onions are crisp-tender, usually about 20 minutes. Allow to cool in the liquid. Drain some to serve as a flavorful condiment, storing the others in their liquid in a tightly capped jar under refrigeration.

ORCHIDS

Of the more than 24,000 different kinds of Orchids known to occur in the wild (the family is the largest of flowering plants), a considerable number are utilized as vegetables in differing parts of the world, by and large on a casual basis.

The Orchid most commonly found in our kitchens is Vanilla. The so-called "beans" of culinary commerce are the cured seed capsules of a viny plant (*Vanilla planifolia*), which is produced in commercial plantations from Mexico to the Malagasy Republic and Tahiti. Vanilla extract is found on practically every kitchen shelf, and the whole "beans" are frequently called for in gourmet recipes.

The ground tuberous roots of certain Old World Orchids, notably of the genus *Orchis*, form salep, a granular powder made into a porridge or mixed with honey, generally fed to invalids or puling children.

Though all parts of most Orchid plants are very bitter to the taste, certain Orchids find random use as condiments and seasonings, the fleshy juvenile leaves, pseudobulbs, and even flowers and seed pods being eaten in varied form—more often for medical rather than strictly culinary benefit.

OXALIS

There are more than 400 different kinds of Oxalis, mostly natives of South Africa, with others in this hemisphere, especially in South America. Many of these are popular with gardeners as ornamentals and are grown for their usually three-parted, stalked leaves and airy sprays of showy flowers. But in such lands as Peru and Bolivia, the subterranean tubers, somewhat like miniature potatoes, form a very important item of the indigenous diet.

In the high Andes the tubers of the Oca (*Oxalis crenata*) have been cultivated since time immemorial; this was a very popular vegetable with the Incas, in fact. Though introduced into Europe and the United

States a long time ago, it has never proved particularly acceptable to culinary gardeners, perhaps because of the bland flavor and moist texture.

Another species of Oxalis (*O. cernua*), from South Africa, is cultivated today in the northern reaches of that continent, and its tubers are on occasion to be found in markets in Marseille and Paris, and, very rarely, in New York. Like the Oca, its flavor is somewhat negative unless it is heavily seasoned, and the texture somewhat soggy. In Mexico a third kind (*Oxalis Deppei*) is cultivated for its tubers, and since this Oxalis is extensively grown in our gardens for its pretty purple-banded leaves and lovely sizable flowers, usually purple, it is a possibility for the epicure. The tubers are, again, sometimes available in European and North African markets, where they have more appeal to the populace.

The Wood Sorrel (*Oxalis Acetosella*) is a native of the eastern portions of the United States and temperate Europe. It is grown in rock gardens and such places, and like a couple of other, rarer members of the genus, its foliage is on occasion used as a sorrel-like salad herb and potherb.

Poisonous oxalic acid is present in some members of this group of plants, hence the gourmet gardener must be positive of the identity of his Oxalis before proceeding to consume any of their parts—whether leaves or tubers.

PALMS

The myriad kinds of Palms distributed throughout the world are among the most important economic plants for man in many regions. The fruits of such well-known species as the Coconut (*Cocos nucifera*) and the Oil Palm (*Elaeis guineensis*) are utilized in multitudinous fashions—as fruits. But in the tropics, where the princely Palms abound, we also find several species of more specialized significance, since parts of them are made use of in vegetable cookery.

In food stores in the United States these days, we can readily find canned hearts of Palm. These are either imported from Brazil or are packed in Florida, where, interestingly, the official state tree, *Sabal Palmetto,* is the source. Elsewhere, the heart buds of several other species of Palm are processed by canners; the hearts are stripped of outer tough coverings and canned, either raw or lightly blanched, in water. They have, depending upon the variety, a more or less bland, delicate flavor that is justly popular with some epicures. As the author of a well-received book on the major kinds of Palms, and a long-time fancier of these splendid plants, I object to the use of hearts of Palm, since their obtaining results in the death of the tree.

Despite this, on special occasions, I convince myself to make use of them on my menus. I must admit that I enjoy them, drained and sliced into thick rounds, then marinated and chilled for some time in a piquant vinaigrette dressing, to be presented on a bed of crisp lettuce leaves.

I am also fond of the following elegantly simple Brazilian dish, which is ideal to serve with broiled steak or Picadillo (page 70). It is but one of the treats of the cuisine to be encountered in the metropolis of São Paulo.

Palmito São Paulo
Serves 4.

1 *large can hearts of palm*
Simple Cheese Sauce (*page 254*)
⅓ *cup slivered Brazil nuts*

Prepare the Simple Cheese Sauce. Drain palm hearts—the imported kind, preferably—and slice them lengthwise. Arrange these in a shallow baking dish, top with the sauce, and sprinkle with the Brazil nuts. Run dish under preheated broiler for just a very few minutes until heated through. Serve without delay.

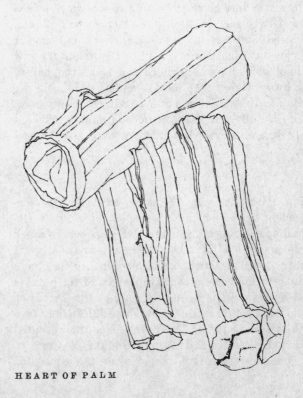

HEART OF PALM

PALM HEART sections, well drained and patted dry, can also be dipped into a light batter and fried in melted lard until rather crisp. Serve these hot, lightly dusted with coarse salt, as a unique appetizer with cocktails or beer.

HERE IS a main dish in which hearts of palm figure with succulent prominence. I should mention here that almost all palms have edible hearts—but there are some few which are violent and usually fatal poisons. So be sure you know your palms before you decide to gather your own.

Palm Hearts and Shrimp
Serves 4.

1 *large can hearts of palm*
2 *tablespoons peanut or soy oil*
1 *tablespoon minced onion*
2 *teaspoons minced green pepper*
3 *tablespoons peeled, chopped fresh tomato*
¼ *teaspoon dried dill weed*
1 *pound medium raw shrimp, shelled*
salt and freshly ground pepper

Thoroughly drain the hearts of palm, reserving the liquid, and cut them into sections about 2 inches long. In a large skillet with cover, heat the oil, and over rather high flame sauté the onion and green pepper, stirring frequently, until they are soft. Add the tomato and reduce heat, continuing to cook until everything is well blended. Add the reserved palm liquid, dill weed, and seasonings to taste. Cover and simmer over low heat for about 15 minutes. Then add the raw shrimp, which have been rinsed and, if desired, halved lengthwise. Cover the skillet again and cook the shrimp for just 5 or 6 minutes, stirring carefully once. Then carefully mix in the sections of palm heart, heat through, and serve without delay over hot steamed rice.

THE PALMYRA Palm (*Borassus flabellifer*) is widespread in tropical Asia. It is a splendid big palmate-leaved species, forming impressive groves over much of its native habitat. Though scarcely known in this country, even in our botanical gardens, in its native haunts virtually every conceivable part of the plant is used by man. In fact, one old song of the Tamils of Ceylon and southern India lists some 801 distinct uses of the Palmyra Palm! These range from the sprouted seeds, eaten roasted and tasting much like chestnuts, to the juvenile root sprout of said seeds, this consumed either roasted or ground into a hearty flour, to the huge leaves, which are dried and used as a kind of paper for strange elongated books.

In almost all other parts of the world, we find palm products of exceptional importance in the cuisine. The fruits of some kinds are cooked prior to being eaten and are considered more as vegetables than as true fruits. One in this unique category of which I am especially fond is the Peach Palm or *pejibaye* (*Guilielma utilis*). This cluster-forming, viciously spiny palm bears masses of sizable fruits which, when boiled, taste very much like mealy peaches. They are justly prized by the natives of Costa Rica, Brazil, and other tropical American countries where the species occurs in abundance. These odd fruit-vegetables, available in cans, have recently begun to be imported into the United States.

AND then we have Sago. This is a long-popular culinary starch, used as a thickening agent and in puddings and soups. It is derived from the soft trunk pith of several different kinds of handsome pinnate palms, notably of the genus *Metroxylon*. These are semi-cultivated in marshy areas in the tropics of the Old World from Ceylon to New Guinea and the Solomon Islands. The obtaining of the starch is a remarkably complicated process involving a lengthy series of stages and a considerable amount of manual labor, often with very primitive tools. Each mature tree, however, may yield as much as two hundred pounds of Sago. Sago, sold as Pearl Sago or Seed Sago, is found at reasonable cost in many of our markets.

PAPAYA

The Papaya, though long well known and justly prized in the warmer parts of the globe, has only in relatively recent years become widely available in our domestic markets. Today this delicious melonlike fruit is gaining in popularity with good cooks throughout the nation, and is being grown commercially in south Florida and Hawaii, and in the Bahamas. It is a native to tropical America and is naturalized in many lands.

The Papaya (*Carica Papaya*) is one of the tropics' most extraordinary plants. It is not a tree—despite its appearance and its growth to ten feet or even more in height—but rather, a woody herbaceous plant, one of the most rapid-growing species known when main-

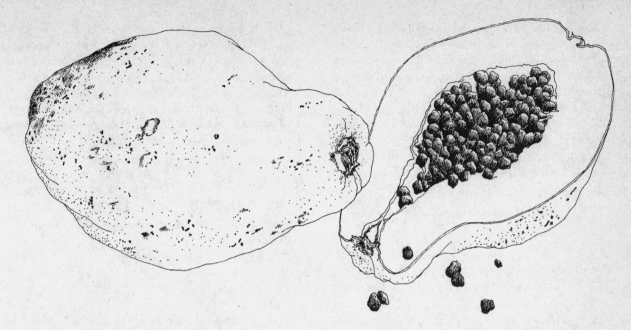

tained under optimum cultural conditions of rich, moist soil and consistently warm temperatures. The seeds from a Papaya acquired at your corner store will quickly sprout, and even in northern areas you can enjoy the "tropical" appearance of the plant in a windowsill pot, or in the garden until chill weather cuts it down.

Today we have many selected varieties of Papayas, these particularly developed in south Florida, where the showy plants thrive and bear with often incredible abundance virtually throughout the entire year. In markets, the fruits are usually offered when only semiripe; they mature in a warm, shaded spot in the kitchen with some rapidity, the smooth skin usually turning from bright green to orange, though some forms retain a greenish cast even when ripe. Although the Papaya—called *fruta bomba* in some areas, *papayer* in French, and Pawpaw—is known primarily as a salad or dessert fruit in its ripe state, the immature fruits are extensively utilized in various parts of the tropics as a nutritious and distinctive vegetable. For use in this way, Papayas should be very firm to the touch, and the flesh distinctly green or yellow-green, not orange or red.

THE SPECTACULAR large, long-stalked, hand-shaped leaves of the Papaya are edible and are prominent in the cuisine of several tropical lands such as the Malagasy Republic (the island formerly known as Madagascar), many parts of tropical Africa, Indonesia's myriad isles, and, in this hemisphere, from the Antilles to Brazil. These leaves have a distinctive flavor, vaguely reminiscent of dandelions combined with spinach. As is so often the case with greens such as this, the simplest method of cookery is the best one.

Papaya Greens
Serves 4.

30 *to* 50 *fresh young papaya leaves*
butter
salt and freshly ground pepper

Use only the very freshest, smallest leaves available. Trim off the stalks. Bring lightly salted water to a rolling boil in a large kettle and plunge in the whole trimmed leaves. Bring again to the boil, and cook for about 4 minutes. Drain, add more salted water, and again bring to the boil. Cook just until the leaves are crisply tender and not bitter, drain very thoroughly, and serve with big pats of butter and salt and freshly ground pepper to taste.

WHEN suitably prepared, the immature fruit of the papaya is a singular delicacy as a vegetable. The flavor and texture of the green papaya is a bit like that of a sweet squash, though it possesses, in my opinion, a uniqueness that will appeal to the connoisseur.

Baked Green Papaya
Serves 4.

2 *medium or* 4 *small firm green papayas*
2 *to* 3 *tablespoons papaya seeds, mashed*
butter
salt and freshly ground white pepper

Cut the washed papayas lengthwise into halves. Scoop out the seeds with their gelatinous coverings, wash off the gelatin, and mash seeds with a mortar and pestle. Blanch papaya halves in a large kettle of rapidly boiling salted water until the flesh is somewhat tender. Drain thoroughly and place halves cut side up in a shallow baking dish. Put some mashed seeds in the hollow of each half, with liberal dollops of butter. Run papayas under preheated broiler until they are bubbling hot and fork-tender. Serve at once, well seasoned with salt and white pepper.

THE GREEN papayas can also be peeled and cooked in lightly salted water, then put through a potato ricer and made into the following exceptional casserole. I first encountered this dish in a small German restaurant in the Organ Mountains of Brazil, not far from the fantastic Dêdo do Deus, "God's Finger." It was served to accompany a mammoth array of, of all things, spicy sauerbraten with authentic potato pancakes.

Brazilian Papaya Casserole
Serves 6.

6 to 8 cups cooked, riced green papaya
1 cup grated fresh coconut
1 cup fresh orange juice
2 teaspoons grated orange zest
¼ cup sugar
4 eggs, beaten lightly
1 cup milk
salt and pepper

In a large bowl, thoroughly blend together the cooked, riced papaya with the coconut, orange juice, and orange zest. Mix in the sugar, then the eggs, milk, and salt and pepper to taste (be rather generous with seasonings). Combine very thoroughly and pour into a liberally buttered casserole. Bake in preheated 325° F. oven for about 45 to 50 minutes, or until the mixture is lightly firm and delicately golden-brown on top. Serve hot.

THE PREPARATION of meat tenderizer from green papayas is today an important adjunct to the commercial production of these adaptable fruit-vegetables. The fruits, hanging on the plant, are scored longi-

tudinally a number of times, and when the milky juice coagulates, it is scraped off and processed. Papain, an enzyme found in this juice, breaks down the tough fibers of meat at an amazing rate (it actually partially "digests" them).

The green fruit forms the basis for a savory pickle and a unique relish, both of which are ideal as accompaniments to curries and most stews.

Florida Papaya Pickle
Makes about 2 quarts.

8 cups green papaya, peeled, sliced into bite-size pieces
4 cups water
4 cups sugar
2 cups cider vinegar
12 peppercorns
8 whole cloves
1-inch length cinnamon bark
2 medium-size bay leaves

In a saucepan, boil the papaya slices in the water for 3 minutes. Drain papaya and reserve. In a large heavy saucepan, combine the sugar and vinegar and bring it just to the boil. Add peppercorns, cloves, cinnamon bark, and bay leaves, and again bring to the boil. Add the drained papaya slices, and over medium heat cook for 15 minutes, stirring carefully to avoid breaking the fruit. Pour into hot sterilized jars and seal immediately. Allow to mellow for at least a week before serving.

Green Papaya Relish

8 cups coarsely grated green papaya
⅓ cup papaya seeds, mashed
¼ cup red wine vinegar
3 tablespoons finely chopped fresh ginger root
3 to 8 drops Tabasco sauce
½ teaspoon salt

Thoroughly combine all ingredients and allow to mellow at room temperature for at least 24 hours prior to using. This relish will retain its texture and flavor, refrigerated, for about 2 weeks.

THE FOLLOWING simple recipe is a marvelous method of serving green papaya as a vegetable. It is particularly suitable with baked ham or sautéed pork chops, but it is amazingly adaptable and admirably supports other meats or fish or fowl. The dish has a pleasantly distinctive "tropical" character.

Glazed Green Papaya Slices
Serves 4.

2 *medium or 4 small firm green papayas*
½ *cup guava jelly*
6 *tablespoons butter*
3 *tablespoons fresh lime juice*

Cut papayas into halves lengthwise, remove seeds, and peel. Cut into slices about 1 inch thick, and place them in a flat baking dish, not overlapping. Thoroughly combine the guava jelly, butter, and lime juice. Bake the papaya slices in preheated 375° F. oven, turning them once, and basting frequently with the guava mixture, until they are very tender and lightly browned.

FINALLY, here is a rich soup concocted from green papaya. This is a recipe which was created in my Coconut Grove kitchen (admittedly after considerable happy experimentation) following the arrival of a big basket of the green fruit on the doorstep from Andros in the Bahamas. The soup has a rather provocative flavor and should be garnished to individual taste with chopped scallion tops and tiny crisp croutons.

Green Papaya Soup
Serves 4 to 6.

8 *cups coarsely grated green papaya*
1½ *quarts rich chicken broth*
3 *tablespoons grated onion*
4 *tablespoons butter*
1 *cup light cream*
⅛ *teaspoon nutmeg*
salt and freshly ground white pepper
chopped scallion tops
crisp tiny croutons

Combine the coarsely grated green papaya with the rich chicken broth and the grated onion. Bring to the boil, then reduce heat, and simmer for 15 minutes, stirring often—the soup should be rather thick. Stir in the butter, light cream, nutmeg, and salt and white pepper to taste. Simmer for 15 minutes more, and serve hot with side dishes of chopped scallion tops and croutons to be added as desired at the table.

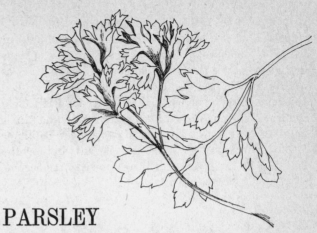

PARSLEY

Though in many kitchens in this country utilized primarily as a garniture or seasoning for various dishes, Parsley (*Petroselinum hortense,* of the Carrot Family) is a delicious vegetable in its own right. In foreign cookery, it finds its way into a number of distinctive recipes, several of which have become justifiably popular hereabouts.

Parsley is so well known as almost to preclude description, though it should be mentioned that there are a number of selected cultivated variants, with variously coarse or finely dissected, flat or curled foliage. Widespread in the wild in Europe and the Near East, this relative of carrots, celery, and parsnips is naturalized in other parts of the world where it is cultivated.

It has been important to man since long before the Christian era, and today is prized as one of our best sources of vitamins A and C. The overdeveloped Hercules wore a pretty crown of parsley when he had just beaten some particularly difficult adversary. And certain of the more elegant ancient Greeks and Romans considered bunches of the lively foliage the acme of decor in their palatial dining halls.

Fresh Parsley, chosen in your favorite market, is a joy to the senses. It is singularly attractive in appearance, it gives off a delicate, yet characteristic scent, its flavor is sublime, and it even feels good when crushed between one's fingers! To maintain Parsley at its peak in your kitchen, thoroughly wash it under cold running water, then shake out as much moisture as possible, and put at once into a jar with tight lid and refrigerate. In this fashion, it will keep in perfect condition for upward of two weeks.

PARSLEY Butter is among the most utilitarian sauces in any good cuisine. It should be used, with more or less discretion, to anoint such vegetable delicacies as boiled potatoes (especially those lovely tiny ones—unpeeled, of course), cooked asparagus or kohlrabi or cardoons or carrots or parsnips or Brussels sprouts or lightly sautéed cabbage chunks. It also appears as a dressing for sautéed scallops of veal or broiled chicken or broiled or pan-fried fish. And, since I am a confirmed shrimp addict, I often serve individual little bowls of the following recipe, kept hot over candle or alcohol burner, as a simple and elegant dip for the boiled or broiled version of those luscious crustaceans.

Parsley Butter
Makes 1 cup.

½ cup finely chopped fresh parsley
1 cup melted butter
¼ teaspoon freshly ground white pepper

Combine all ingredients, heat through, and use while very hot.

Note: If desired, one can add small amounts of such extraneous but sometimes worthy things as minced chives or scallion tops, paprika, slivered toasted almonds, or even Worcestershire sauce to this basic recipe. I do not really approve of these, although a touch of fresh lemon or lime juice is not to be frowned upon when creatures from the ocean are proffered underneath the Parsley Butter.

PARSLEY Bread is one of those delectable things that has been around for a very long time, but that has—in my bailiwick at least—been reinstated only in rather recent years. Almost any sort of bread can be utilized, from crusty Cuban or French or Italian to those admirable little loaves of "party" rye or pumpernickel now happily in our good shops. Sourdough bread, if available, is stupendous! Serve the Parsley Bread thinly sliced with appetizers or light soups, and in robust chunks with steaks and stews and other staples such as pastas.

Parsley Bread

Use various sorts of bread, sliced thick or thin, as the occasion dictates, spread rather freely with butter, sweet or salted. Liberally sprinkle each slice with finely chopped parsley, a touch of freshly ground pepper, and, if desired, a tiny bit of garlic salt. Wrap bread in foil and place in preheated 375° F. oven for 15 minutes. Serve while hot, resealing the foil around the bread after removing the necessary number of slices.

WHEN I was a child, Parsley Jelly appeared on our table on festive occasions to accompany a roast of lamb that was crusty with salt and lots of freshly ground pepper, and pinkly moist inside as it was sliced. Little unpared potatoes, boiled until just tender, were broken open on one's plate and dotted with homemade butter. A crisp salad of lettuce and cucumber slices, often with Kay's Boiled Dressing (page 255), and maybe something like carrots or Hubbard squash purée, and hot rolls—and that made the meal memorable. Parsley Jelly is seldom encountered these days, but it deserves to be revived.

Parsley Jelly
Makes 4 glasses.

2 cups firm-packed parsley leaves
2¼ cups water
2 tablespoons lemon juice
green food coloring (optional)
3½ cups sugar
½ of a 6-ounce bottle liquid fruit pectin

Place the washed parsley leaves (stems removed) in a large saucepan and crush well with a pestle or mallet. Add the water and bring to a quick boil. Remove from heat, cover, and let stand for 10 minutes. Then strain through cheesecloth. Measure 1½ cups, and using a big, deep saucepan, combine the parsley infusion with the lemon juice, and if desired, just a drop or two of green food coloring. Add the sugar, and mix thoroughly. Over high heat, bring to a full, rolling boil, then stir in the half-bottle of liquid pectin, and again bring to full, rolling boil. Boil for 1 minute, stirring constantly. Remove from heat, and skim off any foam. Pour into hot, sterilized jelly glasses, immediately cover with hot paraffin, and, when jelly has cooled, cover glasses with lids.

WASHED, dried sprigs of Parsley can be deep-fried in light olive oil for use in the delicious Italian *fritto misto* and served piping hot, deliciously crunchy, and very lightly salted. Or such compact sprigs make a very enterprising addition to the ingredients of a big batch of Japanese Tempura (page 255).

Now how about luscious, light Parsley Dumplings? These, served with chicken or beef stew, or with your favorite kind of boiled dinner, are a marvelous invention. I like them, too, in many kinds of homemade soups—a rich chicken stock with pieces of chicken and these dumplings floating around is succulent and satisfying.

Parsley Dumplings
Serves 6.

½ *cup finely chopped parsley*
2 *cups sifted all-purpose flour*
3 *teaspoons double-acting baking powder*
1 *teaspoon salt*
1 *tablespoon butter*
3 *egg yolks*
¾ *cup milk*

Into a large bowl, sift together the flour, baking powder, and salt. Using pastry blender or two knives, cut in the butter until mixture is like coarse cornmeal. Beat the egg yolks with the milk, fold in the chopped parsley, and quickly and gently mix this into the flour mixture. Drop the dough, by tablespoons, into boiling soup, or onto meat or vegetables in boiling stew. Cook dumplings, covered, for about 17 minutes. Serve without any delay.

THERE is a special kind of parsley (*Petroselinum hortense* var. *tuberosum*) which produces smallish, white, carrot-shaped roots. Known as Hamburg Parsley, Root Parsley, or Turnip-Rooted Parsley, this is an interesting vegetable, seldom seen in this country outside of select kitchen gardens. The seeds of the plant, however, are readily available from garden-supply stores, and the cultivation is of the easiest.

The roots are eaten raw, or boiled in lightly salted water, then scraped and served with butter or a light cream sauce. Their flavor is distinctive, vaguely reminiscent of celeriac with a hint of parsley. The foliage of Hamburg Parsley, incidentally, can be used just as one does the more ordinary varieties.

PARSNIP

With the Parsnip (*Pastinaca sativa,* of the Carrot Family), there seems no middle ground as to desirability. You either dote on this slim, pristine-pale creation or you simply cannot abide it. In fact, it has oft been stated that the Parsnip is the most neglected and least enjoyed of all root vegetables.

I have been a special fan of this species for a great many years. My first (and most successful) theatrical appearance was as a rather gawky parsnip, while in the second or third grade in school. Perhaps this has something to do with my fondness for this vegetable.

Like so many of our cultivated edibles, the Parsnip originated in Europe, where it was prized long prior to the advent of Christianity. Both the Greeks and Romans were fond of it, and indeed the infamous emperor Tiberius had the roots specially imported from France and Germany to his clifftop eyrie on the Isle of Capri. The plant has, in our time, gotten naturalized in some parts of the world, including the United States, and it can become a rather pestiferous weed.

The old saw that Parsnips must be frozen in the ground to be usable was long ago proved to be erroneous, yet the belief persists today. But the roots can be left in the ground through the winter and dug first thing in the springtime. The seeds are slow to germinate, and the crop may require upward of nine months to harvest. Despite this, Parsnips are usually offered, when available, at very reasonable prices.

If asked to describe the texture of a Parsnip, one might liken it, raw, at least, to a somewhat spongy carrot. But I suspect that the flavor, delicate and singularly appropriate with a great many things, can only be identified as "like a Parsnip."

IN MY kitchen the Parsnip receives very careful attention. My favorite way with them, I think, is the fashion in which my grandmother prepared them in Maine, first parboiling them, then sautéing the longitudinal slices in butter (see recipe below). Another specialty is Parsnip Purée, which is also described below. Both of these recipes are (as Parsnips are in all ways) particularly appropriate with such diverse things as roasts of beef, pork, or lamb, stews made with these meats, chicken (especially broiled), and shellfish and fish.

Grandmother's Parsnips
Serves 4 to 6.

2 *pounds parsnips*
4 *tablespoons butter*
salt and pepper

Boil the unpeeled parsnips (cut in half crosswise if they are overly large) in lightly salted water until a sharp fork easily pierces them. Drain and peel. Cut the roots into medium longitudinal pieces and pat them dry with paper towels. Melt the butter and slowly sauté the parsnips until they are nicely browned on all sides. They can be allowed to become rather crisp, if desired, with lovely results. Season with salt and pepper, and serve while hot.

This simple recipe can be jazzed up in all sorts of ways. More butter can be added at serving time, or, if special elegance is desirable, either Béchamel or

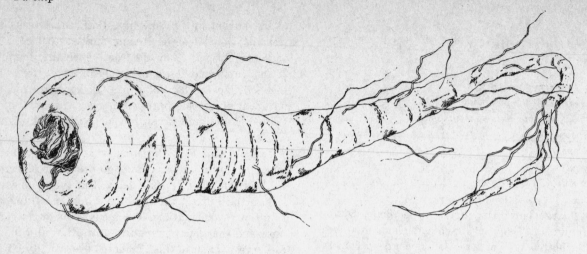

Hollandaise sauce is suggested. If desired, a light sprinkling of fresh minced parsley is not untoward here, either.

Parsnip Purée
Serves 6.

2 pounds parsnips
butter
light cream
salt and pepper
minced parsley and/or chervil
buttered bread crumbs

Boil the unpeeled parsnips in lightly salted water until they are very tender. Drain and peel them, then run parsnip chunks through fine chopper of a food mill while still hot. To each cup of purée, add a goodly hunk of butter (at least the equivalent of 3 tablespoons), a dash of light cream, salt and pepper to taste, plus a touch of minced parsley and/or chervil. Whip the purée with a wire whisk, then turn into a buttered, rather shallow baking dish. Top liberally with the buttered bread crumbs, place in a 375° F. oven, and bake until top of purée is lightly browned.

PARSNIP Salad may sound a bit esoteric to the non-initiate. But a favorite version of these roots at my house has long been the following, which is simplicity itself. I like this with sautéed or broiled pork chops. See what you think.

Simple Parsnip Salad
Serves 6.

2 pounds parsnips
Homemade Mayonnaise (page 255) or Vinaigrette Dressing (page 256)

shredded lettuce
minced fresh parsley

Cook parsnips as indicated under Grandmother's Parsnips, page 173, drain them well, then peel. Cut into pieces about 3 inches long, then into julienne sticks. Chill thoroughly in covered container. Serve on bed of shredded lettuce, with liberal application of Homemade Mayonnaise or Vinaigrette Dressing and sprinkling of fresh parsley.

A PLEASANT way with parsnips is the following one. Reminiscent of especially flavorful potato chips, they make oddly attractive appetizers with beer or cocktails, and I enjoy them with grilled hamburgers and hot sandwiches of roast beef, pork, ham, or lamb.

Parsnip Chips
Makes a lot.

2 pounds parsnips
ice water and ice cubes
lard or light cooking oil
coarse kosher salt

Wash and scrape the parsnips. Cut into very thin strips lengthwise, discarding any part of the core that is hard or woody. Place strips in a large bowl of ice water, add ice cubes, and soak for 1 hour. Drain strips thoroughly and pat them dry with paper towels. Fry, just a few at a time, in hot lard or light oil (not olive oil), until lightly browned. Remove with slotted spoon and drain thoroughly on paper towels. While hot, dust lightly with coarse kosher salt and eat them either hot or after cooling. These chips do not store well, unfortunately.

THE NEXT time you prepare a big roast of beef, pork, or lamb, add lightly parboiled, peeled parsnips for the last half-hour or so of cooking. Baste the vegetable frequently with the savory juices from the meat.

And when you make a big batch of Tempura (page 255), do not neglect the parsnip. Parboil briefly, then peel, and cut into thin longitudinal strips for dipping into the special light batter and quick-frying in oil.

FINALLY, let us consider a very British Parsnip Pie. Recipes for this rich delicacy originating in Elizabethan times are still used with frequency in many good English kitchens. Traditionally topped with a lattice crust, it is a favored harbinger of spring, with fresh primroses set on the lattice crosses.

English Parsnip Pie
Serves 6.

2 *pounds parsnips*
2 *teaspoons salt*
4 *to 6 tablespoons light honey*
¼ *teaspoon ground ginger*
⅛ *teaspoon ground mace*
½ *teaspoon ground cinnamon*
½ *teaspoon grated orange zest*
1 *tablespoon lemon juice*
3 *egg yolks, lightly beaten*
pastry for 2-crust 9-inch pie

Boil the unpeeled parsnips in lightly salted water until they are very tender. Drain and peel them, then, while still hot, run through fine chopper of a food mill. Thoroughly blend in all other ingredients except pastry, of course. Taste the mixture—it should be spicy and quite sweet. Meanwhile, partially bake 9-inch pastry shell. Turn parsnip mixture into cooled shell, and top with latticework of pastry strips. Bake in preheated 450° F. oven for about 20 minutes, or until pastry lattice is nicely browned. Allow to cool slightly before serving, garnished, if desired, with fresh primrose blossoms.

Peas

PEAS, FRESH AND DRIED

The Pea is one of the most universally popular of all vegetables. Originally native to Europe, this annual tendril-climbing viny plant (*Pisum sativum*, of the Legume Family) has been cultivated since pre-Christian days for its rich-flavored young seeds, the mature dried seeds, and, in a special variant, the sweet edible seed pods (see Edible Pea Pods, page 180).

There are a great many distinctive named varieties available today, these making the Pea—or Garden Pea or English Pea, as it is also called—an exceptionally adaptable household staple. Seasonally, in American markets, one can find fresh "peas in the pod," to be shucked at home in the old-fashioned way. The green Peas are also available canned (I consider the tiny, tiny ones particularly desirable), or frozen, often in sauces with butter, wee pearl onions, and the like. Dried peas, excellent for famous hearty soups, come in yellow or green or gray-green, whole or split, and these days we even find this form of the vegetable as a powder.

In France, we find the common garden variety Pea known as *pois* (usually little peas, *petit pois*, an epithet which has also been adopted in several of the Latin-American lands, such as Cuba and Mexico); in Germany, they are known as *Erbsen*; in Italy, *pisi* or *piselli*; in Spain, as *guisantes*; and so on.

STOUT soups prepared from dried Peas figure prominently in the cuisines of many lands, from the Netherlands and Scandinavia to the United States and Canada. Superlative Canadian dishes were often served at my ancestral home in Maine, years back, and through the years I have valued the following marvelous soup from New Brunswick. The dried yellow variety of Pea is traditional, but of course the green kind can be substituted, the whole ones being preferable.

Canadian Pea Soup
Serves 4 to 6.

1 *pound dried yellow peas*
3 *quarts cold water*
½ *pound salt pork, diced*
¼ *cup finely chopped carrots*
¾ *cup chopped onion*
⅛ *teaspoon garlic powder*
1 *small bay leaf*
salt to taste
freshly ground black pepper

In a large heavy kettle with cover, place the picked-over, rinsed peas (whole rather than split peas are preferred) in the water with the salt-pork dice. Cover and bring to a quick boil, and boil for 2 minutes. Remove from heat, still covered, and allow to stand for 1 hour. Add all other ingredients except pepper and simmer, covered, until the peas are falling apart—usually from 1 to 3 hours. Season rather liberally with freshly ground pepper and serve, unstrained, with croutons or crisp pilot crackers.

A PURÉE prepared from dried peas is a marvelous dish to accompany virtually any meat course. Here is a simple basic recipe.

Purée of Peas
Serves 6.

1 *pound dried green or yellow peas, whole or split*
1 *large clove garlic, mashed*
1 *cup coarsely chopped onion*
3 *tablespoons light cream*
3 *or 4 tablespoons butter*
salt and freshly ground pepper to taste

In a kettle with cover, place the picked-over, rinsed peas with the garlic and onion, and add cold water to cover. Put the lid on the kettle and bring to a quick boil; let boil for 2 minutes. Remove from heat, still covered, and allow to stand for 1 hour. Continue to cook over medium-low heat, adding water as needed, until the peas are very soft, stirring often. Drain off any excess liquid and rub the vegetables through a sieve. While hot, beat in the cream, butter, and seasonings to taste. Serve while very hot.

USING this luscious purée, consider the following attractive and superlatively flavorful canapé, to be served piping hot from the oven to commence a festive repast.

Pea-Shrimp Canapés
Makes 1⅓ cups of spread.

1 *cup pea purée*
¾ *cup minced cooked shrimp*
⅛ *teaspoon ground dill weed*
fresh toast rounds or strips

Prepare the pea purée (the green variety is prettier in this instance) as in the preceding recipe. Thoroughly stir in the minced shrimp and dill weed. Check for seasoning and spread liberally on trimmed toast rounds or strips. Run under broiler for just a few seconds, and serve the canapés while very hot.

WHETHER fresh or frozen, peas must be cooked quickly, just until they are firm-tender. I believe they

are best appreciated if simply dressed with butter and a touch of salt and freshly ground pepper—white pepper, if such aesthetic details are important to you. This vegetable is exceptionally adaptable, perfect with every main course one can offer, from red meat roasts to seafood.

Peas are also served in a light cream sauce with pleasant results. A touch of chopped fresh mint can be added to the pot at the last moment, and many European chefs like to sprinkle the just-cooked peas with a teaspoon or so of chopped fresh fennel. And, if you are so inclined, add a small quantity of slivered toasted almonds, and toss the peas lightly just seconds prior to dishing up at the table.

ONE OF the most famous of French ways with *petits pois* is *à la bonne femme*—"in the style of the good lady," whoever she was. Consider serving this the next time you prepare chicken in your favorite fashion—maybe *coq au vin*?

Peas à la Bonne Femme
Serves 4.

2 *pounds fresh peas, shelled, or 1 10-ounce package frozen peas*
¼ *pound lean salt pork, cut into tiny dice*
1 *dozen tiny white onions, peeled*
1 *teaspoon flour*
1 *cup rich chicken stock*
2 *tablespoons chopped fresh parsley*
salt and white pepper

Shell fresh peas, or defrost frozen peas. Parboil the tiny dice of salt pork in a little water for 2 minutes, drain thoroughly, then fry in a sizable heavy pan with cover. When the pork dice begin to brown, add the tiny peeled onions and continue to cook until onions are tender and pork dice are crisp, stirring often. Drain off all but about 1 tablespoon of the fat, sprinkle the pork and onions with flour, and stir for a minute or so. Add the chicken stock, and bring to the boil. Cover and simmer until onions are fully tender. Add the peas to this sauce, with the parsley, a bit of salt and white pepper to taste, cover, and boil gently until peas are just tender.

FRESH or frozen peas prepared in the following epicurean manner are a favorite at my house with a broiled ham steak, fluffy riced potatoes (snipped chives added at last minute), and a topnotch bottle of well-chilled rosé wine.

Green Peas Gourmet

Serves 4.

2 *pounds fresh peas, shelled, or 1 10-ounce package*
   frozen peas
1 *cup thinly sliced celery*
¼ *cup minced scallions, with tops*
1 *teaspoon salt*
1 *cup chicken broth or bouillon*
¼ *cup dry white wine*
4 *tablespoons butter*
freshly ground black pepper to taste
2 *teaspoons cornstarch*

In a saucepan with cover, combine the peas, celery, scallions, salt, and broth or bouillon. Cover and cook over low heat until the peas are almost tender—the celery will still be rather crisp. Stir in the wine, butter, pepper, and additional salt if needed. Combine the cornstarch with 1 teaspoon warm water, and blend in thoroughly. Cook, stirring carefully, for a moment until the sauce thickens and peas are done.

BRAISING peas with lettuce leaves imparts to them a subtlety which has long been relished by good cooks both here and in Europe.

Braised Peas

Serves 4 liberally.

2 *pounds fresh peas, shelled, or 1 10-ounce package*
   frozen peas
1 *large head leaf lettuce*
1 *teaspoon sugar*
1 *teaspoon monosodium glutamate*
½ *cup boiling water*
salt and freshly ground black pepper
butter

Line a heavy saucepan having a tight-fitting cover with washed lettuce leaves. Add the peas, fresh or frozen, sprinkle with sugar and monosodium glutamate, and add boiling water. Cover with washed lettuce leaves, cover the saucepan, and cook over medium heat for about 15 to 18 minutes, or until the peas are just tender. Discard the lettuce leaves, season peas to taste with salt and freshly ground pepper, and dress liberally with butter.

PEAS are not made use of in salads as often as they should be, in my opinion. One of my favorite cool medleys for summery days or nights is the following, to be accompanied by an assortment of crisp crackers and a suitable beverage, such as fresh limeade. The excellent frozen vegetable is perfect here.

Charlie's Pea Salad

Serves 4 to 6.

2 *packages frozen small peas*
2 *cups diced cooked ham*
1 *cup thinly sliced fresh mushrooms*
3 *or 4 medium boiled potatoes, thinly sliced*
shredded lettuce for base
¼ *cup Vinaigrette Dressing (page 256)*
1 *tablespoon freshly snipped chives*

Cook the peas according to package directions until they are just firm-tender. Drain, cool, and chill. Chill ham, mushrooms before slicing, potatoes before peeling and slicing, and lettuce. At serving time lightly toss the peas, ham, and mushrooms together. On individual salad plates arrange a good bed of crisp shredded lettuce, top with thin potato slices, then add the pea mixture, pour the Vinaigrette Dressing over (your own or a commercial version), sprinkle liberally with the chives, and serve.

A CHARMING Japanese family of my close culinary circle consistently creates distinctive dishes. On the occasion of my last visit to their lovely garden home, a superb "main, main entrée" of fresh shelled peas and luscious Florida shrimp was served at dinner. As is customary, there were several other major creations forthcoming on the table, but this was a particularly exceptional recipe, which my hostess kindly passed along to me. Unless you are making it a part of a multicourse Japanese repast, accompany this with individual bowls of hot steamed rice, following a clear soup, and if desired such a salad as Nikko Salad on page 49. Hot tea is the perfect beverage, and a fruit sherbet an ideal finale.

Mrs. Kawakami's Peas and Shrimp
Serves 6.

3 *pounds fresh peas, shelled*
1 *pound raw medium shrimp, shelled*
2 *tablespoons peanut or soy oil*
2 *cups thinly sliced fresh mushrooms*
2 *cups finely chopped scallion tops*
2 *cups rich chicken stock*
1 *teaspoon sugar*
½ *teaspoon monosodium glutamate*
3 *tablespoons Japanese soy sauce*

If desired, cut the shrimp into halves or quarters. Using a wok or large shallow skillet, heat the oil and stir-fry the shrimp over high heat until they just turn color. Add the mushrooms, scallion tops, and fresh peas, and continue to stir-fry for 1 minute. Add all other ingredients, reduce heat, and simmer, stirring carefully, for 3 minutes. The vegetables should retain considerable firmness of texture. Serve without delay.

BLACK-EYE PEA

When one attempts to find some semblance of system in the common names applied to various sorts of legumes—the beans, peas, and their myriad edible relatives—a feeling of inadequacy and hopelessness eventually results. Here is a pertinent example, which I will call the Black-Eye Pea and simply note that most botanists agree that its scientific name is *Vigna sinensis.*

It is, technically, a bean—one that has been extensively cultivated since prehistoric times. As a result, it labors under an incredible assemblage of vernacular names, several of which also apply to other, totally different plants. The best known "alternate" epithets for our multi-guised legumes are Cowpea, Cornfield Pea, Tonkin Pea, Jerusalem Pea, Marble Pea, and, in Spanish, *frijol de carita.*

All this, of course, really makes no great difference to the good cook, although in many recipes a particular, precise variety of pea (or bean) will be acceptable, while others will not. Some familiarity with the varied names applied to the same vegetable is therefore indeed helpful.

This Black-Eye Pea is actually just one of more than 250 differentiated named agricultural variants of the single species, *Vigna sinensis.* Another common form is an albino, called White Cowpea, with somewhat less positive flavor than its better known dark-marked brother. Both of these are available in our markets today dried in packets, frozen in partly cooked condition, and canned cooked, often with the addition of onion. If you grow the vines in your home garden, as is often done, particularly in our Southern states, do not neglect picking a mess of the little pea pods when they measure only two or three inches long. These are exceptionally flavorful, adapting themselves to almost any recipe for which Green Beans (page 37) are suggested. The fresh peas are available in our large markets with increasing frequency, in their rather lumpy rusty-green pods. Shucked and cooked, preferably with salt pork or fatty bacon, they are delightful fare, even though considered somewhat plebeian by many Americans.

The dried seeds themselves—whether called peas or beans—are highly popular in our country, notably in the deep South, and also form an important item of diet abroad, from Africa to India. These are washed, brought quickly to the boil in salted water, then, like the fresh peas, usually cooked with some kind of pork —salt, fatback, or fatty bacon—until tender, then served with butter and appropriate table seasonings.

A traditional Southern dish served on New Year's Day is Hog Jowls with Black-Eye Peas. This savory combination is thought to bring the eater good fortune during the year to come.

I find it amusing to note that there is a Black-Eyed *(sic)* Pea Society of America, with present headquarters in Richmond, Virginia. With regret, I must report that my communications addressed to this select organization have thus far remained unanswered.

Black-Eye Peas can well, and often do, take the place of Pigeon Peas in the famous Bahamian delicacy Peas and Rice (page 181), this especially appropriate with fish in its many forms. They should not be ignored during the preparation of big cauldrons of vegetable soups and such things, and are essential to the production of Cuba's famous Bollitos (pronounced bo-*yee*-toes). These unique, tasty little balls, most often eaten as hot snacks, can be found in the Spanish colonies of such Florida cities as Key West, Tampa, and Miami.

Bollitos
Serves a lot of happy folks.

    1 pound dried black-eye peas
    2 large cloves garlic, mashed
    ½ to ¾ cup chopped onion
    2 teaspoons salt
    lard for deep frying

Soak the peas overnight in water to cover. Slip the skins from the peas by rubbing them between the hands—this is very important! Discard skins. Wash and drain peas thoroughly. Grind the peas, garlic, and onion in a food mill several times, until the mixture becomes a rather smooth paste. Add the salt, then beat the mixture until it takes on the consistency of heavy cake batter. Chill, covered, for about 1 hour, until the mixture is rather firm. Drop by tablespoonsful into deep lard heated to 350° F. Fry until nicely browned, a few at a time. Drain thoroughly and serve while hot.

AN INTERESTING main luncheon dish from Georgia makes memorable use of our good old black-eyes. Serve it with hot rolls, individual platters of thinly sliced tomatoes and cucumbers dressed with wine vinegar and freshly ground white pepper, and a beverage such as beer, iced coffee, or tea.

Black-Eye Peas Savannah
Serves 6.

    6 cups cooked, drained black-eye peas
    6 slices lean bacon, diced
    1 teaspoon salt
    ¼ teaspoon freshly ground pepper
    1 cup light cream

    ¾ cup buttered coarse bread crumbs
    6 thick slices lean bacon, broiled

Fry the bacon dice until crisp. Remove pieces from skillet with a slotted spoon and allow to drain on paper towels. Combine the bacon dice with the cooked black-eye peas, salt, pepper, and cream, and turn this mixture into a well-greased shallow baking dish. Top with the buttered bread crumbs and bake in preheated 350° F. oven for 20 minutes—the dish should be just slightly moist. Arrange the broiled bacon on top of the casserole, and serve while very hot.

BLACK-EYE peas are important to the cuisine of many of the countries of West Africa. This good cookery is gradually becoming known in the United States, and friends to whom I have offered the following delicacy come back for seconds.

Nigerian Black-Eye Peas
Serves 6.

    2 cups dried black-eye peas
    1½ cups chopped onion
    1 cup chopped fresh tomato
    ½ cup chopped green pepper
    1 or 2 teaspoons crushed dried red peppers
    2 tablespoons tomato paste
    ¼ teaspoon oregano
    2 7-ounce cans white tuna (albacore), undrained
    3 large firm-ripe bananas, cut into ½-inch slices
    1 teaspoon salt
    1 cup peanut or soy oil

Pick over and wash the peas, then drain them. Place in a large kettle with cover, add fresh cold water, and bring to a quick boil. Remove from heat, cover, and allow to soak for 1 hour. Then simmer, covered, over very low heat until tender, adding a bit more water if necessary. Add the onion, fresh tomato, green pepper, and dried red peppers (substitute several good healthy dashes of Tabasco sauce for the last, if desired), cover again, and cook over medium heat for 15 minutes, stirring occasionally. Add the tomato paste, oregano, and undrained tuna, mix carefully through the peas, cover and simmer for 10 minutes. Remove the cover and simmer for an additional 5 minutes. Meanwhile, towards the last of cooking, salt the banana slices, and fry them in the hot oil, a few at a time, until they are golden-brown. Drain on paper towels, and serve while hot with the peas-fish mixture.

Now we come to a very famous black-eye pea recipe —Hoppin' John. I cannot find anyone who knows just who John was, or why he was hippety-hopping, but the dish is a great favorite on many good tables in parts of Florida and in other Southern states. I like Hoppin' John with pan-fried thin pork chops and Brazilian Cucumber Salad (page 101).

Hoppin' John
Serves 6 liberally.

1 *cup dried black-eye peas*
¼ *pound smoked bacon or salt pork, diced*
1 *hot red-pepper pod, diced, or several dashes Tabasco
    sauce*
3 *cups cooked rice*
salt and pepper to taste

Pick over and rinse the peas, then soak them in water to cover overnight. Drain and cover with fresh cold water, and cook with the bacon or salt pork and diced pepper pod (or Tabasco sauce) until the peas are very tender. Add the rice, and salt and pepper to taste. Pour into a casserole, cover, and bake in preheated 350° F. oven until the liquid is absorbed and the dish is heated through. Serve hot, with fried shrimp or chicken, or baked stuffed fish.

EDIBLE PEA PODS

The special kind of garden pea extensively cultivated in the Orient (and now, happily in this country) for its edible pods is botanically a variety of the common pea (*Pisum sativum* var. *macrocarpon,* of the Legume Family). These fragile delicacies—otherwise known as Chinese Peas, Snow Peas, Sugar Peas, *ho-lon-dow* or *ho-lang-dau* (Chinese), or *chabo-endo* (Japanese)— are today available in their fresh state in many superior domestic markets.

Frozen Edible Pea Pods are also for sale, but in my opinion they lack the unique crisp texture—and, to a large degree, the remarkable sweet flavor—of the freshly plucked vegetable.

Edible Pea Pods are common additions to a great many superb Oriental dishes. The flattened pods, tapering to both ends, are usually of a particularly vivid green color. They measure up to about three inches in length, with a breadth of about three-quarters of an inch. The tiny peas themselves can be seen through the almost translucent pods.

They should be soaked briefly in cold water, both ends trimmed off (with any little string that comes off along with the tips), drained thoroughly, and refrigerated until cooking time. They should be used as promptly as possible, but if tightly wrapped in culinary plastic, they will retain their freshness for almost a week. In many instances, the trimmed pea pods can be refreshed by soaking for an hour or so in ice water, then thoroughly drained and patted dry with paper towels.

When using Edible Pea Pods—in all sorts of things from clear soups (see Bitter Melon Soup, Korean, page 145) to Sukiyaki (page 164) or mélanges with other vegetables and pork, shrimp, fowl, or beef—the good cook will add these lovely vegetables for just the final two or three minutes of heat. When the least bit overcooked, they become limp and uninspiring to the palate.

A FAVORITE recipe with Edible Pea Pods is the following one—simplicity itself.

Edible Pea Pods with Mushrooms
Serves 4.

1 *pound fresh edible pea pods*
1 *pound fresh mushrooms*
2 *tablespoons peanut or soy oil*
1 *to 3 teaspoons Japanese soy sauce*

Prepare the pea pods as indicated above. Cut the mushrooms, caps and stems, into thin slices. Heat the oil in a wok or large shallow skillet, and stir-fry the mushrooms for 2 minutes over high heat. Add the whole pea pods and stir-fry for a minute or so more. The pea pods must be very crisp-textured when served —scarcely cooked at all, just heated through. Add the soy sauce, mix through, and serve at once. Marvelous!

PIGEON PEA

The Pigeon Pea (*Cajanus indicus*, of the Legume Family) is an erect shrubby plant, sometimes reaching a height of ten feet. It has been cultivated for a very long time, and is probably of African origin. With fuzzy leaves and sprays of yellow and maroon- or red-marked flowers, the hairy pealike pod is lumpy, with constrictions between the rather numerous edible seeds contained within it.

Essentially a tropical legume, the Pigeon Pea is extensively grown in such regions as the West Indies, Africa, and India. A number of vernaculars are on record for this plant, including Congo Pea, Congo Bean, Goongoo Pea (Jamaica), Hoary Pea, No-Eye Pea, *gandul* (Spanish), *dhal, grandul, toor, urhur,* or *paripu* (India and other Asiatic countries). There are several distinct variants, some being relished by the human species, others particularly grown for use as fodder for farm animals.

The seeds, usually dark gray or yellow, are the size of small common peas. They are essential items of the diet in a great many warm lands, especially for use in soups, curries, and in the making of the famous Asiatic dish Dhal (page 133). The Pigeon Pea is an exceedingly prolific plant, thriving even in the poorest of soils, hence is a favorite crop in many parts of the world where other legumes do not flourish.

In this country its cultivation is largely restricted to the Southeastern states, though the dried peas—frequently split into halves—are commonly sold in most of our large cities. Flash-frozen green Pigeon Peas are to be found these days, too, and cooked ones in cans are on occasion seen on store shelves.

PEAS and Rice is perhaps the most famous indigenous vegetable dish of the Bahamas, that glorious string of islets lying off the coast of Florida and Cuba. In the most authentic form of this dish, Pigeon Peas are obligatory, but the Black-Eye Pea may also be utilized with happy results. This savory casserole is most often served with seafood, but it is admirably adaptable to virtually every other kind of meat, from fowl to pork to pot roast of beef.

Bahamian Peas and Rice
Serves 4 to 6.

1 cup dried pigeon peas
6 cups water
¼ pound salt pork, coarsely diced
1½ cups chopped onion
2 medium cloves garlic, mashed
1 cup coarsely chopped fresh tomatoes
1½ cups raw long-grain rice, washed
salt and pepper to taste
¼ cup chopped fresh parsley
¼ teaspoon dried thyme

Pick over and wash the peas, and drain them well. Place in a large heavy kettle with cover, add the 6 cups water, put on the lid, and bring to a quick boil. Remove from the heat and allow to stand, still covered, for 1 hour. Return to medium heat, and begin to cook again. Fry the salt-pork dice in a skillet until rather crisp, then remove pieces with slotted spoon and drain them on paper towels. Drain off all but about 2 tablespoons of fat from the skillet, and in it sauté the onion, garlic, and tomato, stirring often, over rather high heat, until the onion is soft. Turn this mixture into the peas, and continue to cook them, still covered, until they are very soft. Add the washed rice, season rather liberally with salt and pepper, and mix in the parsley and thyme. Cover again and continue to cook until the rice is tender and the mixture is almost dry. If necessary, a small amount of water can be added during this period.

PEPPER

Basically, edible Peppers as a vegetable can be relegated to two major, though rather vague, categories— Sweet and Hot. In the United States, Pepper typically refers to *Capsicum annuum* and varieties, a member of the same family as the potato, tomato, and eggplant. The vernacular nomenclature of these popular, extensively utilized vegetables—today myriad in number, and formidable in diversity of form, dimension, color, and flavor—is terribly confused in this country. And when one considers that they are known elsewhere under such names as Capsicum (England), *aji* (Spanish America), Chile, with various designating specific epithets—*poblano, serrano, jalapeño,* etc. (Mexico), *pimenta* (Brazil), *peperoni* (Italy), *piment* or *piment doux* (France), and *lombok* (Indonesia), the confusion becomes international in scope.

These Peppers, whatever their regional epithets may be, are presumably natives of tropical America. They were, however, introduced into Europe, and thence into the torrid lands of Asia and Africa, at an early date, and quickly became naturalized so extensively there that they were long considered to be true indigenes.

The black or white pepper, commonly used as a spice, is the dried berry of a completely different plant (*Piper nigrum,* of the Peperomia Family).

In the United States, the most widely encountered Sweet Pepper—borne on more or less shrubby annual or biennial plants—is the large, inflated Bell or Globe Pepper, generally known as Green Pepper—although, perversely, it turns bright red when mature! There are many other named forms, including Golden King, Monstrous, Squash, and Brazilian Upright.

The Green Pepper in its commonest form is found throughout the year in all our domestic markets. Its flavor, raw or cooked, is distinctive and delicious, and adapts to all sorts of fine dishes, from soups and stews to salads. Several commercial firms offer the chopped green vegetable in a dried form, for judicious addition as a seasoning.

As with all of the Sweet Peppers, when purchasing the fresh vegetable, choose only very firm specimens—whatever their color—with no wrinkling nor soft spots. Store the Green Peppers in the refrigerator and use them as quickly as possible, and cutting them up at the last moment before incorporation in the recipe, to retain optimum savor. The thin inner pulp is customarily discarded, and even in the finest "sweet" varieties the flat seeds may be pungent, so these are usually carefully rinsed away.

MY COLLEAGUE both in cookery and horticulture, Ed Flickinger, often offers his friends the following delicious spread containing these luscious, sweet Green Peppers.

Mama Flick's Green Pepper Spread

1 small green pepper
½ pound light-yellow extra-sharp cheese
mayonnaise to taste

Using the medium blade of a food grinder, grind the cheese and trimmed, seeded pepper together. Add enough mayonnaise to this mixture to make it just

spreadable. Serve at room temperature with crisp crackers, or as a delightful sandwich filling.

FIRM green peppers, or the more mature red phase of the same vegetable, are delectable when simply roasted in the oven and served as a vegetable. Although available in cans or jars in good Italian markets, the freshly prepared kind is so superior that it must be recommended.

Roasted Green Peppers

firm small green peppers
olive oil

Cut peppers into halves or quarters, remove all pith and seeds, and rub liberally, inside and out, with oil. Place in a shallow baking pan, put into a preheated 400° F. oven, and roast until the peppers are firm-tender, turning the pieces from time to time. Allow to cool slightly before serving seasoned with a bit of salt and freshly ground pepper, if desired. Or add to a Vinaigrette Dressing (page 256) for future use in an antipasto.

HANDSOME big green peppers are stuffed with an amazing variety of ingredients in the cuisine of such lands as Mexico, Spain, Italy, and the Near Eastern countries. Here is a personal favorite version of these, essentially a pretty, nutritious meal-in-one.

Green Peppers Alejandro
Serves 4 to 6.

8 medium-size green peppers
½ cup raw rice
1 pound ground lamb, uncooked
1 cup tomato juice
½ cup finely chopped onion
3 tablespoons minced fresh parsley
1½ teaspoons salt
½ teaspoon black pepper
⅛ teaspoon mixed herbs
3 tablespoons butter
½ cup finely chopped onion
1 small can chopped mushrooms
2 cups tomato juice
½ teaspoon salt
⅛ teaspoon black pepper
⅛ teaspoon dried thyme
3 tablespoons freshly grated Parmesan or Fontina cheese

Cut tops off green peppers and carefully remove

seeds and membranes. Meanwhile cook the rice according to package directions until it is half done, and drain thoroughly. In a large bowl, completely combine the rice, ground lamb, the 1 cup tomato juice, ½ cup chopped onion, the parsley, salt, black pepper, and mixed herbs. Stuff the pepper shells rather firmly with this mixture. (If any remains, make small firm balls of it and cook them separately in a small ovenproof casserole.) Place the stuffed peppers in a shallow baking dish, with about one-half inch of water. Bake in preheated oven for about 60 to 70 minutes, basting the peppers frequently with the water, and adding a bit more if needed. In a saucepan, combine the remaining ½ cup onion, which has been sautéed in butter until just limp, together with the undrained mushrooms, 2 cups tomato juice, the ½ teaspoon salt, ⅛ teaspoon black pepper, and the thyme. Simmer this sauce, covered, over very low heat for an hour. To serve, carefully remove cooked stuffed peppers from the pan, drain, arrange on individual plates, pour liberal quantities of the sauce over them, and sprinkle with the grated cheese.

I HAVE a good friend who was born in Turkey, of Greek parentage, and who prior to his residence in this country lived in Brazil, Costa Rica, and Cuba. One of his specialties is an extraordinary chilled salad prepared with green peppers. It is an adaptable dish with such seemingly diverse things as pot roast, shish kebabs of lamb, and virtually any red meat or fowl stew.

Anatolian Green Pepper Salad
Serves 4.

2 *medium green peppers*
3 *tablespoons plumped seedless yellow or white raisins*
⅓ *cup finely chopped scallion tops*
2 *tablespoons pine nuts (pignoli)*
⅓ *cup light olive oil*
1 *to 2 tablespoons lemon juice*
¼ *teaspoon paprika*
salt and freshly ground pepper to taste

Remove seeds and pith from green peppers and slice into very thin julienne strips. Soak the raisins in a little warm water for 15 minutes or so, then drain them thoroughly. Lightly toss together the green peppers, raisins, scallion tops, and pine nuts, and dress them with a thorough mixture of the remaining ingredients, which has been allowed to mellow for about 30 minutes prior to use. Serve at once.

THE VARIOUS dishes of Chinese origin which are so justifiably popular in the United States include a number of handsome, flavorful medleys utilizing green peppers. Here is one that my authoritative Oriental cronies tell me is not terribly authentic—but it is assuredly successful when offered at table. This should not be confused with the other kind of pepper steak called *steak au poivre*, which is a thick steak coated with freshly crushed black peppercorns and broiled or pan-broiled.

Chinese Pepper Steak
Serves 4 to 6.

2 *large green peppers, cut into chunks*
2 *pounds flank steak*
4 *tablespoons peanut or soy oil*
salt and freshly ground black pepper
⅓ *cup diced onion*
1 *medium clove garlic, mashed*
¾ *cup diagonally cut celery stalks*
1 *cup rich beef bouillon*
1 *tablespoon cornstarch*
2 *tablespoons warm water*
2 *tablespoons Japanese soy sauce*

Using a very sharp knife or meat slicer, cut the flank steak on the diagonal into slices about ⅛ inch thick. In a large heavy skillet with tight-fitting cover, over very high heat, brown the steak slices, a few at a time, in the oil, this seasoned with salt and black pepper. Remove the slices with slotted spoon as they are done and keep warm. Then add the green pepper, onion, garlic, and celery to the skillet. Stirring often —still over high heat—cook vegetables until they start to become tender. Add beef bouillon (or stock), return the meat slices, mix well, cover the container tightly, and cook over high heat for 2 or 3 minutes— the vegetables must still retain considerable texture. Mix together the cornstarch, water, and soy sauce, and blend into the skillet. Reduce heat and cook, uncovered, a minute or so, stirring constantly but with care, until the sauce thickens. Serve immediately with hot steamed rice.

THE SOMEWHAT elongate tapering sweet peppers that vary from bright emerald-green to yellow labor, as one would expect, under a variety of names. Sweet Green Chile Pepper seems to be the most widespread vernacular generally accepted in this country, but I have encountered the vegetables in markets as Italian Sweet Pepper, Sweet Banana Pepper, just plain Banana Pepper, and so on.

In any event, consider utilizing these flavorful, subtle vegetables in the following succulent recipes, both of Latin origin. If perchance the fresh peppers are not available, substitute the excellent canned variety available from California and Texas.

Ajoqueso (pronounced *ah-hoe-kay-soe*) is an insidious business, typically offered with beer or cocktails to begin a Mexican repast. Its name means, literally, "garlic-cheese," which is appropriate.

Ajoqueso
Serves 4 to 8.

½ pound fresh sweet green chile peppers
½ cup minced onion
2 or 3 large cloves garlic, mashed
¼ cup light olive oil
2 tablespoons flour
1 cup light cream
½ pound Cheddar or Jack cheese, shredded

Seed the peppers and cut them into rather small dice. Sauté the peppers, onion, and garlic in the oil until just wilted. Add the flour, stirring constantly, then stir over medium heat for 3 minutes. Gradually add the cream and stir until very smooth. Add the shredded cheese, mix through, and heat until it melts. Keep warm in a chafing dish to serve as a superb dip with pieces of crisp tortilla, corn chips, fresh toast, or unsalted Cuban crackers.

THEN we have a hearty kind of cheese custard, studded with these sweet green chile peppers, to be served as a main dish for meatless meals or to accompany such things as broiled pork chops, cold baked ham, or fried chicken.

Sweet Chile Casserole Mexique
Serves 6.

1 pound sweet green chile peppers
1½ cups diced sharp Cheddar cheese
2 eggs
2 cups milk
½ cup sifted flour
1 teaspoon salt
½ teaspoon freshly ground black pepper

Liberally butter a 1½-quart casserole. Cut peppers into pieces about 1 inch square, first rinsing off all seeds, and arrange half of the pieces over bottom of the casserole. Arrange half of the cheese dice over these. Repeat, topping with the cheese dice. Lightly beat the eggs, then mix in the milk, flour, and seasonings. If there are some lumps, do not worry about them. Pour mixture over the cheese and peppers.

Bake casserole in preheated 350° F. oven for 45 to 50 minutes, or until custard is set and nicely browned on top. Serve while very hot, or reheat if serving later.

THE MULTITUDINOUS hot peppers, whose pungency varies from delicate to dangerously volcanic, are extremely diversified in size (though usually smallish), shape (most globular to more or less cylindrical), and color. Red is the best-known hue—as in such plants as Tabasco Pepper and the perennial, shrubby Bird Pepper (the species *Capsicum frutescens*)—but these fiery delights also come in shades ranging from vivid canary yellow to mottled green to rich chocolate or black-purple.

The *very* hot peppers must be approached with some caution. When using them, fresh or dried, or in their various pickled versions, carefully scrub your hands after touching even the smallest amount, and never bring unwashed fingers close to eyes or mouth. These fiery little vegetables are very important as seasonings in the cuisines of such lands as Mexico, Guatemala, and, in other sectors of the globe, Africa, Indonesia, and Korea.

No MEXICAN table, however elegant or humble, is ever complete without a bowl of Salsa Fría—which means "cold sauce." The preparation of this staple varies almost from home to home, but invariably it should be added to various dishes with discretion. Despite its adaptations in the "chili parlors" of the United States, authentic Mexican food is seldom hot, per se—the Salsa Fría is what gives it its sometimes breathtaking quality. Here is a rather good version, I think. Store it, tightly covered, and it will remain usable for upward of a month, though gaining in intensity all the time!

Salsa Fría

1 to 3 small hot peppers, finely chopped
⅓ cup finely chopped green pepper
3 firm-ripe tomatoes, peeled, coarsely chopped
½ cup finely chopped onion
1 or 2 medium cloves garlic, mashed
1 tablespoon minced fresh parsley
1 teaspoon salt
1 teaspoon chopped fresh coriander (*cilantro*), or ½ teaspoon ground coriander
Tabasco sauce to taste

Thoroughly combine all ingredients and allow to mellow for several hours prior to using as a hot condiment with Mexican and Guatemalan dishes. Serve (with discretion) at room temperature.

THE PIMIENTO is a particular variety of the shrubby hot pepper; it has been developed primarily in Spain and Portugal, from whence it is largely imported into the United States in cans or jars, already cooked and peeled, then preserved in a light briny liquid. Much confusion has been caused by the misspelling of its name as *pimento*. Pimento is one of the authentic vernaculars of the Allspice, a totally different plant product originating from a splendid tree (*Pimenta officinalis*), of the Myrtle or Eucalyptus Family, which is grown especially in Jamaica.

Pimientos are relatively "sweet" hot peppers, extensively used in the fine cuisine of people of Spanish, Portuguese, and Italian ancestries. Often used simply as a pretty garnish for salads, stews and soups, the vegetable really comes into its own in such dishes as the following handsome, flavorful appetizer from Portugal. Serve this with crisp rusks.

Pimiento Hors d'Oeuvre Lisbôa
Serves 4 to 6.

4 *large canned pimientos, drained*
1 *can Portuguese boneless sardines in oil*
¼ *cup chopped fresh parsley*
¼ *cup light olive oil*
2 *tablespoons wine vinegar*
1 *teaspoon lemon juice*
1 *teaspoon grated onion*
⅛ *teaspoon freshly ground pepper*

Cut drained pimientos into large slices and arrange on a salad platter with the sardines, these drained and sprinkled with parsley. Prepare a dressing by thoroughly combining remaining ingredients. Pour this over the salad at the last moment before serving.

MENTION must be made here of Paprika—a spice, vivid red in color when at its peak of potency, which is highly important to the superb cookery of Hungary and Spain. The basic fruit from which this powder is obtained, through drying and varied preparation prior to grinding, is the same as the "sweet" pimiento. This is often known as Long Cayenne, since it also figures in the production of so-called Cayenne pepper—and, for that matter, of chili powder as well. There are many distinct varieties of Hungarian Paprika, these differing markedly in power, and to a somewhat lesser degree the same applies to *pimentón*, the special Spanish Paprika.

PERILLA

Perilla (botanically *Perilla frutescens* and varieties, of the Mint Family) is a rather esoteric vegetable, one of those grown primarily by Chinese and Japanese epicures as a special seasoning. Originally native to an immense area stretching from the Himalayas to Japan, it is cultivated to some extent in Hawaii and California. Usually, seedlings only a few inches tall are offered for sale, these gathered into bunches of somewhat hairy, smallish leaves. This foliage is usually dark purple underneath and lustrous bronze-purple-green on its upper surface (dark purple-brown forms are also known), and because of this feature the plants are sometimes encountered as ornamentals.

Perilla is cultivated in India, Korea, and Japan, as the source of an oil somewhat like linseed oil. Another member of the genus, *Perilla arguta*, which appears to have no well-known vernacular name, is also cultivated in the Orient (probably not at all in the United States). All parts, from seeds or just-germinated seedlings to mature foliage and flowers, are used as powerfully spicy ingredients of the specialized cuisine.

THE "COMMON" Perilla, when cut, gives off a rather pervading odor and flavor reminiscent of cinnamon. The Chinese, who call it *che-so*, and the Japanese, who call it *shiso*, use it in such things as the following pleasant condiment.

Perilla-Cucumber Relish

1 *bunch fresh perilla*
1 *medium-size firm cucumber*
2 *teaspoons salt*
3 *to 4 tablespoons canned tiny shrimp*
3 *tablespoons Japanese rice vinegar*
1 *tablespoon Japanese soy sauce*
1 *teaspoon sugar*

Wash perilla and shake it as dry as possible. Shred the leaves and tender parts of the stems. Peel the cucumber, cut in half lengthwise, scoop out seeds, then slice thinly. Add salt and allow to stand for 10 minutes or more. Wash cucumber, press out excess moisture, and put into a bowl with the shredded perilla. Cut the drained tiny shrimp into halves lengthwise and mix into the bowl, adding all other ingredients. Allow to stand for at least 30 minutes, and serve either at room temperature or lightly chilled.

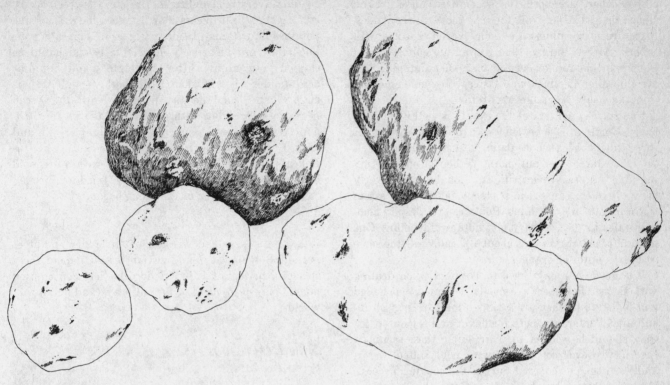

POTATO

The Irish, White, or Round Potato is among the most important of all of the world's vegetables, figuring, sometimes with . overwhelming prominence, in the everyday diet of countless millions of people.

The Potato is not, in its origins, Irish at all, though this is its best known vernacular name. It is, rather, a native of the high valleys of Peru, Bolivia, and Chile, extending northward to Mexico, with a somewhat distinctive form in the mountains of Colorado. It is a member of the huge Nightshade Family (Solanaceae), an assemblage that also includes the tomato and the eggplant. Botanists know it as *Solanum tuberosum,* a species of which there are countless recorded phases.

The history of the Potato is a picturesque one. The Spaniards, who found it in the Inca Empire of Peru, introduced the plant to Europe early in the sixteenth century. It was cultivated largely as a curiosity in botanical gardens at first, and indeed was reputed to be deadly poisonous for many years. But following its introduction into England (by neither Sir Walter Raleigh nor Sir Francis Drake, though both famed gentlemen have been given the credit in past writings), it gained in popularity with gourmets who could afford the considerable expense of the tubers.

In 1663, the Royal Society of London recommended that the Potato be introduced into Ireland, to avoid the famines that periodically swept that green land.

Outside of Ireland, until about the middle of the eighteenth century, it remained a rather infrequently grown crop, this due in large part to the low quality of the tubers. Selective breeding brought about improved varieties, larger and with better flavor, and the use of this novel vegetable became more widespread.

The terrible potato blight that struck Ireland in 1846—the country had become essentially a one-crop economy, totally dependent upon this plant—caused the death of an estimated 600,000 persons. This catastrophe, which ended two years later, pointed up, in a tragic way, the dangers of depending on one crop alone.

The Potato was introduced into the United States in 1719, though the tubers were earlier known as rare imports, these presumably having come from Bermuda. The French were long reluctant to accept the Potato, and only through the efforts of the respected scientist Parmentier was the vegetable popularized, and finally admitted to the ranks of *haute cuisine.*

Potato production in this country today is big agricultural business. Maine, Idaho, and California lead in production of the crop, but most other states boast of fields of one or more varieties of the vegetable. A planting of Potatoes, when in bloom, is very attractive —the white to blue or violet flowers are showy and fragrant. The plant is a somewhat compact, rich-green array, in certain phases tending to vinyness. The edible tubers are borne on specialized underground stems, these distinct from the true roots. In the Andes, there are many unusual regional varieties, some with tubers scarcely larger than a walnut, colored lurid purple, bright red, or even almost polka-dotted. These are a bit alien to our *yanquí* tastes, being much moister than the mealy vegetables we prefer.

The starchy content of the Potato is well known. In many North American homes, in fact, the serving of these tubers at least once daily, in some form or other, as "the starch" is automatic. When properly prepared, Potatoes are nutritious, though a diet overly heavy in them can prove seriously deficient in essential minerals and vitamins. Potatoes are, despite common tales to the contrary, not notably fattening. One medium-size Potato totals about 100 calories—the same as a large apple or orange.

The good cook pays heed to Potatoes when dealing with them. The tubers are not to be boiled and boiled and boiled until they are a sodden mass of grayish inedibility. Preferably, both for flavor and for nutrition, they should be cooked in their skins, these scrubbed carefully. Cover completely with cold salted water, and keep the pot covered during the cooking process. Cooked potatoes can be peeled thinly, thus retaining the prime nutritive portions that lie just under the skin.

Potatoes can be utilized in such an overwhelming variety of fashions—from soup to dessert, literally—that selecting recipes for notice herein is a problem. Since I am a native of Aroostook County, in northern Maine—the largest potato-growing area in the world —I am quite naturally partial to these tantalizing tubers. Here are some personal favorites in which the Potato figures prominently.

WHEN LITTLE new Potatoes are on the scene, consider the following attractive and somewhat unusual array. The bologna or Canadian bacon is absolutely essential to the success of the repast.

Yankee Little Potatoes
Serves 4 liberally.

2 *pounds tiny new red-skinned potatoes*
1½ *pounds fresh green or pole beans*
4 *tablespoons butter*
salt and freshly ground black pepper
½ *pint light cream*
½ *cup whole milk*
bologna cut into ¼-inch-thick slices, or Canadian bacon slices

Wash but do not peel the little potatoes, which should be very firm and fresh. Prepare the green beans, cutting them into pieces 2 or 3 inches long. Cook the potatoes and beans in salted water, in separate pots, until they are just nicely done—the beans should be started a few minutes after the potatoes, and should be crisp-tender when finished. Drain both vegetables thoroughly, and combine the potatoes with the green beans in a large pot with cover. Add the butter, salt, and freshly ground pepper to taste, light cream, and milk. Gently toss the vegetables in the sauce, once, as it heats through—do not boil. Serve with additional butter if desired, accompanied by fried or broiled thick slices of bologna or Canadian bacon.

ANOTHER excellent version of little new potatoes is the following, of Scandinavian origin, named for a special Norwegian lady friend who has contributed much to my enjoyment of the culinary (and botanical) world.

New Potatoes Kari
Serves 4 to 6.

2 *pounds tiny new potatoes*
⅓ *cup melted butter*
1 *teaspoon grated lemon peel*
1 *tablespoon fresh lemon juice*
1½ *tablespoons chopped chives*
salt and freshly ground black pepper
dash of nutmeg

Cook the tiny potatoes until just tender, drain, peel, and dry over medium heat, shaking the pan gently but steadily. Lightly toss them, while still very hot, with the melted butter, lemon peel, lemon juice, and the chives. Season to taste with salt and pepper, and a tiny dash of nutmeg. Serve at once. Particularly good with seafood.

FOR YEARS, my potato pancakes were kitchen disasters. My friends assure me that these are not difficult to prepare, but until I encountered the following version, success was not mine. This recipe seems infallible —even for me.

French Potato Pancakes
Serves 4 to 6 liberally.

6 *large raw potatoes, peeled, grated*
1 *cup heavy cream*
salt and freshly ground pepper

2 *tablespoons melted lard*
2 *tablespoons grated sharp cheese*
peanut or soy oil

Thoroughly combine the grated potatoes, cream, salt and pepper to taste (be rather liberal here), lard, and cheese. In a small heavy skillet heat a little oil, and spread with a thin layer of the potato mixture. Over rather low heat, brown the pancake on the bottom. Then sprinkle with a little oil and place under a pre-heated broiler to brown nicely on top. Carefully remove with slotted spatula, and serve at once. Repeat until all of the potato mixture is cooked, serving the individual pancakes immediately they are done.

I SPENT considerable time in Cuba in happier days there. Potatoes are very important in the diversified cookery of that island—rather more so than in many other Latin lands, where rice predominates as the starch in daily menus. This Cuban version of potato salad is a superb creation that can be made a show-piece with little effort and expense.

Salad Siboney

Allow 2 or 3 tiny cooked new potatoes per serving. Peel and slice these and arrange them on an attractive serving platter, avoiding overlapping them as much as possible. Next, arrange chilled drained canned green beans over the potato slices. Next arrange wafer-thin slices of sweet red or Bermuda onion rather liberally over the platter. Then set 2 or 3 ripe olives and 2 or 3 green Spanish olives per serving attractively around the platter. Garnish as you wish with any or all of the following authentic addenda: chilled canned aspara-gus tips, cooked chilled artichoke hearts, thin slivers of roasted green pepper, and thin slices of canned pimiento. Pour over all your favorite vinegar-and-oil dressing, well herbed and seasoned. Place platter (or platters) in refrigerator and allow the salad to mari-nate and chill for at least 2 hours prior to serving.

FEW things are as satisfactory with steaks, chops, or even the often maligned hamburger or frankfurter as is a perfectly done baked potato. The customary way to prepare these beauties is to scrub the Idaho baker, then rub it with oil (this gives the savory skin a special crustiness), pierce in a couple of places with a sharp fork, and bake in a preheated 400° F. oven until done. I am of the old school that prefers lots of butter, a bit of salt, and several turns from the pepper mill to sour cream, chives, chili sauce, and such oddments. (One can even purchase "ready-made" baked-potato stuffings these days, which from my limited personal

experience are rather ghastly. I do not approve of foil-wrapped baked potatoes, either, but this opens up a grand field of vociferous argument.)

Using good, firm Idaho baking potatoes, we can also create a simple but handsome dish that originated in Sweden. I am told that the good Swedes customarily add a modicum of sugar to it, but I have not experi-enced this. Perfect with the next big roast you prepare.

Swedish Browned Potatoes
Serves 4.

4 *large baking potatoes*
½ *cup melted butter*
salt

Thinly peel the baking potatoes and slice them thinly crosswise, without cutting all the way through. Place them in a shallow baking pan, brush liberally with melted butter, and sprinkle with salt. Bake in 325° F. oven, brushing them frequently with the butter—or use some of the juices from a roast, if this is being cooked alongside. The potatoes are done when they are tender if pricked with a sharp fork and when the tops of the "accordion pleats" are golden brown.

AS MENTIONED previously, our friends in Cuba have a wonderful way with the *papas* that figure in their cookery. My staunch colleague in the fine points of Cuban cuisine, Sra. Benita Robaina, prepares the most memorable Fried Potatoes I have ever encountered. They are done in this simple Havana style.

Fried Potatoes Havana
Serves 4.

4 *to 5 large firm potatoes*
lard
salt

Peel the potatoes and cut them into sticks about 3 inches long by less than ½ inch thick. Wash in run-ning cold water and, if not being used immediately, re-frigerate in fresh cold water. Melt enough lard in a sizable skillet to make 1 inch of liquid fat—the lard should be very hot. Drain the potato sticks and pat them dry with a copious supply of paper towels. Cook the potato sticks, not too many at one time, until nicely browned and as crisp as desired—the sticks will shrink somewhat during this process. As they cook, remove the potatoes with a slotted spoon and drain on paper towels. Dust to taste with salt, and serve quickly.

I MUST recommend the following version of Scalloped Potatoes, from the busy kitchen of my friend Edward A. Flickinger. The dish is most appropriate with such things as baked ham, fried or broiled chicken, and sautéed lamb, mutton, or pork chops.

Eduardo's Scalloped Potatoes
Serves 6.

3 *pounds potatoes, peeled, cut into ¼-inch slices*
2 *medium onions, cut into ¼-inch slices*
4 *to 6 tablespoons butter*
2 *tablespoons flour*
1 *teaspoon salt*
¼ *teaspoon freshly ground pepper*
¼ *teaspoon paprika*
2 *cups milk*

Butter a 2-quart ovenproof casserole. Parboil the potato and onion slices in salted water for about 8 minutes, then drain thoroughly. Arrange a layer of the potato slices in the casserole, top with layer of onion slices, then dot with part of the butter, and sprinkle with flour and part of the salt and pepper. Repeat layers, finishing with onion slices. Carefully pour in milk, top with rest of butter, salt, pepper, and the paprika. Bake, uncovered, in preheated 375° F. oven until the potatoes are tender when pricked with a sharp fork, and nicely browned—usually about 35 minutes.

SINCE I spend most of my time in the tropics, I delight in using our goodly potato in chilled salads, admirably suited to warm days. I have three favorite recipes for Potato Salad (in addition to Salad Siboney, page 189), and since I cannot possibly choose among them, here is the entire trio.

Mashed Potato Salad
Serves 4 liberally.

2 *pounds baking potatoes*
salt and black pepper
butter
light cream
2 *or 3 hard-cooked eggs*
½ *cup finely chopped onion*
1 *cup finely chopped celery, with some tops*
6 *to 8 little gherkins, finely chopped*
1 *small can tiny peas, drained*
canned pimientos, sliced
stuffed olives, sliced
Kay's Boiled Salad Dressing (page 255)

Cut the scrubbed, unpeeled potatoes into quarters and cook them in lightly salted water until tender. Peel when cool enough to handle, rice or mash, and, while still warm, season to taste with salt and pepper. Add a goodly amount of butter and enough light cream to moisten, and mix well but gently. Allow potatoes to cool at room temperature. Coarsely chop half the amount of the hard-cooked eggs you are using, and lightly mix into the mashed potatoes with the onion, celery, gherkins, peas, and enough of Kay's Boiled Salad Dressing so that a savory—but not soggy—medley is attained. Arrange salad in a serving bowl, and attractively garnish top with remaining egg, sliced or sieved, pimiento slices, and stuffed olive slices. Chill for at least 1 hour prior to serving.

Potato Salad Tropique
Serves 4 to 6.

5 *cups cubed cooked potatoes*
3 *large stalks celery, sliced thin*
2 *scallions, with tops, sliced thin*
1 *medium onion, finely chopped*
¼ *cup thinly sliced ripe olives*
1 *cup canned kidney beans, drained*
1¼ *cups mayonnaise (or Kay's Boiled Salad Dressing,*
  page 255)
¼ *teaspoon oregano*
salt and freshly ground pepper to taste
1 *medium-size firm cucumber, peeled, diced*
3 *hard-cooked eggs, sliced*
paprika

In a large, attractive serving bowl, combine the potatoes, celery, scallions, onion, olives, and kidney beans. Fold in mayonnaise (or Kay's Boiled Salad Dressing for added zing), oregano, and salt and pepper to your taste. Mix gently but thoroughly and chill for at least 1 hour. Meanwhile, chill cucumber and eggs. Just before serving, mix in the diced cucumber and garnish the salad bowl with the chilled slices of egg and dusting of paprika.

Florida Holiday Potato Salad
Serves 4 to 6 liberally.

6 *cups cubed cooked potatoes*
2 *cups thinly sliced celery*
¾ *cup coarsely chopped onion*
1 *teaspoon mixed salad herbs*
6 *slices cooked bacon, drained, crumbled*
½ *cup slivered sharp cheese*
¼ *cup grated carrot*
¼ *cup thinly sliced pitted ripe olives*
¼ *cup thinly sliced radish*
1½ *cups mayonnaise*

salt and freshly ground pepper to taste
3 hard-cooked eggs, diced
fresh parsley for garnish

Combine all ingredients except hard-cooked eggs and fresh parsley in a large, attractive serving bowl, mixing them gently but thoroughly. Chill for at least 1 hour. Half an hour prior to serving, add the diced eggs, mixing them into the salad. Return to refrigerator. Garnish with fresh parsley. Admirable with grilled frankfurters and/or hamburgers.

THERE ARE many luscious soups manufactured from the potato. The classic French potato and leek one, for instance—which becomes vichyssoise when subtly altered and chilled. Or the spicy potato mulligatawnies of India. Or the hearty, heavy pottages based on potatoes of the Middle European countries.

Here is an exceptional New England Potato Chowder, more robust than the average soup, which makes memorable eating on a chill evening. Serve it with pilot crackers, if you can locate them.

New England Potato Chowder
Serves 4 to 6.

3 cups diced raw potatoes
½ pound salt pork, diced
1 cup coarsely chopped onion
¾ cup coarsely chopped celery, with some leafy tops
¼ cup finely chopped carrot
4 cups milk
1 cup water
2 cups canned cream-style corn
1 cup shredded sharp Cheddar cheese
salt and pepper to taste
butter

In a heavy soup kettle with cover, fry salt pork dice, turning often, until crisp. Add onion and celery, with leafy tops, and cook for a few minutes, until they start to soften. Add potatoes and carrot, and cook, stirring occasionally, for about 10 minutes. Then add the milk and water, mix through, cover kettle, and simmer over low heat until vegetables are tender, usually about 12 to 15 minutes. Stir in corn and cheese, season to taste, simmer uncovered for a few minutes, and serve each very hot portion with a goodly piece of butter atop.

POTHERBS, MISCELLANEOUS

In the United States, dozens of different kinds of plants are used as potherbs, or edible greens, or pot-

herb vegetables. In other lands the number of edibles in this category rises literally into the hundreds. Through centuries of experimentation man, wherever he may have lived, has discovered that many of the plants around him are edible. (One must wonder what happened to all the men who discovered, too late, which plants were *not* edible!)

In this volume I have taken up a considerable number of the potherbs of greatest general use in the United States—those to be found with greater or lesser frequency in our markets or in our kitchen gardens. But I am sure that readers of this book are intimately familiar with many other plants, perhaps wildlings of his regional woods and fields, whose young shoots and juvenile foliage can be eaten—and which often are, as prized seasonal delicacies. The space limitations of this work obviously preclude discussion of all of these.

PUMPKIN

The Pumpkin is one of those extraordinary cucurbit fruits, botanically referable to the species *Cucurbita Pepo* (of the Squash-Gourd Family), which is treated as a vegetable in our kitchens. The Pumpkin (often colloquially mispronounced Punkin in parts of the United States, and also known as Pie Pumpkin and Field Pumpkin) is a large—sometimes immense—round to oblong vegetable, maturing late in the season and generally vivid orange in color. The thick, hard rind keeps the vegetable for months, and sometimes upward of a year. Though for the cook it bears scant similarity to the patty-pan squash, the yellow summer crookneck squash, or the zucchini, technically it is the same thing. The West Indian Pumpkin, another related plant, is considered under its well-known Spanish name, Calabaza (page 67).

Pumpkins are readily available in our markets, principally during the autumn months. But with modern processing the vegetable appears on our grocery shelves frozen and canned, for use at other seasons as well. Pumpkin appears in a tasteful variety of ways—in soup, boiled or puréed as a hot vegetable, and in one of our most famous national dishes—the Yankee Pumpkin Pie.

FRESH PUMPKIN BLOSSOMS—as well as those of most other kinds of cucurbits, from squash to zucchini—are eminently edible. These pretty, orange or yellow blooms, with their little stems, are sometimes to be found in specialty vegetable markets, notably those whose proprietors are of Mediterranean ancestry. My favorite way with them is the simplest one, which allows their full delicacy of flavor to come through without impairment.

Pumpkin Flowers
Serves 3 or 4.

25 to 30 fresh pumpkin (or squash) flowers
2 tablespoons light oil or melted butter
sprinkle of salt

Quickly rinse the flowers in cold water and shake them dry. Place oil or melted butter in a sizable skillet with tight-fitting cover. Add flowers, all in one layer, crowding them as needed. Sprinkle lightly with salt, cover container, and, over high heat, cook for not more than 5 minutes. Serve at once.

PURÉED or mashed pumpkin is the basis for the following quick one-pot recipe. I like to serve this with Pineapple Cole Slaw (page 61), hot cornmeal muffins, and tall glasses of iced coffee.

Vermont Pumpkin Casserole
Serves 4 liberally.

4 cups mashed or puréed pumpkin
1 cup rich white sauce
1½ cups diced cooked ham
3 tablespoons halved seedless raisins
1 cup coarsely grated sharp cheese
3 hard-cooked eggs, thinly sliced
½ cup broken soda crackers
⅓ cup coarsely grated sharp cheese
2 tablespoons butter

Thoroughly combine the pumpkin, white sauce, ham, raisins, and 1 cup grated cheese. Place half the pumpkin mixture in a sizable ovenproof casserole, then top with a layer of the sliced hard-cooked eggs; top with remaining pumpkin. Sprinkle coarsely broken-up crackers over the pumpkin, then the ⅓ cup sharp cheese, and dot with butter. Bake in preheated 350° F. oven for 30 minutes and serve while very hot.

ONE OF my favorite ways with pumpkin is an old-fashioned dessert from New Brunswick, Canada. I prefer these tasty custards at room temperature rather than chilled.

Pumpkin Custards
Makes 6.

⅔ cup cooked, mashed pumpkin
1½ cups whole milk
2 tablespoons light honey
⅛ teaspoon ground nutmeg
⅛ teaspoon ground cloves
2 eggs, beaten well

Briefly whirl pumpkin with milk, honey, and spices in electric blender, or use a rotary beater to accomplish the same thing. Blend in the beaten eggs. Divide mixture among 6 buttered custard cups. Set these in a shallow pan of hot water and bake in preheated 325° F. oven for 20 minutes, or until custards are set and nicely browned on top. Allow to cool to room temperature before serving.

MY HORTICULTURAL and culinary colleague, Ed Flickinger, bakes an especially pleasant Pumpkin Pie. It comes from his part of Pennsylvania, Newport, on the shores of the Juniata River. He often serves it with rich mango or vanilla ice cream.

Pumpkin Pie Juniata
Serves 4 to 6.

2 cups cooked, mashed pumpkin
1 9-inch unbaked pastry shell
4 eggs, separated
1 cup sugar
½ teaspoon ground cinnamon
¼ teaspoon ground allspice
¼ teaspoon ground ginger
1½ tablespoons flour
3 tablespoons butter, melted
½ cup light cream
¼ teaspoon salt

Bake pastry shell in preheated 400° F. oven for 10 minutes; remove from oven. Meanwhile combine the pumpkin with beaten egg yolks, sugar, cinnamon, allspice, ginger, and flour. Combine the melted butter and cream with lightly beaten egg whites, add salt, and mix into the pumpkin. Turn into pie shell. Reduce oven heat to 325° F., and bake pie for about 45 minutes, or until it is firm and lightly browned on top. Turn off heat and leave pie in oven for 15 minutes more, to set perfectly.

PURSLANE

Purslane or Pusley is *Portulaca oleracea* (of the Portulaca Family), a very widespread prostrate weedy plant that grows in the sandy soil of many lands, from our own Southwest to Europe. Connoisseur gardeners in this country often pull the tender shoots for use as a tasty, though somewhat slippery, potherb. The French, who dote on such things to a greater degree than we do, have long cultivated some selected variants of the plant as a vegetable under the name *pourpier*. These are more erect-growing than the wild plant, with larger, more tender stems and leaves of superior flavor. These are prized for use in salads, or are served after brief cooking, usually accompanied by a butter or cream sauce, or are pickled in seasoned vinegar as an unique condiment.

Winter Purslane (*Montia perfoliata*, of the Portulaca Family) is the epicure salad-maker's delight in the regions in which it grows wild, or on occasion is cultivated. The plant has roundish or spatula-shaped leaves, often reddish-green, and strange, elongate, cup-like racemes of little white or roseate blossoms. These vegetables often grow in considerable abundance as weeds in wet places, in the wild in mountainous areas from Quebec to California, and as naturalized specimens in portions of the West Indies and Europe. In Europe the names Blinks, Water Chickweed, Blinking Chickweed, and Water-Blinks have been applied to the species.

The fresh leaves are washed, patted dry, and chilled prior to using in salads—with the lightest possible of dressings. Or if available in sufficient quantity, they can be steamed in a small amount of lightly salted water and offered dressed with butter and suitable seasonings. The texture is interesting and the flavor is piquant.

Winter Purslane is sold by several commercial specialists in wild plants in the United States. It thrives when cultivated much as watercress does.

QUINOA

The Quinoa (*Chenopodium Quinoa*, of the Goosefoot Family) is a very important food plant in western South America. It has been cultivated there for centuries for the small, glossy, bitter seeds. These vary in color from white to red, and, usually after soaking and protracted boiling, are made into bread, porridge, added to soups, and even fermented to give an intoxicating beverage.

In recent times, Quinoa seeds have been imported, principally from Peru, and are offered as a culinary curiosity by some specialty shops in our large cities.

RADISH

There are many different kinds of Radish, the basic species probably originating in the Oriental part of

temperate Asia, but unknown in the wild in historic times. Botanists call these *Raphanus sativus,* and place it—along with many of our common cultivated vegetables—in the Crucifer Family. Considerable doubt still exists whether the Radishes of the Orient (India, China, and Japan, principally) are the same botanical entity as the European ones, though this interpretation is generally followed.

Whatever their scientific status, Radishes are popular in virtually all parts of the globe. Red-skinned Radishes are the ones most commonly seen in our markets. But they also display delicate white-skinned (some closer to pale tan) forms, more elongate than the round, red variety, and even Radishes with black or lurid purple skins. The distinctive white Oriental Radish, Daikon, is discussed on page 194.

Radishes, by and large, are very easily and quickly grown from seed. A rich, friable soil is best, and often the vegetable is in perfect condition for use three or four weeks after sowing.

Though Americans usually relegate the Radish to the relish tray, its culinary uses are far more extensive. In Europe, particularly in France, the chilled raw vegetable is often served as a special course, thinly sliced, with salt and butter, the latter being spread liberally on the seasoned wafers. There is even, as we might expect from the French, a special radish dish designed expressly for use at table on such occasions.

At their peak of fresh development, the juvenile leaves of the Radish are often added to salads, to which they impart a pleasant spiciness. If a sufficient quantity is available, such Radish greens can also be steamed until just barely tender, then served with butter and customary seasonings.

ALL Radishes, whatever their outer color, can be cooked. A favorite version is simple steaming of the firm roots, as follows. This recipe is a piquant addition to the menu with such relatively bland meats as fowl or veal.

Steamed Radishes
Serves 4 to 6.

> *3 bunches firm red or pink radishes*
> *¾ cup coarsely chopped scallions, with tops*
> *¼ cup butter*
> *¼ cup water*

Trim off leaves (use these in salad if they are fresh) and scrub the radishes. In a heavy saucepan with tight-fitting cover, sauté the scallions in the butter until they are soft. Add the radishes and water, cover, and raise heat for 2 minutes. Lower heat, and steam vegetable until just firm-tender—usually about 5 minutes. Do not overcook. Drain. Serve while hot, with a bit of butter and perhaps some salt.

These Steamed Radishes also can be anointed with a cream sauce if desired, or with a bit of the rich gravy from the meat with which the dish is served, then simmered for just a moment prior to placing on the table.

ONE OF the most attractive vegetable appetizers I have ever encountered was a well-chilled platter of crisp white radishes, cored carefully and stuffed with a mixture of butter, sharp Cheddar cheese, and minced parsley. Use only the firmest radishes, of uniform dimension, for this purpose.

AND THEN we have a delectable, very easily prepared Oriental salad, in which radishes figure with prominence.

Sweet-Sour Radishes
Serves 4 liberally.

3 *bunches firm red or pink radishes*
¾ *to 1 teaspoon salt*
3 *tablespoons light-brown sugar*
3 *tablespoons wine vinegar*
1 *teaspoon sesame-seed oil*

Trim off ends of radishes, scrub them, and drain thoroughly. Crush the radishes slightly with a plate or bottom of a jar. Sprinkle with the salt and allow to stand for 30 minutes. Drain off the liquid. Arrange the crushed radishes in a serving dish. Thoroughly combine all other ingredients and pour over radishes. Serve promptly, so that the vegetable does not lose its crispness.

THE RATTAILED Radish (*Raphanus sativus* var. *caudatus*) is a horticultural curiosity not often seen in the United States. It is grown not for the swollen tap-root, but rather for its enormously elongate seed pods, these often reaching lengths of a foot or so. These, with much the same "bitey" flavor as the common root, are eaten raw, or are pickled in vinegar. They are especially popular in Southeast Asia, where they are used as a condiment with curries and such things.

ORIENTAL Radish is technically the same species as the European kinds (*Raphanus sativus* sometimes with the addition of the designating var. *longipinnatus*), but it is a very distinctive plant. It produces white roots from one to six inches in diameter, up to three feet in length, and up to fifty pounds in weight apiece. Available throughout the year, these heavy vegetables are eaten raw by Chinese, Japanese, and Koreans (and by knowledgeable Occidentals, too), and they are pickled and cooked in a variety of fashions.

Most often sold in markets in Hawaii and our Western states under its Japanese name, Daikon (pronounced *dye*-kon), it is also known by its Chinese name, *loh-bak choi*. Three types are usually encountered—spherical, oblong, and cylindrical. The oblong variety, seldom more than four inches long by two inches thick, is preferred by the Chinese, while the others are favorites of the Japanese.

The texture of these Oriental Radishes is usually a bit more spongy than their Western relatives, but the flavor is very much the same.

Daikon is best known to non-Oriental cooks in this country in its preserved version, pieces of the vegetable being pickled in a combination of soy sauce, seaweed derivatives, and other flavorings. Imported from Hawaii or directly from Japan, this pickle, thinly sliced and well chilled, is essential for many of us who enjoy serving Oriental and Indonesian menus. It is even a happy accompaniment to such American delicacies as hamburgers and hot dogs.

Daikon seedlings—called *kokonoka daikon* in Japanese, *loh-bak choi-chai* in Chinese—are frequently cultivated for their pretty, vivid green foliage, which is widely appreciated as a special green vegetable. The plantlets are customarily offered in markets tied into bundles of twenty or so, each with a long, slender, white taproot; this is customarily discarded when the leaves are cooked, briefly, as a pungent green.

The Daikon root is frequently carved into a variety of shapes—roses, for instance—and chilled for use as a garnish. For festive Japanese occasions, an amazingly intricate and beautiful "fishnet" is carved from the raw root and used to adorn a cold whole cooked fish. And in its shredded raw state it traditionally forms a bed for the fabulous raw fish, *sashimi*, which graces many a Nipponese table. This raw shredded vegetable is also frequently served in small portions as a condiment with such things as sukiyaki, or is incorporated into the warmed soy sauce–sake dip that accompanies tempura.

MIZUTAKI is a delectable Japanese dish, a kind of boiled sukiyaki, generally utilizing either chicken or a firm-fleshed fish. Fresh Daikon is essential to its success. It is customarily prepared in one of those

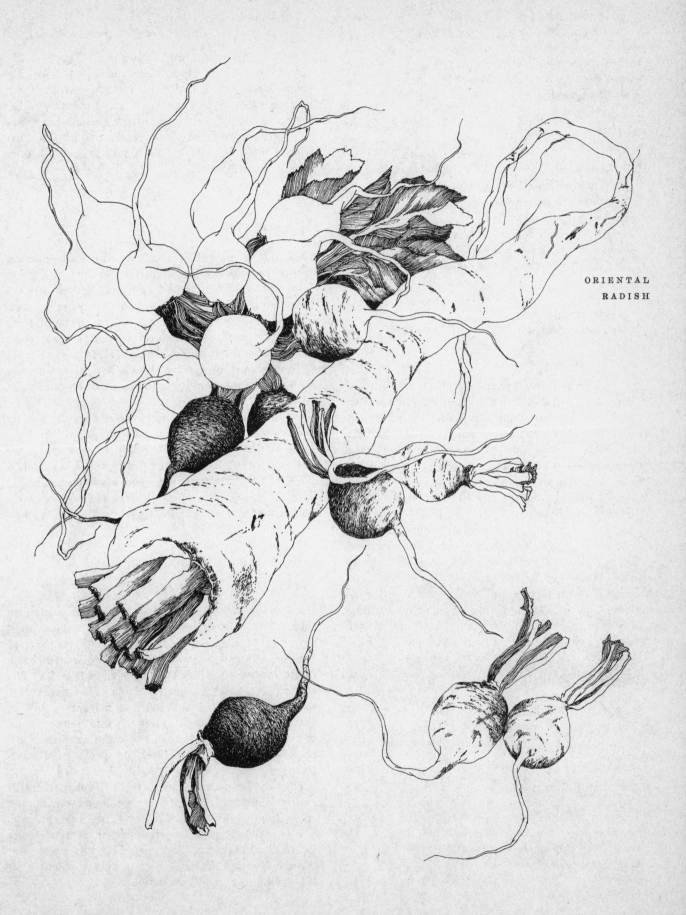

ORIENTAL
RADISH

ingenious Mongolian cookers (called *sin-sul-lo*), but an electric skillet can well be used instead.

Here is the version of Mizutaki I serve on special occasions—accompanied by ample supplies of hot steamed rice, my favorite Nikko Salad (page 49), and hot tea or warmed sake.

Mizutaki
Serves 4.

1 *medium Oriental radish (daikon), freshly grated*
1 *young chicken, boned, cut into bite-size pieces*
8 *dried Japanese black mushrooms*
1 *cup 1-inch cubes canned tōfu*
1 *can bamboo shoots, thinly-sliced lengthwise*
1 *medium Chinese cabbage, thinly sliced*
1 *small eggplant, unpeeled, thinly sliced*
2 *medium onions, thinly sliced, in rings*
12 *scallions, cut into 2-inch lengths*
6 *cups rich chicken stock*
⅓ *cup Japanese soy sauce*
¼ *teaspoon minced fresh ginger root*
2 *or 3 drops Tabasco sauce*

Soak the dried mushrooms in about one cup of warm water until soft, usually about 30 minutes. Cut these into thin slices, and add liquid to Mongolian cooker (*sin-sul-lo*) or electric skillet. As in Sukiyaki (page 164), arrange mushroom slices, chicken, *tōfu* cubes, bamboo shoots, Chinese cabbage, eggplant, onion rings, and scallion sections attractively on two or more platters. Add the rich chicken stock (fresh, preferably) to the cooking utensil, and heat to the bubbling stage. In the meantime, thoroughly combine the daikon, soy sauce, ginger root, and Tabasco sauce, and place in individual side dishes. Seat your guests, furnish each with chopsticks, and allow them to select from the chicken and vegetable array, lowering each piece into the bubbling liquid in the cooking container at table. When pieces are done to individual choice, they are removed with chopsticks and dipped into the spicy daikon sauce before eating.

THE FOLLOWING colorful salad from Mindanao, in the Philippines, is appropriate with such things as chicken or pork medleys, especially those cooked with rice.

Daikon Salad Davao
Serves 4 liberally.

1 *medium Oriental radish (daikon)*
3 *or 4 tablespoons coarse kosher salt*
3 *tablespoons malt vinegar*
water

2 *cups fresh orange segments*
2 *large firm-ripe tomatoes, unpeeled, diced*

Scrape the daikon, and, using a very sharp knife, cut into wafer-thin slices. Place these in a pot with the coarse salt, vinegar, and water just to cover. Refrigerate overnight. When ready to use, drain the daikon very thoroughly and toss lightly with the orange sections (from which all white membrane and pith have been removed) and the diced tomatoes. Chill thoroughly prior to serving.

RAPE

Rape is a member of the complicated cabbage alliance (*Brassica Napus,* of the Crucifer Family), which has been cultivated for such a long period that its original home is today unknown. Also known as *rapa* or *colza,* it consists of several distinctive forms. Some of these are grown expressly for farm animal forage; others are of value for the oil expressed from the seeds; and still others are prized for the stalked green leaves, a rather strong-flavored vegetable used especially by persons of Italian ancestry.

Rape greens are to be encountered, usually during the summer and fall months, in many of our markets, often under the name of *broccoli di rapa.* They are best prepared in the manner suggested for Boiled Kale (page 129), and are good accompaniments to such things as highly spiced Italian sausages, or pasta with a well-seasoned meat sauce of Sicilian or Neapolitan origin.

RHUBARB

Rhubarb or Pieplant is a large, showy perennial vegetable (*Rheum Rhaponticum,* of the Buckwheat Family), probably originally from the southern parts of Siberia, but now extensively cultivated in temperate lands for its juicy, acid, thickened leaf stalks. The plant is a singularly ornamental one, often several feet tall, with huge leaves that make an attractive show in the garden during their prime. In this country, commercial production often includes the artificial forcing of special variants of the basic species, with abortive leaves but large, usually red-flushed stalks.

In our domestic markets, fresh Rhubarb is still mostly a seasonal vegetable, being found during the springtime. It is available, however, in frozen packets, and it is also canned, sometimes in an oversweetened liquid. The stalks are used particularly to make pies, tarts, cakes, and dessert sauces. A rather potent wine is also obtained from these petioles.

Rhubarb Pie seems a very American delicacy. I have offered it to visiting European friends, who have been thoroughly aghast that we would eat—and indeed enjoy—such an abominable creation. Virtually every domestic cookbook contains good instructions for this authentic delight, but I would like to mention two dessert sauces I often serve, which date, I think, from my childhood in Maine. There we always had a patch of Rhubarb growing out in the back garden.

Here is a delicious Rhubarb sauce that I like to serve as a dessert for special luncheons. If you go in for flaming things, the addition of the brandy will be obligatory.

Rhubarb Donna
Serves 6.

1 12-ounce package frozen rhubarb
½ cup dry red wine
½ to ¾ cup sugar
⅛ teaspoon salt
1 tablespoon cornstarch
6 thin slices firm pound cake
6 thick slices French vanilla ice cream
2 ounces brandy (optional)

In a chafing dish (or saucepan at the stove, if you must!), bring the wine to the boil. Add rhubarb and simmer until just tender, usually about 5 minutes. Blend together the sugar, salt, and cornstarch, and mix into rhubarb-wine thoroughly. Cook, stirring constantly, until the sauce is thickened and clear. Serve each person a small slice of pound cake topped with French vanilla ice cream and the rhubarb sauce. If desired, heat the brandy until fumes just rise, then pour over rhubarb sauce in chafing dish. Set alight, and ladle this sauce (flaming or not) over each portion of the dessert.

USING either the fresh rhubarb or the frozen kind, prepare the following luscious sauce to serve atop such things as waffles, pancakes, biscuits, or even toast. I like to make this up and keep it on hand in a tightly covered jar in the refrigerator for a sweet snack at some illogical time of night.

Rhubarb-Raspberry Sauce
Serves about 6.

1 pound fresh rhubarb, trimmed and prepared, or 1 12-ounce package frozen rhubarb
1 package frozen raspberries
½ cup sugar

Combine the ingredients and cook over very low heat, stirring often, until the rhubarb is tender. Do not overcook. Use the sauce either warm or chilled.

IN MY school days in Orlando I used to be invited on occasion to the house of a Finnish school chum for dinner. The food was memorable and unique. One of Armas's mother's specialties was a refreshingly tart soup made out of rhubarb. She served it with a kind of flat rye bread, liberally spread with sweet butter.

Finnish Rhubarb Soup
Serves 4 to 6.

3 cups trimmed rhubarb, cut into 1-inch pieces
1 quart rich chicken stock, strained
½ pound chicken livers
2 or 3 whole cloves
2 or 3 tablespoons lemon juice
salt and freshly ground white pepper
wafer-thin lemon slices

In a heavy kettle with cover, bring the rich, well-seasoned chicken stock to the boil. Add the rhubarb, chicken livers (whole or cut into halves), cloves, lemon juice, plus seasonings to taste. Cover kettle and simmer until rhubarb and livers are tender. Serve very hot, each bowl topped with a lemon slice.

RICE

The growing and use of Rice began before the time of records. The first mention of this member of the Grass Family (*Oryza sativa*) in formal history occurred in 2800 B.C., when a Chinese emperor wrote a ceremonial ordinance for Rice planting. The word "rice" in Chinese means "agriculture" or "culture." Some historians have traced the cultivation of this vegetable (a grain) to a plant called *newaree* which was grown in India in an even earlier period, 3000 B.C.

Today, at least 7,000 varieties of Rice are known. These can be divided generally into three main groups: short-grain, medium-grain, and long-grain. The American Rice Council defines these categories as follows:

Long-Grain Rice. This rice is four to five times as long as the grain is wide. When cooked, the grains tend to separate and are light and fluffy. Long-grain rice may be preferred for salads, curries, stews, chicken or meat dishes.

Short- and Medium-Grain Rice. These varieties have short, plump grains which cook tender and moist, with the particles tending to cling together. They are favored by many cooks, and are especially good for croquettes, puddings, or rice rings, which require a tender rice that is easily molded.

In the United States, in particular, we encounter specialized precooked and otherwise prepared kinds of Rice, which enjoy wide and often justified popularity. Rice connoisseurs often view these modernities with considerable disdain, but they do have a certain place in our cuisine.

Rice is used in a great variety of fashions by man, other than as an eminently edible vegetable grain. Important examples include rice flour, rice oil, and sake, the fabled Japanese wine. And then we have the myriad breakfast cereals created from the grains.

In lands other than ours, Rice—the nutritious, flavorful, unpolished kind—appears on the menu every day. Among many populations, in fact, it appears at every meal of every day, often with little else. In the United States the vegetable is most commonly served in the South and Southwest, but it is becoming increasingly popular in other parts of the country.

Rice can be served on any occasion, for any course, from beginning to termination of the meal. As an appetizer, I can think of few things as unique and tasteful as an array of the marvelous Japanese Rice *sushi*. These creations are so popular in their native islands that *sushi* stands in the hundreds, purveying solely varieties of these delights, occur everywhere.

Sushi (pronounced *soo*-shee) are typically a special version of Rice cooked with vinegar, then formed into small patties or balls, and either sandwiched or topped with diverse flavoring items. These range from raw, thinly sliced fish, cooked mashed fish or shellfish, tiny soy-touched omelets, to a considerable number of vegetables, raw or chilled after brief cooking, from sliced mushrooms to shredded seaweeds. Traditionally, the *sushi* are accompanied by tiny individual bowls of soy sauce (to which a bit of slivered ginger root has been added, if desired) and the hot green Japanese horseradish, Wasabi (page 238).

HERE IS a basic recipe for Sushi Rice. Rice-wine vinegar is a delicate liquid, available in this country from Oriental specialty shops. If one cannot locate it, substitute white cider or white wine vinegar in the following recipe.

Sushi Rice
Makes a lot.

    3 cups polished white rice
    3¼ cups water
    ¼ cup rice-wine vinegar or white vinegar

    1 teaspoon salt
    ½ teaspoon monosodium glutamate
    ¼ cup sugar

Three hours prior to cooking rice, wash it carefully and place in a colander to drain. In a pot with tight-fitting lid, bring the water to the boil, add the rice, stir, cover tightly, and again bring to the boil. Reduce heat and cook for 20 minutes. Remove covered pot from heat, and allow to stand for 5 minutes. Turn rice out into a large shallow pan and pour over it the vinegar, which has been thoroughly combined with salt, monosodium glutamate, and sugar. Then, mixing lightly with a fork or chopsticks, and fanning with your favorite hand fan (or small portable electric fan), quickly cool the rice.

Now form the *sushi meshi* into smooth balls or ovals, and top with the desired flavoring material, as in the first column, this page. If the idea of raw fish is repellent, start off your experiments with some mashed fresh-cooked or canned seafood—prime white tuna (albacore) or chilled boiled shrimp are good ones for the *sushi* novice. But I will bet that once you have been introduced to the delights of *sashimi* (raw fish) and of the various special seaweeds, you will bcome a serious devotee of *sushi* prepared thus authentically.

RICE, of virtually all varieties, is frequently incorporated into soups, both here and abroad. In particular, the savory rich broths—made from chicken or veal, as a rule—which are graced with bits of green or root vegetables are customarily served with a small amount of rice, this cooked until just tender. A superlative example, in my opinion, is the Escarole Soup Lake Como described on page 111.

THOUGH cooked hot Rice is served just as is, as a rule, in the cuisines of many lands, we in this country normally put "things" into it, to vary flavor and, often, texture. Some of these dishes are almost overwhelmingly involved, and indeed the eater may forget that the basis of it all was rice.

Rice medleys should not be hodgepodges indiscriminately made from leftovers. Tastefully prepared with top-caliber ingredients, they can be prime examples of the good cook's art. Paella (pronounced pah-*eh*-ya) is an excellent instance of a superb single-dish creation based upon rice. As is well known, this Spanish and Latin-American specialty occurs in a number of "authentic" variants. Here is one whose authenticity I can affirm, and whose succulence I can enthusiastically recommend.

Paella
Serves 8 to 10.

2 cups raw long-grain rice
¼ cup light Spanish olive oil
3-pound chicken, cut in serving-size pieces
1 chorizo (spicy Spanish sausage), sliced
2 medium cloves garlic, mashed
1½ cups chopped onion
1 cup chopped green pepper
3 ripe tomatoes, peeled, coarsely chopped
½ to 1 teaspoon oregano
1½ pounds raw medium shrimp, shelled
12 small clams in shells, scrubbed
3 cups hot water
1½ teaspoons salt
¼ cup coarsely chopped parsley
¼ to ½ teaspoon Annatto (page 16)
2 cups diced cooked lobster meat
1 cup tiny canned peas, drained
1 7-ounce jar whole pimientos
2 packages frozen artichoke hearts, cooked, drained
1 package frozen asparagus tips, cooked, drained

Heat oil in paellero or large skillet or wok. Brown chicken pieces with the chorizo slices for about 10 minutes over high heat. Add garlic and onion, and cook for 3 minutes. Add green pepper, tomatoes, oregano, raw shrimp, and clams in their scrubbed shells. Cook rapidly until clam shells open, usually about 5 minutes. Remove clams and keep them warm. Stir rice into mixture. Add water, salt, parsley, and annatto (or equivalent of saffron). Bake in preheated 325° F. oven until rice is just tender. Carefully stir in diced lobster, tiny peas, and half of the pimientos cut into large pieces. Garnish with reserved clams in their shells, artichoke hearts, asparagus tips, and remaining pimientos. Heat through and serve at once, while very hot.

A HANDSOME side dish, with fowl or fish in particular, is the following Green Rice (risoverdi), rice baked with several species of vegetable greenery in the style of northern Italy.

Green Rice
Serves 4 to 6.

1 cup raw long-grain rice
2 tablespoons light olive oil
2 tablespoons butter
1 cup finely chopped scallions, with tops
1½ cups finely chopped raw spinach
¼ cup finely chopped parsley
2 cups hot, rich chicken stock
1 teaspoon salt
¼ teaspoon white pepper
1 cup freshly grated Parmesan cheese (optional)

In a heavy skillet, heat oil and butter, and sauté the scallions, stirring often, for 5 minutes. Add the spinach and parsley, and continue to cook for about 1 minute. Stir in the rice, mixing well, then add chicken stock, salt, and white pepper. Turn into a 2-quart casserole, cover, and bake in preheated 350° F. oven until the rice is tender and has absorbed the liquid, usually about 30 minutes. Toss lightly with a fork and serve each portion, if desired, with a light sprinkling of the fresh-grated cheese.

FROM the Balkans to India, rice is frequently prepared in a fashion known as pilaf (or pilaff), pilau, or pilaw. Such delectable dishes generally are cooked in butter, a light oil, or a stock, and usually include such admirable addenda as bits of cooked (or raw) meat, vegetables, and even fruits, so that in many cases the final superlative product is essentially a meal in one. Here is a special pilaf from the shores of the Bosporus that well fills that definition. Serve it with a light green salad, one including cucumbers, with a light oil-and-lemon-juice dressing, hot crusty bread (the Arab kind, if available), and tea or beer.

Turkish Liver Pilaf
Serves 6.

2 cups raw long-grain rice
½ cup butter
2 tablespoons pine nuts (pignoli)
1 cup finely chopped onion
⅓ cup finely chopped green pepper
1 quart hot rich chicken broth
salt and freshly ground pepper
⅛ to ¼ teaspoon ground allspice
¼ cup seedless white or yellow raisins
2 tablespoons tomato paste
2 tablespoons butter
1½ cups diced raw calf's liver
½ teaspoon grated lemon peel

In a large heavy skillet with cover, melt the ½ cup butter and sauté the pine nuts, onion, and green pepper over medium heat for 10 minutes, stirring often. Add the rice and continue to sauté, stirring, for 5 minutes. Add the hot broth, salt and pepper to taste (be a bit heavy-handed here), allspice, raisins, and tomato paste, mix well, cover tightly, and remove from heat to soak for 30 minutes. In a skillet, melt the 2 tablespoons butter, and over high heat, quickly sauté the liver dice until browned—just a minute or two. Sprinkle with lemon peel, then lightly stir into rice mixture, cover again, and cook over low heat for about 10 minutes. The rice should be just perfect at this point, but test it, and if necessary, cover again and simmer for a moment more. Serve without delay.

HERE IS another version, this one called Pilau, of Asiatic tendencies and superlative content. My basic recipe, it will be noted, contains rice, seasonings, and several fruits and vegetables. Our vegetarian friends often prepare the dish just this way, with an array of condiments but without the addition of meats. But most of us will wish to add one or more meats and seafoods to the basic mixture. I am very fond of a combination of diced boiled chicken and diced baked ham. Cubed roast lamb is another favorite, and if one wishes to get really fancy, chunks of cooked shrimp and/or lobster, or even firm-fleshed fish will create an entirely different and perfectly delicious type of pilau.

This enterprising, highly adaptable dish should be served much like a curry, with a variety of condiments in suitably attractive little side dishes. These should include a good mango chutney, mashed hard-cooked eggs (yolks and whites separate), little thin omelets cut into strips, quick-fried 1-inch sections of scallion tops, chopped raw scallions, chopped cucumber, chopped firm banana, chopped salted peanuts and/or almonds and/or cashews, chopped preserved ginger, tiny bits of watercress and/or parsley, shredded coconut, crumbled crisp-cooked bacon, minced boiled shrimp, and so on and on. . . . Oh, yes, and a fine bottle of well-chilled white or rosé wine.

Basic Pilau
Serves 6 liberally.

2 cups long-grain rice
¼ pound (1 stick) butter
1 teaspoon salt
¼ teaspoon saffron or Annatto (page 16)
¼ teaspoon freshly ground pepper
3 10½-ounce cans chicken consommé
1 cup diced green pepper
6 scallions, with tops, sliced
2 tart green apples, peeled, diced
1 cup chopped seedless raisins
diced cooked meats or seafood
4 large onions, sliced wafer-thin
assorted condiments

In a large heavy skillet with cover, melt half of the butter. Add the rice and cook over moderately low heat, stirring often with a spatula, until it becomes golden-brown. Add salt, the saffron or annatto, and black pepper, and mix thoroughly. Then add the canned chicken consommé (or equivalent quantity of rich chicken broth), and mix very well. Add the green pepper and scallions, again mix, then cover and bake in preheated 325° F. oven until rice is tender, usually about 20 minutes. If needed, more chicken consommé can be added—the rice will absorb a great deal of liquid. Stir in the apples, rinsed, drained raisins, and meats (see above for suggestions). Cover skillet again and heat through. Meanwhile, in another skillet, melt the remaining butter, and in it cook the slices of onion until they are soft and yellow. Arrange the pilau in a pyramid shape on an attractive large serving platter. Pour the onions and their butter sauce over the pyramid. Serve with assorted condiments (see above for suggestions).

ONE OF my favorite ways for rice with "things" is the following. It is easy, attractive, and ideal for service with such diverse foods as shrimp or poultry or red meat in just about any form.

Rice Calcutta
Serves 4 to 6.

2 cups raw long-grain rice
5 cups water
1½ teaspoons salt
¼ cup seedless white or yellow raisins
½ cup toasted slivered almonds
1 teaspoon sugar
2 tablespoons grated coconut

In a heavy saucepan with tight cover bring the water plus salt to the boil. Add the rice, cover, and bring again to the boil. Boil rapidly for about 8 minutes, or until rice is barely tender. Drain and rinse under running cold water. Meanwhile, soak the raisins in warm water until they plump up. Preheat oven to 250° F. Spread the drained, rinsed rice on large cooky sheets. Dry in the oven for 30 minutes, tossing rice carefully with a fork every 10 minutes. Turn rice into a large serving bowl and toss lightly with well-drained raisins, almonds, sugar, and coconut. Serve without delay.

FRIED rice, as served all too often in the average Chinese restaurant in most American cities, is a rather uninspired affair concocted of whatever leftovers the cook happens to have on hand. When carefully prepared, however, using fresh ingredients, a true culinary showpiece appears. Try this version, which I named for the exotic port of Macao. It is virtually a meal in itself when served with iced (or hot) tea and maybe lime or pineapple sherbet for dessert.

Macao Fried Rice
Serves 4.

1 cup raw long-grain rice
1 pound lean pork, cubed
¼ cup peanut or soy oil
1 large clove garlic, mashed
¾ cup chopped onion
1 teaspoon salt
¼ teaspoon freshly ground pepper
1 3-ounce can sliced mushrooms
1¾ cups water
2 cups cooked shrimp, in bite-size pieces
½ cup chopped scallions, with tops
¼ cup chopped green pepper
2 eggs
salt and pepper
soy sauce, Japanese preferred

Cut pork cubes into tiny julienne strips. In a large skillet with cover, over high heat, brown pork strips in hot peanut or soy oil with garlic and onion, stirring constantly. Remove pork and vegetables with slotted spoon and reserve them. Add rice to hot oil and cook, stirring constantly, until lightly browned. Add salt, pepper, mushrooms (with their liquid), and water. Bring to the boil, then cover, reduce heat and simmer until rice is almost tender. Return pork strips, garlic and onions, plus the shrimp, chopped scallions, and green pepper. Mix well but with care, and cook for about 10 minutes, stirring often. Meanwhile beat eggs with salt and pepper to taste, place in hot greased small skillet, and fry until firm, turning once. Cut omelet into thin strips, mix through the rice, and serve at once, with soy sauce on the side.

CHILLED rice dishes, popular in Europe, are not as widely known as they should be in American homes. They offer the desirable qualities of handsome appearance, high nutrition value, and exceptional tastiness. Here is a particularly showy cold rice mold, served with an exceptional dressing. To accompany it, offer an assortment of cold cuts, sliced roast ham, and fried chicken.

Chilled Rice-Vegetable Mold
Serves 6.

2 cups raw short-grain rice
¼ cup butter
2 cups orange juice
3 cups water
1½ teaspoons salt
1 8-ounce can sliced beets, drained
1 cup thinly sliced celery
1 cup thinly sliced unpeeled cucumber
1 ripe avocado, peeled, thinly sliced
¼ cup chopped scallions
Orange French Dressing (page 255)

Melt butter in a heavy saucepan with cover, and add orange juice, water, and salt. Bring to the boil and slowly add the rice. Cover and reduce heat; cook until rice is tender and liquid has been largely absorbed, usually about 20 minutes. While rice is still hot, pack into lightly oiled 8-inch ring mold. Refrigerate. Chill remaining vegetables thoroughly (do not cut avocado until last moment). Unmold the rice onto a chilled platter, place vegetables attractively in the middle, and serve with Orange French Dressing in a bowl on the side.

How LONG has it been since you and the family enjoyed a good rice pudding? My favorite version of this famous old dessert is the one delineated below, which combines two citrus fruits—oranges and lemons—with the rice to piquant advantage. Serve it at room temperature with heavy cream. Short- or medium-grain rice is preferable here.

Tropic Rice Pudding
Serves 6.

2 cups cooked short- or medium-grain rice
2 eggs
1 cup milk
⅓ cup orange juice
¼ teaspoon salt
3 tablespoons sugar
2 tablespoons softened butter
½ teaspoon vanilla extract
½ teaspoon grated lemon rind
½ teaspoon grated orange rind
1 teaspoon lemon juice
⅓ cup seedless raisins

Butter a 1½-quart baking dish. Preheat oven to 325° F. Beat the eggs and combine thoroughly with milk, orange juice, salt, sugar, butter, and vanilla extract. Fold in the cooked rice and all other ingredients, mixing well but gently. Pour into the baking dish and bake until pudding is firmly set—usually about 40 minutes. Serve warm or at room temperature.

I MUST not neglect description of a superb method of serving rice as a dessert—Calas. I often serve these pretty puffs as one of the prime items on a festive brunch table, with an assortment of fresh fruits of the season and tiny individual bowls of maple or cane syrup, warmed, for surreptitious dunking. Also found on the menu would be a selection of cheeses, broiled ham and Canadian bacon slices, and eggs available either scrambled or poached. It is an easy menu, and one which has found considerable favor with many of my culinary cohorts.

Calas
Makes 2 dozen.

1½ cups cooked short-grain rice
½ package yeast, active dry or compressed
½ cup warm (not hot) water
3 eggs, beaten
1¼ cups sifted flour
¼ cup sugar
½ teaspoon salt
¼ teaspoon nutmeg
fat for deep frying
confectioners' sugar, granulated sugar and cinnamon, or
  warmed syrup

Be sure the rice is cooked until very soft. Mash rice and cool to lukewarm. Soften yeast in warm water and stir in the warm mashed rice. Mix well, cover and let rise overnight. Next day, shortly before use, add eggs, flour, sugar, salt, and nutmeg. Beat until smooth. Let stand in a warm place for 30 minutes. Drop by tablespoons into deep hot fat (360° F.) and fry until golden brown, about 3 minutes. Drain on absorbent paper towels, and serve sprinkled with powdered sugar, or granulated sugar mixed with cinnamon, or warmed maple or cane syrup.

MENTION must be made of Glutinous Rice, a series of special varieties of this grain (sometimes afforded botanical recognition as a distinct species, known as *Oryza glutinosa*). This rice is beloved by many Orientals. The grains contain a sugary, rather than starchy, material, and when cooked they have a texture that is, at first, quite alien to Occidental palates. Glutinous Rice is, however, essential to the production of many desserts in the Far East—little cakes flavored

with various kinds of beans, the Chinese version of candies, and the like. And in such lands as Vietnam, Laos, Cambodia, and Thailand, boiled "sticky" rice is frequently served in preference to the ordinary variety, usually anointed with potent sauces made from such dubious delights as putrid fish.

Glutinous Rice is available as an import in Oriental specialty shops in this country. From it, one can prepare the following interesting—and admittedly exotic—congee.

Lotus Seed Rice
Serves 6.

1 cup glutinous rice
½ cup dried Lotus seeds (page 140)
1½ quarts water
½ cup finely chopped scallion tops
3 tablespoons soy sauce
2 tablespoons sugar

Cover the dried lotus seeds with hot water and soak until their skins can be removed. Remove the tiny bitter green embryos with a pick. Rinse lotus seeds and place in the boiling water to simmer at lowered heat, covered, for about 30 minutes. Add the rinsed glutinous rice, mix through, cover again, and cook until rice softens. Add the scallion tops toward end of cooking, mixing through. Remove from the heat, add soy sauce and sugar, mix well, and serve while hot.

ROCAMBOLE

Rocambole (*Allium Scorodoprasum*, of the Lily Family) is an unusually interesting vegetable, of considerable culinary potential, little known in the United States, although long popular in the French-speaking parts of Canada and in its native southern Europe and eastern Mediterranean regions. A relative of the garlic, it is also known as Giant Garlic, or as Sand Leek or Everlasting Leek.

Both its long, flattish, pale-green leaves and its underground bulbs—made up of "cloves," much like those of the better-known garlic—are possessed of a garlicky scent and flavor, though this is rather subtle. After the small flowers fade, a cluster of tiny bulbils forms at the top of the spirally twisted stalk. These are edible, though pungent, and are used sometimes when pickled.

The foliage of the Rocambole is snipped, as is that of chives, for seasoning in salads and sauces, and the bulbs, broken into cloves, form an acceptable and delicate spice vegetable, to be used in the fashion of true garlic. If sufficient plants are on hand—they are very easily cultivated in the kitchen garden in most parts of the country—the very young leaves can be braised in stock, like scallions or leeks.

ROCKET

Rocket (*Eruca sativa,* of the Crucifer Family) is one of the green spring and autumn vegetables much favored by many people of Europe and the Middle East as a salad and potherb. The young, tender leaves possess a flavor reminiscent of horseradish, and their shape is somewhat like those of common mustard. The pretty yellow flowers are also edible and are often cooked along with the leaves or sprinkled over salads for their pungency.

Also known as *roquette* (France), *tira, rucola* or *arugula* (Italy), *roka* (Greece), *rokka* (Turkey), and Rocket-Salad (England), it is a rather coarse weedy annual, originally from southern Europe, but now naturalized in parts of this country, Canada, Mexico, and Australia. The plant has been cultivated since ancient days, and is extensively grown today in northwestern India and Pakistan as the source of jamba oil.

ROCKET is an infrequent vegetable in our markets, although the seeds are readily available and the plant is of the easiest cultural requirements. Its unique prickly flavor is well displayed in the following elegantly ornate Greek salad, as served at the famous old Louis Pappas Restaurant in Tarpon Springs, Florida. It is almost a meal in itself.

Louis Pappas' Famous Greek Salad
Serves 4 Greeks.

PREPARE A POTATO SALAD FROM THE
FOLLOWING ITEMS:

  6 *boiled potatoes*
  2 *medium onions or 4 scallions*
  ¼ *cup finely chopped parsley*
  ½ *cup thinly sliced scallions*
  ½ *cup salad dressing*
  salt to taste

GREEK SALAD INGREDIENTS:

  12 *fresh rocket leaves, plus some flowers*
    if available

  1 *large head iceberg lettuce*
  3 *cups potato salad (see above)*
  2 *tomatoes cut into 6 wedges each*
  1 *peeled cucumber cut lengthwise into 8 fingers*
  1 *medium-size ripe avocado, peeled, cut into wedges*
  4 *portions Feta cheese*
  1 *green pepper, cut into 8 rings*
  4 *slices canned beets*
  4 *peeled and cooked shrimp*
  4 *anchovy fillets*
  12 *ripe olives (Greek style, if possible)*
  4 *fancy-cut radishes*
  4 *whole scallions*
  ½ *cup distilled white vinegar*
  ¼ *cup olive oil*
  ¼ *cup salad oil*
  oregano

Line a large platter with outside lettuce leaves. Place 3 cups of potato salad in a mound in center of the platter. Cover with the remaining lettuce, this finely shredded. Arrange the rocket leaves and flowers on top of this. Place the tomato wedges around the outer edge of salad, with a few on top, and place the cucumber fingers in between these, to make a solid base of the salad. Place the avocado slices around the outside. Arrange slices of the Feta cheese on top of the salad, with green pepper rings over all. On the very top, place the sliced beets with a shrimp on each beet slice and an anchovy fillet on the shrimp. The olives, radishes, and green scallions are arranged to taste. The entire salad is then sprinkled with the vinegar (more may be used) and then with the two oils which have been thoroughly blended together. Lightly sprinkle a bit of oregano over all, and serve at once, preferably with hot crusty bread liberally anointed with crushed garlic.

RUTABAGA

Though most of us categorize the Rutabaga side by side with the common turnip, botanical studies have shown that it is an evolutionary offshoot of a weedy relative of the cabbage, with the scientific name of *Brassica campestris* var. *Napo-Brassica* (Crucifer Family). The common Turnip (page 235) is a distinct species (*Brassica Rapa*).

The Rutabaga, or poorly-named Yellow Turnip (there is also a form with white flesh, popular in parts of Europe), is a reasonably recent vegetable develop-

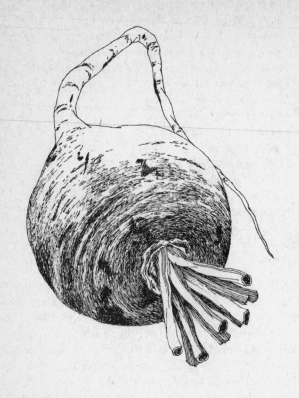

1 *inch boiling water*
1 *teaspoon salt*
1 *teaspoon sugar*
2 *tablespoons butter*
⅛ *teaspoon freshly ground pepper*
1 *tablespoon minced onion*
2 *eggs, separated*
2 *tablespoons grated sharp cheese*
chopped fresh parsley

Combine rutabaga, water, salt, and sugar in a saucepan; bring to the boiling point, uncovered. Boil for 3 minutes. Cover and boil until tender, 12 to 15 minutes, then drain. Mash until fluffy, then add butter, pepper, and onion, mixing well. Beat egg yolks thoroughly and stir into the mashed rutabaga. Beat egg whites until stiff and fold into the mixture. Pour into a 1-quart casserole. Bake in preheated 325° F. oven for 55 minutes. Sprinkle the grated sharp cheese over top, and return to the oven until it has melted, about 5 minutes. Sprinkle with the parsley and serve at once.

ment. First printed reference to it was in 1620, by the great Swiss botanist Caspar Bauhin. It is variously considered to have originated in Scandinavia or Russia, and today is extensively cultivated in that part of the world, the British Isles (where known as Swede or Turnip-Root Cabbage), France (called *chou-navet*), and Canada. Most of our heavy round or ovoid Rutabagas come from Canada, where varieties—notably the Laurentian—with particularly delicate sweet-flavored flesh have been developed in recent times. To retard spoilage, most of these roots arrive in our markets with a wax coating. This, with the peel, should, of course, be removed prior to cooking.

The Rutabaga is abundantly favored with easily digestible nutrients, its flavor is distinctive, and its cost—particularly during the winter months—is usually low.

CONSIDER this splendid soufflé utilizing Rutabaga. This is especially good with such things as roast turkey or chicken, but adapts equally well to beef.

Rutabaga Soufflé
Serves 6.

4 *cups diced rutabaga*

THE FOLLOWING rutabaga dish is excellent with baked ham or pork chops. It is delectable reheated as a leftover, too—a characteristic of most recipes for this succulent root vegetable.

Rutabaga Chips
Serves 6.

2 *pounds rutabaga*
⅓ *cup butter*
1 *cup rich chicken broth*
1 *teaspoon salt*
⅛ *teaspoon black pepper*
3½ *tablespoons sugar*

Pare rutabagas and cut into eighths. Then cut into strips ¹⁄₁₆ inch thick. Combine butter, chicken broth, salt, pepper, and 1½ tablespoons of the sugar. Heat to the boiling point. Add the rutabaga and cook for 10 minutes. Turn into a buttered 1-quart casserole. Sprinkle with the remaining sugar and bake in preheated 375° F. oven for 45 minutes.

MASHED or riced rutabagas have long been a tradition with turkey and chicken in many American homes, especially those near the Canadian border. Here is a particularly tasty version for your festive table.

Rutabaga Supreme
Serves 6.

6 cups diced rutabaga
2 cups diced potatoes
2 cups boiling water
1 bouillon cube
2 teaspoons salt
1 tablespoon sugar
¼ teaspoon ground pepper
1 cup grated sharp cheese
2 tablespoons minced onion
chopped fresh parsley

Combine the rutabaga, potatoes, water, bouillon cube, salt, and sugar in a saucepan. Bring to boiling point and boil for 3 minutes, uncovered. Cover and boil for 12 minutes, or until vegetables are tender. Rice or mash, and add pepper, cheese, and onion. Beat until fluffy. Garnish with chopped fresh parsley and serve while very hot.

RYE

Probably originally from southwestern Asia, Rye (*Secale cereale*, of the Grass Family) is another of the grains that have been cultivated since time immemorial. Though known from ancient days, it is, however, a "newer" grain than wheat or barley.

Today Rye is more or less extensively grown in almost all countries of the northern hemisphere, the seeds of this grass being ground to make an important flour. This is the basis of rye bread and coarse, heavy, wonderful black bread. Through various complex processes, Rye is distilled into various alcoholic delights, among them whiskey and vodka. The roasted grain is sometimes sold as a coffee substitute in some parts of Europe.

Rye flour is to be found in most large markets in this country and enjoys a rightfully distinct position in our good cookery.

SALSIFY

Also known as Oyster Plant, Vegetable Oyster, and, in French, *salsifis*, Salsify is a delectable vegetable which is not as yet particularly well known by cooks in the United States. It is a member of the prodigious

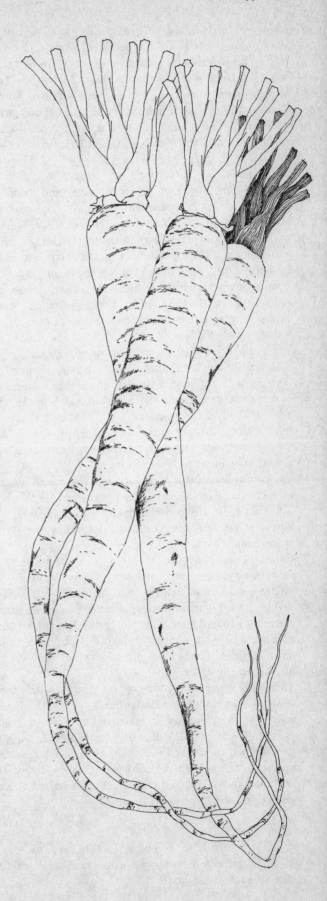

Daisy Family, known scientifically as *Tragopogon porrifolius*. A native of the southern parts of Europe, it has been cultivated in this country on a rather casual scale for a very long time. It has, in fact, become naturalized in many parts of the United States. Though considered a weed, it is showy when in flower. The sizable daisy-shaped purple blooms close prior to noon—hence, in Great Britain, the plant has been given the vernacular name of "John-go-to-bed-at-noon."

The young, narrow, grassy leaves and terminal heart are justly popular—especially when well bleached—raw in salads, or lightly cooked and served with butter and customary seasonings. But we know it better for its fleshy taproots, up to about ten inches in length and two inches in diameter on top. The skin is grayish-white or grayish-yellow, while the flesh is white, with a milky white juice. A black-skinned related plant is the Scorzonera or Black Salsify (page 209).

The flavor of Salsify, when properly cooked, is indistinguishable from that of the oyster, though the texture is considerably firmer than that marvelous mollusk. Improved varieties, developed both in this country and abroad, are very prolific, and the vegetable should be far more widely appreciated here than is presently the case. Excellent canned Salsify is available, imported from France.

To prepare, scrape the roots, cut them into lengths of a couple of inches, and place in cold water to which a few drops of lemon juice or cider vinegar have been added to prevent discoloration. Cook in a variety of ways, from simple boiling in salted water (again with the addition of a touch of lemon juice or vinegar), to stewing or sautéing in butter or in a court-bouillon.

Mashed or riced Salsify, well dressed with butter, salt and freshly ground pepper, and a touch of lemon juice, is superb with such things as broiled chicken and sautéed pork chops. If desired, fold in a tablespoon or so of finely chopped parsley for each 4 cups of mashed vegetable.

Salsify is very amenable to various delicate sauces —Béchamel, Mornay, Hollandaise, or light cheese-cream—but care must be taken not to mask the delicacy of the vegetable's flavor. This comes through to greatest degree when the Salsify is served hot, in my opinion, though many European epicures fancy the roots cooked until just tender, then marinated and chilled in a vinaigrette dressing.

SALSIFY HAPPILY accompanies almost any meat. Here is an excellent recipe utilizing this attractive root vegetable with veal.

Salsify with Mustard Veal
Serves 4 to 6.

1 *can or jar (about 15 ounces) salsify*
2 *pounds veal, cut into sizable cubes*
2 *tablespoons butter*
2 *tablespoons flour*
chicken broth
2 *teaspoons Dijon mustard*

In a large heavy skillet with cover, melt the butter and in it brown the veal cubes, a few at a time. Remove the veal as browned, using a slotted spoon. Add the flour to the skillet and carefully cook it, stirring frequently, until browned. Add the liquor from the can or jar of salsify to enough rich chicken broth to comprise 1½ cups of liquid. Add this to the skillet, mixing thoroughly with the browned flour. Return the veal, and add the Dijon mustard (please do not use any other variety here). Bring to the boil, then reduce heat, cover, and simmer for 1 hour, or until the veal is fork-tender. Add the salsify and heat thoroughly to serve.

SALSIFY Fritters are often encountered on good tables in France and, to a degree, in northern Italy. Here is a favorite recipe that I delight in serving as a separate special course at dinners of festive proportions.

Salsify Fritters
Serves 4.

1 *pound salsify*
salted, lightly acidulated water
¼ *cup light olive oil*
1 *to 2 tablespoons lemon juice*
2 *tablespoons finely chopped parsley*
salt and freshly ground white pepper
batter
deep fat or oil

Scrape the salsify roots and cut them into rounds or lengths of equal dimensions. Cook in salted water to which a touch of lemon juice or cider vinegar has been added until just firm-tender. Drain well and arrange in a bowl. Add olive oil (peanut or soy oil can be substituted), lemon juice, parsley, and seasonings to taste. Allow to marinate for 30 minutes or so. Remove salsify pieces with slotted spoon, dip into a light batter, and fry in hot deep fat or oil until nicely browned. Drain on paper towels and serve while hot.

SAMPHIRE

This is a fleshy-stemmed perennial herb (*Crithmum maritimum*, of the Carrot Family), growing above the high-tide mark along rocky coasts of many parts of Europe, including the British Isles. Also known as St. Peter's Herb, Sea-Fennel, Parsley-Pert, and *bacile* (French), the aromatic crisp-textured leaves and juvenile stems have been collected, principally during the autumn months, for centuries as a special vegetable.

These are eaten fresh in salads (typically served with a light vinaigrette dressing), are chopped and used as a pleasant salty condiment with cold meats, and are pickled in vinegar much in the manner of gherkins. The very young parts can also be slightly cooked in a cream sauce, with flavorful results.

Samphire is cultivated on a modest scale by gourmet gardeners in the United States, but the bunches of succulent grayish-green leaves and stems of European produce markets seldom appear in ours. This is an interesting and unusual vegetable, one which warrants further attention from North American cooks.

SCALLION

The Scallion is botanically known as *Allium fistulosum*, and, like the allied onion, garlic, chives, shallot, and leek, is a member of the Lily Family. This highly utilitarian but attractive vegetable is also known as Welsh Onion (a distinct misnomer, since the species is indigenous to Siberia!), Green Onion, Spring Onion, Stone Leek, and Cibol.

The Scallion is no longer just a springtime vegetable; it is now extensively cultivated throughout the year, so that it is always available in tidy bunches in our good produce markets. It is somewhat similar in appearance to a juvenile onion, with erect clusters of vaguely angled tubular bright-green leaves, but the base is only slightly enlarged, never forming a large bulb.

Scallions are often used raw—both green tops and white or whitish basal parts—for mixed tossed salads. They have a pleasant, delicate flavor and somewhat crisp texture when very fresh, as they should be for kitchen use. The vegetable is also incorporated into a considerable roster of recipes of varied origin. It has been suggested that Scallions can be substituted when the allied shallot is not available, but I consider the two very distinctive in flavor, each occupying its particular favored niche in our good cookery.

KOREAN cookery is not unlike that of certain parts of China and of Japan. Yet it has many distinctive characteristics (some of the most widely appreciated dishes are far "hotter" than many of us non-Koreans generally enjoy!), and many delicacies, such as this light soup.

Korean Scallion Soup
Serves 4.

> 2 cups coarsely chopped scallions, with tops
> 1 quart rich chicken broth
> 2 teaspoons peanut or soy oil
> 3 eggs, beaten well
> 2 to 3 tablespoons soy sauce, Japanese preferred

Heat the rich chicken broth, freshly prepared, preferably, to the boiling point, covered. Using a large shallow skillet, heat the oil and pour in the thoroughly beaten eggs. Cook these into a thin omelet until firmly set and lightly browned on the bottom. Turn omelet out onto a plate and cut into strips measuring about 2 inches by ¼ inch. Add these, with scallions and soy sauce, to the boiling chicken broth, cook for just 1 minute, and serve.

SCALLIONS are widely utilized in Oriental cookery. I typically add them to Sukiyaki (page 164) and Tempura (page 252). They are delicious when done in the same way as Asparagus Nipponese (page 22), or in the following dish in combination with soybean curd, ideally the imported canned kind.

Scallions and Bean Curd
Serves 4.

2 *big bunches scallions*
5 *squares soybean curd, cubed*
4 *tablespoons peanut or soy oil*
2 *tablespoons sake (or dry sherry)*

Rinse and trim scallions, then cut on diagonal into 1-inch lengths. In a wok or large skillet, heat the oil over high flame, add the scallions, and stir-fry for just a few seconds. Add the bean-curd cubes and continue to stir-fry for about 1 minute. Combine the sake (or sherry), and soy sauce, add this to skillet, and continue to cook for about 30 seconds. Serve without any delay.

ELEGANCE personified is to be found in the following recipe—whole scallions in a savory sauce, in the Greek style. This is a perfect dish to set before family or guests with seafood, fowl, or with lamb, in particular, although it can also be served with other foods.

Scallions à la Grecque
Serves 4 to 6.

4 to 6 *bunches scallions*
⅓ *cup light olive oil*
2 to 3 *tablespoons wine vinegar*
⅓ *teaspoon finely chopped garlic*
½ *cup dry white wine*
½ *teaspoon salt*
¼ *teaspoon freshly ground pepper*
2 *tablespoons finely chopped parsley*
1 or 2 *drops Tabasco sauce*

Rinse and trim scallions, leaving them whole. Combine all other ingredients. Arrange the scallions in a flat pan and pour the sauce over them. Add enough water so that the scallions are just barely covered, and cook them, uncovered, over medium heat until just tender—do not overcook them! Allow the scallions to cool in the broth, then carefully remove to a serving dish. Over rather high heat, cook the broth until it is reduced by half, then pour it over the scallions. Allow to cool, and chill thoroughly before serving.

VARIOUS sorts of quiche often make a happy appearance at my table, these containing on differing occasions such ingredients as bacon (as in the famed quiche Lorraine), crabmeat, chicken, and a wondrous series of vegetables—including scallions, as in the following delicacy.

I like to offer the rich French cheese pie as a separate course—sometimes as an appetizer, or before the meat—accompanied by a suitable wine, usually a Chablis or some such white. With a pleasant light salad alongside, hot crusty bread, and, of course, wine, the pie makes a superlative supper as well.

Quiche Ciboule
Serves 4 to 6.

1 *cup finely chopped scallions, with tops*
2 *unbaked 9-inch pastry shells*
4 *eggs*
salt and pepper
2 *cups light cream*
2 *cups grated Swiss cheese*
¼ *cup grated Fontina or Parmesan cheese*
2 *tablespoons chopped pimiento*

Partially bake the pastry shells. Allow them to cool slightly prior to use. Rinse and trim the scallions, then chop them finely. Beat together the eggs with salt and pepper to taste, then fold in the cream (half cream and half evaporated milk is very acceptable). Mix in all other ingredients. Pour the mixture into the pastry shells and bake in preheated 350° F. oven for about 40 minutes, or until the tops of the pies are nicely browned. Cut into wedges and serve hot, or use leftovers (if any) chilled, as unique appetizers.

CRISP-TENDER hot scallions are supreme vegetables when served on toast; with a rich cheese or Hollandaise sauce, as a special preliminary course. Though oftentimes only the white basal parts are used for such delights, I prefer to take advantage of the complete vegetable.

Scallions on Toast
Serves 4.

4 *big bunches scallions*
2 *tablespoons butter*
2 *tablespoons hot water*
½ *teaspoon salt*
4 *slices crisp fresh toast*
cheese or Hollandaise sauce

Rinse and trim the scallions. In a sizable heavy skillet or large saucepan with tight-fitting cover, place scallions with butter, hot water, and salt. Cover and steam over rather high heat for 4 or 5 minutes—the scallions should be partially cooked, yet still retain a pleasant degree of texture. Drain, arrange on toast, and top with sauce to taste. Serve at once.

SCORZONERA

Scorzonera, or Black Salsify (*Scorzonera hispanica,* of the Daisy Family), is an unusual vegetable, closely related to the "white" Salsify (page 205), but at once distinguished by the black skin of the elongate fleshy taproot. The flesh is white and somewhat similar to that of the better known ally in flavor and texture.

Scorzonera—from the Catalán word for "viper," because in olden times in its native Spain, it was utilized as an antidote for the bite of that venomous reptile (Viper's Grass is an alternate vernacular)—is occasionally encountered in United States markets today, though it is nowhere near as common as salsify.

Its preparation and culinary uses are precisely those indicated under Salsify (page 205).

SEA KALE

Sea Kale (*Crambe maritima,* of the Crucifer Family), mentioned earlier, is a rather stout perennial plant, often more than three feet tall, native along the coasts of Europe and occasionally encountered as a select vegetable in choice markets in this country. It is only vaguely allied to true kale, but does somewhat resemble that plant in its large, heavy, intricately crisped and cut grayish-green or blue-green masses of leaves.

On the Continent—notably in Ireland and England, where it is a favored table item—the young shoots are often bleached in the field and served much as one does Belgian endive hearts, though their flavor is a bit more acrid.

Selected varieties developed in Great Britain and available from seedsmen here are particularly sweet-flavored when properly bleached, and are enthusiastically recommended. The broad leaf stalks are the parts most often eaten, although the crisp leaves are delicious when cooked until tender, then drained and served with butter, crumbled bacon, and suitable seasonings. Many French gourmets delight in a salad made from the unbleached foliage of the Sea Kale (which they call *chou marin*), tossed with a vinaigrette dressing to which has been added some freshly snipped chives and a pinch of tarragon.

The bleached shoots of Sea Kale, typically appearing during the winter and early spring months in shops, are variously steamed, boiled, or simmered in a stock. The peak of their unique flavor is kept by steaming. Dress with butter or top with a light white sauce, perhaps garnished with some sieved hard-cooked egg yolk, and serve especially to accompany poultry or veal.

SEAWEEDS

In recent years, with our erupting population, much has been said of the foods which must be grown to support future generations. Seaweeds are very frequently noted among these vital foods of the future. Until the past decade or so, unless he had visited Japan or frequented Oriental colonies in Hawaii and California, the average American knew little about the numerous edible algae.

The Japanese have long considered these marine plants essential to their superb cuisine, and indeed have cultivated several kinds for many years, in remarkable underwater "farms." Our nutrition experts inform us that we, too, must soon consider such commercial exploitation of these vegetables.

The Seaweeds, as an assemblage, include several thousands of different species of plants, extremely diversified in dimensions and appearance. There are those consisting of a single green or blue-green cell, microscopic in size; there are those like sargassum, which we find in coarse, intricately branched bunches dotting our beaches; and there are the kelps or tangles, gigantic treelike structures forty and fifty feet in length.

Most of the Seaweeds of culinary importance are used in moderate amounts as flavorings, seasonings, or condiments. Some few, though, are consumed as is, out of hand. For example, when I was a child in Maine, one of the periodic delights for a special snack was a fistful of Dulse. This is a dried marine alga, of a dull reddish-purple color, which has a subtle flavor reminiscent of the scent of a wave-battered strand, and a texture strangely like that of chewing tobacco! It may sound grim, but I still adore it! Dulse (also spelled Dulce) is, interestingly, to be found in bars of some of our larger cities, being served in place of the omnipresent drab potato chips. The dried fronds—to be found in shops specializing in health foods—are also chopped and added to stews and ragoûts, imparting a delicate reddish color and subtle flavor to the sauce, which it also thickens slightly.

Kombu (or Konbu) is one of the very important Oriental Seaweeds (the species is *Laminaria japonica*, for the most part), also known as Tangle or Japanese Kelp. The leathery fronds of these very large marine plants, are usually shredded or powdered, after drying, to be sprinkled on rice as a unique seasoning, or added to soups and sauces. Sizable pieces of the alga are readily available in Oriental specialty shops in this country; in this form they are added to meat dishes, or eaten as a distinctive, somewhat iodine-flavored vegetable, or pickled, and even made into a kind of confection. I have several times served it as a side dish with Sukiyaki or Tempura in the following fashion; it is odd, but of definite connoisseur interest.

Kombu
Serves 4.

1 4-inch square dried kombu
1 cup water
½ teaspoon Japanese soy sauce
½ teaspoon lemon juice

In a saucepan, place the square of kombu in the water and bring to the boil. Remove container from heat and allow to set until seaweed is well softened, usually 20 minutes or so. Remove seaweed from liquid and cut it into thin strips with a sharp knife. Return to the saucepan with soy sauce and lemon juice. Simmer until kombu is somewhat tender, yet still retains its pleasant texture. Serve small portions hot, in tiny individual side bowls at table.

This seaweed is an essential ingredient of one of the most widely utilized of Japanese culinary stocks, *dashi*. The other vital item in this very important recipe is *katsuobushi*, oven-dried bonito fish which has been allowed to develop a greenish mildew to increase its flavor, after which the fish is shredded. *Dashi-no-moto*, a sort of "instant" dried form of the stock basis, is now available from Japan, the little individual packets being much like our tea bags. Boiled with water, the resultant broth has a pleasant subtle fishy flavor, with wonderful overtones of the perfume of the sea. I use it very often as a soup base, and as a starter for many sauces for Oriental dishes.

For the purist who wishes to prepare fresh Dashi, using our big kelp, kombu, here is a simple recipe.

Dashi
Makes about 4 cups.

1 square-inch piece dried kombu
4⅓ cups water
½ cup shredded katsuobushi (*dried bonito*)
⅛ teaspoon monosodium glutamate

In a saucepan, bring the seaweed with the water to the boil, preferably notching the kombu all around the edges so the flavor comes out into the broth more quickly. Remove kombu and discard. Add the shredded dried fish to the water and again bring to the boil. Add the monosodium glutamate, remove saucepan from heat, and strain at once, using the liquid as a superior stock.

Kombu is also available in our specialty stores in various prepared delicacies, usually preserved in a seasoning sauce in imported tins. One of these is reminiscent of rich forest-green ravioli in appearance, another is a little soft-leathery soy-sauce-flavored roll tied with an edible "string" of seaweed. I like to serve these, slightly chilled, as a prelude to a multicourse Oriental dinner. They are invariably received with pleasure by my guests—even after they have been informed of what they have eaten!

Using the basic Dashi stock above, the inventive cook can readily create a fascinating variety of soups with Oriental overtones. One example is the fabulous Japanese thick soup, Misotaki (page 44). Now here is a clear soup, *suimono*, which includes another of the very important Oriental edible seaweeds, the Purple Laver (*Porphyra tenera*). This is available in many of our specialty markets as very thin dried sheets, packaged, imported from Japan (where it is called *nori*) or China (where it is called *jee-choy*). When using this alga, be sure to rinse off all bits of sand which might adhere to the fronds.

Seaweed Soup
Serves 4.

¼ pound purple laver
5 cups Dashi (above)
⅓ cup thinly sliced canned abalone
1 teaspoon Japanese soy sauce
½ teaspoon monosodium glutamate
1 tablespoon minced scallion tops

Rinse the seaweed in 2 or 3 changes of tepid water, carefully washing off any grit. Press out moisture, then cut laver into thin strips or slivers. Heat the Dashi in a kettle over high flame, add the abalone slices, boil for 2 minutes, then add seaweed bits. Continue to boil for 5 minutes more, then stir in soy sauce and monosodium glutamate. Serve at once, each bowl sprinkled with scallions.

PURPLE laver is also used as a wrapping for the elegant "jelly-roll" kind of Sushi (page 198), known as *norimaki-zushi*. The rinsed, softened pieces of this alga also figure in the service of raw fish, *sashimi*, and are incorporated into the distinctive Japanese vinegared salads called *sunomono*.

THERE are dozens of other edible seaweeds. These include the various Brown Algae of Oriental oceans, several species of which (especially the Arame, *Ecklonia bicyclis*) are dried, then added, chopped, as a special seasoning to rice dishes. Still others, with high gelatin content, such as one of the Red Algae (*Gelidium Amansii*), are manufactured into agar or *kanten* jelly. One of the more unusual Oriental desserts consists of tiny, variously flavored and colored cubes of this odd product. And still other seaweeds in the Far East are made into one type of translucent culinary noodle, a sort of shirataki.

ALMOST all of the peoples of the Pacific Islands make use of differing kinds of seaweeds. In Hawaii, for instance, enterprising cooks often serve the several dark-colored kinds of Limu in soups, vegetable-meat medleys, and in such things as the following distinctive tropical hors d'oeuvre. There are a number of species of Limu, of various botanical identity, to be found in Honolulu markets, and on occasion in stores on the Mainland as well. They are well worth searching for and experimenting with.

Limu Seaweed Appetizer
Serves 4 to 6.

> 1½ *pounds fresh limu*
> 1 *pound large curd cottage cheese*
> ½ *cup freshly grated Daikon (page 194), or red radish*
> 2 *tablespoons minced scallion tops*
> 2 *teaspoons Japanese soy sauce*
> *salt and freshly ground pepper*
> *ripe mango slices*

Rinse the limu in several changes of tepid water and drain. Chop into fine shreds with a very sharp knife, and salt lightly. Thoroughly combine with the cottage cheese, daikon, scallions, soy sauce, and seasonings to taste. Form into compact walnut-size balls and

chill for 1 hour. Serve on a chilled plate surrounded by mango slices.

I BELIEVE that within ten years the regular diet of many Americans, and possibly of much of the world population, will include myriad products manufactured from these extraordinary marine and freshwater vegetables of the future.

SHALLOT

The Shallot (*Allium ascalonicum*, of the Lily Family), which is a relative of the onion, garlic, and the like, figures prominently in fine cookery. Presumably from Syria or thereabouts in Asia, it has been cultivated for a very long time for the grayish or brownish bulbs (cloves), small, pointed and borne in tight little clumps. These are utilized for flavoring and are reminiscent of a very mild onion, with perhaps a touch of garlic added. The leaves are small and hollow, slightly pungent, and are on occasion chopped for the seasoning of salads.

Shallots are absolutely essential to the intricacies of French *haute cuisine*. Much has been made of the imported vegetable, but precisely the same thing is easily grown in the home garden in the United States, at a remarkably lower tariff. I keep my Shallots in pots, in a rather sandy soil, and find they thrive and multiply so rapidly that I have given starts to just about every culinary friend I have hereabouts. When pulled, the bulbs are amazingly long-lasting, often persisting in perfect condition for eight to twelve months in a cool, dry place.

The French, who call it *échalote,* prepare an excellent seasoning spread from the Shallot, by peeling the little cloves, blanching them until tender, then grinding in a mortar with an equal amount of butter. This is served with various cold hors d'oeuvres, incorporated into certain elegant sauces, and is used especially on hot broiled meats. When white wine and various other ingredients are added to this spread, and the mixture is served hot, it is the famous *beurre Bercy.*

For such things as broiled, grilled, or fried steaks, sliced leftover roast beef, and hamburgers, the following marvelous Shallot Wine Sauce is well-nigh perfection. For fish or fowl, substitute a white wine, such as Chablis, for the red.

Shallot Wine Sauce

    5 tablespoons minced shallots
    2 tablespoons butter
    1 teaspoon salt
    1 cup dry red (or white) wine
    ¼ cup lemon juice
    ½ teaspoon freshly ground pepper

In a heavy saucepan, melt the butter, add shallots and salt, and cook over medium heat, stirring often, until shallots are soft. Stir in other ingredients and simmer for 15 minutes, prior to use as a sauce, marinade, or basting liquid.

SNAKE GOURD

The Snake Gourd (*Trichosanthes Anguina,* of the Squash Family) is a remarkable cucurbit from the Asiatic tropics, often cultivated as a culinary curiosity elsewhere, including the United States. A stout quick-growing annual vine, it produces slender cylindrical green or whitish-green fruits which may attain lengths of six feet. When grown in choice gardens for use as a vegetable, it is the custom to tie a stone to the apex of the developing fruit so that it does not become contorted, as it often does when left to grow normally.

These gourds—the species is also known as Snake Squash or Club Gourd—are reminiscent of zucchini when picked young and thinly sliced, to be used as in the recipes for that vegetable (page 248). The elongate gourds are infrequently seen hereabouts except in fine Oriental markets, but they are considered great delicacies throughout much of the Far East and Southeast Asia, and well warrant further attention by connoisseurs in the United States.

Two other members of the genus *Trichosanthes* have edible fruits as well, both of them cooked as vegetables. These are the *dummella* of India and Ceylon (*Trichosanthes cucumerina*), whose cucumberlike fruits are much valued in vegetable curries, and the Japanese Snake Gourd (*T. japonica*), whose young fruits are pickled in soy sauce, and whose sizable roots are made into a culinary starch. Both of these oddities are available in tins as imports, but have a very limited appeal in this country.

SORGHUM

Sorghum (*Sorghum vulgare*) is a grass which has been cultivated since time immemorial in Asia and Africa, where even today the population in many areas subsists in large part on the seeds.

As is usually the case with plants which have been grown for a very long time, there are endless, more or less distinct varieties of Sorghum. Certain kinds are grown expressly for the making of brooms, others are raised extensively for the sweet syrup obtained from them, and still others—those which particularly interest us—for their abundant, often down-hanging bunches of grains.

This last category includes such forms as Kaffir Corn, Egyptian Rice Corn, Guinea Corn, African Millet, *milo* and *doura.* The ripe seeds, or grains, are usually coarsely ground, often roasted, then made into porridges, puddings, or thick soups, or formed into flattish cakes to be baked until crisp. Some types are fermented into a powerful beer.

In the United States, as yet, this grain is largely relegated to the status of fodder for farm animals and birds.

SORREL

In this country, Sorrel applies to several species of the genus *Rumex* (of the Buckwheat Family), both native and naturalized, the sizable, rather thick root leaves of which are much valued by gourmets. These, variously sour or acid in flavor, are justly praised when used in crisp salads, as a potherb, and in soups.

Sour Grass is another well known North American vernacular, and the name Dock is also applied regionally to some of these plants, such as the Belleville Dock (*Rumex Acetosa*), Spinach Dock (*Rumex Patientia*), the Curled or Narrow-Leaved Dock (*Rumex crispus*), the Bitter or Broad-Leaved Dock (*Rumex obtusifolius*), and so on.

In the United States the green, often red-suffused leaves are usually gathered from wild plants, but in Europe a number of these utilitarian vegetables are cultivated. They are perennial in habit, and for the most part singularly easy of growth. In a few markets of our larger cities, bunches of fresh Sorrel (or Dock) leaves and stems can today be encountered during the spring months, but these are customarily quickly bought up by connoisseurs. Seeds of a variety of these plants, including some of the exceptional European species, are available from dealers here, and their more extensive home cultivation is very much to be encouraged.

The degree of sourness present in the leaves, caused by oxalic acid, fluctuates markedly from species to species of Sorrel, some of the most prized kinds being headily puckery and decidedly an acquired, though delectable, taste.

As with all fresh greens, the foliage and tender stems should be made use of as quickly as possible. After rinsing to remove any grit, they are plunged into salted boiling water, to cook only until barely wilted and still retaining most of their crisp texture. Drain, to serve at once dressed with butter and seasonings, for a memorable treat. In France, where Sorrel is called *oseille* and is far more available than here, the vegetable is often coarsely puréed and served with a light cream sauce or heated heavy cream, or sautéed briefly in butter.

For salads, the rinsed, chilled leaves with young stems of Sorrel are lightly tossed with a delicate vinaigrette dressing, possibly with some sieved hard-cooked egg yolks—anything more would be heresy.

SORREL SOUP is a splendid creation, in my opinion, and a regrettable rarity at my house, since the various wild plants do not occur in this part of Florida. On exceptional occasions, though, I have received bunches of the greens via air, and have prepared the following delicate, wondrously refreshing potage. (An attractive tinned soup is now available from French sources, too.)

Sorrel Soup
Serves 4.

2 *cups tightly packed, coarsely chopped sorrel leaves and tender stems*
6 *cups rich chicken broth*
2 *egg yolks*
½ *cup heavy cream*
1 *tablespoon cooking sherry*
salt and pepper

In a kettle, heat the rich chicken broth, fresh, if possible, and add the chopped sorrel, to cook over medium heat for 10 minutes. In a bowl, beat together the yolks with the cream and the sherry. Gradually add about a half-cup of the hot soup to this, beating all the while, then turning this back into the soup kettle. Heat, but do not boil, season to taste, and serve without delay.

SOYBEAN

The Soybean (*Glycine Soja*, of the Legume Family) is a truly remarkable vegetable with numberless uses to man. A native of China and Japan, the bushy plant has been cultivated since before the era of recorded history. There are countless varieties, with beans ranging in color from brown or black to red, yellow, and green—some of which are grown as forage for animals, others expressly for human consumption.

In the Orient the Soybean is second only to rice in importance as a food. In the United States, in addition to its culinary uses, it is utilized in the manufacture of such products as paints, oilcloth, linoleum, and liquid shampoo.

In the Orient and increasingly in markets in such places as Hawaii and California in this country, green Soybeans are for sale as a fresh vegetable. The plants have pod-laden branches, each short, narrow, very hairy pod containing three or four edible seeds. The fresh Soybean pods are washed, then boiled in lightly salted water until they are soft. Drained, they are seasoned to taste with soy sauce and a bit of sugar, then served, the beans being shucked from the pods at table.

THESE GREEN BEANS of the Soybean, after cooking, can well be incorporated into chilled salads with other vegetables, to be anointed with a rather positive dressing at serving time. They also adapt well to a variety of flavorful casseroles, such as this one.

Miss Diddley's Green Soybeans
Serves 4.

2 cups cooked drained green soybeans
2 tablespoons peanut or soy oil
½ cup coarsely chopped onion
¼ cup coarsely chopped green pepper
½ teaspoon minced garlic
½ pound lean sausage meat
salt and pepper
½ cup grated sharp Cheddar cheese

In a skillet, sauté the onion, green pepper, and garlic in the oil until vegetables start to brown. Crumble in the sausage meat and continue to cook until it is rather well browned, stirring often. Add the soybeans, season to taste, and mix through. Turn into a 1-quart casserole, sprinkle with the cheese, and bake in preheated 350° F. oven for 20 minutes, or until cheese has melted and is lightly browned.

THE DRIED beans of the soybean are commonly available these days, notably in health-food stores. Very high in protein, they are often used as a nutritious additive to such dishes as meat loaf, hamburger patties and pasta-meat medleys.

Roasted soybeans are ground into a meal and into flours of various degrees of coarseness; these are then incorporated into a wide array of edibles—breakfast foods, special foods for infants, crackers, breads, cakes, biscuits, pasta, ice creams, candy bars, and are even used as a substitute for coffee. The meal is frequently combined with wheat or other flours, and adds its unique nutritional benefits and nutty flavor to many baked products.

Sprouted soybeans are much like the bean sprouts grown from Mung Beans (see page 48), though their flavor is subtly different. Soybean sprouts are available in cans and frozen packets in many of our superstores. As with mung bean sprouts (which can be used in this recipe), do not remove the hulls, for these are loaded with vitamins.

Soybean Sprouts Cantonese
Serves 4.

1 pound fresh soybean sprouts
4 tablespoons peanut or soy oil
½ cup finely slivered green pepper
2 tablespoons sake
1 to 2 tablespoons Japanese soy sauce
1 tablespoon sugar

Rinse bean sprouts thoroughly under running cold water—but do not soak them. Using a wok or large shallow skillet, over high flame, add the oil and quickly stir-fry the green-pepper slivers for about 1 minute. Add drained bean sprouts and stir-fry for just 30 seconds, then add sake, soy sauce to taste, and sugar, mixing thoroughly but with care. Serve immediately.

SOYBEAN oil is widely used in American kitchens as a light, bland cooking and salad oil.

SOY SAUCE, called *shōyu* in Japan, is the most important seasoning in the cuisine of that country, and is increasingly used by American cooks as well. It is commercially produced by fermenting a special variety of soybean, to which malt and salt have been added. I recommend the Japanese imported brand called Kikkoman, which is neither too salty nor too strong, as are most others available in this country. Soy sauce in modest amounts adds tremendously to all sorts of dishes. Because of its salt content, cut down a bit on seasoning with salt when adding soy sauce to a recipe.

TŌFU is the curd of cooked, mashed white soybeans, which has been precipitated, then pressed into cakes. It is perishable, hence most conveniently bought in cans, water-packed. The rather soft but firm cakes—sometimes baked or even fried prior to canning, and respectively known as *yakidōfu* and *aburage*—have a bland flavor, vaguely reminiscent of a custard. It is just this suavity which makes *tōfu* so valuable, since it quickly absorbs the flavors around it in such things as soups, sukiyaki, and mizutaki, yet retains its exceptionally pleasant substance. *Tōfu* is to be found in many of our domestic markets, imported from Japan. With its high content of readily digestible protein, it should be better known by all Americans.

MISO is a special Japanese seasoning paste made of fermented cooked soybeans, red or white, often in combination with rice or other ingredients. Usually rather salty, it is used particularly in the superb thick soups known collectively as *miso-shiru*. The paste is available frozen in many of our specialty shops. I often prepare my own version of *miso*, using dried navy or other white beans (see page 44), instead of utilizing the commercial imported variety.

SPANISH OYSTER PLANT

The Spanish Oyster Plant, alias Golden Thistle, is a long-rooted, very prickly member of the Daisy Family, *Scolymus hispanicus*. An indigene of southern Europe, notably the Iberian peninsula, its large coarse leaves are irregular and dark green with pale-green spots, and it has rather drab yellow flower heads. The taproot is reminiscent of salsify, a related plant, but grows to lengths of more than a foot. Lighter in color, the flesh is somewhat intermediate in flavor between salsify and parsnip.

Spanish Oyster Plant is infrequently seen in our markets, though its seeds are available from commercial sources here, and it is a rampant grower. The young leaves and stalks are prepared in the manner suggested for Cardoon (page 71), and are relished by good cooks in Spain and Portugal. The root is used as suggested for Salsify (page 205).

SPINACH

Spinach, an important vegetable in our American diet, has been cultivated for literally thousands of years in its presumed native haunts, the southwestern parts of Asia. Botanists know it as *Spinacia oleracea* and include it in the odd Goosefoot Family.

There are many different varieties of Spinach now available, these having been developed largely through the efforts of professional plant breeders in this country. The handsome, characteristically rather arrowhead-shaped leaves that we eat are borne directly from the roots, and they vary in color from rich, almost black-green to a pale yellowish-green, and in texture from plane to markedly crumpled. In the United States, Spinach is most often grown on an extensive commercial scale during the autumn and spring months, but bunches of the attractive greens are seldom absent from our large markets at other seasons.

As is the case with all vegetables, Spinach should never be overcooked. Boiling the richly flavored leaves until they are scarcely more than mush not only results in an unappetizing dish but also effectively removes almost all of the nutritional benefits.

Most Spinach found on our produce stands these days is labeled encouragingly ''cleaned.'' But one must still carefully wash the vegetable to remove the grit that persistently adheres to it. Trim off all but the youngest, most tender of stems and midribs, and tear the leaves into large pieces. Then place in a large pot of cool water and swish around for a moment or two. Do not allow to soak. Remove the vegetable to a colander and discard the water in the pot. Repeat the process at least once more, again draining the Spinach, and discarding the water with any residual sand.

The best method of cookery for Spinach is, to many of us, the simplest. Bring to the boil a large pot of

salted water and place the washed, drained vegetable in it. Return to the boil and cook for not more than 2 or 3 minutes, depending upon the age and dimensions of the leaves. Quickly drain in a colander and serve immediately with lots of butter, salt and freshly ground pepper to taste, and, if desired, a tiny touch of freshly ground nutmeg.

Though the fresh vegetable is preferred, the modern flash-frozen chopped Spinach in packages does away with the tedious advance preparation of washing and draining. The frozen product can, of course, be substituted for almost all of the recipes given herewith.

Spinach is an adaptable vegetable. Its uses are myriad, ranging from soups and salads to omelets and main meat entrées. It is particularly prominent in the cuisine of Middle Eastern lands. It is also justifiably popular in such places as Switzerland, where it is grown in tidy fields with splendiferous mountain backdrops.

HERE IS a favorite Swiss way with Spinach from the Hôtel Richmond in Geneva.

Swiss Spinach
Serves 4 to 6.

2 pounds fresh spinach
6 tablespoons butter
½ cup finely chopped onion
1 small clove garlic, minced
2 tablespoons flour
½ teaspoon salt
⅛ teaspoon freshly ground pepper
⅛ teaspoon nutmeg
½ cup light cream

Wash the fresh spinach thoroughly, drain it very well, and chop—not too fine. In a large heavy skillet with cover, sauté the onion and garlic in 4 tablespoons of the butter until they are just limp. Add the chopped spinach and combine with the onion and garlic. Sprinkle with flour, salt, pepper, and nutmeg, then add the cream, and mix thoroughly but with care. Cover skillet and cook over rather high heat for 3 minutes—no longer! Stir in the remaining butter and serve at once.

A GREAT many Armenian dishes contain spinach in some form or other. Here is a special Armenian soup —a robust conglomeration which should be served with few other accompaniments. Bulgur is readily available in specialty markets these days; some additional uses for it are discussed on page 243.

Armenian Spinach Soup
Serves 6 to 8.

1 pound washed raw spinach, finely chopped
2 cups minced onion
4 tablespoons butter
2 quarts rich beef stock
1½ cups oatmeal
½ cup bulgur
1 teaspoon salt
⅛ teaspoon freshly ground pepper
½ cup warm water
2 tablespoons tomato ketchup
2 teaspoons lemon juice

In a large soup kettle with cover, sauté the onion in the butter, stirring often, until just barely limp. Add the rich beef stock and bring to the boil. In a bowl, thoroughly combine the oatmeal (not the quick-cooking variety) and the bulgur with the salt and pepper. Add the warm water and mix with the fingers until the mixture is firm. Form into balls about ¾ inch in diameter. Drop the balls into the hot soup, cover the kettle, and simmer for 20 minutes. Add the ketchup, lemon juice, and the spinach, cover again, and simmer the soup for 3 to 5 minutes. Serve while very hot.

HERE IS another memorable soup utilizing spinach.

Cream of Spinach Soup
Serves 4 to 6.

2 pounds washed raw spinach, finely chopped
½ cup finely chopped onion
2 tablespoons butter
3 cups chicken stock or bouillon
1 cup light cream
1 cup dairy sour cream
¼ cup minced scallions, with tops
dash nutmeg
salt and white pepper to taste
lemon slices

Sauté the onion in the butter over high heat, stirring constantly, until limp but not browned. Add the finely chopped spinach and cook, still stirring, for about 1 minute, until the spinach is just wilted. Heat the chicken stock or bouillon and add the onion-spinach mixture. Turn into an electric blender and whirl briefly—the mixture should contain little flecks of greenery. Return to the soup pot, add the light cream and sour cream (both at room temperature), plus scallions, nutmeg, and salt and pepper to taste.

Heat thoroughly, but do not allow to come to the boil. Serve, garnished with thin slices of lemon, while very hot—or, for a change, thoroughly chilled.

HAVE you ever noticed how many professional men are avid—and excellent—amateur cooks? Here is a recipe given me by a good friend, a doctor of considerable renown, which is a favored easy luncheon dish at his lovely home in Coral Gables.

Parke's Spinach-Stuffed Tomatoes
Serves 4.

½ package frozen spinach soufflé
2 tablespoons water
½ pound lean ground beef
monosodium glutamate, salt, and pepper to taste
4 large firm tomatoes
4 slices white toast

Cook the half-package of spinach soufflé very slightly and drain thoroughly. In a skillet, bring the 2 tablespoons of water to the boil, then add the ground beef and cook, stirring constantly, for 1 minute. Drain off any excess liquid and combine the cooked beef with the spinach. Season rather liberally with monosodium glutamate, salt, and pepper. Meanwhile, cut tops off tomatoes, and carefully remove pulp and seeds. Stuff the tomato shells with spinach-beef mixture and bake in preheated 300° F. oven for 20 minutes. Serve at once, each spinach-stuffed tomato set on a slice of crisp, fresh toast.

OMAR KHAYYAM'S Restaurant in San Francisco is one of the most famous in that metropolis. The special Spinach Salad is a prime specialty of the house, served with such delicacies as shish kebab. Here is their recipe, used through their kind courtesy, although it never tastes quite as wonderful as in its indigenous haunts. Atmosphere must have something to do with it. . . .

Spinach Salad Omar Khayyam's
Serves 4 to 6.

2 pounds fresh spinach
2 tablespoons salad oil
1 tablespoon lemon juice
1 large can asparagus tips, chilled
2 firm ripe tomatoes, in wedges
2 hard-cooked eggs, finely chopped
Omar's Dressing (page 256)

Wash spinach thoroughly, discarding all stems. Cut

the leaves into strips an inch or so wide and drain them in a towel, patting as dry as possible. Dress spinach strips with salad oil (I use either peanut or soy oil) and lemon juice, arrange on a platter and chill for 1 hour. When ready to serve, garnish the platter with drained asparagus tips and tomato wedges, and sprinkle with the chopped egg. Serve Omar's Dressing separately.

A VERY simple salad with fresh spinach is this one, especially suitable with grilled hamburgers or almost anything involving lamb.

Syrian Spinach Salad
Serves 4.

1 pound fresh spinach
1 teaspoon salt
6 scallions with tops, finely sliced
2 tablespoons lemon juice
2 tablespoons olive oil
½ cup coarsely chopped salted pecans or walnuts

Wash the spinach carefully and remove and discard coarse stems. Drain thoroughly, shaking to remove as much moisture as possible, and pat dry in one or more clean kitchen towels. Tear spinach into large hunks and place in a sizable shallow pan. Sprinkle with the salt, roll and toss the spinach by hand, and allow to stand for 15 minutes. Drain and squeeze dry. Place in salad bowl, add scallions, lemon juice, and olive oil. Toss lightly. Sprinkle with chopped nuts and serve at once.

AND YET another salad, this decidedly a personal favorite, to serve as a special separate course, or with broiled chicken.

Super Spinach Salad
Serves 4 to 6.

2 pounds fresh spinach
8 slices lean bacon, diced
2 cups small, firm bread cubes
¼ teaspoon garlic powder
3 tablespoons lemon juice
salt and freshly ground pepper
⅛ teaspoon Dijon or Düsseldorf mustard
3 tablespoons olive oil
6 tablespoons peanut or soy oil

Wash the spinach thoroughly and discard any tough

stems. Drain the leaves and pat dry with clean towels. Wrap in a clean towel and refrigerate for at least 1 hour. Fry the diced bacon until crisp, remove pieces with slotted spoon, and drain on paper towels. Drain off all but 2 tablespoons of bacon drippings. Sprinkle bread cubes with garlic powder, tossing lightly, and sauté in the bacon drippings until lightly browned, stirring them frequently. Remove bread cubes and allow them to drain on paper towels. Prepare a vinaigrette dressing by stirring salt and freshly ground pepper to taste (be rather liberal with the latter) and the mustard into the fresh lemon juice; combine the two oils and gradually beat the mixture into the lemon juice. At serving time, lightly toss together the chilled spinach leaves, torn into bite-size pieces, with the crisp bacon, browned bread cubes, and dressing. Serve without delay.

AND NOW for a main dish in which spinach figures prominently, here is an odd but delectable recipe from Iran.

Spinach-Beef Teheran
Serves 4 to 6.

2 pounds fresh spinach
½ cup melted butter
1½ pounds lean beef, cut into ½-inch cubes
4 tablespoons butter
1 pound assorted dried fruits—pears, apricots, peaches, and prunes
⅓ cup lemon juice
1 teaspoon salt

Drain the thoroughly washed spinach and chop coarsely. In a large skillet with cover, add the spinach to the melted butter and cook, covered, until it just wilts. Remove lid, and continue to cook, stirring constantly, until spinach becomes dark green in color. Remove from heat at once. Using another skillet, melt the 4 tablespoons of butter and sauté the little cubes of beef until they are well browned on all sides. Add the beef cubes to the spinach, together with the assorted dried fruit (this cut into suitable pieces), the lemon juice, and the salt. Add just enough water to cover, cover the pan, and cook over very low heat for about 45 minutes, or until the fruit is tender. Serve over hot steamed rice.

THERE are infinite interesting ways to serve spinach as a hot vegetable. For example, the addition of a goodly dollop of yoghurt or dairy sour cream or even buttermilk to hot, just-cooked spinach is highly recommended. Also, one can quickly cook the leaves in a small amount of rich chicken or beef stock, drain the vegetable, then serve with butter and customary seasonings. Or, consider the following delicious recipe, which adds a touch of the Orient.

Spinach Sesame
Serves 4.

1 pound fresh spinach
3 tablespoons sesame seeds
3 tablespoons soy sauce, Japanese preferred
¼ cup melted butter
salt and freshly ground pepper

Wash spinach carefully, discarding all coarse stems. Put sesame seeds in a small heavy skillet, place in preheated 350° F. oven, and stir and shake occasionally until they turn rather dark brown. Cook the spinach, torn into bite-size pieces, in a small amount of lightly salted water in covered pot over high heat; shake the pot a couple of times. This should not require more than 2 minutes. Drain spinach, toss lightly with the toasted sesame seeds, and place in warmed serving dish. Pour the melted butter over and add salt and freshly ground pepper to taste.

OUR ITALIAN friends do wonderful things with spinach. They frequently incorporate it into stuffings for various sorts of pasta—ravioli are probably the best known in the United States. They make several splendid thick soups from the leaves. And they concoct the following delectable main dish, this to be served with side dish of pasta (usually spaghettini or linguine), with a hearty meaty bolognese sauce over both Spinach Balls and pasta.

Italian Spinach Balls
Serves 4 to 6.

2 pounds fresh spinach
lightly salted boiling water
3 tablespoons melted butter
3 tablespoons grated onion
3 tablespoons minced scallion tops
3 tablespoons freshly grated Parmesan or Romano cheese
2 eggs, beaten lightly
2 cups fine dried bread crumbs
⅓ cup butter

Trim off coarse stems from spinach, wash leaves

very thoroughly, and drain. Coarsely chop the leaves and smallest stems, and add to lightly salted boiling water to cover. Over high flame, bring water again to the boil, and then quickly drain the spinach. Allow to stand in the colander, pressing out as much moisture as possible. Turn spinach into a big bowl, and combine very thoroughly with melted butter, onion, scallion tops, cheese, eggs, and 1 cup of the bread crumbs. Allow to stand for about 15 minutes, then form into balls about the size of a walnut. Roll these in the remaining bread crumbs. Melt the ⅓ cup butter in a large skillet, and fry the spinach balls a few at a time until they are brown and crisp on the outside, turning them often and with care. Serve as is, or with your favorite meaty pasta sauce, while very fresh and hot.

AND THEN we have Spinach Frittata, again of old Italian ancestry, and today encountered in many subtle and not so subtle variants. This is handsome to the eye, easily prepared, and simply delicious. Any leftovers are tasty when chilled, too.

Spinach Frittata
Serves 4.

1½ cups coarsely chopped fresh spinach leaves
3 tablespoons light olive oil
¾ cup thinly sliced small white onions
8 large fresh eggs
½ teaspoon salt
¼ teaspoon freshly ground black pepper
¼ teaspoon sweet basil
2 tablespoons minced fresh parsley
⅓ cup freshly grated Parmesan cheese
2 medium-size firm-ripe tomatoes, thinly sliced
6 pitted ripe olives, thinly sliced

Preheat oven to 350° F. In a heavy iron skillet, heat the oil and sauté the onion slices, stirring often, until they are soft. In a large bowl, beat the eggs with a wire whisk, then fold in salt, pepper, basil, spinach, parsley, and Parmesan. Turn into the skillet containing the onion, and cook on top of stove over low heat, lifting from bottom with a spatula as the eggs set. After about 3 minutes of this, arrange tomato and olive slices attractively on top, then place *frittata* in preheated oven until it is firmly set and slightly browned. Serve directly from the skillet while very hot, or chill any leftovers.

SQUASH

As pointed out elsewhere in this book, the common nomenclature of the numerous kinds of vegetables known as Squash is almost hilariously confused. These plants are all cucurbits, and virtually all of those in general cultivation bear names that vary markedly from region to region. Some of them, of the important genus *Cucurbita*, are taken up below; the reader is referred as well to entries under Calabaza, Pumpkin, Snake Gourd, and Zucchini (see Index).

There are dozens and dozens of different kinds of Squash. In some parts of the United States, and Canada, the names Squash and Pumpkin are used almost without discrimination for the same thing. And of course, in each foreign land in which these cucurbits are eaten, indigenous vernaculars abound in overwhelming array.

While all of this unseemly confusion makes little difference to the average cook, let us attempt to make some semblance of sense out of the muddle by taking up the basic Squash groups one at a time, with their most prevalent common names and brief selection of pertinent recipes.

The Summer Squashes are mostly variants of the botanical species *Cucurbita Pepo*, an exceedingly diverse entity whose origins are probably in the Himalayan mountains—like most of these plants, it has been cultivated for such an incredibly long time that its home is unknown. Here we find the Summer Crooknecks (yellow, white, and green), Pattypan (Cymling), Butternut, Scallop, and the distinctive ornamental gourds. Here, too, oddly enough, botanists place the North American Pumpkin (page 191) and the West Indian Pumpkin, which is considered on page 67 under its well-known Spanish name of Calabaza.

In most of our domestic markets, Summer Yellow Crookneck Squash is among the most consistently available kind throughout most of the year. As with all such vegetables, the smallest, firmest specimens available should be chosen for use in the kitchen. All the recipes suggested for Zucchini, commencing on page 248, are suitable for this vegetable charmer. And do refer to Ratatouille, on page 108. Do not peel this Squash—much of its unique, delightful character lies in its vibrant color and crisp peel. This vegetable can also be had frozen and in cans.

HERE IS a tasty main-dish version of this lovely Squash with the elongate name. I like it with hot cornbread sticks and iced coffee.

Summer Yellow Crookneck Squash Potpourri
Serves 6.

10 *small summer yellow crookneck squashes, in*
    ⅛-inch rounds
1 *cup chunks of green pepper*
½ *cup thinly sliced onion*
2 *tablespoons light oil*
2 *large firm-ripe tomatoes, coarsely chopped*
salt and pepper to taste
1½ *cups diced cooked ham*
1 *tablespoon butter*
1 *cup tiny stale bread cubes*
¾ *cup grated sharp cheese*

In a skillet, over high heat, sauté the squash rounds with the green pepper and the onion in the oil, stirring gently, for 2 or 3 minutes. Add the tomatoes, season to taste, mix well but with care, and cook for 1 minute more. Remove from heat. In another skillet, sauté the ham dice in the butter until nicely browned. Turn squash mixture into a suitable shallow casserole and top with the ham. Sprinkle with bread cubes and cheese and place under preheated broiler, about 8 inches from the flame, just until the cheese melts.

THE PRETTY Pattypan Squash (also called Cymling), the Butternut Squash, and the Scallop Squash are utilized much in the same way in our kitchens. Often baked until tender (halved, in most instances), to be served with butter and seasonings, including, if desired, brown sugar or honey, they can also be stuffed with various savory mixtures. Use a sharp melon-ball cutter to scoop out the centers. Here is a favorite method.

Stuffed Pattypan Squash
Serves 6.

6 *pattypan, butternut, or scallop squashes*
6 *slices lean bacon*
½ *cup finely chopped onion*
½ *teaspoon salt*
½ *teaspoon freshly ground pepper*
½ *teaspoon basil*
1 *tablespoon finely chopped parsley*
butter
½ *cup sauterne*

Cut tops off squash and carefully scoop out centers, leaving a firm shell. Discard pith and seeds, or, if desired, roast the latter for snacking later on. Coarsely chop the squash flesh. In a skillet, fry bacon until crisp, then drain it and crumble. Pour off all but about 2 tablespoons of bacon fat, and in this sauté the onion until soft, stirring often. Add squash flesh and cook for about 3 minutes, stirring often. Mix in crumbled bacon, salt, pepper, basil, and parsley. Spoon this stuffing into squash shells, top rather liberally with butter, and arrange in a shallow greased baking pan. Pour wine over stuffed squash, cover the pan with aluminum foil, and bake in preheated 350° F. oven until squash is tender, usually about 30 minutes. Remove foil for last 5 minutes or so, to allow the topping to brown.

The flesh of these tasty squashes is also highly recommended when boiled or steamed until tender, to be served riced or puréed and liberally dressed with butter, salt and pepper, and if desired a tiny touch of nutmeg or cinnamon.

THE WINTER Squashes are referred to either *Cucurbita maxima* or *C. moschata* by the botanists. The former is presumably an American indigene, since certain forms of it were found growing with corn in Indian fields when Columbus arrived on our shores. The second species probably originated in the Asiatic tropics, but here again its precise original home is today unknown.

In this admittedly vague category we include the hard-skinned squashes such as Banana, Acorn (Danish), Hubbard, Turban, Mammoth, Cushaw, Canada Crookneck, and Winter Crookneck. These are often encountered under distinctive regional vernaculars that vary in differing parts of the world.

These diverse squashes, by and large, are either peeled and the flesh boiled or steamed till tender, to be used like Pumpkin (which see, page 191), or cut into suitable portions and baked, with or without stuffing mixtures of various sorts. In the United States these cucurbits are especially prominent at table during our winter feasting holidays, Thanksgiving and Christmas. And do consider utilizing this kind of squash boiled in salted water until just firm-tender, then cooled, thinly sliced, and offered as an unique salad on lettuce leaves, with vinaigrette or Thousand Island Dressing, and sprinkled with fresh-snipped chives, if desired.

Here is an exceptional version of baked Acorn (Danish) Squash, from Polly Dross, good culinary

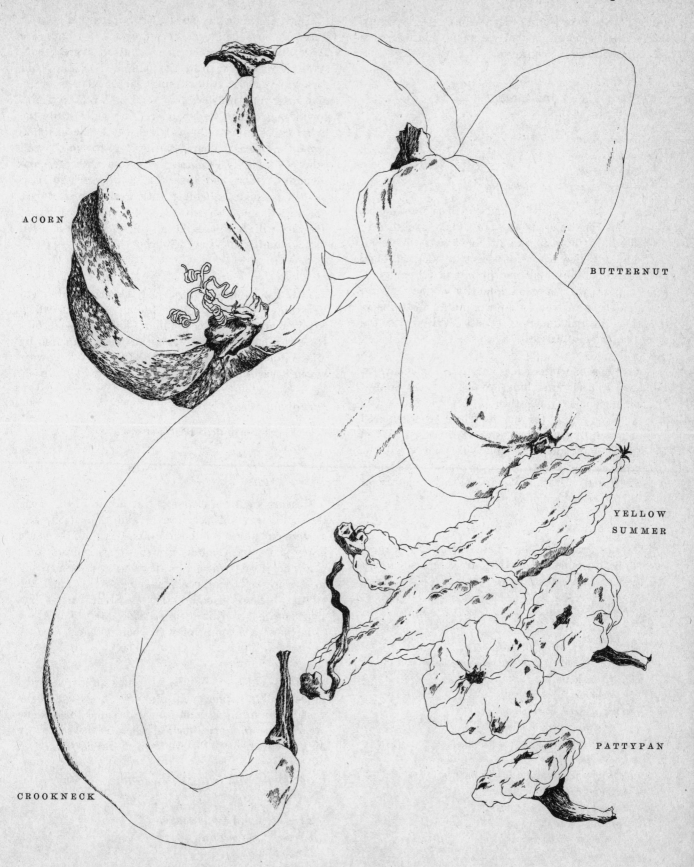

ACORN

BUTTERNUT

YELLOW
SUMMER

PATTYPAN

CROOKNECK

crony of St. Petersburg, Florida. Mrs. D. typically serves this as one of several vegetable side dishes to accompany turkey or chicken.

Mrs. Dross's Acorn Squash
Serves 4.

　2 *firm acorn squashes*
　butter
　cooking sherry
　whole canned cranberries, drained

Wash the acorn squashes and cut them into halves, but do not remove seeds and pulp. Bake squashes in preheated 375° F. oven, in a little hot water in a shallow pan, until they are tender—usually about 30 to 40 minutes. Scoop out seeds and pulp, and fill cavity of each squash with a good quantity of butter and sherry. Return to oven for a few minutes, and at serving time fill remainder of squash cavity with the whole canned cranberries.

SOME types of winter squash are gigantic cucurbits. Hubbard squashes weighing upward of forty pounds are not uncommon, and when kept in the dirt cellar will supply a family for months. These are often seen in our produce markets during their season. When the fresh mammoth vegetables are not available, frozen or canned squash purée is available and may be substituted for Pumpkin in the manufacture of pies, tarts, turnovers and such.

PUMPKIN (page 191) or Calabaza (page 67) can, of course, be used instead of the puréed squash in this lovely West Indian dish.

Tobago Squash Pie
Serves 4 liberally.

　6 *cups puréed cooked Hubbard or other winter squash*
　3 *tablespoons butter*
　⅓ *cup finely diced onion*
　¼ *cup finely diced green pepper*
　1 *cup finely diced cooked ham*
　1½ *cups finely chopped cooked shrimp*
　⅛ *teaspoon dried thyme*
　2 *tablespoons finely chopped fresh parsley*
　2 *tablespoons chopped pimiento*
　salt and pepper
　1½ *cups stale bread cubes*
　1 *medium clove garlic, mashed*
　¼ *cup peanut or soy oil*
　butter

Using fresh or frozen squash, prepare a smooth purée. In a skillet, over rather high heat, sauté the onion and green pepper in the butter, stirring constantly, until soft. Add the ham and shrimp, and continue to cook, still stirring, for about 2 minutes. Mix in thyme, parsley, pimiento, and rather liberal sprinklings of salt and pepper. Meanwhile, sauté the bread cubes in the oil—in which the garlic has mellowed for at least 1 hour—until nicely browned on all sides. Thoroughly combine the squash with the ham-shrimp mixture, and turn into a well-greased deep pie tin or plate. Sprinkle with garlic bread cubes, pushing them down into the pie slightly, and dot liberally with butter. Bake in preheated 375° F. oven for 20 minutes, and serve while hot.

JAMAICAN cooks do marvelously flavorful and inventive things with their West Indian pumpkin, which is taken up in this book under Calabaza (page 67). Here is a most unusual Jamaican jam, originated by Miss Vinnette M. Walters, of the Parish of Trelawny, which is easily adapted to our big old winter squash.

Squash Jam

　4 *cups coarsely grated raw winter squash*
　1 *orange*
　1 *lemon*
　4 *cups sugar*

Measure 4 cups of coarsely grated raw, ripe squash. Grate the rind of the orange and the lemon, and squeeze out juice from both fruits, straining this. In a heavy saucepan, combine grated squash, sugar, fruit rind and juice, and mix until sugar dissolves. Bring to a slow boil, and cook, stirring often, until the mixture becomes smooth and thick. Skim if necessary. Pour into hot sterilized jars at once, and seal. Allow to mellow for a couple of weeks before using.

THERE ARE many kinds of soups prepared from squash and the other cucurbits in various parts of the world. But in my opinion, few can equal this unique creation, again from Jamaica, where it was served by Mrs. Fay Gearing in the hill town of Mandeville.

Country Style Squash Bisque
Serves 4 to 6.

　2 *pounds peeled winter squash*
　1 *pound ripe tomatoes*
　¼ *cup barley*
　1 *medium clove garlic, mashed*

2 bay leaves
¼ teaspoon dried marjoram
⅛ teaspoon dried thyme
2 tablespoons finely chopped scallion tops
1 tablespoon Pickapeppa Sauce
few grains allspice
1 teaspoon sugar
salt and pepper to taste
2 quarts rich beef stock
2 tablespoons cooking sherry
2 slices lean bacon, fried crisp, crumbled
2 tablespoons finely chopped fresh parsley

Peel squash and cut into pieces. Peel the tomatoes and add them, along with squash, barley, and listed ingredients through salt and pepper to the rich beef stock. Cover and simmer over medium heat, stirring often, for 1 hour, or until vegetables are falling apart. If desired, whirl the hot soup in an electric blender until smooth. Correct seasoning, add sherry, and serve while very hot, sprinkled with crumbled bacon and parsley. Offer saltine crackers or fried croutons on the side.

SUSUMBER

The Susumber, alias the Gully Bean (*Solanum torvum,* of the Potato-Tomato Family) is a prickly big-leaved bush, widespread in waste places in many parts of the tropics. In Jamaica, in particular, it has long been cultivated to some considerable degree, and the species has recently been introduced into Florida.

It bears abundant round berries, less than a half-inch in diameter, which are very popular in the native cuisine of Jamaica. Utilized when immature and firm, they possess a distinctive puckery flavor which is most refreshing when cooked in combination with such things as dried salt codfish or freshwater crawfish, or when appearing in soups or stews.

Here is an attractive and singularly flavorful dish I recently relished during a tour of Jamaica, one combining Susumbers and chicken. This odd vegetable's name, by the way, is pronounced soo-*soom*-ber.

Susumber Toss-up
Serves 4.

½ pound susumbers
1 2-pound broiler-fryer chicken, disjointed

2 teaspoons salt
1 teaspoon freshly ground black pepper
⅛ teaspoon dried thyme
2 tablespoons finely chopped scallion tops
1 hot chili pepper, minced
½ cup fine-chopped onion
1 cup chopped peeled tomato
2 cups water
1 cup coarse bread crumbs
¼ pound (1 stick) butter, softened
1½ cups hot mashed potatoes

Pick over and wash susumbers. In a sizable heavy kettle with cover, place the susumbers, chicken, and all listed ingredients through water, and cook over medium heat, covered, for about 35 minutes, or until chicken and susumbers are tender. Allow to cool, and cut chicken into dice, discarding bones and, if desired, skin. In a rather shallow baking dish, arrange a layer of the chicken, sprinkle with ⅓ the bread crumbs and dot with butter, top with layer of susumbers and other vegetables and a bit of the broth, then repeat layers. Finish with bread crumbs and remaining butter, and decorate with hot mashed potatoes. Bake in preheated 350° F. oven for 20 minutes, until potatoes are nicely browned, and serve while very hot.

SWEET CICELY

Sweet Cicely (or Cicily) is a very pretty large perennial plant of stream banks in Europe, the stems set with large downy gray-green highly dissected leaves, and topped by small white, very fragrant flowers.

Botanists know it as *Myrrhis odorata,* and place it in the Carrot Family. It is also cultivated as Myrrh, which is confusing, for the best-known Myrrh, that of the Bible, is the coagulated resin of several African and Indian trees of the genus *Commiphora* (Bursera or Gumbo-Limbo Family) which are not in cultivation. And, just to confuse things still further, North American Myrrh is *Osmorhiza* (also of the Carrot Family), a totally distinct plant, the roots of which have been eaten by our Indians for centuries, though seldom except in times of want.

The foliage of Sweet Cicely is used, generally coarsely chopped, as a sweetish aniselike flavoring in salads, soups, and stews—in moderation, since it is a very positive thing. It is grown by many persons of European antecedents in this country but is very rarely encountered in our markets.

SWEET POTATO

As is amply evident throughout this book, there are many examples of confusing duplications of common names for totally distinct vegetables in different parts of the world—and, indeed, in different parts of the United States. A prime example of this is found in the widely grown, justifiably popular root tuber which botanists call *Ipomoea Batatas,* and which in the United States is encountered interchangeably as Sweet Potato and Yam.

The plant involved is not in the slightest degree related to the common white ("Irish") potato. And the vegetables correctly known as Yams (genus *Dioscorea*) are little known outside of the tropics, although they are widely grown and important in many of these warm lands—and ideally this name should never be applied to our *Ipomoea.* The confusion here is, however, a rather logical one, Yam being a corruption of the African word pronounced *nyam* (see *ñame,* for *Dioscorea,* in Spanish), which refers to a number of different kinds of root-tubers familiar to the Africans who were transported to this country during the terrible days of slavery. Especially in our Southern states—where Sweet Potatoes are even today grown on an extensive scale—the slaves in many instances subsisted in considerable part on these starchy "yams."

The Sweet Potato—since we must use this singularly inaccurate epithet—is originally from the tropical parts of the Americas, but its precise home is not known to science. *Ipomoea* is a member of the Morning-Glory Family (Convolvulaceae), and though many different varieties of Sweet Potato have been developed through the centuries, the pretty flowers of the vine remain very characteristic in form. In modern times, Sweet Potatoes form an extremely important item of daily diet for countless millions of persons in the tropics, from Brazil to New Guinea.

Two principal types of Sweet Potato are grown in this country, one with a mealy flesh, after cooking, of some dryness, usually yellowish in color, the other moister, softer, and sweeter, and orange or even reddish-orange in color. Technically, the Boniato (see page 226) is a variant of the first named of these.

In many cookbooks, the Sweet Potato is considered in close conjunction with the white potato. This is possibly logical, though confusing, since it can be prepared in many of the ways suggested for the "Irish" vegetable from the Andes of South America.

In our markets today, fresh Sweet Potatoes are found in bountiful array throughout the year. They are often colored with a red dye, which is soluble in the water in which they should be scrubbed prior to cooking. In choosing them in the market, consider the smallest specimens on display—provided, of course, that they are very hard when pressed. These are the youngest vegetables, and they do not possess the fibers which may be present in overly large ones.

Best nutritive value is obtained from Sweet Potatoes if they are cooked without peeling. They are usually either baked or boiled in lightly salted water until done to the degree desired, then prepared in an interesting variety of fashions.

These utilitarian vegetables are often served with pork or ham, though they admirably accompany beef, veal, lamb, and chicken or duck.

INITIALLY, let us consider a delectable soup prepared from Sweet Potatoes, this with happy overtones of Brazilian cookery.

Sweet Potato Soup Rio
Serves 6.

> 4 cups peeled, diced sweet potatoes
> 3 tablespoons butter
> ½ cup thinly sliced onion
> 3 tablespoons coarsely chopped parsley
> 1½ teaspoons salt
> ½ teaspoon freshly ground pepper
> 4 cups water
> ½ teaspoon grated orange zest
> pinch mace
> 2 tablespoons cornstarch
> 3 cups milk
> ½ cup coarsely chopped salted peanuts
> 4 tablespoons butter

In a heavy kettle with cover, melt the 3 tablespoons butter and add the sweet potatoes, onion, parsley, salt, pepper, and water. Cover kettle and bring mixture to a boil, then reduce heat somewhat and cook until the vegetables are tender. While still hot, mash the vegetables—some degree of texture should remain. Add the orange zest, mace, and cornstarch thoroughly blended with a bit of the milk, mixing completely into the soup. Add the remaining milk, peanuts, and the 4 tablespoons of butter, and heat through, stirring constantly. Serve while very hot.

HERE is another soup, this one from West Africa's picturesque land of Liberia. Like much food from this part of the world, it is normally very "hot stuff," but in this recipe the amount of hot pepper sauce to be added is left to individual discretion.

Liberian Sweet Potato Soup
Serves 6 to 8.

1 *pound sweet potatoes, peeled, diced*
3 *tablespoons butter*
¾ *cup diced celery*
¼ *cup diced green pepper*
½ *cup diced onion*
6 *cups rich chicken stock*
salt and freshly ground black pepper
1 *teaspoon tapioca*
½ *cup coarsely chopped salted peanuts*
1 *cup light cream*
dash nutmeg
Tabasco sauce to taste

In a large heavy kettle, melt the butter, and add the sweet potatoes, celery, green pepper, and onion. Sauté the vegetables, stirring frequently until they are rather soft. Stir in the chicken stock, season with salt and pepper to taste, and simmer for 10 minutes, stirring often. Allow soup to cool slightly, then whirl in electric blender until smooth. Return purée to the kettle, add the tapioca, and cook over low heat until tapioca is tender. Add the peanuts, stir in the cream, nutmeg, and Tabasco sauce to taste, heat through—do not boil—and serve while very hot.

CONSIDER, too, the following attractive, simple salad made from these tasty root vegetables.

Sweet Potato Salad Miami
Serves 4.

3 *cups cooked sweet potatoes, in 2-inch by ½-inch sticks*
1 *cup thinly sliced celery*
1 *cup drained canned or fresh pineapple chunks*
1 *cup cubed cooked ham*
mayonnaise
crisp lettuce leaves
cucumber slices

Be sure that all ingredients are well chilled before assembling the salad. Very lightly toss the sweet-potato sticks, celery, pineapple, and ham with just enough mayonnaise (homemade, preferably) to bind the mixture. Serve without delay on a bed of crisp lettuce leaves—tiny hearts of Romaine are perfect—garnished with thick slices of unpeeled, scored cucumber.

AMONG the many Sweet Potato dishes originating in the Antilles is Haitian Sweet Potato Pie. This is actually a pudding, redolent of spices and raisins, and

with bananas to give it an extra fillip. An amazingly adaptable recipe, it is most often served hot from the oven, with ham, pork, or chicken. But leftovers are excellent when chilled and offered in thin slices, perhaps with an assortment of cold cuts or cold ham and chicken.

Haitian Sweet Potato Pie
Serves 4 to 6.

2 *cups cooked mashed sweet potatoes*
2 *small bananas, peeled, mashed*
1 *cup milk*
2 *tablespoons sugar*
½ *teaspoon salt*
⅛ *teaspoon nutmeg*
⅛ *teaspoon cinnamon*
2 *egg yolks, beaten well*
3 *tablespoons chopped seedless raisins*

In a large bowl, thoroughly blend the mashed sweet potatoes and mashed bananas. Add milk gradually, and mix until very smooth. Add the other ingredients and mix thoroughly. Pour mixture into a well-buttered 1-quart casserole. Bake in a preheated 300° F. oven for about 50 minutes, or until the "pie" is well-set and firm and the top a nice golden-brown color. Serve either hot or chilled and thinly sliced.

IF COOKING over a charcoal grill is your specialty, then consider the following skewered delights. These are excellent with pork or ham—or hamburgers or frankfurters, for that matter.

Sweet Potato-Pineapple Kabobs
Serves 4 to 6.

3 *large sweet potatoes*
1 *large can pineapple chunks, drained*
½ *cup melted butter*

Parboil the sweet potatoes until they are partially cooked but still rather firm. Allow to cool. Peel and cut into cubes or slices an inch or so thick. String on skewers (preferably soaked bamboo ones) alternately with pineapple chunks. Brush liberally with melted butter and grill over very hot coals, turning often and basting frequently with the butter, until nicely browned—usually about 15 minutes. Serve at once.

A SHOWY and festive version of sweet potatoes comes to us from Louisiana, one of the major areas of production for this luscious vegetable. Since the dish is rather sweet, serve it with fowl, particularly.

Louisiana Sweet Potatoes Waldorf
Serves 8.

4 *medium-size sweet potatoes, cooked, peeled*
4 *baking apples*
1 *tablespoon sugar*
¼ *cup water*
¼ *cup milk*
2 *tablespoons butter*
2 *tablespoons dark brown sugar*
½ *teaspoon salt*
⅛ *to ¼ teaspoon cinnamon*
2 *tablespoons dark seedless raisins*
2 *tablespoons chopped pecans*

Core the unpeeled apples and cut each one crosswise into three slices. Reserve the top slices and place remaining slices in a 3-quart rectangular baking dish. Sprinkle with sugar, and add water to bottom of dish. Bake in 375° F. oven for 15 minutes. Meanwhile, mash the sweet potatoes with the milk, butter, brown sugar, salt, and cinnamon. Peel and chop the reserved apple slices and stir into the mashed sweet potatoes with the raisins and pecans. Top each apple slice with about ½ cup of the sweet-potato mixture. Sprinkle with additional chopped pecans, if desired. Bake 15 minutes longer and serve.

SWEET POTATOES may also figure with prominence in the wonderful Japanese Tempura (page 252), cooked in a manner akin to "French frying." In fact, firm sticks of the vegetable are delectable when "French fried" as one does the white potato.

COOKIES prepared from sweet potatoes are old-fashioned favorites in many kitchens of our Southern United States. Here is a particularly tasty form of this famous recipe.

Sweet Potato Cookies

2 *cups cooked mashed sweet potatoes*
2 *cups flour*
1 *cup butter, softened*
½ *teaspoon salt*
¼ *pound coarsely ground walnut meats*
¼ *cup butter, softened*
¼ *cup dark brown sugar*
powdered sugar (optional)

Thoroughly combine the sweet potatoes, flour, 1 cup butter, and salt, to form a dough. Using a floured board, roll this out into a thin sheet, and cut into circles 1½ inches in diameter. Slash designs with the point of a knife on half of each circle. On the other half of each circle place a teaspoon of a mixture made by thoroughly combining the walnuts, ¼ cup butter, and brown sugar. Turn over like half-moon pies and crimp the edges. Bake cookies in preheated 350° F. oven until they are nice and brown. If desired, roll in powdered sugar while still hot.

SWEET POTATOES as a dessert enjoy tremendous popularity in many tropical lands from Mexico to the Philippines, particularly in the form of this recipe.

Sweet Potato Camote
Serves 6.

6 *raw medium-size sweet potatoes, peeled*
1½ *cups dark brown sugar*
¾ *cup water*
4 *tablespoons butter*
½ *teaspoon salt*

Cut the peeled sweet potatoes into quarters lengthwise. In a heavy saucepan, combine all other ingredients and bring to a boil. Add the sweet-potato pieces, adjust heat so the liquid just barely simmers, cover the pot, and cook until potatoes are tender. Allow sweet-potato pieces to cool in the syrup, then arrange them on a rack to drain and dry. When dry, chill prior to serving as a sort of candy or as dessert.

BONIATO

The Boniato (pronounced bone-ee-*ah*-toe) is one of the "new" vegetables that has made its way into our big-city markets in recent years. Long a staple in Cuba and other parts of the Antilles, it is a distinct form of the sweet potato, with brown or red skin and handsome white flesh. This flesh becomes delightfully mealy in texture when properly baked or steamed; it is much drier than its better-known domestic relative.

The flavor of the Boniato is somewhat more bland than other varieties of the sweet potato; hence it admirably adapts itself to the following rather spicy recipes. Baked Boniatos are great favorites at my house, served piping hot and dressed with lots of butter and salt and freshly ground pepper to taste. These, and the dishes described below, are especially appropriate with pork chops, roast pork, or baked ham.

Today Boniatos are raised to an extensive degree in Florida. In Dade County alone, for example, more

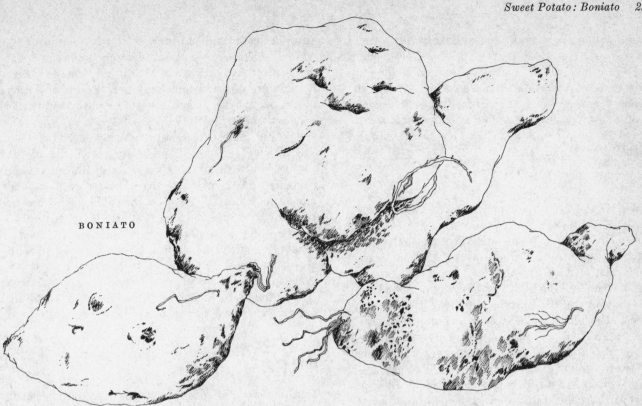

BONIATO

than one thousand acres are planted to this intriguing tropical root vegetable to fill the demand from Miami's large Cuban colony.

Ordinary sweet potatoes can be substituted for Boniatos in these recipes, although the end results will be quite different.

FRITTERS (*frituras*) made from the mealy Boniato are favored food in virtually all of the West Indian isles. They should be served as soon as possible after they are done. To get the proper flavor, lard is essential for frying.

Boniato Fritters
Makes about 30 fritters.

5 or 6 medium boniatos
1 tablespoon cornstarch
1 teaspoon baking powder
1 teaspoon salt
¼ teaspoon nutmeg
⅓ cup halved seedless raisins
2 eggs, beaten well
½ cup melted lard

Bake the unpeeled boniatos until they are tender. Peel; mash the pulp. Measure 3 cups of mashed pulp and combine thoroughly with the cornstarch, baking

powder, salt, nutmeg, raisins, and beaten eggs. Melt the lard in a smallish heavy skillet, and drop the boniato mixture into it by heaping tablespoonfuls. Fry until delicately browned on all sides. Drain on absorbent paper towels; serve without delay while hot.

BONIATO with Orange (*con naranja*) is a rather ornate but exceptionally tasty way to prepare this delectable root vegetable, and particularly good with boiled tarragon chicken, or sautéed pork chops.

Boniato with Orange
Serves 6 to 8.

4 medium boniatos
3 tablespoons butter
¾ teaspoon ground cinnamon
¼ teaspoon ground nutmeg
salt and freshly ground pepper
½ cup tiny marshmallows
½ cup broken pecan meats
½ cup seedless raisins
2 seedless oranges, unpeeled, sliced

Cook the boniatos in their skins in boiling salted water until they are tender. Drain thoroughly and peel. While still hot, mash them, and blend in the butter, cinnamon, nutmeg, and salt and freshly ground pepper to taste. Fold in the marshmallows, pecan meats, and raisins, and correct seasoning. If the mixture seems too dry, add a bit more butter. Arrange the unpeeled orange slices on a liberally buttered cooky sheet, and top each with a mound of the boniato mixture. Bake in preheated 325° F. oven for 15 minutes and serve without delay.

TACCA

The genus Tacca (of the small Tacca Family) contains two species of extraordinary perennial herbaceous plants which are of some importance as vegetables. These are the Tahiti or Fiji Arrowroot (*Tacca pinnatifida*) and the Hawaiian Arrowroot (*T. hawaiiensis*). The plants have stalked, handsomely incised big leaves, and produce fantastically complicated clusters of usually purple-black flowers, surrounded by great winglike and elongate taillike bracts—a unique characteristic that endears them to collectors of tropical ornamentals and gives them the appropriate common name of Bat Plant.

The profuse subterranean tuberous root stocks are very starchy, and the plants have long been cultivated for these, sometimes on a rather extensive scale, in the Pacific region. The tubers are often sizable, and occasionally are eaten, after boiling, in the areas where they are grown. They possess a bland flavor and moist texture, not unlike a poor-quality potato.

TALINUM

Talinum triangulare (of the Portulaca Family) is an exceptionally valuable summer green vegetable which for some years has been available in choice markets in Florida, where it is raised on a casual basis in dooryard gardens. Sold usually as Talinum or Suriname Purslane, it is a native of the American tropics, but the original seeds were introduced from Java into our area years ago by the great horticulturist David Fairchild. Talinum does not seem to have been taken up by culinary gardeners in other parts of this country, though it thrives under adverse conditions during the hottest weather, when other greens customarily perish, and is raised as a rather important crop in places as far afield as Ghana and the Malagasy Republic.

This Talinum (at least one other kind is cultivated in greenhouses as a showy ornamental) is a rather shrubby, thick-leaved, rapid-growing plant. The tender juvenile shoots and leaves are delicious when properly cooked, having a pleasant texture and somewhat spinachlike flavor. High in vitamin content, the thick clumps grow with astounding vigor, and a new crop of greens can be picked every few days during the peak season.

The vegetable is most often quickly cooked in boiling salted water, then dressed with butter and offered piping hot with suitable seasonings. But it can be parboiled, then run through a blender or sieve and added to a hearty cream soup—add some Coconut Cream (page 254) for a particularly luscious tropical potage—this to be served very hot. Or use the tender shoots in a stir-fry dish, in a bit of oil, seasoned with a touch of mashed garlic, a pinch of sugar, and soy sauce to taste.

Talinum is a delicious vegetable that certainly deserves more widespread attention everywhere.

TARO

Taro is a sort of all-encompassing term for a small yet diverse, botanically confused group of primarily tropical plants with edible tubers and, in some instances, foliage. As is so often the case in extensively and long-cultivated edible plants, even today the botanists cannot agree as to the precise scientific epithets for the various forms, though generally all of the Taros are placed in a single genus, *Colocasia*.

These plants belong to the widespread Arum Family (Araceae), a large aggregation which also includes such well-known, nonedible species as the jack-in-the-pulpit, the calla lily, and the anthuriums, philodendrons, and monsteras of our homes, greenhouses, and gardens.

Taro has been cultivated by man since long prior to the birth of Christ. The ancient Egyptians prized it, and today varieties of this vegetable with its attractive "elephant-ear" foliage are grown extensively in North Africa, Italy, and such parts of the Near East as Syria and Lebanon. In these lands, and indeed in a great many others from Cuba to Japan, Taro tubers are utilized daily as a starchy food, in place of, or in conjunction with, rice, potatoes, and the like.

In the Southern United States, the variety of Taro in frequent cultivation is known as Dasheen, and under this name it appears today in many mainland produce markets. In Hawaii and many other parts of the Pacific, the vegetable is known as Taro, or by an overwhelming number of indigenous vernaculars. Further south in the Americas, Taro is largely usurped in the native diet by the Malangas and Yautías, which are discussed under Malanga, page 141. In

Jamaica, Barbados, and Trinidad, though, we find Taro grown as *coco, eddo,* and *baddo,* with the leafy tops generally called Callaloo (see under Chinese Spinach, page 92).

As would be expected when considering such a long-grown group of plants, there are infinite and subtle variations of Taro. By and large, though, the tubers —too acrid to be eaten raw—are somewhat like medium-size white potatoes, with prominent rings and warty lateral buds. Their flesh, when pared, varies from whitish to the more common bluish-white, gray, or purplish.

Many forms, notably those of the Pacific region, have edible heart-shaped leaves that form an important item in the indigenous cuisine. It must be emphasized, though, that the foliage and tubers or thickened root stocks of many of these "elephant-ear" plants—including a considerable proportion of those types cultivated in this country as ornamentals—cannot be eaten, even after cooking, as they contain toxic crystals of calcium oxalate.

In Hawaii, and to a lesser degree in some of our large mainland markets, we can on occasion find a marvelous tropical delicacy—the forced young sprouts of Taro, often under the Chinese name of *woo-sun* or the Japanese *imonome.* These are palest greenish-white in color, seldom more than four inches in length, and, when properly prepared, as suggested below, are fabulous fare.

They are particularly adapted to serving with roast or broiled chicken, roast pork liberally basted with lime juice, or baked fish. Like most such fragile vegetables, the Taro sprouts should be purchased only if very firm to the touch and very pale in color.

Taro Sprouts
Serves 4.

    1 *pound taro sprouts*
    1 *teaspoon cider vinegar*
    2 *teaspoons salt*
    2 *cups water*
    butter
    salt and freshly ground pepper

Trim off any discolored parts of the sprouts; wash the sprouts thoroughly. Close to serving time, combine the vinegar, salt, and water in a sizable kettle, bring to a quick rolling boil, and lower the taro sprouts into it. Bring to a boil again and cook, uncovered, until the sprouts are just barely tender, usually less than 5 minutes. Drain immediately and serve while very hot, dressed with butter, salt and freshly ground pepper to personal taste.

BOILED taro tubers are prepared like boiled white potatoes. They are reminiscent of potatoes in flavor, with a pleasant nutlike flavor added, though consistency is oftentimes a bit moister.

Baked Taro is a good way with these adaptable tubers. Parboil them, scrubbed but unpeeled, for about 10 minutes in heavily boiling water, then bake in preheated 375° F. oven until thoroughly tender when pierced with a sharp fork.

As is the case with a number of root vegetables, taro tubers can be made into savory crisp chips to accompany everything from cocktails to hamburgers or frankfurters. Many knowledgeable cooks prefer these chips to those made with potatoes.

Taro Chips

Peel taro tubers and slice them as thinly as possible. Spread slices on absorbent paper towels and allow them to dry for 30 minutes or so, patting them with more towels to absorb all moisture possible. Heat a considerable amount of lard or light oil, and fry the chips, a few at a time, until they are delicately browned. Drain on fresh paper towels. Salt the chips, preferably using coarse kosher salt. These chips will keep rather well in a large, tight-capped jar.

SOMEWHAT in this culinary alliance, delicious thin sticks of fried taro are prepared—in precisely the same fashion as Benita's Fried Potatoes (page 189). These are superlative with fried fish or roast pork.

As mentioned previously, good cooks in Hawaii utilize taro in many different and delicious dishes. Every visitor to the Islands partakes of poi at least once, but often not more than once, since this odd paste is very much an acquired taste. Here are a couple of other taro recipes from Hawaii that are received with more consistent acclaim.

Taro Biscuits

    1 *cup cooked, mashed taro*
    ¼ *cup shortening*
    1½ *cups all-purpose flour*
    3 *teaspoons baking powder*
    2 *teaspoons sugar*
    ½ *teaspoon salt*
    1 *egg*
    ¼ *cup milk*

Thoroughly combine the cold cooked, mashed taro with the shortening. Sift together the dry ingredients and blend these into the taro with a pastry blender or two knives. Beat the egg with the milk, add this to the dough, and mix thoroughly. Place dough on lightly floured board and pat it down to ½ inch in thickness. Cut into small rounds with a lightly floured biscuit cutter, and place biscuits on lightly floured baking sheet. Bake in preheated 425° F. oven for 15 minutes, or until nicely browned on top. These are best served while very hot.

THE FOLLOWING elegant chicken-and-taro recipe is a Honolulu specialty.

Taro Chicken Breasts
Serves 3.

4 *tablespoons cooked, mashed taro*
3 *tablespoons butter*
3 *tablespoons finely chopped celery*
3 *tablespoons finely chopped onion*
1 *egg yolk*
½ *teaspoon salt*
⅛ *teaspoon pepper*
1½ *teaspoons poultry seasoning*
3 *boned, flattened chicken breasts*
3 *tablespoons whole cranberry sauce*
1 *tablespoon light brown sugar*
2 *tablespoons butter*

Melt the 3 tablespoons butter in a skillet, and sauté the celery and onion, stirring often, until they are soft. Add the egg yolk, taro, salt, pepper, and poultry seasoning. Spread this mixture over the chicken breasts. Combine the cranberry sauce with the brown sugar and spread this over the taro stuffing. Roll up the chicken breasts, and tie or skewer them to keep the stuffing contained. Melt the 2 tablespoons butter in a shallow ovenproof dish, and bake the chicken breasts at 300° F. for 30 minutes, or until they are very tender.

THIS NEXT taro casserole is a delicious concoction especially appropriate with roast meats. It is even more flavorful when reheated.

Taro Casserole Roberto
Serves 4 to 6.

2 *pounds taro tubers*
3 *tablespoons butter*
Simple Cheese Sauce (page 254)
⅓ *cup halved seedless raisins*
½ *cup buttered coarse bread crumbs*

Wash and scrub the unpeeled taro tubers, then boil in lightly salted water until very tender. Drain, peel, and put through potato ricer. In a well-buttered casserole, place a layer of the fluffy taro, dot with butter, then pour over part of the Simple Cheese Sauce and sprinkle with part of the raisins. Repeat layers, finishing with the bread crumbs. Bake in preheated 375° F. oven until crumbs and topping are nicely browned, and serve hot.

MENTION must be made here of taro stalks, or *woo-harp* (Chinese), or *imokuki* (Japanese), which are an exciting vegetable sometimes found in produce markets in Hawaii, California, and New York. There are several distinct variants, often of special forms of taro raised expressly for this purpose. These vary in dimensions from a foot or so, each stalk ¾ inch thick, and variously purple or green in color, to the *towimo*, a prized form with petioles to six feet long and four inches in diameter. These vegetables are generally boiled, cut into suitable sections, in one or more changes of salted water, then served with a light soy sauce-seasoned dressing.

TOMATO

The history of the Tomato is among the most fascinating of any of our vegetables. The plant was cultivated by the Indians in Peru long before the arrival of Columbus in this hemisphere. Early exchange between the Mexican and Peruvian cultures extended its range northward, and our word tomato is, in fact, a derivative of the Aztec *zitomate*.

The fruit—for the Tomato is one of those fruits which is most often utilized as a vegetable—was transported from Peru to Italy in the fifteenth century. Initially, this "love apple" or "golden apple" was viewed with extreme distrust and was considered by most people to be deadly poisonous. This is somewhat understandable, since many Tomato relatives of the Deadly Nightshade Family (Solanaceae—an immense group which also includes the eggplant, the potato, and the petunia and tobacco plant) are indeed dangerously toxic when eaten.

But, gradually, it was discovered that these splendid juicy globes were edible—and among the most adaptable of all fruits (or vegetables) in the kitchen. Thomas Jefferson grew some of the first Tomatoes to be seen in this country. Even as late as 1894, they were uncommon enough in markets to cause articles in the press.

Today there are literally dozens of different kinds of Tomatoes in cultivation in the United States—red, yellow, and green ones, varying in size from scarcely

larger than a marble to four and five inches in diameter —and the Tomato in its multitudinous prepared forms and derivatives is an essential ingredient in American and foreign cookery.

ONE OF my favorite salads, simple and suitable for service with all sorts of things from a platter of nicely displayed cold cuts to a grandiose pot roast or broiled pork chops, is the following one.

Tomatoes Oregano
Serves 4.

2 or 3 large just-ripe tomatoes
2 tablespoons light olive oil
1 tablespoon wine vinegar
1 tablespoon oregano
salt and freshly ground pepper to taste

Slice the tomatoes, peeled or not, as you wish, very thinly, and arrange them for individual servings on salad plates. Pour over them the oil and vinegar. Sprinkle on the oregano and salt and pepper to taste. Refrigerate for 1 hour prior to serving.

Thinly sliced, firm-ripe avocado can be added to this, if desired.

AND THEN we have these splendiferous chilled tomatoes, to be served with your favorite crisp crackers or party bread for a most unusual luncheon entrée, or as a special dinner salad. The recipe is named to honor Vizcaya, the magnificent old Deering estate on the palmy shores of Biscayne Bay, one of Miami's prime showplaces of art and architecture.

Tomatoes Vizcaya
Serves 4.

4 large firm-ripe tomatoes
3 hard-cooked eggs
1 small can deviled ham
1 tablespoon mayonnaise
½ teaspoon salt
¼ teaspoon black pepper
lettuce leaves for base
1 tablespoon minced fresh parsley

Slice tomatoes two thirds through on their sides, like an accordion. Mash the eggs with a fork and mix very thoroughly with deviled ham, mayonnaise, salt, and pepper. Place a small amount of this filling in each opening of the tomato, press tomato back into shape, and chill for at least 1 hour. Arrange tomatoes on crisp lettuce leaves and serve garnished with minced fresh parsley.

ANOTHER excellent all-purpose salad is the following one, which I first encountered aboard an airplane traveling to South America. I have never tasted it since, save at my own table. A suggested menu with this tomato salad is filet mignon or other steak, done to your taste, Fried Potatoes Havana (page 189), a good robust red wine, and assorted French pastries for an excellent conclusion.

Tomato Salad Aéreo
Serves 4.

2 large ripe beefsteak tomatoes
crisp escarole or lettuce leaves for base
12 spears canned asparagus
8 tiny canned potatoes, thinly sliced
commercial French dressing
1 cup crisp garlic croutons
salt and freshly ground pepper

Slice the beefsteak tomatoes—the biggest and the very best that you can find—and arrange the slices on the crisp greenery on 4 chilled salad plates. Top with the asparagus spears (preferably the all-green ones) and sliced potatoes. Liberally dribble commercial French dressing over all (I like Milani's 1890, which is not "French" at all, if we wish to be accurate), then scatter the crisp garlic croutons on top—these made by sautéeing firm, trimmed bread cubes in oil in which garlic to your taste has mellowed for at least 1 hour. Season the tomatoes with salt and pepper individually at table.

PHILIPPINE food is infrequently found on most North American tables, which is unfortunate, since it is imaginative and by and large most acceptable to our palates. Serve these unique stuffed tomatoes, Manila style, well chilled to accompany pork, chicken, or seafood.

Philippine Stuffed Tomatoes
Serves 3 to 6.

6 medium firm-ripe tomatoes
1½ cups crushed pineapple, drained
1 tablespoon commercial French dressing
½ cup chopped salted peanuts
additional salt to taste
Romaine or other lettuce leaves for base

Skin tomatoes, using your favorite method, then cut off tops and carefully remove seeds. Chill tomato shells for at least 2 hours. Meanwhile, combine the pineapple, French dressing, and chopped salted pea-nuts, and add a bit of extra salt if needed. Chill. When tomatoes are well chilled, carefully stuff them with the pineapple-peanut mixture and chill, until ready to serve on crisp Romaine or other lettuce leaves.

BROILED and baked tomatoes appear in ever so many ways. The simplest versions, to me, seem the best, since they retain the full luscious flavor of the vegetable. Beautiful firm cherry or midget tomatoes are particularly appropriate here, as they have the texture and taste that has been lost in some of the larger modern varieties of the beast.

Here are three pertinent recipes that can accompany almost anything in the meat, fish, or fowl line. Larger tomatoes can, of course, be utilized, but be sure that they are just firm-ripe, and not soft to the touch.

Baked Little Tomatoes

Place 3 or 4 unblemished, firm-ripe cherry or midget tomatoes for each serving in a shallow oven-proof dish. Pour over them about 2 tablespoons good quality olive or peanut oil for each serving, sprinkle with a pinch of thyme or sage or basil or oregano per serving, plus some salt and freshly ground pepper. Carefully shake the tomatoes in the seasoned oil so that they are well coated, and place in preheated 400° F. oven. Bake for 5 or 6 minutes, or until the skins start to split. Do not overcook, and serve immediately.

Little Tomatoes Parmigiana

Cut firm-ripe cherry or midget tomatoes in half, allowing about 3 or 4 tomatoes per serving. Place on cooky sheet and sprinkle the cut surfaces liberally with freshly grated Parmesan cheese. Place under preheated broiler and broil for just a moment, until cheese is melted and bubbly. Serve at once.

THE LAST recipe of the three can be a little time-consuming to prepare, but the results are flamboyant. This can be served as a distinctive hot hors d'oeuvre for luncheon or late supper.

Elegant Little Tomatoes

Allow 3 or 4 unblemished, firm-ripe cherry or midget tomatoes per serving. With a very sharp knife, cut off tops of each one, and, using a melon-ball scoop,

carefully remove the pulp. In a skillet, fry per serving ½ slice lean bacon, diced, until crisp. Drain and combine with the mashed tomato pulp, plus 1 teaspoon grated sharp Cheddar cheese, and a pinch each of salt and freshly ground pepper for each tomato. Stuff each little tomato and place, cut side up, in a well-buttered shallow ovenproof dish. Bake in preheated 400° F. oven for 5 or 6 minutes, or until the cheese has melted and is bubbling. Serve while very hot, on individual fresh toast rounds if desired.

FIRM little cherry or midget tomatoes, fresh from the field or market basket, make exceptional appetizers when stuffed in the following savory fashion. You may, in fact, even wish to make a light meal out of them, accompanied by rolls and a suitable beverage.

Cherry Tomatoes Italienne
Serves 6 to 8.

2 dozen firm-ripe cherry tomatoes
2 hard-cooked eggs, mashed
1 3¼-ounce can white tuna (albacore), drained and flaked
1 teaspoon minced fresh parsley
salt and freshly ground pepper
¼ teaspoon dried basil
2 to 3 tablespoons mayonnaise
3 tablespoons finely chopped pine nuts (pignoli)

Cut off tops of tomatoes, plus a tiny sliver off bottom so they will sit upright. Carefully scoop out pulp and seeds. Thoroughly combine mashed eggs, flaked, drained tuna, parsley, salt and pepper to taste, basil, and mayonnaise. Stuff the tomato shells, and dip their tops in the pine nuts. Chill thoroughly before serving.

TOMATOES figure with considerable prominence in the superb cuisine of many parts of Italy. But the cookery indigenous to the peninsula from about Naples southward, and including the island of Sicily, is often a bit heavy-handed in its use of the tomato. In particular, the sauces offered with the diverse kinds of pasta are inclined to be a bit too tomato-y, particularly those encountered in Italian restaurants in the United States.

Here is my favorite pasta sauce. Though it contains liberal amounts of canned tomatoes, in 4 forms, the end result is a satisfactory smoothness. Though I customarily serve it over spaghettini cooked just al dente, its robust character recommends it for use with such things as lasagne, rigatoni, and the like. The order of addition of ingredients is vital to preparation, please note.

Caterina's Pasta Sauce
Serves 6 to 8.

¼ pound (1 stick) butter
2 tablespoons olive oil
3 to 8 cloves garlic, peeled, mashed
2 cups coarsely chopped onion
¾ cup coarsely chopped green pepper
1 small can tomato paste
1 small can warm water
2 small cans tomato sauce
1 can condensed tomato soup
1 soup can warm water
1 1-pound 12-ounce can Italian-style tomatoes
¼ cup minced fresh parsley
½ cup chopped dried Italian mushrooms (preferably),
   or 2 small cans mushrooms (stems and pieces)
1½ tablespoons sugar
½ to ¾ teaspoon oregano
¼ teaspoon dried basil
2 teaspoons salt
½ teaspoon freshly ground black pepper
1 pound lean ground beef
2 tablespoons light olive oil
1½ pounds lean ground beef
3 tablespoons light olive oil

In a large heavy kettle with cover, melt the butter, add the 2 tablespoons olive oil, and slowly sauté the garlic, onion, and green pepper until they are very limp and starting to brown. Thoroughly combine the tomato paste with the small can warm water, and add this to the kettle, a little at a time, mixing well after each addition. Then add the tomato sauce, tomato soup plus can of water, and can of Italian-style tomatoes, breaking these up. Mix thoroughly and bring the sauce to the simmer. Add parsley, mushrooms (soak the dried ones in a bit of hot water for 15 minutes prior to chopping), sugar, oregano, basil, salt, and black pepper. Reduce heat and allow the sauce to simmer very slowly, covered, stirring occasionally. About 1 hour after starting the sauce, brown the 1 pound ground beef in a skillet with the 2 tablespoons olive oil. Add the meat and its juices to the kettle, mixing well. Continue to simmer sauce for 2 hours more, still covered, stirring often, being careful that it does not stick to the kettle and scorch. After a total of 3 hours' cooking, form the 1½ pounds ground beef into very small, walnut-size balls, and brown them slowly in the 3 tablespoons oil, turning them often and carefully. Add these to the kettle, and allow them to simmer for at least 30 minutes before serving. Serve the sauce and attendant meatballs generously over hot spaghettini or other pasta, offering freshly grated Parmesan or Romano cheese on the side, to be added to individual choice.

TOPI-TAMBO

The Topi-Tambo (*Calathea Allouia,* of the Maranta Family) is an important food plant in many parts of the American tropics, and to a degree in some warm countries in the Old World. Of the numerous vernaculars which are also applied to it, the following are important: Sweet Corn Root, *lerenes* or *llerenes* (Spanish America), *topinambour* or *topi* (Haiti), and *topee-tambu* (Ceylon). The epithet used here is from Trinidad, whence on occasion of late the small white tubers have been imported into large city markets in the United States.

These tubers are much like little egg-shaped potatoes, and are borne on stalks from the underground stem-like rhizome of the plant. The vegetative parts are very attractive, with stalked paddlelike leaves upward of four feet tall, light green above, pale silvery-gray underneath. Produced in large bunches, their stalks often striped with dull red, these leaves are usually prettily wavy-margined, and have long found favor with horticulturists as showy greenhouse or warm-country garden specimens. The flowers, though intricate in structure, are insignificant.

The tubers of the Topi-Tambo were the principal food source of the aboriginal inhabitants of the Antilles, and today the plant is widely cultivated in such islands as Cuba, Hispaniola, and Puerto Rico. The tubers' flavor is bland but pleasant, the texture crisp though often a bit moist.

Topi-Tambos (what a cheery name!) are usually boiled, then scraped and served whole, dressed with butter, salt, and perhaps a touch of grated onion. They can also be incorporated into soups, stews, and the like, but like almost all such tropical tubers, they must never be overcooked as they become mushy with disconcerting rapidity.

The Calatheas, of a large genus of marantads, are very well known to connoisseur greenhouse gardeners in the United States, being cultivated for their spectacular large bunches of leaves, these frequently of striking combinations of color. In some species, the flower spikes are showy as well, and in one kind (*Calathea macrosepala,* called *chufle*) the juvenile flowers with their attendant bracts are fried, usually in a light batter, as an interesting food.

The sometimes immense paddle-shaped leaves of some members of the group are formed into temporary baskets, or shaped into impromptu umbrellas, or used as thatch in their native haunts in the American tropics.

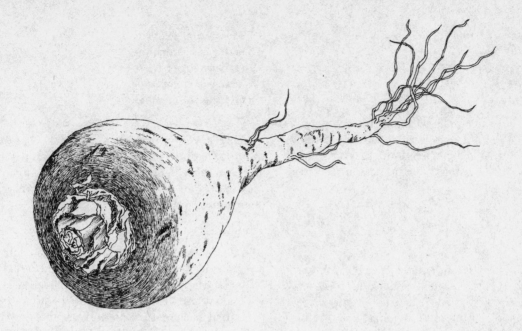

TURNIP

The Turnip is one of our very old vegetables, having been cultivated by man for its edible young leaves and for its tuberous white or purple-white roots for more than four thousand years. Its origins are unknown but are presumably either temperate European or Asiatic. Scientists refer it to the species *Brassica Rapa* (of the Cabbage Family), a distinct entity from the Rutabaga (page 203), which is often known by the inaccurate name of Yellow Turnip.

Known as *navets* in France, Turnips are extremely popular in the elegant French cuisine, being cooked in many inventive fashions that are as yet little known in the United States. Their refreshing flavor is singularly appropriate with such diverse meats as duck or goose, pork, ham, and sausages of almost all kinds.

The finest Turnips appear in our markets during cool weather. Typically offered with their leaves intact, the vegetable is at its best when only a couple of inches in diameter, with firm unblemished skin. The leaves should be used for greens (in the manner described for Boiled Kale, page 129) as promptly as possible. The roots should be peeled and cooked as recommended below. Older, larger winter Turnips may require preliminary blanching in salted water to remove the slight bitterness that is often present.

Turnip greens are especially popular in our Southern states, and excellent canned and frozen versions are now available, oftentimes with diced turnip roots added. The Chinese know these flavorful greens by the musical name of *mu-ching-choi-chai*, and the Japanese call them *kokonoka kubura*.

Turnips can be made into soufflés or timbales; they can be boiled and served with parsley butter; they can be riced or puréed, braised and glazed, and pan-fried in butter. Thin crisp slices are appropriate for inclusion in Japanese Tempura (page 255) or Italian Bagna Cauda (page 72)—or served, well chilled, as a distinctive snack with preprandial beverages. I like Turnips added, in moderation, to hearty vegetable soups, and many stewlike creations have evolved in my kitchen into which their pleasing flavor has been incorporated.

Here is a very simple medley that admirably displays the crisp texture and palate-piquing qualities of this ancient root vegetable. Use only the smallest tenderest Turnips available. And see if you don't find this delicious with roast stuffed chicken.

Turnips Juliette
Serves 4.

1 pound small young turnips
1 pound tiny white onions
2 medium-size green peppers
⅓ to ½ cup butter
salt and pepper to taste

Peel turnips and onions, and with the green peppers, cut into very thin julienne strips. Quickly sauté these in the butter, stirring often, until they are just barely tender yet still distinctly crisp. Season to taste and serve without delay.

TURNIPS, braised in the succulent French style, are often placed in the pan around a duck or piece of pork which is being roasted. The meat's juices are used to give a final basting to the vegetable, and it in turn imparts a degree of its own delicate flavor to the roast.

Braised Turnips
Serves 4.

1 pound small young turnips
3 tablespoons butter
1 cup rich chicken or beef stock
salt and freshly ground pepper

Peel the little turnips and cut them, if desired, into thick slices, halves, or quarters. In a heavy saucepan with tight-fitting cover, melt the butter and heat the stock (preferably fresh) and add turnips to the liquid. Season with a touch of salt and pepper, cover the pot, and cook over medium heat until turnips are just tender but not overcooked, usually about 15 minutes. Serve with additional seasoning at table.

THE CUISINES of the Orient make rather extensive use of the turnip root—it is called *mu-ching* in Chinese, *kubura* or *kabura* in Japanese. The roots are thinly sliced and pickled in a rather piquant soy-flavored sauce. They are cubed or slivered to be added to stir-fried assemblages, with other vegetables and such meats as beef or pork or poultry, much like sukiyaki. Or they are utilized in the following chilled salad, which I offer at home with Chinese-style spare ribs and hot rice.

Turnip Salad
Serves 4.

V. Good

1 pound small young turnips
2 tablespoons sesame oil
1 teaspoon sugar
¼ teaspoon ground ginger
2 tablespoons soy sauce
2 tablespoons cider vinegar

Using a very sharp knife, cut the peeled turnips into the smallest possible slivers. Thoroughly combine all other ingredients, and marinate the turnip bits in the mixture for several hours prior to serving, in small quantities.

WHEN cooked until nicely tender, then run through a potato ricer, turnips may be seasoned rather lightly, butter and cream added, and the whole then blended with equal parts of whipped white potatoes to afford a delightful mélange. Or parboil the roots until barely tender, scoop out their centers, and stuff with diced cooked pork or ham in a white sauce thickened with bread crumbs and containing, if desired, some cooked tiny peas.

Here is a delicious casserole combining turnips and pork, which seem to have an affinity for each other.

Turnips and Pork Kentucky
Serves 4.

1 pound small young turnips
8 lean pork chops, cut ½ inch thick
1 tablespoon lard
1 large onion, thinly sliced
1 can cream of mushroom soup
½ soup can water
salt and pepper to taste

Cut the peeled turnips into slices about ½ inch thick. In a skillet, sauté the pork chops in lard until they are nicely browned on both sides. Remove and keep warm. Drain off most of the fat and sauté the onion, separated into rings, until it is soft. Remove with slotted spoon. In a 1½-quart casserole, arrange a layer of the turnip slices, then a layer of pork chops, then some of the onion rings. Repeat, finishing with onion rings. Combine the mushroom soup and water, and add this to the casserole. Season lightly and bake in preheated 350° F. oven for about 20 minutes, or until turnips are tender.

Lemon Turnips
3 med turnips, peeled + cut into strips
2 T. butter   1 t. chopped onion
1 T. parsley, snipped   1 t. lemon juice

turnips
Cook in small amt. of boiling salted water till crisp. Add chopped onion, parsley, lemon + butter. Toss. Add s + p.

HERE IS a beautifully seasoned Turnip and Pork Pie with an especially fine crust.

Quebec Turnip and Pork Pie
Serves 4 to 6.

1 *pound small young turnips*
2 *slices lean bacon, diced*
1½ *pounds cubed lean pork*
½ *cup finely chopped onion*
½ *cup finely chopped celery*
1 *large clove garlic, mashed*
2 *tablespoons flour*
1 *cup rich beef stock*
1 *teaspoon salt*
½ *teaspoon chervil*
¼ *teaspoon mace*
1 *small bay leaf, crumbled*
Pastry (see recipe below)
1 *tablespoon butter, melted*

Peel turnips, and cut into smallish cubes. In a large skillet, over low heat, lightly brown the bacon. Add pork cubes, onion, celery, and garlic. Cook, stirring often, until meat is lightly browned. Add cubed turnip, sprinkle flour over the top, and mix. Add beef stock, salt, chervil, mace, and bay leaf, mix again, and cook slowly until the mixture thickens. Cover and cook slowly for 30 minutes. Allow to cool for 10 minutes. Roll one of the pastry balls into a circle an inch larger than the top of a 9-inch pie plate; line plate with this crust. For top crust, roll remaining pastry ½-inch larger than the pie plate, and make several small slashes in center of crust. Fill the crust-lined plate with turnip-pork mixture. Moisten crust rim; cover with top crust, fold edges under, and flute edge. If desired, decorate with pastry leaves. Brush with melted butter. Bake in preheated 425° F. oven for 15 minutes, then reduce heat to 350° F. and bake for about 25 minutes. Serve while piping hot.

Turnip Pork Pie Pastry
Makes crust for one 9-inch pie.

2 *cups sifted flour*
1 *teaspoon salt*
⅔ *cup lard*
1 *egg, beaten*
2 *tablespoons water*

Sift flour and salt into mixing bowl; cut in lard with pastry blender or two knives. Add egg and water; mix until dry ingredients are moistened. Form into two balls; use as directed in above recipe.

UDO

The Udo is *Aralia cordata,* an attractive member of the Ivy or Aralia Family. Extensively cultivated in its native Japan.

Udo is a very pretty plant, attaining heights from four to eight feet, shrubby in habit, with masses of intricately cut vivid-green foliage. It is cultivated as an ornamental to a small degree in temperate parts of this country.

Introduced into the United States by Barbour Lathrop and David Fairchild in 1903, Udo was given considerable enthusiastic publicity by the latter great horticulturist in his various publications. Despite his affection for it, today the plant is grown only by select gourmet gardeners, and by some Japanese in California who raise small quantities of the stocky young shoots, blanched artificially during growth, for their own markets.

The shoots of Udo have a fairly positive flavor of turpentine, which may in part explain its lack of acceptance by the Occidental cook here. But this can be dispelled by boiling the stalks in salted water for ten minutes or so, then refrigerating in ice water for a couple of hours. The vegetable, thus prepared, is crisp and delicious when reheated and served hot with butter and seasonings (including a touch of Japanese soy sauce, and if desired, a modicum of sake or dry sherry); or thinly sliced and left chilled, it may be used as a salad ingredient.

Another kind of aralia, the Chinese Angelica Tree (*Aralia chinensis*), which grows up to forty feet tall, with a somewhat prickly trunk and large multiparted attractive leaves, is cultivated to some extent in the Orient, not only as a desirable ornamental, but for the burgeoning juvenile leaves, which are eaten, after boiling in several changes of water, as a vegetable, usually with rice or in soups.

UNG-CHOI

Ung-choi is a member of the same genus as sweet potato, known botanically as *Ipomoea reptans* (Morning-Glory Family). In Hawaii this plant, from India and China, is known as Swamp Cabbage, a name which in the mainland United States is generally applied to the aroid *Spathyema foetida* (also known as Skunk Cabbage).

The Chinese are very fond of Ung-choi, cutting the apical sprouts of the aquatic fleshy vine into pieces about three inches in length, then rapidly cooking them in a bit of peanut or soy oil, to be served without delay, lightly seasoned with salt or soy sauce.

WASABI

Wasabi (*Eutrema Wasabi,* of the Cabbage Family) is a rather ornamental perennial plant of Japan, where it has long been cultivated for its fleshy roots. These are grated after drying to make a delectable and powerfully hot condiment, known either by the Nipponese vernacular or as Japanese Horseradish.

The desiccated powder is available, happily, in many specialty shops in this country, and in my opinion should be present in every good kitchen. The powder is mixed with a small amount of water to make a smooth paste of an attractive green hue. It is used—with discretion—with all sorts of foods, from appetizers to ornate main dishes.

One of my favorite culinary authors, Paula Peck, recommends draining ordinary commercial bottled horseradish of its liquid, blending in a bit of Wasabi paste, and using the delicate green result. A felicitous suggestion, indeed, and one which immediately became a staple condiment in my house when I heard of it.

Here is a superb Wasabi dipping sauce for such things as Japanese-style raw fish (*sashimi*), or *sushi* or tempura or fried shrimp or broiled lobster.

Wasabi Dipping Sauce
Makes enough.

2 teaspoons wasabi powder
½ cup Japanese soy sauce
4 teaspoons sake
2 teaspoons sugar

Blend a small amount of water into the wasabi powder to make a smooth paste. In a saucepan, combine all other ingredients, and simmer for 3 or 4 minutes. Remove from heat and allow to cool. Gradually blend the soy sauce mixture into the wasabi paste, and serve as a dip.

WATER CHESTNUT

The Chinese Water Chestnut (*Eleocharis dulcis,* of the Sedge Family) has long been cultivated, particularly in rice paddies, in the Orient and parts of Southeast Asia. The name Water Chestnut has also been applied to the Jesuits' Nut, a totally different plant (see page 127). The "chestnuts" are the roundish, flat-based tubers of a rather nondescript-looking kind of rush. Known in Chinese as *ma-tai,* and in Japanese as *kuro-kuwai,* these little corms have a dull or glossy brown or ebony skin and firm white flesh.

The fresh vegetables are encountered on occasion in specialized markets in Hawaii and California, principally from July to the end of September, and are indeed worth searching out. But when they are not available, the excellent canned ones, packed in water, are to be found on every good grocer's shelves as imports from Hong Kong or Japan. Water Chestnuts are favorite, essential ingredients in a wide array of famous dishes of the Far East.

After peeling or draining, the tubers are either cut into thin slices or quartered or diced. They possess a crisp texture which is largely retained even after the brief cooking to which the vegetable should always be subjected, and the distinctive nutty flavor adapts admirably to a tremendous variety of kitchen creations.

I like to add wafer-thin slices or tiny dice of Water Chestnut to tossed green salads, at the last moment prior to the dressing, or to a clear consommé or other clear soup, toward the end of cooking.

THERE ARE many other things we can do with the Water Chestnut. Consider the following unusual little meatballs, to be offered, hot and savory, as an appetizer. Keep them warm in a chafing dish—they are not very good when cold.

Water Chestnut Meatballs
Makes about 2 dozen.

3 tablespoons finely diced water chestnuts
1 pound lean ground beef
2 tablespoons peanut or soy oil
2 tablespoons minced onion
1 small clove garlic, mashed
¼ teaspoon grated fresh ginger root
2 tablespoons brown sugar
¼ teaspoon monosodium glutamate
3 tablespoons sake or cooking sherry
½ cup Japanese soy sauce

Thoroughly combine the ground beef with the water-chestnut dice and form into balls about the size of large marbles. In a large shallow skillet heat the oil and in it sauté the onion and garlic, stirring often, until they are browned. Combine the ginger root, brown sugar, monosodium glutamate, sake or sherry, and soy sauce, and allow to stand for an hour or so, stirring occasionally. Remove onion and garlic from oil with slotted spoon, and add them to the soy-sake mixture. In the seasoned oil, fry the tiny meatballs, a few at a time, until they are well browned on all sides. As they brown, remove them and keep them warm. When all the meatballs are done, drain off excess fat, then return meatballs to the skillet, and pour the sauce over them. Simmer the meatballs, uncovered, for 20 to 30 minutes, carefully shaking them from time to time in the sauce. Serve balls warm, in the sauce, skewered on picks.

ONE OF the best known Polynesian appetizers is Rumaki, a luscious concoction of water chestnut and chicken livers wrapped in bacon, then broiled to succulent perfection. Here is a special version of Rumaki, one involving a felicitous marinating process, which was created by Edward A. Flickinger, South Florida's renowned tropical horticulturist, who is a marvelous, inventive amateur chef as well.

Ed's Rumaki
Serves 6 to 8.

> 1 *small can water chestnuts*
> ½ *pound fresh chicken livers*
> 6 to 8 *slices lean bacon, halved and cut lengthwise*
> 1 *cup milk*
> *toothpicks or cocktail picks*

Rinse chicken livers and cut each in half. Rinse again. Cut drained water chestnuts into halves or quarters. Wrap a piece of water chestnut and half of a chicken liver as firmly as possible with a thin strip of bacon, and impale with a pick. Marinate the rumaki in the milk, under refrigeration, for 3 to 4 hours. At serving time, drain rumaki very thoroughly, and broil rather close to the flame under preheated broiler or over a good bed of charcoal until the bacon is rather crisp—usually about ten minutes. Serve immediately as a hot hors d'oeuvre.

ANOTHER delicious variation of rumaki utilizes water chestnuts but substitutes fresh chunks of pineapple for the chicken livers. This is not marinated in milk, but otherwise is treated as Mr. Flickinger's recipe, above.

AND THEN, please consider the following simple and delectable water chestnut creation.

Water Chestnut Biscuits

Cut drained canned water chestnuts into tiny dice and place into split fresh-baked buttermilk biscuits, which have been bountifully buttered and lightly sprinkled with sharp Cheddar cheese. Pop these back into a preheated oven until the cheese has melted and serve at once, especially with roast meats or stews.

HERE IS an exceptional and exceptionally easy casserole that well illustrates the qualities of the water chestnut. Accompany with a cool salad of chilled thinly sliced peeled oranges, on shredded lettuce, with perhaps Thousand Island Dressing, hot rolls, and your favorite beverage.

Water Chestnut-Tuna Casserole
Serves 4 to 6.

> 1 *7-ounce can water chestnuts*
> 2 *7-ounce cans white tuna (albacore)*
> 1 *3-ounce can crisp chow mein noodles*
> 1 *can condensed cream of mushroom soup*
> ¼ *cup coarsely chopped salted cashews*
> ⅓ *cup finely chopped scallions, with tops*
> *salt and pepper to taste*

Drain water chestnuts and slice thin, or dice coarsely. Drain tuna and flake it. Reserve about 3 tablespoons of chow mein noodles. Lightly combine all other ingredients, and turn into a buttered 1-

quart casserole. Sprinkle with reserved crisp noodles and bake uncovered in preheated 350° F. oven for 40 minutes.

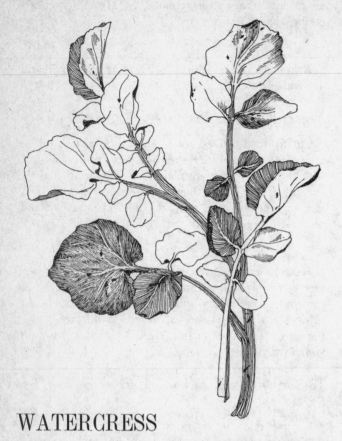

WATERCRESS

Cress, in culinary parlance, is applied to several different kinds of plants with edible, pungent foliage, all members of the botanically very complicated Crucifer Family. In various parts of the world at least five totally distinct species of plants are known as Cress. In the United States the best known of these is Watercress (usually called *Roripa Nasturtium,* though even this scientific epithet is controversial), a hardy perennial herb which grows often partially submerged in fresh, running streams. Though originating in Europe, it is now extensively naturalized in North and Central America. (See also Cress, page 99.)

Watercress frequently appears in our markets, sold in tight bunches of crisp succulent stems set with crunchy little leaves. It should be purchased only when it is a bright vivid green—yellowing indicates staleness—and very firm to the touch. I always untie the bunches as soon as possible after I get them home, and wash them in ice water. Then I shake off as much moisture as possible and wrap the Watercress in a clean towel, to be refrigerated until use—which should be within a day or two.

Seed of Watercress is available from several domes-

tic sources, but the culinary gardener must remember that this plant requires fresh, cool, moving water and very rich soil to succeed.

Watercress has been used in fine cookery since ancient times. In fact, the old Greeks believed that if eaten in quantities with vinegar, it was a sure cure for a deranged mind! And if one nibbled its fresh, crispy leaves while drinking, the imbiber would remain sober. Whether these old tales are valid or not, the vegetable is very rich in minerals and in vitamins A and C.

Watercress is all too often relegated to the position of a garnish with steaks and other meats—and often remains uneaten. It should not be so neglected, for its crispness is a perfect accompaniment to red meat, and it figures in some superb culinary delicacies in its own right.

THOUGH generally only the little leaves are utilized, the stems, if small and young, can readily be added to all of the dishes here discussed. If, by chance, one's garden brook boasts of a large rich planting of Watercress, then consider this gourmet's showpiece:

Bill Straight's Watercress

Wash thoroughly a considerable quantity of fresh watercress—at least a pound—then drain. Chop coarsely, using both stems and leaves, and steam, covered, in a very small amount of lightly salted water, until just wilted and still firm-textured. Drain off all moisture and serve at once, dressed liberally with butter, with additional salt plus freshly ground pepper to taste.

WATERCRESS sandwiches have elegant Victorian overtones, yet are relished even in these hectic times by many connoisseurs. Crisp the leaves and smallest stems in ice water, drain, dry with absorbent paper towels, and chill until the last possible moment. Spread sweet butter liberally on thin slices of firm white bread, trimmed of their crusts. Arrange watercress leaves in abundance on the buttered bread, top with second buttered slice, and cut into triangles. Serve without delay.

ANOTHER exceptional sandwich made with this luscious green is the following European one:

Watercress-Cheese Sandwiches

Slice fresh Roquefort or Stilton cheese rather thickly, and put between trimmed slices of buttered firm-textured white bread, with a thick layer of fresh crisp watercress. Accompany with a fine ripe pear and a glass or two of your favorite chilled wine.

ONE OF my favorite places in this hemisphere is the province of Chiriquí, in western Panama. The scenery is spectacular, the botanizing is consistently fascinating, and the rustic little mountain hostelries so favored by visitors from the Canal Zone offer extraordinarily good food. Watercress grows in abundance in many of the frigid rushing streams, and one of the specialties of the region is the following superb soup utilizing it to excellent advantage.

Watercress Soup Chiriquí
Serves 4 to 6.

2 *bunches fresh watercress, washed and drained*
2 *cans condensed cream of celery soup*
2 *soup cans milk*
2 *tablespoons chopped scallions, with tops*
1 *tablespoon lime peel*
salt and freshly ground white pepper

Reserve enough sprigs of washed watercress for garnishing each serving. In your electric blender, place the remaining watercress, the soup, milk, scallions, lime peel, plus salt and white pepper to taste (be rather liberal here). Run blender for 1 minute at high speed, but no longer. Chill thoroughly, and serve in chilled cups or bowls with reserved watercress sprigs as garnish.

AS A SALAD, well-crisped leaves of watercress patted dry are ideally served with the simplest of additions— just several grinds from the pepper mill, or, if desired, a very light dressing of top-quality oil and vinegar with pepper at the final moment.

Here, too, is a marvelous combination of crisp watercress with chilled seedless or seeded oranges. This is particularly tasty with beef (pot roast to grilled hamburgers), lamb in any form, or chicken, especially broiled.

Watercress-Orange Salad
Serves 4.

1 *large bunch fresh watercress*
3 *firm oranges, chilled*
salad dressing of your choice
freshly ground black pepper to taste

Thoroughly wash and drain the watercress, discard any coarse stems, and pat dry the leaves and tiny stems to chill until serving time. When ready to assemble the salad, peel the chilled oranges, slice them into very thin crosswise slices, and discard any seeds. Arrange slices on individual chilled salad plates and scatter with crisp watercress. Use your favorite salad dressing (a good piquant vinaigrette or one of the commercial "French" dressings, for instance) and freshly ground pepper to taste. Serve without delay.

OUR FRIENDS in France do some very fine things with watercress, including the following remarkable biscuits. Their distinctive flavor is good with fish and shellfish, sautéed veal, and veal roast. Consider them, too, with seafood or fowl salad for that party luncheon.

Watercress Biscuits
Makes a dozen.

⅔ *cup finely chopped watercress leaves and stems*
2 *cups sifted bread flour*
3 *teaspoons baking powder*
½ *teaspoon salt*
dash Cayenne pepper
½ *teaspoon onion juice*
5 *tablespoons melted butter*
¾ *cup milk (about)*

Sift together the flour, baking powder, salt, and Cayenne. In a dry towel, gently press out moisture from the finely chopped watercress (use only the small tender stems with the foliage). Then blend the cress thoroughly with the flour mixture. Combine the onion juice, melted butter, and part of the milk, and add to the flour mixture, using enough milk to make a soft dough. Roll this out on a floured pastry board until it is just about ½ inch thick. Flour a biscuit cutter, and cut dough into rounds. Place these on an ungreased baking sheet and bake in preheated 450° F. oven for about 12 minutes, or until the biscuits have become nicely browned on top. Serve while very hot.

ORIENTAL cooks, who fully appreciate so many kinds of vegetables and treat them with the tender care they deserve, are fond of watercress. In Chinese, it is known as *sai-yong-choi*, in Japanese as *kawara-chisa*. Here is an unusual recipe from Hawaii, to be served as a special course at your next Far Eastern feast. The dried jujubes, the fruits of the tree *Zizyphus mauritiana*, also known as red dates or *hong-cho*, are available in select Chinese stores.

Chinese Watercress Pork
Serves 4.

   2 *large bunches watercress*
   1½ *pounds lean pork*
   1 *teaspoon peanut or soy oil*
   ½ *teaspoon minced fresh ginger root*
   ½ *teaspoon salt*
   1 *quart water*
   6 *dried jujubes*

Thoroughly wash and drain the watercress. Break or cut into 2-inch lengths. Thinly slice the pork. Using a heavy kettle with cover, heat the oil over rather high flame, add the ginger root and salt, and the pork strips. Stir-fry the pork for about 3 minutes, then add the water and the jujubes. Lower heat, cover the kettle, and cook for 1 hour. Add the watercress and cook for 5 minutes. Serve while very hot, with steamed rice.

WATER DROPWORT

Belonging to the same family, Water Dropwort (*Oenanthe stolonifera*) somewhat resembles juvenile plants of celery. Its root system, however, is fibrous, and the stems up to a yard tall are connected by underground—or underwater, since the plant is normally an aquatic in nature—stolons.

A native of the Mediterranean area, including northern Africa and Asia Minor, the plant has long been cultivated in such places as Vietnam, China, and Japan. It is grown to some extent today in Hawaii, where bunches of its pretty green leaves (often with the roots, also edible, attached) are found in markets with frequency.

The juvenile shoots and growths are customarily blanched quickly in boiling water, then allowed to cool in the liquid. Roots, stems, and foliage are cut or broken into smallish lengths and added to chicken or fish soup. Since the flavor of the Water Dropwort—also known as *sui-kan* in Chinese, as *seri* in Japanese—is quite positive, only a half-dozen or so bits of the cooked vegetable should be added to each serving of the soup.

The Water Parsley of our Pacific Northwest is another species of *Oenanthe* (*O. sarmentosa*). It produces smallish black-skinned tubers which, when boiled, have long been relished by the Indians of the region for their sweet, creamlike texture and flavor.

WATER PENNYWORT

The Water Pennywort group (genus *Hydrocotyle*, of the Carrot Family) is a sizable one, widespread in temperate and tropical parts of the world, often growing in moist or boggy spots. The usually creeping stems produce small, round, rich green leaves, often like diminutive umbrellas, and clusters of tiny, mostly whitish, flowers.

At least one species of Water Pennywort, *Hydrocotyle asiatica*, of tropical Asia, is cultivated to some degree for its leaves, which are eaten either raw or lightly cooked in salted water, and usually served with rice. Their flavor is fresh and rather pungent.

WEST INDIAN GHERKIN

The Gherkins of our North American stores are tiny cucumbers of a special variety. The West Indian Gherkin is another species of the same genus, *Cucumis Anguria* (Squash Family). Also known as Bur Cucumber and Gooseberry Gourd, this slender, rough vine is grown to some extent in the warm parts of the United States.

These fruits, used as a vegetable, measure only one to three inches in length, are borne on a slender elongate stalk, and are reminiscent of a fat, blunt-end cuke, pale green when young, but becoming lemon-yellow with maturity. The Gherkins are more or less copiously set with flexible spines up to a quarter-inch in length. The flesh is usually greenish, with numerous small smooth white seeds.

When very young, only an inch or so in length, the vegetables are added, whole or halved, to soups in such places as Jamaica. Or they are boiled, then offered hot with butter and seasonings, which include rather liberal dashes of hot pepper sauce. In the West Indies the mature Gherkins are pickled exactly as our domestic cucumber pickles are.

Though West Indian Gherkin is the generally accepted common name for this cucurbit, research has shown that it is of African origin. It was probably introduced into this hemisphere during the period when slaves were brought from the Dark Continent, and has long been considered an indigene to this part of the world.

WHEAT, BULGUR

Wheat is one of the extremely ancient grains, having been cultivated in its myriad variants by man for countless centuries. As we know it today, it includes descendants of several kinds of grasses, of the genus *Triticum*. The nomenclature of the Wheats is very complex and confusing, but for our casual attention at this time we should consider the Common Wheat (*Triticum vulgare*), the Durum Wheat (*T. durum*), the Spelt Wheat (*T. Spelta*), and the Poulard Wheat (*T. turgidum*).

The kernels—the seeds—of all of these grasses are prepared in many fashions, both before and after roasting and grinding into flours of various degrees of fineness. From them most of our breads and other bakery products, as well as the majority of our pasta and breakfast foods, arise. Beers and various alcoholic beverages are also prepared from special forms of Wheat.

Bulgur, or Bulghour, is the parched, crushed seed of the Common Wheat (*Triticum vulgare*, of the Grass Family). It is extremely important in the cuisine of most Near and Middle Eastern lands, and today is readily available here in many markets and health-food stores. With its delicious nutlike flavor and interesting texture, it has gained many fans in this country outside of the Arabic colonies where it is eaten often, almost daily. Persons of Arab extraction know it under the name *burghol*.

One of my favorite ways with this nutritious, tasty grain is in an elegant pie made from kibby (or kibbee), the national dish of Syria and Lebanon. I first encountered this in Jamaica, where Mrs. H. Haddad of the metropolis of Highgate sent it along for our adjudication at the National Culinary Arts Competition in which I had the privilege of participating. I like to serve it with Syrian Spinach Salad (page 217), and iced tea, with the wonderful puffy Arab bread rounds now to be found in many of our stores.

Lamb can, of course, be substituted for beef, though it seldom appears in the Jamaican version.

Bulgur Kibby Pie Haddad
Serves 8.

2 cups bulgur
2 pounds lean beef, finely chopped
⅓ cup finely chopped green pepper
3 sprigs fresh parsley
½ cup chopped onion
2 teaspoons salt
¼ teaspoon black pepper
¼ teaspoon cinnamon
cracked ice
2 tablespoons peanut or soy oil
½ cup minced onion
1½ pounds lean ground beef
salt and pepper to taste
¾ cup peanut or soy oil

Rinse the bulgur in cold water and drain thoroughly. Mix well with listed ingredients through cinnamon, using your hands, and run twice through the fine grid of a food mill. Moisten with some cracked ice and knead well. Meanwhile, in a smallish skillet, heat the 2 tablespoons oil, and over medium flame cook the onion and ½ pound ground beef, with seasonings to taste, until onion is almost tender and meat is crumbly. In a greased 9-inch cake pan with low edge, spread a layer of the ground bulgur-beef mixture (kibby). Press this down to a thickness of ½ inch. Place the cooked ground beef stuffing on top, ½ inch away from the sides, spreading it evenly and pressing it down with fingers. Top with remaining kibby, and press this down very evenly. Cut into 8 equal wedges, and pour the ¾ cup oil over. Bake in preheated 450° F. oven for 1 hour, and serve either hot or warm.

BULGUR is utilized in a great many fashions in the Arabic kitchen. Kibby *neeyee*, or raw kibby, is a savory combination of the rinsed bulgur with ground lamb or beef, this uncooked, plus grated or ground onion, and seasonings and oil to taste. Distinctive additions are often made to this unique medley—chopped sautéed pine nuts (pignoli) or almonds or filberts or walnuts, or yoghurt and/or cinnamon. Frequently the raw kibby is made into balls or football-shaped portions, these eaten variously as appetizers or as part of the elegant multicourse repasts that characterize the cuisine of the Arabic lands.

HERE IS a sumptuous salad made with cooked bulgur that I find delightful. Though it is particularly recommended for use with shish kebabs and such things, I find it very acceptable with steaks or broiled hamburgers or lamb patties as well.

Bulgur Salad Aqaba
Serves 4 to 6.

1½ cups bulgur

3 *tablespoons butter*
2 *cups water*
¼ *cup light olive oil*
2 *tablespoons lemon juice*
¼ *teaspoon dried mustard*
¾ *teaspoon salt*
¼ *teaspoon freshly ground pepper*
½ *teaspoon grated lemon rind*
2 *teaspoons finely snipped chives*
1 *cup shredded lettuce*
1 *cup chopped fresh orange pulp*

In a sizable skillet with cover, over rather high heat, brown the bulgur in the butter, stirring constantly. Stir in the water, bring to the boil, cover the skillet, and simmer for 15 minutes. Uncover skillet and toss bulgur for a few seconds over heat so that it dries out—but do not overcook it. Remove from heat and allow to cool. Meanwhile, make a dressing by thoroughly mixing together the oil, lemon juice, dried mustard, salt, pepper, lemon rind, and chives. Turn cooked bulgur into a bowl, and chill for 1 hour, turning the kernels occasionally with a fork. At serving time mix in the thoroughly blended dressing, with lettuce and orange pulp. Serve at once.

WILD RICE

Wild Rice, despite its name, is a plant totally removed from ordinary rice. Both are grasses, but this is a wild species known by the fancy botanists as *Zizania palustris*. Perennial in habit, it is native along the margins of lakes and ponds in the north-central portions of North America, with an allied species found in similar habitats in northern Asia.

Our indigenous plant, also known as Indian Rice or Water Oats, is an attractive aquatic with stems up to nine feet tall, which during their season produce large terminal panicles somewhat like airy candelabra, hung with the seeds. These seeds are relished by waterfowl as much as by humans.

Wild Rice is largely gathered in Minnesota and Wisconsin, where by law it can only be harvested by the Indians in the old-time way—by paddling through the marshes in a canoe, bending the grass over the boat, and beating the kernels into it. In recent times attempts are being made (by a packager of Chinese convenience foods) to cultivate it. Wild Rice is available in many of our specialized food shops, and the price of small packages in which it is sold can cause a serious shock to one's wallet. But, when cooked, the little grains expand measurably, so that a small quantity of the dried product goes a long way.

My late culinary colleague, G. A. Jagerson, of Neenah, Wisconsin, was an expert with this extravagant delicacy. He recommended washing the grains very thoroughly—three or four times—and cooking them until they split open to expose the white inner portions. He believed, as do I, that one should use Wild Rice with loving care, tampering little with the delicate flavor of this exotic grain.

Mr. Jagerson considered the following simple Wild Rice Casserole "excellent for use with any game meats, especially wild duck. To accompany it, I prefer a tossed green salad with orange slices and crisp raw onion rings. And for dessert, how about Peaches Melba?"

Wild Rice Casserole
Serves 4 to 6.

1 *cup wild rice*
¼ *pound (1 stick) butter*
⅓ *cup chopped onion*
½ *cup chopped green pepper*
½ *pound sliced fresh mushrooms*
½ *cup slivered almonds*
3 to 4 *cups duck (or chicken) broth*
salt and white pepper to taste

In a large skillet, melt the butter and in it sauté the onion, stirring often, for about 5 minutes. Add the green pepper and continue to cook until onion is yellow. Add the mushrooms and almonds, and cook, stirring carefully and often, for about 5 minutes more. Add the thoroughly washed wild rice, plus the broth, mix well, and turn into an ovenproof casserole. Cover this and bake in preheated 325° F. oven for 1 hour, stirring occasionally. Add more broth as needed. When the rice is done, remove the casserole cover for a few minutes prior to taking dish from the oven.

HERE IS a superb blending of the rich yet delicate flavors of wild rice and fresh chicken livers. I would serve this with individual little heads of Bibb lettuce, with oil and vinegar to taste, and a chilled bottle of a fine dry white wine.

Wild Rice with Chicken Livers
Serves 4.

1 cup wild rice
⅛ teaspoon dried thyme
2 tablespoons chopped fresh parsley
3 cups rich chicken broth
1 pound fresh chicken livers
¼ pound (1 stick) butter
salt and freshly ground white pepper to taste
additional butter

In a large skillet with cover, combine the washed wild rice with the thyme, parsley, and chicken broth. Cover and cook over low heat, stirring frequently, until rice is just done. In another skillet, sauté the chicken livers quickly in butter until done to taste. Gently combine the wild rice with the chicken livers and butter, season to taste, turn into a casserole, dot with additional butter, and bake, covered, in preheated 325° F. oven for 30 minutes, removing lid of casserole for final 5 minutes or so.

WILD RICE as a stuffing is fantastically savory. It can be used in almost anything stuffable, from Cornish game hens or duck (wild or otherwise) to lamb chops.

Wild Rice Stuffing

1 cup wild rice
¼ pound (1 stick) butter
1½ cups minced onion
1 teaspoon ground sage
2 tablespoons minced parsley
½ cup chopped green celery leaves
4 cups rich stock (beef, duck, chicken, etc.)
salt and freshly ground pepper to taste
1 ounce sweet vermouth

In a large heavy skillet with cover, sauté the onion in the butter, stirring often, until it takes on color. Add sage, parsley, and celery leaves, and cook for 3 to 5 minutes more, stirring often. Add the thoroughly washed wild rice, rich stock, seasonings to taste, and sweet vermouth, mix well, and simmer, covered, for 40 minutes, or until rice is done and liquid is absorbed.

HERE IS a bit of a fillip your guests might enjoy with this costly but lovely delicacy.

Popped Wild Rice

2 cups wild rice
deep fat
salt

Thoroughly wash the rice, then drain it, and dry each kernel completely. Heat a quantity of deep fat to 375° F. and drop the rice, 2 tablespoons at a time, into it to cook until it pops. Drain on paper towels, salt lightly, and serve while hot.

FINALLY we have wild rice incorporated into an Oriental creation, Mr. Jiggs Jagerson's superb version of *yok chow fon*. He notes that a great many standard recipes for regular rice are nicely adapted to use with the wild cousin. And that "the door is always open for adaptations, especially in the realm of seafood, as the tastes are all on the quiet side, and complement rather than overpower each other."

Yok Chow Fon Jagerson
Serves 6.

4 cups cold cooked wild rice
3 tablespoons peanut or soy oil
4 scallions, with tops, chopped
2 cups thinly sliced Chinese cabbage or Swiss chard
1 tablespoon finely chopped fresh ginger root
½ pound Chinese roast pork, diced
salt and pepper to taste
Mei Yen seasoning powder to taste
½ teaspoon sugar
2 tablespoons Japanese soy sauce
3 eggs, beaten
½ cup chopped fresh parsley

In a wok or other type of shallow large skillet, heat the oil to high degree and add the scallions and rice, mixing well and cooking until heated through. Add the Chinese cabbage or Swiss chard, and stir-fry the mixture for 4 minutes. Add the ginger and diced Chinese pork (this available from your local Oriental restaurant or specialty food market), with salt and pepper, Mei Yen, sugar, and soy sauce. Stir well, heat through, and then make a hole in the mixture, adding the beaten eggs. Fry for 3 minutes, and mix thoroughly through the rice. Serve at once, sprinkled with the chopped parsley.

YAM

In this country, the word Yam has long been used as a synonym for sweet potato, the two names being oddly interchangeable in most areas. This is unfortunate and confusing, since the true tropical Yams —totally distinctive vines producing diverse, delicious underground (and above-ground) tubers—have long been found in our Latin American and Oriental markets, and today are increasingly to be found in general supermarkets.

The true Yams are referable to the fascinating genus *Dioscorea* (of the Dioscorea Family), an assemblage of some 250 species and numberless horticultural variants, mostly from the warm countries of the world. The vines twine clockwise, often have strongly angled or winged stems, and support dense, glossy, pretty leaves varying from heart-shaped to several-lobed. Some of these plants are grown as ornamentals, and a considerable number are cultivated extensively as food. Interestingly enough, some produce abundant tubers well up the stems, giving them the apt vernacular of Air Potato; these are rather reminiscent of common white potatoes. These aerial tubers are edible, although often so bitter that they require cooking in several changes of water.

The Dioscoreas most important to us are those producing subterranean tubers. In some of these the oblong tubers measure only a few inches in length and weigh but a pound or so. These have white or yellowish flesh, and when properly prepared, in the opinion of many of us who enjoy them, they excel the finest of white potatoes. The best varieties (very little critical development of choice kinds has been done here, despite the importance of the group) are known as *ñame* (pronounced *nyah*-may) in Cuba and Puerto Rico, *yampi* or *yampie* in Jamaica and Panama, and *cush-cush* in Trinidad and Guyana.

Then there is the prodigious Giant or White Yam, today widely cultivated in the tropics under a wealth of other names. This is a showy profuse vine (*Dioscorea alata* and variants) with underground tubers weighing as much as one hundred pounds, and attaining lengths of more than eight feet! The texture and flavor of most of these forms are inferior to those of their smaller brethren, but they are important food plants, often encountered in native markets from the Antilles to India.

Other large-tuber kinds of Yams include the Oriental or Chinese Yam—also known as Chinese Potato, Cinnamon Vine, *tai-sue* (Chinese), or *nagaimo* (Japanese)—with cylindrical, oblong, often irregular roots up to two feet long and six inches thick. Their outermost skin is gray or blackish, the inner one purple, and the flesh is white and rather moist. These very flavorful Yams are often to be found today in markets in Hawaii, California, and New York.

Yams can be utilized in all ways recommended for potatoes and other such tubers. Roasted or baked, boiled, steamed, or fried, they are nutritious and extremely adaptable vegetables, and they well warrant more extensive attention from good cooks in this country. Some of the selected types of small Yams boast of a mealy texture and a subtle nutlike flavor, and even the very large, rather coarse kinds have a definite valued place in tropical cuisine. Choose your Yams with care, and pursue their preparation with interest.

IN THE lovely islands of St. Kitts and Nevis, tiny tasty Yam Chips are served at every table with beer or cocktails. I can only wish that some enterprising entrepreneur would make them generally available for this purpose in the United States.

Yam Chips

Peel and slice raw yam tissue-thin, in pieces about an inch across. Soak for 2 to 3 hours in cold salted water. Drain and thoroughly pat dry with paper towels. Just before serving, drop a few at a time into a quantity of smoking-hot deep fat, lard, or oil, to fry until golden-brown. Drain thoroughly, sprinkling with coarse salt while hot.

CONSIDER the following Yam Poofs, which are especially acceptable as hot appetizers or snacks. Again, they owe their pleasant origin to the West Indies. Fry them in deep lard for optimum effect.

Yam Poofs
Makes dozens.

> 4 cups finely grated raw yam
> 2 egg yolks
> 1 tablespoon dark rum
> 1 tablespoon finely snipped chives
> 2 teaspoons salt
> ½ teaspoon freshly ground pepper
> deep hot lard for frying

Peel yam and rinse, then grate, using finest grid. Lightly beat the egg yolks and blend them into yam with rum, chives, salt, and pepper. Beat thoroughly with a rotary beater for a minute or so. Heat a quantity of lard—there must be enough to float the poofs —and drop teaspoons of yam batter into it. Fry, a few at a time, until nicely browned, remove and drain on paper towels, to serve while hot.

HERE IS a Jamaican casserole made with yams— preferably the smallish ones called *yampis* there—

which is perfectly delectable with such things as chicken, pork, or beef.

Yam Scallop
Serves 4.

> 1 pound small yams
> 2 medium onions, thinly sliced
> salt and freshly ground pepper
> 2 teaspoons flour
> butter
> 2 cups Coconut Cream (page 254)

Peel the yams, cut them into slices ¼ inch thick, and immediately place in salted water to soak for 1 hour. Butter a baking dish liberally, and in it put a layer of drained yam slices, then a layer of onion slices, then sprinkle rather liberally with salt and pepper, and with part of the flour. Repeat layers, dotting top heavily with butter. Gently pour the coconut cream over. Bake in preheated 350° F. oven until yams are tender and lightly browned on top.

THE SPANISH word *buñuelo* (boon-yoo-*el*-oh) is variously translated "fritter" or "patty" or even "doughnut." All the tropical root vegetables are variously used in their preparation in different parts of the Americas, and especially in the Caribbean islands these tasties are commonly offered for sale, piping hot, by curbside vendors.

A favorite version is made with the true yam or *ñame*. These delights are most often served as a sweet snack or as a dessert. Dust with sugar (granulated or confectioners'), or offer while very hot with some honey or melted guava jelly poured over them. Messy but good.

Ñame Buñuelos
Makes about a dozen.

> 1 pound small yams
> 2 quarts salted water
> 4 tablespoons butter
> 2 tablespoons light cream
> 6 tablespoons flour
> 1 egg, beaten well
> ½ teaspoon salt
> 2 teaspoons sugar
> lard for frying

Peel the yams, cut into sizable pieces, and boil in the salted water, covered, until very tender, usually about ½ hour. While hot, put through potato ricer, then add butter, cream, flour, beaten egg, salt, and sugar, mixing very thoroughly. Allow to stand for 15 minutes or so, then drop by tablespoonfuls into hot lard to fry until nicely browned. Remove with slotted spoon, drain on paper towels, and serve hot, dusted with sugar, or with a small amount of honey or melted guava jelly poured over them.

ZUCCHINI

The general confusion in the common names of virtually all of the vegetables known collectively as cucurbits is again the case with this tasty, nutritious, and widely cultivated plant. Botanically it is a variant of the common pumpkin grown for use in pies and such things (*Cucurbita Pepo*), but to the good cook it is variously known as Vegetable Marrow, Italian Squash, Green Squash, Cocozelle, and—perhaps most widely in this country—Zucchini.

This is an extremely desirable vegetable, yet, except in the kitchens of persons of Mediterranean antecedents, it is somewhat neglected in the United States. Italians and Greeks, in particular, are very fond of these elongate, rich dark-green squashes. Both the foliage and tender stems of the juvenile vines are to be encountered in specialized domestic markets, for quick cooking as greens, and the rich orange buds of

the flowers are favored for an oil- or butter-sautéed dish, or for addition to omelets or scrambled eggs.

When choosing Zucchini, try to obtain the smallest, youngest specimens possible. If these are only three or four inches in length, they are indeed ambrosial in flavor, delicate and memorable in a variety of fashions. These squashes, unless they are very old, never need peeling—simply wash them and trim off both ends.

THE ZUCCHINI is a singularly adaptable vegetable. Consider, for instance, the unusual and most attractive chilled hors d'oeuvre that follows. Crisp wheat or sesame seed crackers are a good accessory.

Alex's Zucchini
Serves 4 to 6.

1 *pound small zucchini, unpeeled, thinly sliced*
3 *tablespoons light olive oil*
⅓ *cup chopped onion*
1 *small clove garlic, mashed*
1 *teaspoon salt*
½ *teaspoon freshly ground black pepper*
1 *cup commercial sour cream*
1 *teaspoon finely chopped chives*

Prepare the zucchini by washing them, trimming off

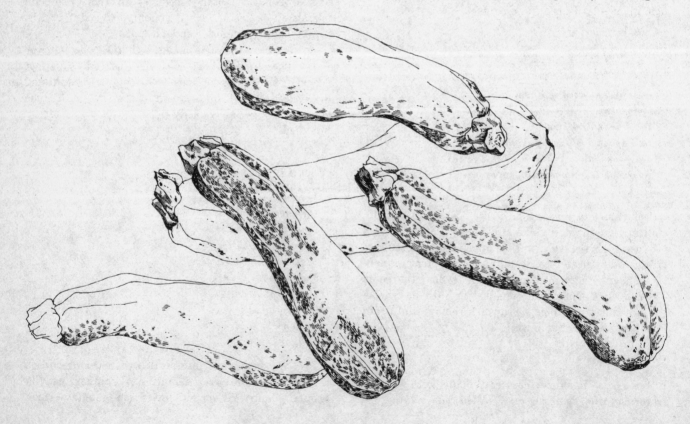

ends, then slicing very thinly. In a large skillet with cover, heat the oil and add the onion and garlic. Over high heat, quickly stir-fry these for about 5 minutes. Add the zucchini slices and continue to stir-fry, taking care not to break the slices any more than necessary. Add salt and pepper, and cook, covered, for about 5 minutes. The zucchini must retain much of its delightful crispness. Remove skillet from heat, uncover, and allow to cool. When at room temperature, fold in the sour cream, and arrange in a serving bowl. Chill thoroughly and serve garnished with the chopped chives.

FIRM, unblemished little zucchini, quickly sautéed in the Italian manner, are favorites at my house. The dish is ideal to accompany entrées from Italy or Spain or Greece or Portugal or the Near East—and I like it with good old American hamburgers. If any leftovers remain, chill these and serve on crisp lettuce as a unique salad.

Zucchini Sauté
Serves 4 to 6.

1 *pound small zucchini, unpeeled, thinly sliced*
3 *tablespoons light olive oil*
1 *cup chopped onion*
1 *medium clove garlic, mashed*
1 *medium can Italian-style (peeled) tomatoes*
½ *teaspoon salt*
¼ *teaspoon freshly ground pepper*
⅛ *teaspoon oregano*

Prepare zucchini as indicated above. In a large skillet with cover, heat the oil and add the onion and garlic. Over high heat, quickly stir-fry these for about 5 minutes. Add the zucchini slices, and continue to stir-fry for just 1 minute, taking care not to break the slices any more than necessary. Add tomatoes, breaking them up with fork or fingers. Add seasonings, mix through, cover skillet, reduce heat, and simmer for 10 minutes.

COLACHI (pronounced koe-*lah*-chee) is a wondrous medley combining zucchini with a variety of tasty vegetables plus bacon plus seasonings. A hearty dish that goes well with a sautéed veal or pork chop and crusty hot rolls, for an easy and perfectly delightful dinner.

Colachi
Serves 4 to 6.

1 *pound small zucchini, thinly sliced*

4 *strips lean bacon, diced*
3 *tablespoons (or less) light olive oil*
1 *cup chopped onion*
1 *small clove garlic, mashed*
1 *medium can Italian-style (peeled) tomatoes*
1½ *cups corn niblets*
1 *tablespoon cider vinegar*
½ *teaspoon sugar*
1 *teaspoon salt*
½ *teaspoon freshly ground pepper*
⅛ *teaspoon oregano*
¼ *cup finely chopped fresh parsley*

Prepare zucchini by washing and slicing thinly. In a large skillet with cover, fry the diced bacon until just barely browned. Remove bacon bits with slotted spoon and drain on paper towels. Add some of the oil, and over rather high heat, lightly brown the onion with the garlic, stirring often. Add all other ingredients except the parsley and stir-fry the mixture with care until the zucchini slices are just beginning to be tender, adding a bit more of the oil as needed. Cover the skillet, reduce heat, and simmer for about 5 minutes more. Stir in the parsley about 2 minutes before serving, while very hot.

MAUDE DRUM is one of the more famous culinary "characters" (I use the term with her permission) of my acquaintance. She resides in a quaint establishment, embowered by rare tropical flowers and overrun with loquacious Siamese cats. An invitation to dine might include edible delights such as the following, oftentimes served with a marvelous mixed grill of meats and resin-baked potatoes.

Zucchini à la Maude
Serves 4.

1 *pound small zucchini, halved lengthwise*
3 *tablespoons light olive oil*
1 *can beef consommé*
2 *or 3 tablespoons freshly grated Fontina (or*
    Parmesan) cheese
salt and freshly ground pepper to taste

In a large skillet with cover, sauté the halved zucchini in the oil until lightly browned on all sides. Add the consommé, undiluted, and simmer covered until the cucurbit is just barely tender. Remove zucchini and drain well. Top with the grated cheese, arrange in a shallow ovenproof pan, and place under preheated broiler until cheese has melted. Add salt and pepper to taste and serve without any delay.

HERE IS an elegant hot casserole whose antecedents are Mexican. I first enjoyed a version of it in a rough palm-thatched hut with a spotless earthen floor, well up in the glorious mountains of Oaxaca. My hosts were some Indian friends and a charming elderly American who has spent much of his life exploring the spectacular forests of the area for botanical novelties. This casserole, with a boiled and spicily seasoned (but slightly scrawny) chicken, fresh-made tortillas, and rich mountain coffee comprised our welcome meal.

Mexican Zucchini-Corn Casserole
Serves 6.

  1 *pound small zucchini, thinly sliced*
  4 *medium ears fresh corn*
  ¾ *cup diced onion*
  ⅓ *cup diced green pepper*
  3 *medium fresh tomatoes, diced*
  2 *tablespoons light olive oil*
  ⅓ *teaspoon sugar*
  2 *teaspoons salt*
  ¼ *teaspoon freshly ground black pepper*
  1½ *cups diced stale bread*
  ⅓ *cup diced sharp cheese*

Wash and slice the zucchini. Remove kernels from fresh corn, and retain the milk with them (or use 2½ to 3 cups canned corn niblets). In a heavy casserole combine squash, corn kernels with milk, onion, green pepper, tomatoes, oil, sugar, salt, and black pepper. On top of stove, over medium heat, cook, stirring often but with care, for about 15 minutes, or until zucchini is just tender—but not overdone. Sprinkle with bread and cheese dice, and place in preheated 350° F. oven until cheese melts and bread is crisp. Offer while very hot.

This European version of zucchini is to be encountered in a few good restaurants on this side of the ocean as well. It is particularly appropriate with husky stews made from beef, veal, or pork.

Sweet and Sour Zucchini
Serves 4 to 6.

  1 *pound small zucchini*
  2 *tablespoons butter*
  ⅓ *cup chopped onion*
  1 *teaspoon paprika*
  1 *teaspoon butter*
  1 *teaspoon flour*
  ¼ *cup cider vinegar*
  ½ *cup water*
  ¼ *teaspoon dill seeds*
  1 *teaspoon sugar*
  ¼ *teaspoon salt*

In a heavy skillet with cover, sauté the onion in the 2 tablespoons of butter until just soft, but not browned. Cut the washed, unpeeled zucchini into strips of the dimensions of French-fried potatoes. Add these and the paprika (Hungarian preferred) to the skillet, and over high heat cook for 2 minutes, turning often. Mash the 1 teaspoon butter with the flour and add this to the skillet with all other ingredients. Cover and simmer over reduced heat until the zucchini is just crisp-tender.

assorted vegetables

When one serves shish kebabs or other versions of skewered meat, old practice used to call for broiling an assortment of vegetables along with the meat cubes—on the same skewer. This is impractical, since the two require different cooking times. So consider the following delicious and simple way with crisp-broiled vegetables, done in the Turkish manner, and ideal for service with lamb, pork, or beef—whether skewered or not.

Turkish Vegetables
Serves 4 to 6.

1 *lemon, juiced*
1 *tablespoon light olive oil*
⅓ *cup peanut or soy oil*
salt to taste
1 *small eggplant*
1 *large green pepper*
2 *semiripe tomatoes*
1 *small can onions, drained*
6 to 12 *medium-size fresh mushrooms*

In a large bowl, combine the lemon juice, both oils, and salt to taste. Correct flavor to personal taste, adding more lemon juice or more oil, as desired. Cut unpeeled vegetables (canned onions already are peeled, of course) into rather sizable chunks, the mushrooms into halves or quarters, and marinate in the sauce, turning often but with care, for at least 1 hour. Arrange drained vegetables in shallow pan, and broil about 3 inches from flame of preheated broiler for 3 or 4 minutes. Serve without delay.

IN MANY parts of the world, notably India in the East and the West Indian isles from St. Kitts and Nevis to Trinidad, attractive flavorful curries containing an assortment of vegetables appear at table.

Many persons in India, or of Indian ancestry, are vegetarians, and for us carnivores such a dish makes a pleasant diversion for a meatless meal.

Just about any vegetable imaginable, or available, can be incorporated into these elegant medleys. Suggestions include onion, carrot, sweet potato, true yam, malanga, taro, chayote, turnip, okra, cabbage, tomato, green bean, pumpkin, green papaya, green pepper, and so on. Choose a combination of vegetables with compatible flavors and textures, and similar cooking times.

Here is the excellent version of curried raw vegetables that I find so adaptable to myriad uses in my home.

Raw Vegetable Curry
Serves 4.

2 *cups raw vegetables, cut into small neat pieces*
4 *tablespoons butter*
¼ *cup finely chopped onion*
1 or 2 *teaspoons curry powder*
1 *cup hot water*
1 *teaspoon salt*
½ to 1 *teaspoon lime juice*
1 *tablespoon grated coconut*
¼ *cup finely chopped onion*

Melt butter in a skillet with cover, and fry the first ¼ cup onion, over rather high heat, stirring constantly until soft. Add curry powder, mix through, and continue to cook for 2 minutes. Add hot water and salt, and bring to the boil. Add lime juice, coconut, and the second ¼ cup fine-chopped onion, plus selection of raw vegetables. Mix through, reduce heat to medium degree, cover skillet, and cook until vegetables are just tender. Do not overcook! Serve with or over hot boiled rice.

ONE CAN also prepare a good curry by making use of leftover vegetables of various kinds. For me, this lacks the special texture and fresh flavor of the above recipe, but it is an inventive and popular way in many tropical lands to cook remnants. The vegetables are added to this sauce just long enough to heat through —no further cooking should occur.

Cooked Vegetable Curry
Serves 4.

2 cups cooked vegetables, cut into small neat pieces
4 tablespoons butter
⅓ to ½ cup finely chopped onion
1 or 2 teaspoons curry powder
1½ teaspoons flour
1 teaspoon guava jelly
½ to 1 teaspoon lime juice
1 cup hot chicken or beef stock

Melt the butter in a skillet with cover, and over rather high heat, fry the onion, stirring constantly, until soft. Add curry powder and flour, mixing well, then blend in guava jelly and lime juice, to cook over medium heat for a moment. Blend in the stock, cover the skillet, and simmer for a few minutes before adding cooked vegetables to heat through very quickly over increased heat. Serve with or over hot boiled rice.

THE TIMBALE (pronounced tahm-*bahl*) is a staple on many a European table but, oddly enough, relatively rare in our own country. Although it looks festive, this is a utilitarian creation, in which cooked vegetables, meats, and what have you are baked in a rich egg custard. Leftovers take on a new and happy guise when incorporated into timbales. They do not require the constant close attention of the somewhat allied soufflé, and they can be reheated without problem.

Here is a basic recipe for the timbale. For our purposes, just about any flavorful vegetable obtainable can be added to the dish. Fresh or leftover, frozen or canned, by themselves or in combination with suitable meats, unadorned or anointed with a sauce of your choice, these are delectable, economical, nutritious affairs that well warrant the serious attention of all good cooks.

Basic Timbale Recipe
Serves 4.

1 to 1½ cups finely chopped or sieved cooked vegetable
   and/or meat

½ cup light cream
1 cup rich chicken stock
3 or 4 eggs
½ teaspoon salt
¼ teaspoon pepper

In a sizable bowl, beat the cream, stock, eggs, and seasonings together with a wire whisk or rotary beater. Fold vegetable (or vegetables) and/or meat (or meats) into mixture. Lightly butter 4 custard cups and fill them ⅔ full of the mixture. Set them on a rack in a pan filled with hot water, the level of this up to that of the timbale mixture in the cups. Bake in preheated 325° F. oven until custards are firm, usually about 20 minutes. If desired, serve with a suitable sauce.

TEMPURA (pronounced tem-*poo*-ra) is Japanese in origin, but during its peregrinations from those islands to other parts of the globe, it has acquired special characteristics which doubtless puzzle the purist Nipponese cook.

This grand medley of elegant cuisine (the name means "deep frying") is exceedingly popular in its native land, where literally thousands of restaurants, most of them small, devote themselves to the careful preparation of this dish, to the virtual exclusion of all else. Tempura, because of its attractive appearance and delectable combinations of fresh flavorful ingredients, is today justifiably popular with many connoisseurs everywhere.

I prefer to cook Tempura in an electric skillet, although authentically it is done on a hibachi, where a steady, high heat must be maintained. Each guest selects from the handsomely arranged platters—traditionally seafood on one, chicken (if being used) on a second, and vegetables on one or more others—just what he or she wishes, pops it into the batter, then into the hot oil for quick cooking. With chopsticks, or food tongs if need be, the cooked pieces are removed to the plate and rapidly and enthusiastically consumed. Small individual dishes of a special dipping sauce are placed at the side of each setting.

All of the Tempura ingredients, except the batter (which must be made fresh at the last moment and, ideally, replenished once or twice if the meal is a protracted one), can be prepared ahead of time, arranged on their display serving platters, and refrigerated, covered with wax paper or foil. Rice, hot tea, and if desired Nikko Salad (see page 49) with some thin slices of pickled daikon are served on the side. Dessert should be simple—perhaps chilled canned lychees or longans or a light sherbet.

Tempura
Serves 4 liberally.

TEMPURA BATTER:

½ cup flour
½ cup cornstarch
⅛ teaspoon salt
¼ teaspoon monosodium glutamate
2 eggs
½ cup warm water

Sift dry ingredients together. Beat eggs and add water. Add slowly to dry ingredients, mixing thoroughly. It is very important that this batter be made fresh, hence it is recommended that it be re-prepared at intervals as the meal progresses.

The pieces of seafood, chicken (if desired), and assorted vegetables are dipped into this batter, drained, then lowered carefully into a considerable quantity of soy or peanut oil heated to about 375° F.

The following ingredients are suggested for the Tempura repast, although with a little ingenuity additions can well be made.

SEAFOOD: Shrimp (raw, peeled, with tails left on), scallops (whole or halved), lobster (meat removed from shell, cut into bite-size pieces), firm-fleshed fish (cut into bite-size pieces).

CHICKEN (if desired): (boned, cut into bite-size pieces).

VEGETABLES: Sweet potatoes (strips about 2″ long, ¼″ diameter); parsnips (same); carrots (same); green beans (precook for 5 minutes, cut into 2″ lengths); onion rings; scallions (cut into diagonal 2″ lengths); eggplant (unpeeled pieces 2″ long, ½″ thick); pineapple (chunks of either fresh or canned); etc.

TEMPURA DIPPING SAUCE:
Serves 4.

¼ cup Japanese soy sauce
⅓ cup water
1 tablespoon saké
small slice fresh ginger root, unpeeled, or ¼ teaspoon ground ginger
½ teaspoon monosodium glutamate
2 tablespoons finely chopped scallion tops

In a heavy saucepan, heat first 5 ingredients together. Serve warm, in individual dipping dishes, each portion sprinkled with scallion tops.

ONE OF the perennial favorites in the realm of salads manufactured from a select array of vegetables at my abode in Coconut Grove is a version of famed Salade Niçoise, from the French Riviera. It can be made with all sorts of raw or cooked vegetables, with select seafood and eggs, and a superb herby dressing.

I like to serve individual helpings of this nice Nice salad to family and friends, rather than placing everything all together in one big bowl or platter. And I very much recommend using it as the entrée for a meal, with crusty bread and a compatible beverage, perhaps chilled beer.

Salade Niçoise
Serves 4 to 6.

1 large head iceberg or other lettuce, shredded
8 to 12 tiny new potatoes, cooked, peeled
½ pound cooked green beans
1 16-ounce can artichoke hearts
2 7-ounce cans white tuna (albacore), drained
4 to 5 medium tomatoes, quartered
4 to 6 hard-cooked eggs, quartered
1 small red onion, sliced into thin rings
1 small can midget sardines in oil, or 1 2-ounce can anchovy fillets in oil, drained
1 package dried Italian salad dressing mix
¼ cup wine vinegar
½ cup salad oil
¼ cup olive oil
½ teaspoon dried basil
1 teaspoon parsley flakes
1 teaspoon salt
¼ teaspoon freshly ground pepper
ripe olives, unpitted
green olives, unpitted

Chill all listed ingredients from shredded lettuce through red onion. Drain the sardines or anchovies. Thoroughly combine the listed ingredients from Italian dressing mix through freshly ground pepper, and allow them to mellow at room temperature for an hour or so. On individual big salad plates (or your favorite large white platter or shallow bowl, if you wish), spread the crisp shredded lettuce as a base. Slice the potatoes and use your imagination to arrange these attractively with the green beans, artichoke hearts, tuna, tomatoes, eggs, red onion rings, and sardines or anchovies. Garnish with both kinds of olives, and serve the dressing in a separate pitcher or bowl, to be added at table to individual taste.

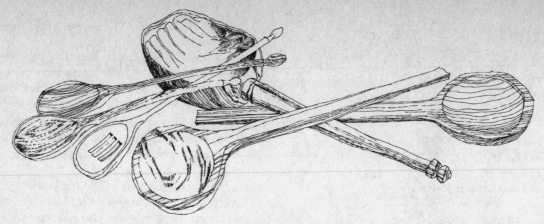

sauces and salad dressings

Simple Cheese Sauce
Makes about 1¾ cups.

2 tablespoons butter
2 tablespoons flour
¼ teaspoon salt
⅛ teaspoon black pepper
¼ teaspoon dry mustard
⅛ teaspoon garlic salt
1 cup whole milk
¾ cup diced sharp cheese

In a saucepan or top of a double boiler, melt the butter. Slowly and carefully blend in the flour and seasonings, mashing out all lumps. Stir in the milk a little at a time, allowing a moment between each addition, and stirring constantly. When sauce is very smooth and slightly thickened, add the diced cheese, and cook, stirring constantly, until it has melted and the sauce is again smooth. Serve while hot, or reheat over hot water in top of a double boiler.

THE LIQUID contained in the coconut is vitally important to good cuisine in many tropical parts of the world. Most often the liquid, as it comes from the cracked nut, is termed "coconut milk." Clear as water, or faintly cloudy, it is more properly called "coconut water," and coconut milk (and cream) are derived as described below. The water possesses a delicate, pleasant flavor, and can well be substituted for genuine water in the cooking of various foods such as rice and most green or yellow vegetables, seafoods, or chicken.

True Coconut Milk and Coconut Cream are prepared as follows:

Coconut Milk (and Cream)

2 cups freshly grated coconut meat
3 cups water

Break shell of coconut, peel off dark outer skin, and grate the meat, from the outside in; this gives more body to the grated product, for some unexplained reason. In a saucepan, combine the grated coconut and water. Bring to a quick boil, stirring, then remove from the heat and allow to stand for 30 minutes. Using your hands, squeeze out the liquid, straining it, if desired, to remove all tiny bits of coconut. This heavy liquid is the true coconut milk. When it is allowed to set for a while, a very thick, extremely rich, utterly delicious cream forms on the top. A weaker batch of excellent cooking liquid can be obtained by again covering the coconut meat with an additional 3 cups of water, and repeating the process.

Some culinary authorities state that the coconut milk (and cream) are manufactured by use of whole cow's milk in place of water, with the grated meat from the nut. Okay.

However one prepares it, the coconut milk or cream can be stored, refrigerated in a tight-capped container, for a week or so. Use it in many of the recipes in this book, as noted, and experiment with it further in your own creative cookery.

MALTA is a quaint little island in the Mediterranean which has given the world a special breed of cats—and a very special sauce for cooked vegetables such as asparagus, broccoli, artichokes, and cauliflower. One sometimes sees the sauce's name spelled Maltese.

Sauce Maltaise
Makes about ¾ cup.

3 egg yolks
¼ teaspoon salt
pinch Cayenne pepper
1 tablespoon lemon juice
¼ cup fresh orange juice
½ cup hot melted butter
1 tablespoon grated orange rind
1 drop red food coloring (optional)

Using a whisk, beat the egg yolks until light and thick, and turn into top of a double boiler over simmering water. Stir in salt, Cayenne, lemon juice, and 1 tablespoon of orange juice. Continue to cook, stirring constantly, and being careful that water does not boil. Very gradually dribble in the hot melted butter, stirring constantly. When sauce is nicely thickened and smooth, blend in remaining orange juice, orange rind, and, if desired, the drop of food coloring. Serve immediately in a heated bowl.

Oriental Cream Sauce
Makes 1¾ cups.

3 tablespoons butter
3 tablespoons flour
⅛ teaspoon freshly ground pepper
1 cup buttermilk
2 tablespoons soy sauce, Japanese preferred
2 teaspoons prepared mustard
½ cup dairy sour cream

In a saucepan, melt the butter, and thoroughly blend in flour and black pepper. Gradually add the buttermilk, soy sauce, and mustard, stirring after each addition. Cook, stirring constantly, until the sauce is smooth and thickened. Blend in the sour cream and heat through—do not allow to come to the boil. Serve the sauce hot, or at least warm, spooned over cooked vegetables such as carrots, cauliflower, cabbage, broccoli, asparagus, peas, or new potatoes.

THERE ARE many different kinds of boiled salad dressings around. In these days of abundant and usually excellent bottled and dehydrated dressings, the homemade species may seem a bit old-fashioned. But the following delight is a staple in my kitchen, and should be in yours, too. Kay was my mother, and from her I learned a great many invaluable things about inspired vegetable cookery.

Use her special, piquant dressing, which keeps well when refrigerated, on salads of crisp greens or crisp-cooked, chilled vegetables—and in general as a superior form of mayonnaise.

Kay's Boiled Salad Dressing
Makes about 2 cups.

1 teaspoon salt
2 rounded teaspoons dry mustard
3 teaspoons flour
4 tablespoons sugar
2 eggs
⅔ cup cider vinegar
1 cup light cream or soured cream

Mix all dry ingredients together in a bowl, then add the eggs and mix them in very thoroughly. Gradually add the vinegar and then the cream, mixing to remove all lumps. Use a whisk, or an electric beater if desired. Cook in a nonsticking heavy saucepan or in the top of a double boiler over boiling water, stirring constantly, until the dressing becomes thick. Cool and refrigerate, to serve cold.

Orange French Dressing
Makes 1½ cups.

1 6-ounce can frozen orange juice concentrate, thawed,
    undiluted
½ cup salad oil
¼ cup cider vinegar
¾ tablespoon sugar
½ teaspoon dry mustard
¼ teaspoon salt
2 or more drops Tabasco sauce

Combine all ingredients in a bottle with tight-fitting cap. Shake until thoroughly blended and refrigerate until serving time, shaking again just prior to use.

Homemade Mayonnaise
Makes 1¼ cups.

2 egg yolks
¼ teaspoon dry mustard
1 teaspoon salt
pinch Cayenne pepper
1 cup salad oil
2 tablespoons lemon juice or wine vinegar

Place egg yolks, mustard, salt, and Cayenne in a smallish bowl, and, using a whisk or electric mixer at medium speed, beat until thick and lemon-colored. Add ¼ cup of the oil, a drop at a time, continuing to beat after each addition, until thickened. Gradually add half of the lemon juice or wine vinegar, then the remainder of the oil, alternating with the lemon juice or wine vinegar, very slowly and beating all the time. Chill before using.

Mustard Cream Dressing
Makes about ⅔ cup.

  2 tablespoons prepared mustard
  1 to 2 teaspoons fresh lemon juice
  salt and freshly ground white pepper
  ⅔ cup light cream

Thoroughly combine the mustard (Dijon or Düsseldorf are excellent choices) with the lemon juice, and rather liberal quantities of salt and white pepper. Add the cream, a little at a time, mixing thoroughly after each addition. Chill slightly before use.

This piquant sauce is excellent with salads containing such things as beets, celery, and celeriac, as well as with cold roast chicken or chilled seafood of all sorts.

THIS IS designed especially for use with Spinach Salad Omar Khayyam's (page 217) by Mr. George Mardikian. But I have also found it an exceptional dressing for a big crisp tossed salad of assorted mixed greens of other types—Romaine, escarole, chicory, watercress, and whatever else is available in prime condition.

Omar's Dressing
Serves 4 to 6.

  1 medium clove garlic
  2 eggs
  ½ cup tomato ketchup
  1 tablespoon sugar
  1 teaspoon Worcestershire sauce
  1 teaspoon salt
  ½ teaspoon paprika
  ½ teaspoon dry mustard
  2 cups salad oil
  ½ cup vinegar
  ⅔ cup tepid water

Rub the cut clove of garlic around the inside of a mixing bowl. Put the eggs, ketchup, sugar, Worcestershire, salt, paprika, and dry mustard in the bowl and, using a rotary beater, combine these ingredients until they form a smooth paste. Slowly add the salad oil (I use peanut or soy oil) alternating with the vinegar, blending well after each addition. Add the tepid water gradually, blending well after each addition.

Vinaigrette Dressing

  3 or 4 parts light olive oil (or other salad oil)
  1 part prime red or white wine vinegar
  salt and freshly ground pepper to taste
  fresh or dried herbs to taste (optional)

This is, of course, the true French dressing. Shortly prior to use, thoroughly combine the oil and vinegar, beating with a fork, then add salt and freshly ground pepper to taste. Test the mixture as you progress, and if more oil or vinegar seems needed, add it. Fresh or dried herbs of your choice can be blended in at last few moments, dependent largely upon what you are serving the vinaigrette with. Store at room temperature and use the dressing as soon as possible for optimum results.

general index

Included are botanical, foreign and vernacular names of plants and plant families, as well as names of people and places and general information mentioned in the book. For the convenience of the cook, there is a separate recipe index, beginning on page 265.

recipe and culinary index

For the convenience of the cook, recipes are listed under name of recipe, name of vegetable and category of recipe (appetizer, soup, etc.). The general and botanical index will be found on pages 257–264.